P9-DMS-821

FOAL

Islamism and Islam

Islamism and Islam

Bassam Tibi

Yale UNIVERSITY PRESS

New Haven & London

Copyright © 2012 by Bassam Tibi.

All rights reserved.

This book may not be reproduced, in whole or in part, including illustrations, in any form (beyond that copying permitted by Sections 107 and 108 of the U.S. Copyright Law and except by reviewers for the public press), without written permission from the publishers.

Yale University Press books may be purchased in quantity for educational, business, or promotional use. For information, please e-mail sales.press@yale.edu (U.S. office) or sales@yaleup.co.uk (U.K. office).

Designed by James J. Johnson.
Set in Granjon type by Westchester Book Group.
Printed in the United States of America.

Library of Congress Cataloging-in-Publication Data

Tibi, Bassam.
    Islamism and Islam / Bassam Tibi.
      p.   cm.
    Includes bibliographical references and index.

    ISBN 978-0-300-15998-1 (cloth : alk. paper)   1. Islam and world politics.   2. Islamic fundamentalism.   3. Islamic renewal.   4. Religious awakening—Islam.   5. Islam—21st century.   I. Title.
    BP173.5.T534 2012
    320.5'57—dc23

                                                                                                2011037442

A catalogue record for this book is available from the British Library.

This paper meets the requirements of ANSI/NISO Z39.48-1992 (Permanence of Paper).

10   9   8   7   6   5   4   3   2   1

Contents

Preface

The first message of this book is that there is a distinction between the faith of Islam and the religionized politics of Islamism, which employs religious symbols for political ends. Many will deny this distinction, including most prominent Islamists themselves. There is no doubt that many Islamists hold the sincere conviction that their Islamism is the true Islam. In fact, however, Islamism emanates from a political interpretation of Islam: it is based not on the religious faith of Islam but on an ideological use of religion within the political realm. Islamism and Islam are thus different entities, not to be confused with each other, and in this book I aim to explain this difference.

In the field of Islamic studies, the difference between Islamism and Islam is largely ignored or even dismissed. But for reasons that will become clear, the distinction is crucial to any belief that Muslims can live in peace with non-Muslims. The religious faith of Islam is not an obstacle to peace or a threat to the non-Muslim other. Islamism, on the other hand, creates deep civilizational rifts between Muslims and non-Muslims. It not only labels "Jews and crusaders" as the enemy but also targets other non-Muslims: Hindus in Kashmir and Malaysia, Buddhists and Confucians in China and Southeast Asia, people of African animist religions in Sudan. Islamism classifies all non-Muslim people as *kuffar*—infidels—and thus "enemies of Islam." Liberal Muslims are not immune either. As well as contributing to polarization between Muslims and the non-Muslim other, Islamism also generates ferocious infighting within the community of Islam. In its jihad against "enemies of Islam," Islamism seeks to excommunicate even liberal Muslims from the *umma*—the worldwide Muslim community. To protect themselves against criticism, Islamists have invented the formula of "Islamophobia" to defame their critics. In contrast, in this book I combine respect for the faith of Islam with a staunch critique of Islamism. It is no contradiction to defend Islam against prejudice and to criticize Islamism.

Islamism is not what Islamic civilization needs today in its current state of crisis. Instead, we need to subscribe to a civil and liberal Islam with a secular perspective. In so doing, we non-Islamist Muslims not only approve pluralism but also seek a place for Islam in the diversity of cultures and religions that makes up the modern world. Liberal Muslims are not, as the journal *Foreign Affairs* characterizes us, "a small slice." To describe us this way, with the implication that we may therefore be ignored, is not only a factual error but a tactical one, as this assumption tends to alienate precisely the non-Islamist secular Muslims who are most friendly to the West.

Diversity is a most precious good. Can the Islamist mindset be admitted in the name of diversity? Can we trust Islamists who forgo violence to participate in good faith within a pluralistic, democratic system? I believe we cannot. Liberal Muslims and unbiased Westerners are able to accomplish the cross-cultural bridging necessary for a pluralist society. For reasons I explain in this book, those who subscribe to Islamism, regardless of whether they engage in violence, only inflame the tensions between secularism and their political religion and therefore cannot be partners in the search for a democratic peace for the twenty-first century. I hasten to point out that this is not a judgment of the personal characteristics of any particular Islamist or on Islamists as a group. It is a statement about the ideology of Islamism.

The second message of this book is that Islamism is a totalitarian ideology in Hannah Arendt's understanding of this term. Its totalitarian outlook is deeply linked to its antisemitism. Antisemitism is, as Arendt notes on the first page of her famous book *The Origins of Totalitarianism,* "not merely the hatred of Jews" but a genocidal ideology. This distinction, too, is important: it is the difference between wishing to relegate Jews to a despised place in society and denying the Jewish people the right to exist.

Islamists speak of a united umma but in reality dig deep trenches and arouse strong and dangerous passions. Living in Germany and having survived attempts on my life by jihadists (as well as by neo-Nazis), I know these passions from up close. Yet as a devout Muslim, raised in Damascus as the son of an *ashraf* family (Muslim nobility), I declare myself immune to the charge of Islamophobia. Hating Islam would require me to renounce myself, my family, my faith, and my heritage. I write not to denigrate these things but in part to defend them.

I write also as a political scientist who has devoted his career to the study of Islam. But my work differs from the currently fashionable American style of Islamic studies. My method is not primarily descriptive, nor is it a cultural-narrative approach. I study Islam within the framework of what I term *Islamology,* a social science–based inquiry that relates Islamic realities to the study of international conflict in world politics. In a way, Islamology resembles the old Sovietology, with the very basic difference that it replaces the latter's cold war mentality with a spirit of intercultural bridging. Nonetheless, I do not overlook what Mark Juergensmeyer has termed a "new cold war" being fought between the secular concept of order and religionized politics.

Islamology deals with the relations of Islamic civilization not only with the West but more generally with the world at large. The pattern of post-bipolar politics generated by the politicization of Islam involves non-Muslims as well as Muslims. As a political inquiry, Islamology studies Islamism, not Islam as a faith; it is also a discipline for studying how political-religious tensions develop into conflicts. The best example of this kind of conflict is the one that has emerged over the past century between Muslims and Jews. Having had the opportunity to study in Frankfurt with the Holocaust survivors Max Horkheimer and Theodor W. Adorno, two great and philosophically astute social scientists, I believe I am one of the few Muslims with some insight into the meaning of the Holocaust. Because this subject is often invoked by Islamists—they claim to be suffering its equivalent in today's Europe—it is important to know something not only of the horrific practices of the Holocaust but also of its underlying ideology. I will show that this ideology has more in common with Islamism itself than with the ideas of those the Islamists claim are oppressing them.

Others will no doubt strongly disagree with this assessment and even accuse me of Orientalism and Islamophobia. Identifying Islamism as a totalitarian ideology mobilizes all kinds of polemics, but name-calling should not be mistaken for serious criticism. All it proves is that, in the academy as elsewhere, polarization often closes the door to rational debate. The sensitivity of the matter makes clear how an academic description, when it relates to deeply disputed political questions, becomes a source of tension among scholars. Even the reviewing process for this book revealed these divisions within the scholarly community.

This book was completed in 2009 at Yale University and passed two rounds of peer review, involving eight reviewers and four passes of editing. After a review by the editorial committee of Yale University Press, there were two additional rounds of reviewing that included three new reviewers. The revisions required by the third and fourth rounds were painful but also a blessing, as they contributed to a tremendous improvement of the book and the way its arguments are put forward. I hope this additional work provides sufficient inoculation to allow the book to stand up to attack in a very contentious realm of inquiry. The bigger hope, however, is that it will spark a fruitful and enlightening debate.

I am convinced that the many complications in publishing this book (eleven reviews) are due neither to the author nor to the publisher but to the theme it broaches. In deference to the sensitivity of my subject, I have done my best to support my arguments with sound evidence. The major idea of the book, that there exists a most significant distinction between Islam and Islamism, is not acceptable to Islamists or to some scholars. Essays reflecting a debate on this at a meeting of the Middle East Studies Association can be found in the book *Islamism: Contested Perspectives on Political Islam.*

There is no denying that in the aftermath of 9/11, the subject of Islamism and Islam has become highly charged and has helped shape the first decade of the new century. The tensions are general, and Western (particularly American) policies made a damaging contribution to them. While the change of administration in Washington after 2008 brought some improvement, it will not, by itself, end the sense of polarization between the world of Islam and the West. People who read Arabic and are familiar with Sayyid Qutb's writings know that Islamists bear their share of responsibility for this polarization. The idea of an imagined war between Islam and the West, however enthusiastically it has been embraced by right-wing parties in the United States and Europe, is also an independent Islamist invention. Therefore it is consequential when the Obama administration abandons the terms "Islamism" and "jihadism."

One has to raise a new question. Is Qutb, the man who first advocated this polarization, really that significant? Am I not, as a questioner at a Washington symposium suggested, giving too much credence to a "marginal figure"? No Islamist would call him marginal. Qutb is the *rector spiritus* of Islamism, and the binary worldview he established in his work is passed on to younger generations as an essential part of Islamist indoctrination. Arendt convincingly shows how important is indoctrination in totalitarian movements.

The puzzle is that Islamists today have advocates in the West on both the left and the right. Why? Some leftists reinterpret Qutb's anti-Westernism as anticapitalism and thus support Islamism out of a mistaken belief that it is an ally against globalization. Some conservatives, by contrast, demonize Islam and Islamism altogether. Yet when the subject turns to "the Jews," especially those who are believed to run Wall Street, one is astounded to see Europeans on both the far left and the far right united with Islamists in their antisemitism and anti-Americanism. As a participant in the student rebellion of 1968 and a onetime member of the editorial board of the Berlin-based Marxist journal *Das Argument,* I find these attitudes on the left especially disappointing. At times it seems that the spirit of enlightenment has been written off or, at least, severely weakened. Doctrines have taken the place of principles. The leftists today who support Islamism do so only because it is against the United States, not out of any sense of shared ideals or values.

The existence of conflict between the Islamic and Western civilizations is not to be confused with a "clash of civilizations." The conflict cannot be reduced to a contest in which the outsize power of the West can be brought to bear; it is a conflict also of values.

My aim in this book is to illuminate these conflicting values and to open a debate on the distinction between Islamism and Islam. To bear fruit, this debate must break certain damaging taboos. In response to the accusation that my research has been based in Western institutions and thus contaminated by a Western worldview, I answer that the knowledge included here was largely obtained in the world of Islam itself. I have studied Islam and its civilization for four decades, working in the Middle East, South and Southeast Asia, and West Africa. Admittedly, I did most of my writing in the West. But most countries of the world of Islam lack the institutions where one may freely conduct such research.

I wrote this book at Yale University, but my home institution over the past four decades has been in Germany. It can be tough and often unpleasant to be a Muslim working on religion in that country. If you visit a church in any German big city on Sunday, you will find either old people in attendance or a yawning emptiness. The same applies throughout Western Europe. Young Europeans seem not only to have lost their religion but to have acquired a nihilistic relativism in their cultural values, making it difficult for them to understand the return of the sacred to politics. Too many social scientists in Europe understand neither how the return of the sacred in a political shape affects politics and society, nor the meaning of religion itself. While in Washington, D.C., during the summer of 2010 to complete the final draft of this book, I became aware that many of the young generation of American political scientists who deal with Islam are not much better informed than their European colleagues.

Academic resistance to critical views of political Islam, particularly in the social sciences, is not restricted to Europe. Political science and sociology are everywhere poorly represented in Islamic studies. Scholars of religious studies, history, and anthropology often write about politics in Islam, but knowledge of the faith of Islam and of its various local cultures does not qualify a scholar as an authority on politics. This is revealed in the bulk of publications in the field. A few mostly senior political scientists of high caliber combine the professional standards of their discipline with knowledge about Islam—Fouad Ajami, John Waterbury, Leonard Binder, and Michael Hudson come to mind—but there are few younger names to add to this list.

This paucity of scholars occurs in an era when the postsecular politicization of Islam and the religionization of politics are advancing throughout Islamic civilization, not only in the Middle East. In addition, Islamism is but one aspect of a global phenomenon of religious fundamentalism that is making similar inroads in other cultures. We live in a global age of religionized politics. This phenomenon was subjected to scholarly scrutiny in a large set of studies entitled The Fundamentalism Project, organized by Martin Marty at the American Academy of Arts and Sciences and published in five volumes. This book is inspired by those volumes but breaks new ground by proposing that we replace the vague and misleading notions of "radical Islam" and "Islamic revivalism" with new concepts of political Islam, Islamism, and religious fundamentalism. To flesh out these concepts I analyze six major features of Islamism: its deeply reactionary vision of the world political order, its embrace of genocidal antisemitism, its predicament with democracy, its use of violence, the shari'atization of law, and its search for authenticity within an Islamic tradition it has largely reinvented out of an obsessive desire for purity. Finally, in an effort that leans heavily on the ideas of Hannah Arendt, I argue that Islamism is best understood as a totalitarian ideology.

This is not how most people in the West think about Islamism. In my view, the return of the sacred in political guise is not well understood. This is not only a matter of academic concern. The West badly needs a better set of policies for dealing with Islamic civilization, and these can come only from a better understanding of how Islamists think, and of the complex reality that Islamism is not Islam. Today, in the light of the "Arab Spring," it is more urgent than ever that we understand the nature of Islamism. The fall of authoritarian regimes (Tunisia, Egypt, Libya) seems not to fulfill the promise of democratization but rather portends the empowerment of Islamism, leading to the envisioned shari'a state. In this book I hope to illuminate these complex issues in a larger context.

Acknowledgments

After retiring in 2009 and determining to leave the stage, I decided that this book—apart from a planned collection of my unpublished research papers—would be my last one. Following twenty-eight earlier books written in German and eight in English, in a time span of some forty years, I end my public and academic life and go private, unless an irresistible window of opportunity opens. This is also my third study published in the United States on political Islam, or Islamism. The first was *The Challenge of Fundamentalism* (1998, updated 2002), and the second was *Political Islam, World Politics, and Europe* (2008). Together, these books reflect the progress of my reasoning and research on Islamism over the past one and a half decades. In view of this book's place in my career, these acknowledgments cover not only the present work but also my scholarly life in relation to the study of Islam.

First, I am most grateful to all eleven reviewers, who compelled me to rethink and rewrite these chapters to make the arguments strong enough to withstand criticism. Some of the reviews were as pleasant as strong medicine, but they convinced me of the need to inoculate the book against misunderstanding.

The backstory of this book and my research on Islam is a long one. It begins in the late 1960s, when I was among the Arab intellectuals who, following the humiliating defeat in the Six-Day War, pinned our hopes for a better future on a new Arab-Muslim enlightenment. (You can read about these efforts in Fouad Ajami's 1981 book *The Arab Predicament*.) In those years, Arab intellectual life was largely secular, and we did not care much about political Islam. But we on the Arab left failed to gain a popular foothold, and we watched painfully as Islamists took our place as opinion leaders. My first physical encounter with Islamism took place in Cairo in November 1979, after I presented a paper entitled "Islam and Secularization" at The First International Islamic Philosophy Conference on Islam and Civilization (November 19–22, 1979, Ain Shams University, Cairo). From that point on I was continuously exposed to threats from Islamists who called my thinking un-Islamic and heretical. Despite much opposition, the paper was published in Arabic by Anis Sayigh in his Beirut-based journal *Qadaya Arabiyya* in March 1980, and then in English by Prof. Mourad Wahba in Cairo. The proceedings of the conference and its publication in Arabic would be unthinkable today: no journal in the Arabic-speaking world would risk the level of Islamist censure it would bring. I am grateful to numerous Arab-Muslim intellectuals who encouraged my work at that time, including Fouad Ajami, Mourad Wahba, Sadik J. al-Azm, and Saad Eddin Ibrahim. There were also many unnamed editors who published my articles in Arabic in Beirut (above all: *Dirasat Arabiyya* and *Mawaqif*), in Tunis (in *Shuon Arabiyya*), and in Cairo (*al-Tali'a*). In the 1970s I sought refuge in Europe. At that time I primarily wrote books on secular issues, especially nationalism and development. My first book on Islam was about the phenomenon some describe as the Islamic revival but which I prefer to call—as I did in that book's title—the Crisis of Modern Islam. In this context I pursued research in Cairo and also lived and taught in Khartoum, Tunis, and Rabat, as well as in Dakar, Senegal, and Yaoundé, Cameroon. In Cairo I worked primarily at al-Ahram Center for Political and Strategic Studies, where I enjoyed the support of Sayyid Yasin, Abdulmun'im Sai'd, Osama Ghazali-Harb, and above all my friend Saad Eddin Ibrahim. Ibrahim was later jailed and subsequently forced to flee his country. In Khartoum, I worked with the late Mohammed Omar Bashir during my tenure at the Institute for African and Asian Studies. In Tunis I worked with many friends at the Centre d'Études et de Recherches Économiques et Sociales (CERES), and published there as well. I also lived and taught in Ankara, Turkey. Throughout the 1980s and 1990s I lectured at universities in Morocco, Algeria, and Tunis, and later in some of the Gulf States. Fearful of imprisonment, I did not go to Qadhafi's Libya, Wahhabi Saudi Arabia, Saddam Hussein's Iraq, or my home country of Syria, where I am outlawed by the Ba'th regime.

Well-informed security people persuaded me to make the heartbreaking decision not to risk going to Damascus to attend the funerals of my father and, later, my beloved mother.

Since 1995 I have found that my study of Islam is most enriched when I travel outside the Middle East. I gained many new insights in South and Southeast Asia, above all in Indonesia. Earlier, in the 1980s, West Africa was most important for me, with appointments in Senegal (where I was inspired by the model of Afro-Islam to unfold my concept of Euro-Islam) and Cameroon. I am especially grateful to Hidayatollah Islamic State University in Jakarta, Indonesia, where I taught as a visiting professor in 2003, and to its president, Ayzumardi Azra. I returned to Jakarta in July 2009 to join the debate on the Prospects of a Progressive Islam (the title of the event) with fellow liberal Muslims. I also had tenures at National University of Singapore/ NUS, and L'Institut des Relations Internationales de Cameroun/IRIC in Yaoundé, where I studied the damaging impact of Saudi Islam in suppressing the more open-minded Islam in Africa. I am grateful to the many friends, colleagues, and students—too many to name here—who encouraged and challenged me in all of these places.

Admittedly, I assembled and digested in the West all the knowledge I obtained in the world of Islam. Next to my home University of Göttingen in Germany I list other institutions in the West that supported my work. On the top I mention Harvard University, where I had several affiliations between 1982 and 2000. Membership in the Fundamentalism Project at the American Academy of Arts and Sciences (where I am especially thankful to the chairmen, Martin Marty and Scott Appleby) and in the Culture Matters Research Project of the Fletcher School, Tufts University (chaired by Lawrence Harrison), had a great impact on my work. I am grateful to Cornell University, which provided me with a six-year tenure as the A. D. White Professor at Large. I thankfully acknowledge the Center for Advanced Holocaust Studies at the United States Holocaust Museum in Washington, D.C., for two opportunities to serve as the Judith B. and Burton P. Resnick Senior Visiting Scholar, in 2008 and 2010.

In addition to the institutions listed above, several individuals supported my research. At the Center for Advanced Holocaust Studies I wish to thank

Paul Shapiro, Suzanne Brown-Fleming, Harriet Shapiro, Jürgen Matthaus, Robert Williams, and many other colleagues. At the Yale Initiative for the Interdisciplinary Study of Antisemitism, the director, Charles Small, and his assistant, Lauren Clark, were most supportive. I am most grateful to Yale University Press director John Donatich, whom I first met in Amsterdam, and executive editor William Frucht, whose efforts accompanied this book through all stages and who became not only a pivotal person in the project but also a friend. In my forty-year career as a writer and an academic book author, I never encountered an editor who devoted so much time and attention as did Bill Frucht to the present book, contributing with vigor not only to the improvement of my prose but also to the strengthening of my arguments. My collaboration with manuscript editor Dan Heaton for a few months in 2011 was briefer than my relationship with William Frucht (2008–12), but it was of the same intensity of cordiality and enrichment.

Though peer reviewing can be painful, I benefited from all of this book's reviews, even (perhaps especially) from readers who were not favorable to the project. One of the latter inspired me to add the chapter on shari'a, an addition that has been a great improvement. Among the reviewers were two who completed lengthy annotations, with helpful recommendations that I mostly followed. I also need to single out one reviewer who stated at the outset that he/she disagrees with my argument but nonetheless strongly recommended that Yale University Press publish the book, not only out of respect for academic freedom and the seniority of the author, but also in the hope that the book would generate a much-needed debate.

For the decade leading up to my retirement in 2009, I worked closely with my full-time assistants Thorsten Hasche and Elisabeth Luft at the University of Göttingen. They and my beloved wife, Ulla, protected me from making unqualified generalizations about Germany and German culture, which I analyze and describe in my feature article, "Ethnicity of Fear?," published in *Studies in Ethnicity and Nationalism*. Elisabeth's unfailing assistance was essential to this book's completion. She word-processed all of the handwritten drafts faxed to her from Yale, and earlier from Cornell and Washington. I am most fortunate to enjoy the assistance of Thorsten Hasche, which continued after I left my office in Germany. In 2010 the fax machine at the Center for Advanced Holocaust Studies connected us across the Atlantic while I completed this draft. Very special gratitude goes to my University of Göttingen colleague Prof. Dr. Franz Walter—he is not a student of Islam but a great scholar of comparative "political parties" research. Out of pure interest in my work and in support for my research, Franz selflessly provided for funds from his Center for Democracy Research for the year 2009–12 to pay my associate Thorsten Hasche. Without Thorsten's research assistance and computer work, the completion of the final draft would not have been possible at all. My very deep gratitude goes to Thorsten Hasche for his commitment to this book.

Among the academic specialists who have been supportive of my work on Islam and Islamism in the past three decades, I single out (again) Fouad Ajami of SAIS; the late Nazih Ayubi, whose 1991 book *Political Islam* remains the definitive introduction to the subject; Bernard Lewis, a mentor and friend, who helped me spend an academic year at Princeton; and the late Muhsin Mahdi, Roy Mottahedeh, the late Samuel P. Huntington, and Herbert Kelman, my colleagues at Harvard from 1982 to 2000. I am also pleased to thank Lawrence Harrison of the Fletcher School, and Martin Marty and Scott Appleby of the Fundamentalism Project. Others who encouraged my work include Shahram Akbarzadeh, Nezar AlSayyad, Shlomo Avineri, Jeffrey Bale, Zeyno Baran, Russell Berman, Davydd Greenwood, Jeffrey Herf, Charles Hill, Roland Hsu, Efraim Inbar, Mark Juergensmeyer, Jamal Kafdar, Ali Karaosmonoglu, Peter Katzenstein, John Kelsay, Fethi Mansouri, Peter Newman, Eric Patterson, Y. Raj-Isar, Anthony Reid, Emad E. Shahin, and Kemal Silay.

In a time in which not only leaders of Islamism but also mainstream Islamic leaders, Western scholars, some journalists, and many others impose limits on what it is permissible to think and say about Islam and Islamism, I am most grateful that Yale University Press has the courage to bring to the market this kind of research. Coming from Syria, where academic freedom—especially on political matters—is severely restricted, I appreciate this freedom and admire those who have the vision to keep it alive, both in the United States and in Europe. This freedom is now at peril in the West itself, not because of dictatorship but in the name of political correctness. This is a great concern that weighed on my mind while I was writing this book. This book is a critical analysis of Islamism that I hope will help bring about a post-Islamism that is not yet in sight.

In the preface I acknowledge that I "write as a political scientist who has devoted his career to the study of Islam," and then I complain about the dismissal of this kind of work by some. For me it is therefore a great pleasure to thank the editors of three recent encyclopedias who admitted my interpretation of Islam and Islamism as authoritative. First I thank the editors of the eight-volume *International Encyclopedia of Political Science* (2011), B. Badie, D. Berg-Schlosser, and L. Morlino, for having selected me as the "authority" to write an extensive entry on Islam, published in volume 5 of the work (pages 1348–53), under the aegis of the International Political Science Association. The same gratitude goes to Professors Mark Juergensmeyer and Helmut Anheier for giving me the same honor in their *Encyclopedia of Global Studies*. Earlier, Professor Mark Bevir accepted for his *Encyclopedia of Political Theory* my entry "Fundamentalism" (volume 2, pages 536–40), in which I present Islamism as the Islamist variety of the global phenomenon of religious fundamentalism. All of these colleagues give me comfort and endorse the perception that scholars are members of a community characterized by rationality and civility. Despite the controversial character of my ideas, I hope this book shall be received by the scholarly community in a mindset for which these colleagues provide the model.

Islamism and Islam

I

Why Islamism Is Not Islam

WHAT IS THE DIFFERENCE between Islamism and Islam? The essential answer is that Islamism is about political order, not faith. Nonetheless, Islamism is not *mere* politics but religionized politics.[1] In this book I look at Islamism as a powerful instance of the global phenomenon of religious fundamentalism.[2]

The notion of "religionized politics" is essential for grasping this book's basic argument. In the case of Islamism, the religionization of politics means the promotion of a political order that is believed to emanate from the will of Allah and is not based on popular sovereignty. Islam itself does not do this. As a faith, cult, and ethical framework, it implies certain political values but does not presuppose a particular order of government. Islamism grows out of a specific interpretation of Islam, but it is not Islam: it is a political ideology that is distinct from the teaching of the religion of Islam.

It follows that Islamism is also not, as it is often described, a revival of Islam. It does not revive but rather constructs an understanding of Islam not consonant with its heritage. Islamism calls for a return of Islamic history and glory, but the state to which it seeks to "return" is, in Eric Hobsbawm's phrase, an invented tradition. The Islamist utopia, an imagined system of divine governance named *hakimiyyat Allah* (God's rule), has never existed in Islamic history.

Islamism and the Invention of Tradition

To understand why and how Islamism invents Islamic tradition, one should first familiarize oneself with the agenda of the Islamist movements. It

represents much more than religious orthodoxy or a political intent to create havoc. The term "radical Islam," which suggests this meaning, is therefore misleading. The same applies to the use of the term "moderate Islam"
to identify those Islamists who forgo violence and pursue their goals peacefully. In fact, all Islamists have a common commitment to a remaking of
the world. Within Islamism there is a distinction between institutional
Islamists and jihadists, but the two differ only over the means to be employed, not over the goal itself. Even those Islamists identified as "radical"
but belittled as "jihadi-*takfiri* pockets" share this political agenda. (The
term "takfiri" refers to jihadist groups that engage in accusing other Muslims of *kufr* [unbelief] and branding them as infidels if they do not share
Islamist views. These groups are not "pockets" but an integral part of the
Islamist movement.

   Islamism exists in a global age characterized by what Daniel Bell has
called a return of the sacred.[3] This recourse to religion takes place under
the conditions of a dual crisis: one is normative and relates to secular modernity, and the other is structural and relates to failed development. But
despite the superficial appearance of a religious revival, the return of the
sacred is not a "religious renaissance." Instead, religion assumes a political
shape. In Islam the religionization of politics is carried out in the name of
an imagined *umma* (community).[4] The resulting political order is known as
a shari'a state. Islamism can therefore be identified as an ideology that con-
nects *din* (religion) with *dawla* (state) in a shari'a-based political order. This
is a religionized political agenda, not a spiritual one. In addition, it is not
local, restricted to countries of Islamic civilization, but also global, as Islamists
propose a remaking of the world at large.

   In their masterpiece *Dialektik der Aufklärung* (*Dialectics of Enlightenment*)[5] Theodor W. Adorno and Max Horkheimer present a case for comparison. Though they never argue (as some wrongly suggest) that fascism
grew from liberal Enlightenment and do not identify the two with each
other, they do see a context of crisis in which the two are related. I propose
a similar relationship between Islamism and Islam. Islamism is a cultural-
political response to a crisis of failed postcolonial development in Islamic

societies under conditions of globalization. Yet even though Islamism is political, it remains religious. Unlike its totalitarian predecessors, communism and fascism, the new totalitarianism is not a secular but a religious ideology. How can we understand Islamism as different from Islam without denying the connection between them? How does one avoid confusing the two? In Europe, the dialectics of Enlightenment in a time of great crises led to communist and fascist rule. Just as these European ideologies contradicted the Enlightenment, Islamism contradicts the humanism of Islam. Continuity and break, tradition and innovation are involved. No prudent scholar would condemn the Enlightenment or all of Europe because of these totalitarian movements. I wish to bring the same insight to Islam and Islamism. This book represents an effort to apply the thinking of global historical sociology to the crisis of Islamic civilization from which Islamism emerges.

I thus take pains to dissociate Islam from Islamism without ignoring their commonalities. In both Islam and Islamism one encounters diversity within unity. Certain beliefs and principles are common to all Muslims, but they are expressed in multiple traditions.

A person is considered to be a Muslim if he or she adheres to the *al-arkan al-khamsah,* the five principles or pillars of Islam. These are to pronounce the *shahadah* (the unity of God and the acknowledgment of Mohammed as His messenger); to perform the *salat* (daily prayers); to fast during the holy month of Ramadan; to pay *zakat* (alms) to the poor; and finally, if financially possible, to travel to Mecca to fulfill the duty of *hadj* (pilgrimage) to become a *hajji* (male) or *hajja* (female). Does Islamism revive these pillars and the traditions related to them? The major creed of Islamism is *din-wa-dawla* (unity of state and religion) under a system of constitutionally mandated shari'a law. This is not faith but the imposition of a political system in the name of faith.

Nor is it based in any plausible reading of history. In this opening chapter I maintain that Islamism does not herald a revival but is rather an invention of tradition. I borrow this term from Eric Hobsbawm[6] because it most accurately captures the relation of Islamism to the past. The Islamic shari'a state advocated by Islamists is not the caliphate—though some Islamist movements, such as Hizb ut-Tahrir, use this notion—but a novelty whose roots are thoroughly modern. The shari'a on which this political order is to be based is likewise a modern invention.

Another invention of tradition is the Islamist definition of the umma as the supposed citizenry of the *nizam Islami,* or new Islamic order. The *umma* is the community of the faithful, based on shared observance of the five pillars of Islamic belief. The historian Josef van Ess[7] mentions in his magnum opus on early Islamic history that umma in early Islam never had the meaning attributed to it by contemporary Islamism. After the death of the Prophet in the seventh century, van Ess writes, Muslims of Mecca and Medina refused to pray behind an Imam who was not a *sheykh* (leader) of their tribe. In his book *Muhammed at Medina,* the historian of early Islam W. M. Watt described the classical Islamic umma as a "super-tribe" uniting various tribes in a "federation of tribes" for purposes of prayer. This umma was not a political entity but the opposite: a means of transcending political boundaries for religious unity.

In contrast, the Islamist umma is explicitly political, what Benedict Anderson termed an "imagined community." But it is an odd variety, sovereign but not inherently limited. In developing his idea of the imagined community, Anderson was attempting to fathom nationalism—to explain why, as he put it, "nation-ness is the most universally legitimate value in the political life of our time."[8] Islamism, however, has a relation to "nation-ness" that is at best ambiguous: not only is it skeptical of the nation-state as the fundamental political unit of the modern world, it rejects many of the concepts underlying modernity. As prerequisites for imagining their polity as a modern-style nation, Anderson writes, people must overcome three ideas: that a particular language has a unique relationship to reality; that the head of state mediates between the divine and the human; and that historical time is equivalent to cosmological time. Islamists fail on all three counts. They thus qualify as truly radical, not in the superficial sense of engaging in political violence but in the sense of opposing certain ideas at a very deep level. It is not clear that most Western scholars and policymakers understand Islamist radicalism in this sense.

The tensions between Islamists' utopian ideals and basic modern notions about the political order inevitably lead to conflict. Islamism flourishes as an ideology of opposition, but when Islamists come to power they not only fail to deliver what has been promised, they also become totalitarian and suppress any dissent to their rule. Even in democratic-secular Turkey the ruling AKP, an Islamist party, undermines the freedom of the press and puts journalists in jail without trial. In November 2010 Turkey was criticized for its media restrictions by the European Union in its annual report on the country's bid to join the EU.

The Basic Issues

It is a mistake for Muslims and Westerners to play down the ideology and practices of Islamism as the work of a few "militant" adherents of "radical Islam," or to simply excommunicate these "radicals" as "un-Islamic." There is no such thing as radical Islam: Muslims who practice their religion even in the most conservative possible manner are not radical any more than the Amish are radical. Instead, there is a totalitarian Islamism presented by a transnational movement that religionizes politics. But Islamists' reference to Islam is not simply instrumental. They think of themselves as true believers and behave accordingly.

If those who belittle Islamists as a marginal minority of "radical Muslims" are mistaken, those who inflate the politics of Islamization into "the other modernity" are likewise mistaken. The growth of Islamism compels others to respond to it in a pragmatic manner. They believe they will be able to accommodate Islamism in dealing with it, and also that the mundane problems of governance will make the Islamists more tractable once they gain power. Islamism, in this view, either will burn out on its own, as extremist movements tend to do, or will eventually accommodate to practical realities. Both predictions are belied by facts on the ground. Post-Islamism is not yet in sight, and Islamism grows, taking full advantage of Islamic symbols for its own use.

An invented tradition cannot be well understood if it is not related to the tradition from which it has emerged. Little understanding of this relationship exists in the West. I shall identify six themes as basic to the relation of Islamism and Islamic tradition. These are:

- the interpretation of Islam as nizam Islami (state order);
- the perception of the Jews as the chief enemy conspiring against Islam, because they are believed to be pursuing a "Jewish world order" in conflict with the Islamist goal;
- democratization and the place of institutional Islamism in a democratic state;
- the evolution from classical jihad to terrorist jihadism;
- the reinvention of shari'a; and
- the question of purity and authenticity, which determines the Islamist view of secularization and desecularization.

These six themes, which help us understand the basic contrast between Islamism and Islam, are each given a chapter. Then, in Chapter 8, I draw on the work of Hannah Arendt to conceptualize the Islamist movement as the new totalitarianism. I do not impose her approach on my subject, but rather use the tools of analysis she developed.

Western readers may legitimately wonder why the list above does not include the issue of gender and Islamism. Women's issues are certainly an important subject in the Muslim world today. But in three decades of reading Islamists' literature, I have found that they have little to say on this topic: it does not seem to interest them much. Sayyid Qutb chastises Western civilization for its promiscuity. Based on his years in New York City, from 1948 to 1950, he saw the emancipation of women as symptomatic of a Western decline of values. Yusuf al-Qaradawi states clearly that men are the leaders of the Muslim umma and that the worst-case scenario would be for a woman to lead the umma. Islamists generally hold the view of traditional shari'a that men are superior to women and thus have an obligation to lead them. There are, of course, varying degrees of patriarchy within the world of Islam, the highest of which are in the Middle East. In Muslim West Africa and Southeast Asia, Muslim woman have more rights than in Arab countries. Female politicians have become heads of state in four non-Arab Muslim countries: Turkey before the AKP, Indonesia, Pakistan, and Bangladesh. Nonetheless, the most powerful Muslim feminists are two Arab women: the Moroccan Fatma Mernissi and the Egyptian Nawal al-Sa'dawi. These women have courageously criticized both traditional Muslim and modern Islamist patriarchy and have fought for gender equality. But Islamists, while they have imposed the cruelest strictures on women, seem to have given little thought to the place of women in their envisioned umma.

There is a key distinction between the totalitarianisms analyzed by Arendt, fascism and communism, and contemporary Islamism. While the earlier phenomena were secular, Islamism is not. Therefore, while a political order is at the forefront of Islamist thinking, one should beware the pitfall of banning Islamists from the Islamic umma. We must not adopt the procedure of the takfiri Islamists themselves, who excommunicate from the Islamic community any Muslims who disagree with them.

The term "Islamism" reflects a common approach of adding the suffix "ism" to reflect the conversion of an original idea into an ideology. For instance, adding an "ism" to the name of Karl Marx reflects an effort to transform the thoughts of this European humanist into an ideology that is not always consonant with Marx's original thought. Marxism was further developed by Leninism to totalitarian communism, which was never Marx's intention. In a similar vein, the politicization of Islam is a process by which this religion is used for the articulation of political concerns that are not in line with Islamic faith. Political religion becomes a means for the pursuit of nonreligious ends. I keep repeating that Islamism is not Islam, yet add that Islamism is a political interpretation of this religion; in other words, it is based in Islam and does not lie outside of it. If these nuances are not properly understood, then one may make the mistake of conceiving Islamism merely as an instrumental abuse of Islam. In my three decades of research on Islamism, I have talked with a great number of Islamists throughout the world, and I know that they honestly perceive themselves as true believers. Their reference to Islam is not merely instrumental.

The politicization by which Islam is transformed into the political religion of Islamism is the core issue that emerges in a crisis-ridden social situation. Consider, for instance, its effect on Islam's claim to universality. The politicization of this universalism results in a political ideology of activist internationalism resembling that of internationalist communism. Both ideologies seek a remaking of the world. No wonder that Islamists, while rejecting many Western ideas (and claiming to reject all of them), borrow from communism the idea of world revolution.

The War of Ideas

For a scholar, taking the distinction between Islamism and Islam seriously is a risky thing to do. It has become common practice to hurl the charge of "Orientalism" at those who fail to comply with established taboos. Orientalism is a term popularized by the late Edward Said, who accused the West of creating an imaginary cultural space called "the Orient" in order to establish hegemony over Asian civilizations. But the issue is not only intellectual: the risks may include more existential threats. Islamism is not a club for free debate. When the scholar is a Muslim accused by Islamists of kufr, he or she may be threatened with death.

The Islamist accusation of heresy or infidelity and the scholarly accusation of Orientalism both reflect a mindset aimed at limiting thought and speech. Some people who are involved in the so-called war of ideas[9] perceive this war as a fight between democracy and Islamist jihadism. They seem unaware that they are echoing the Arabic term *harb al-afkar,* which also means "war of ideas" and was coined by the Islamists themselves. The source of this concept is Sayyid Qutb, who wrote in one of his major pamphlets that a war between *iman* (belief) and kufr (unbelief) takes the shape of a war of ideas. Kufr becomes a label for excluding anything that is seen not to be Islamic. In Qutb's view, the fight against unbelief assumes the character of a cosmic war. He writes: "The battle between the believers and their enemies is in its substance a fight over the religious dogma and absolutely nothing else. . . . It is not a political or an economic conflict, but in substance a war of ideas: either true belief or infidelity is to prevail [*imma iman imma kufr*]."[10] This fight defines the Islamist perspective of jihad in its new meaning of "an Islamic world revolution . . . for an Islamic world peace. It is not a peace that avoids violence at any price . . . for Islam is a permanent jihad . . . to achieve the just order based on Islamic tenets."[11]

These statements inspire the war of ideas that Islamists now fight. They maintain that there is no such a thing as a distinction between Islam and Islamism, but only one essential Islam. Those who agree are "true believers," while all those—including Muslims—who oppose this view stand against Islam. Muslims who do not buy into this argument are accused of *shurk* (heresy), or even kufr; critical non-Muslims are labeled Islamophobes. The reason for this dismissal is more than an expression of religious fanaticism. The distinction helps unravel Islamism and therefore is a fitting target in the war of ideas that Islamists wage.

There is an advantage to Islamists in presenting themselves as the voice of Islam. It helps to insulate them against criticism, as well as against persecution by Muslim rulers whom they identify as "enemies of Islam."

If Islamists have a rational motive for denying the distinction between Islamism and Islam, what can we say of their Western allies? In the Islamic diaspora of Europe—and partly in the United States—it has become common to accept the Islamist deception. Sunni Islamists legitimate *iham* (deception), the willful misleading of "infidels," as part of their war of ideas. In this they have found unwitting allies among those Europeans who view Islamism as a liberation theology and part of a progressive antiglobalization movement. (Some Islamists use these terms as well.) They are abetted by pragmatic American analysts who consider moderate Islamists suitable partners for U.S. diplomatic efforts in the Middle East. A highly disturbing example of this pragmatism is a policy article in *Foreign Affairs* in which the author advocates that the United States cultivate a relationship with the Muslim Brothers in Egypt.[12] In addition to factual errors (for instance, misinterpretations of the ideology and politics of the movement), the arguments for cooperation with the Muslim Brothers, underpinned by a notion of "moderate Islam," are based on ignorance of the movement itself. The Movement of the Muslim Brothers has long been one of the foremost pillars of political Islam in both its violent and nonviolent forms. The group's ideology of a nizam Islami (Islamic system of government) reflects an utterly totalitarian political agenda. Of course, there is a liberal and civil Islam, but the notion of "democratic Islamism" is a contradiction in terms.

The Institutional Islamists and the Jihadists

The distinction between institutional and jihadist Islamists is often referred to in public debates as a distinction between "moderate" and "radical" Islamists, but as I have mentioned, this is a misleading distortion.[13] Many "moderate" Islamists go to the ballot box and participate in politics within institutions, and some, but not all, forgo terror. Yet they do not abandon the Islamist agenda, which is a radical agenda for remaking the existing political order. What is "moderate" about this? It is more useful to speak of institutional Islamists and jihadists.

What makes jihadist Islamists "radical" in Western eyes is their commitment to violence in the form of irregular warfare. Thus the difference between "moderates" and "radicals" has to do only with means and ignores the two branches' common worldview. Moreover, because Islamism is a transnational movement with global networks, Islamists cannot be described as a "crazed gang," as Edward Said called them after 9/11. If they were really a "crazed gang," then they could be chased by police and brought to justice. In fact, Islamists constitute a powerful movement and are truly engaged in a war, of both violence and ideas. Having said that, I add with dismay that the flawed politics and practices of the George W. Bush administration did great damage to efforts to present realistic arguments about jihadist Islamism. Thus the fact of a new irregular warfare is ignored. Many people think that anyone who acknowledges the existence of this war must be a neoconservative. It is deplorable that this notion has been used to dismiss the analysis of jihadism within Islamism. Under the Obama administration the ideological dimension of this war is dismissed altogether, with the result that jihadists are often viewed as individual criminals.

The institutional and jihadist branches of Islamism are two aspects of a single transnational movement. In many countries in the world of Islam this movement is poised to seize power, whether through the abuse of democracy or through terror redefined as legitimate Islamic jihad.

It is also nonsensical to view institutional Islamists as "reformers" and jihadists as "revolutionaries."[14] Though the distinction between jihadist and institutional Islamists is important to understand, violence is only peripheral to the overall phenomenon of Islamism. Two dominant Western obsessions are wrong: the association of Islamism with violence, and the focus on peaceful Islamists as "moderates" and therefore amenable to accommodation with the West.

Denial

It is now time to turn to those who will not find comfort in this book. Basically, there exist three groups of people who will oppose any effort to distinguish Islamism from Islam.

First are the Islamists themselves. They will argue that there exists only one immutable Islam, of which they claim to be the true representatives. This idea of a monolithic Islam is used to legitimize Islamist political activities. But such an Islam does not exist, either religiously or culturally, outside of the Islamist mindset.

In direct opposition to the Islamists, the second group consists of those who demonize Islam altogether and deny any meaningful diversity within it. Adherents of this view contend that there is no distinct Islamism but a general "Islamic threat."

In response, some apologists reverse this argument: they accept the dismissal of a distinction between Islamism and Islam but allege that any threat posed by Islamists is a xenophobic myth. Between the extremes of the first and second groups, the third group tends to attract adherents of political correctness, who are simply against addressing the issues in clear and critical terms if doing so might invite a claim of disrespect to any religious or ethnic group. All of these groups have in common a tendency to overlook nuances and instead to look at Islam, either positively or negatively, as a monolithic entity.

The first group, the Islamists, understandably would not like to see themselves unveiled. Their invented tradition of just one valid Islam is a political construct, useful for discrediting any opposition to their views of the state order. To be sure, many—in fact most—Islamists honestly believe in the notion of one true Islam and place themselves among its true adherents. But these people, while honest, are also naïve. I know of Sunni Islamist leaders who, in a religious borrowing of the Shi'ite notion of *taqiyya* (dissimulation),[15] embrace the mindset of iham. By presenting themselves as the spokesmen of "true Islam," these leaders enable themselves to defame their critics with the equally invented and instrumental notion of Islamophobia.

Some Islamists cultivate a sense of victimization by imagining themselves as the "new Jews" and even speak of a "new Holocaust" against Muslims—a tragic irony when one considers how antisemitic most Islamists are. The accusation of Islamophobia serves as a weapon against all who do not embrace Islamist propaganda, including liberal Muslims. Most followers of Islamism are honest and do not play such games, but many of their leaders do. These leaders fight their war of ideas with all means available. It is worth noting that only some Islamists use the term *al-Islamiyya* (Islamism), which is established in modern Arabic. Most prefer to speak of *sahwa Islamiyya* (Islamic revival)[16] as a way to blur the distinction between Islam and Islamism. This suggests that something old and traditional has returned, and that the political use of Islam is not a modern invention. I argue in this book that Islamism is not a revival of any tradition.

The second and third groups of deniers both consist of groups in the West who conflate Islam with Islamism. The third group does so largely out of political correctness, and this group ultimately ends up—willingly or otherwise—aiding the Islamists by depicting them in a flattering light. Islamism becomes, in the title of a book by Raymond Baker, *Islam without Fear*.[17] The best example of this state of mind is the work of John Esposito, for whom the distinction between Islamism and Islam is totally absent. A close reading of Esposito's books reveals that he is nearly always dealing with the ideology of Islamism, not the religion of Islam.[18] His conclusion that Islam is compatible with democracy translates into approval of Islamism as a democratic movement. As I will show in Chapter 4, this view is utterly wrong. People of this mindset not only dismiss the distinction between Islam and Islamism but also misunderstand the differentiation within Islamism itself. Institutional Islamists and jihadists alike are committed to an Islamic order based on an invented shari'a. The fact that the jihadists employ violence does not make the institutional Islamists any less committed. The politically correct deniers close their eyes to this reality. Within this group are some people who not only prefer the distinction between "moderate Islam" and "radical Islam" but also refuse to hear any talk about an Islamist threat. Esposito makes his position clear in the title of his book *The Islamic Threat: Myth or Reality?* which accuses his critics of blurring those two things. Of course, since he speaks of an "Islamic," not an "Islamist," threat, much of the blurring is done by Esposito himself.

Another example is the French writer Gilles Kepel, who foresees the *déclin d'islamisme* (per the subtitle of his book, unfortunately published in 2000 and shortly belied by 9/11). The "decline of Islamism" is a wrong forecast. Still another popular French writer, Olivier Roy, keeps arguing that we are entering an age of "post-Islamism"—a term that evokes a deliberate parallel with postcommunism. This judgment is equally baseless. The notions of decline and post-Islamism reflect a misconception of the realities on the ground. Islamism is thriving. It results from a particular crisis and is underlain by normative and structural constraints. As long as this underpinning remains in place, Islamism will be a major factor throughout the Islamic world and also in its diaspora in the West, with no post-Islamism in sight.

While the first and third groups described above are apologetic about Islamism, the second not only rejects the distinction between Islamism and Islam but is generally hostile to everything (and everyone) Islamic. The depiction of Islam after 9/11 as "radical Islam" and as a threat to the Enlightenment has become a common Western narrative. If Islamists can be accused of coining the notion of Islamophobia to deter legitimate criticism as a religious defamation of Islam, this fact does not erase the existence of prejudice against Islam. Much popular discourse in Europe and America can be legitimately described as Islam-bashing.

One example of this way of thinking is the intelligent but facile book by Lee Harris, *The Suicide of Reason: Radical Islam's Threat to the*

Enlightenment. Harris is one of those Westerners (like William McNeill)[19] who speak of civilization in the singular and deny a civilizational history to everyone outside Europe and its colonial offshoots. He carries on the tradition of viewing non-Westerners as *People without History.*[20]

Harris speaks reverently of the Enlightenment but seems to be in the dark about the three hundred years of Islamic intellectual history, from the ninth to the twelfth centuries, that contributed to it.[21] During that era, a variety of Islamic rationalism thrived that I sometimes describe as an Islamic Enlightenment. Medieval Muslim rationalists from Farabi to Averroës advocated the primacy of reason, which is what the Enlightenment is all about.[22] This tradition was passed over to Europe and, according to the Swiss historian Jacob Burckhardt, helped shape the European Renaissance.[23] Yet Harris depicts Muslims as a people who have not only never achieved rationalism but are apparently incapable of it. He attributes to all Muslims a "radical Islam" characterized by fanaticism and intolerance. Not only did they commit the attacks of 9/11, but they are willfully bringing about "the suicide of reason."

Though not an expert on Islam, Harris is sufficiently confident of his knowledge to discern that it is dominated by "a populist tradition of fanatical intolerance."[24] This tradition is sustained by the "simple fact that Muslim fanaticism works, and throughout the centuries it has worked with spectacular success."[25] Muslims are essentialized as "intolerant fanatics" (a tautology that is repeated throughout) whom no one can change. "Fanatical intolerance," Harris tells us, "made Muslims . . . impervious to all outside efforts to change their fundamental way of life." The conclusion seems clear: all Muslims are to be viewed as fundamentalists and a "threat to the Enlightenment." One may conclude from these distortions and misconceptions that Harris is knowledgeable neither about the dialectics of Enlightenment and how it relates to fascism nor about the crisis of Islamic civilization that generates Islamism.

Another example of this mindset is the book *Surrender,* by Bruce Bawer.[26] *Surrender,* which excoriates liberal American media and academic institutions for abetting (as the jacket copy describes it) "pressure and intimidation designed to crush the ability of non-Muslims to resist Islamic encroachments on Western freedom," is an alert not about Islamism but about Islam in general. Bawer sees Ayatollah Khomeini's pronouncement of a death sentence against the novelist Salman Rushdie for his book *The Satanic Verses* "as illuminating the eternal nature of Islam itself—and its attitudes toward freedom." He not only makes no distinction between Islamism and Islam but states that there is no such thing as liberal Islam.[27]

The few knowledgeable scholars among this group who are generally hostile to Islam also deny the distinction between Islam and Islamism. One of them is Andrew Bostom, who has published two highly informative anthologies on jihad and on antisemitism.[28] The flaw in Bostom's work, unlike Harris's, is not a lack of knowledge but rather an apparent inability to engage in clear-cut differentiations. This problem is demonstrated by Bostom's confusion of traditional Islamic Judeophobia with modern Islamist antisemitism, and his confusion of classical jihad with contemporary jihadism. I shall not elaborate on these issues here because I discuss Islamist antisemitism and jihadism in later chapters.

The Political Order: The Islamic State and the Remaking of the World

The most important point is what all Islamists share: an ambition for a remaking of the world. Islamism is not about violence but above all about the order of the world. Therefore, the neo-Arabic term *nizam* (system) is central to Islamist ideology. The political order of Islamism is also a new world order. The established world order, based on the 1648 Peace of Westphalia, is secular, while the envisioned one is sacral, based on the concept of a *dawla Islamiyya,* the Islamic shari'a-based state, and on hakimiyyat Allah (God's rule) to replace popular sovereignty. This order vehemently rejects the "Westphalian synthesis" and it is supposed to be enhanced, Islamists say, to an international Islamic system. There existed in the past a universal Islamic order, for which Marshall G. S. Hodgson coined the term "Islamicate." That order united the world of Islam as a kind of a civilizational entity as well as in a political sense. Nonetheless, this should not be confused with the modern system. The notion of world order does not exist in the traditional Islamic doctrine. Its use by Islamists reflects an invention of Islamic tradition using ideas about world order that have been introduced through neo-Arabic terms not known to Islamic heritage.

The origins of political Islam can be traced back to the emergence of the Movement of the Muslim Brothers, founded in 1928 in Sunni-Arab Islam in Cairo. This fact runs counter to a common Western misconception. Islamism did not arise out of the 1979 Shi'ite Khomeinist revolution in Iran. Sunni Islamism is much older than Khomeinism. Therefore, in this book I focus on Sunni-Arab Islamism and explain its spillover to the rest of the Muslim world, while also attending to the Shi'ite impact in such important areas as the transfer of Shi'ite martyrdom in Sunni suicide bombing or the adoption of taqiyya in the new shape of iham.

In terms of the distinction between institutional Islamists and jihadists, the original Muslim Brothers without doubt belong in the jihadist category. They subscribed to terror and practiced it on all possible levels. The founder of the movement, Hasan al-Banna, made this view abundantly clear in his "Risalat al-Jihad," where he writes: "There are some Muslims who are misguided by the view that fighting the enemy is the lesser jihad compared with the greater self-jihad . . . as jihad of the heart. . . . This is a clear distraction from the importance of physical fighting [*qital*] as substance of the jihad. . . . It ranks next to the great profession of allegiance to Islam [*shahadah*]. Jihad means to kill and to be killed on the path of Allah. . . . Oh, Brothers, Allah gratifies in this world and also at heaven the umma that masters the art of death, and knows how to die in dignity. . . . Be advised, death is inescapable, and it happens at once."[29]

This passage does not reflect an "Islamic revival" but instead documents the shift from traditional jihad to jihadism. It gives religious legitimacy to suicidal terrorism that cultivates death on the path of Allah. In a way, al-Banna anticipated the adoption of martyrdom from Shi'ite Islam that took place after 1979. The glorification of death as political sacrifice is more reminiscent of Georges Sorel's *Réflections sur la violence,* one of the sources of European fascism, than of the respectful Islamic ethics of life. In the past, when Muslims fought jihad as a regular war—not as terror—to disseminate Islam, they never glorified death as al-Banna did.

Today, the Muslim Brothers repress their terrorist past and claim to have become a moderate movement of institutional Islam that embraces democracy. Yet they do not dissociate themselves from the al-Banna tradition. This benign pose is taken at face value by some, even in *Foreign Affairs*.[30] But the Muslim Brothers' transformation, if genuine, points only to a difference in means. They have not abandoned their vision of a shari'a-based Islamic state as a political order, the most basic feature of Islamism.

In the West the notion of an "Islamic state" is often confused with the "restoration of the caliphate." Only the Islamist movement *hizb ut-Tahrir* (Party of Liberation) advocates such a restoration. The Muslim Brothers never talk about it. Their concern is the nizam Islami, by which they mean the modern shari'a-based Islamic state. Islamism invents the tradition of a shari'a state and gives it the new name nizam Islami.

Adherents of institutional Islamism agree to elections but shun the political philosophy of civic values or democratic pluralism. Their commitment to democracy is thus highly questionable. The most prominent example of institutional Islamism is the AKP, which has ruled Turkey since 2002.[31] The leaders of AKP are intelligent politicians who know well that the Supreme Court would ban their party if they publicly pronounce their agenda, but they nonetheless practice a politics of "creeping Islamization." One great step in this direction is the plan for a new constitution that allows the judiciary to be simultaneously weakened and reshaped. For the moment Turkey's judiciary is still secular; this is, however, in flux, as will be shown in chapter 6. In the Arab Middle East, other Islamist movements are already involved in the business of government: Hamas[32] is ruling Gaza and is ready to take over the West Bank. The war of 2008–9 weakened Hamas militarily but not politically, and it was foreseeable that the war could not eradicate it. The AKP-supported flotilla incident of May 2010 was a political triumph for Hamas. In Lebanon, Hezbollah[33] is represented in the government and parliament. Most Shi'ite parties in Iraq[34] after the U.S.-led liberation from Saddam Hussein's dictatorship follow Islamist precepts. In Egypt the Muslim Brothers are ready to take over; they are resurgent since the Arab Spring and continue to bill their Islamism as democracy. So where is Kepel's "End of Islamism"?

Islamism's "Jewish Conspiracy" against the Islamist World Order

A second feature of Islamism is a perception of competition over the world order. Sayyid Qutb's book *Our Battle against the Jews* nurtures the Islamist obsession with a Jewish conspiracy against Islam. The Islamized antisemitism that grew from Qutb's writings is different from the secular Judeophobia once embraced by pan-Arab nationalism. It is also different from traditional Islamic Judeophobia. A part of Islamist antisemitism is the adoption of the idea, taken from the fabricated *Protocols of the Elders of Zion,* that attributes to the Jews the aspiration to rule the world. Today this view is combined with anti-Americanism, as Islamists believe that the Jews rule the world from New York and Washington. Thus the Islamic world order envisioned by Islamism is seen as directly threatening, and threatened by, "world Jewry."

The necessity of "countering the Jews" is thus central to the worldview of Islamism and not related to any specific conflict, not even the conflict with Israel. As we will see in Chapter 3, Islamists view the Jews as a "cosmic enemy." Underlying this view is the belief in a deeply rooted rivalry between an Islamic and a Jewish world order. When the Movement of the Muslim Brotherhood was founded in 1928, there existed no state of Israel and obviously no related conflict. Nevertheless, the Muslim Brothers saw themselves as struggling with a "Jewish conspiracy" against besieged Islam. The view that Islamist Judeophobia results from the Israeli-Palestinian conflict, and will disappear once it is resolved, is thus utterly wrong. The history of the Muslim Brotherhood reveals that political Islam takes issue with the Jews regardless of the Middle East conflict. Nonetheless, in British Mandate Palestine there existed a conflation of Palestinean-nationalist and Islamist-universalist antisemitism.

In an Islamist reading of history, the alleged cosmic war between Islam and Judaism began with the creation of the Medina polity in 622. Qutb maintains that the Prophet established in Medina the very first "Islamic state" and that this was opposed by "the Jews." Today, Islam is perceived to be under siege, and Islamists attribute this siege to the "conspiracy" growing out of a supposed war of nearly fourteen hundred years. Their primary concern is clearly not the Israelis and Palestinians. It is to annihilate what Qutb and his fellows view as an "evil." This is the substance of their antisemitism. This is more than a phobia, and it is what makes Islamism a genocidal ideology. The German historians Mallmann and Cüppers disclosed in their book *Nazi Palestine*[35] Islamist plans, designed with the German military, to implement this ideology in a Holocaust "planned for the Jews in Palestine."

Not only my commitment to Muslim humanism prompts me to argue that this murderous ideology is alien to Islam. At issue is also the Islamist claim that the foremost goal of "world Jewry" is to create a world order. This falsehood makes Jews not only an enemy but an enemy with whom no peace is possible. If this idea represents an *Islamic* and not an Islamist antisemitism, how could one ever argue for peace between Jews and Muslims?

Modern antisemitism was introduced to the Middle East by Arab Christians under French influence beginning in 1905, but it later infected the secular Arab-Muslim nationalists. European antisemitism is an ideology that had no roots in the traditional culture and religion of Islam. Many Western writers and experts on this issue not only confuse traditional Judeophobia with modern antisemitism but also confuse pan-Arab nationalism (as embraced by such midcentury figures as Gamal Abdel Nasser) with Islamism. In so doing they fail to understand that two distinct antisemitisms are at work: one secular, the other religionized. The former is imported from Europe and remains at the surface, while the Islamized antisemitism claims authenticity and presents its prejudice as an appealing religious belief. These writers also ignore Hannah Arendt's recommendation that we distinguish between traditional Judeophobia and modern antisemitism: the first is based on resentment, the latter is a genocidal ideology.

Democracy and Democratization

The third subject required for understanding the distinction between Islam and Islamism is the attitude of each toward democracy. The American missionary effort to democratize the world of Islam through wars in Afghanistan and Iraq has put Islamism in a new, highly skeptical stance toward democracy. After toppling Saddam Hussein's regime, the United States had no choice but to cooperate with Saddam's most visible domestic enemies, the powerful Islamist opposition, in the name of promoting democracy. The distinction between institutional and jihadist Islamism thus became highly relevant to U.S. policy. The Obama administration has transformed this difference into a distinction between "moderate Muslims" and nameless "terrorists," and has employed this approach to justify doing business with the former. These were placed in positions of authority. During the Bush years jihadists were declared enemies in a largely unsuccessful "war on terror." The Obama administration has avoided any reference to Islamism and to jihadism to justify its indiscriminate conciliatory policy of engagement toward Muslims and distinguishing them from those "radicals."

Despite their very different policies, both the Bush and Obama administrations have proceeded from unexamined assumptions. While institutional and jihadist Islamists differ in their preferred means of gaining power, they are in agreement about vision, worldview, and the issue of governance related to their ultimate goal of an Islamic shari'a state. How compatible is this envisioned order with democracy? I shall address that question fully in Chapters 2 and 4. Here, two points must suffice. The first relates to the distinction between Islam and Islamism, the second to the compatibility of Islam and democracy. There is no doubt that Islam, as a source of political ethics, in the course of religious reform, can exist in harmony with democracy. But Islamists constitute the foremost and best organized political opposition in the world of Islam. When an election takes place, as happened in Gaza and in Iraq, Islamists often win and take power. In Gaza, their victory in the 2006 elections did not prevent them from a violent, complete takeover in June 2007. Since then, all Hamas detractors have remained in jail without trial. Prospects are uncertain for the fairness of the next election—if indeed it takes place at all.

Institutional Islamists split democracy into two segments, much as they do with modernity itself. They adopt modern instruments and procedures, including electoral politics, while rejecting the values of cultural modernity. Islamists approve the ballot box as a mechanism of voting, thus reducing democracy to an instrumental procedure. But they do not espouse the more important aspect of democracy, democratic pluralism and power sharing. They reject the political philosophy and civic culture of democracy as Western and alien to Islam. Can democratization succeed on such a basis?

Beyond superficial procedures such as holding elections, there are deeper questions of Islamists' adherence to the democratic process. This process requires that all involved parties not only forgo violence but consent to the core values and procedures of democracy. The distinction between institutional and jihadist Islamists makes sense only when the former really abandon all forms of violence and stick to the rules of a civil system. The distinction is blurred to the point of meaninglessness when so-called moderate Islamist movements engage in the ballot-box game while still maintaining violent militias. Hamas in Palestine, Hezbollah in Lebanon, the Supreme Iraqi Council (SIQ) and the Mahdi Movement in Iraq are all represented as political parties in their respective elected parliaments yet also maintain militias.[36] They go to the ballot box, get senior figures elected to the parliament, but continue to practice violence through their militias, which they refuse to disband. How can the combination of the ballot box with the bullet be consonant with democracy?

The only Islamist party I know of that functions without a militia is Turkey's AKP. But even the AKP has been accused—by the general prosecutor of Turkey in a July 2008 trial in the Turkish constitutional court—of pursuing a "creeping Islamization" of the country. The AKP was not fully acquitted of this accusation, although the judges, in their verdict, declined to ban the party in order to save the country from severe conflict. In 2010 the AKP responded by drafting a new constitution that not only changes the constitutional court but also restructures the entire judiciary to the AKP's benefit.[37] The politics of creeping Islamization of secular Turkey becomes more visible. The AKP's Islamism[38] is an exceptional case that, for a variety of reasons, cannot be generalized. But because it is the prime exhibit for those who argue that political participation will lead Islamist movements to adjust to democracy, it merits a brief discussion. Keep in mind that democracy is not merely about ballot boxes and voting booths, it is also, and more basically, about the core values of a civic political culture. There are many reasons to doubt the AKP's commitment to democracy, among which are Turkey's regular attacks on the freedom of the press and arrests of political opponents with no legal procedure. This is a pattern of institutional Islamism. What is happening is not an adjustment of an Islamist party to a secular republic but rather the reverse. Under the AKP we are seeing the desecularization and de-Westernization of a Kemalist republic that was once a model for a secular democracy in the world of Islam. Add to this the increasing closeness of AKP-led Turkey to Iran, Hamas, and Hezbollah, and the picture clearly suggests a drift away from the West.[39]

Classical Jihad and Contemporary Jihadist Terrorism

No one can write about Islamism without touching on the subject of jihad. Islamism is not terrorism, and this book dissociates both Islam and Islamism from violence. Nonetheless, the jihadization of violence in a new warfare not only is much more than terror, it is an important feature of Islamism. The distinction between Islam and Islamism matters especially when we consider the question of the legitimization of violence. In Islam jihad means not only "self-exertion" but also, as the Qur'an prescribes, the implementation of *qital:* physical fighting against the unbelievers for the spread of Islam. When Islamic civilization was highly developed, between the seventh and seventeenth centuries, Muslims engaged in jihad wars for the expansion of the "Islamicate" as an international civilization. According to the foremost historian of Islam, Marshall G. S. Hodgson, Muslims of that time engaged in the "formation of an international political order."[40] This expansion was eventually tamed by the rising West and ended with the decline of Islamic civilization.

The related historical development is summarized in Chapter 2 as a process of a mapping of the entire globe into an international system determined by the "Westphalian synthesis."[41] Today Islamism is the foremost variety of a "revolt against the West," in which the distinction between cultural modernity and Western hegemony is missing. What matters here are the Islamists' responses to the decline of their civilization in the course of the evolution of the modern international system and expansion of international society.[42] These responses are partly a continuation of the Islamic "Shari'a reasoning,"[43] however, in an invention of tradition. In this context, cultural modernity and its reversals in a counterenlightenment[44] also matter to Islamic civilization in its crisis resulting from a predicament with modernity.[45] The contemporary efforts of some scholars with an Islamic background to discard these problems by dismissing the Westphalian international system as an expression of "Eurocentrism" can be qualified as a "defensive culture," not as a contribution to a proper understanding of the issue.[46] How did the Islamic worldview adjust to this change?

The most authoritative institution of Islamic learning in Sunni Islam is the millennium-old al-Azhar University in Cairo. The authoritative textbook *Bayan li al-Nas* (Declaration to humanity), a product of al-Azhar, recommends that followers abandon "armed jihad."[47] A fatwa issued by Sheykh al-Azhar ranks highest in the religious establishment of Sunni Islam. The recommendation against armed jihad is such a fatwa. In a personal meeting in September 1989, the late sheikh Jadu-ul Haq reconfirmed this fatwa to me in a strong condemnation of "armed jihad." Leaders of political Islam, however, dismiss this fatwa and consider this recommendation a submission to the enemies of Islam.

The evolution of classical jihad into modern jihadism was launched by Hasan al-Banna. Sayyid Qutb's concept of an "Islamic world revolution" was later added as "global jihad." This revolution is meant to restore the *siyadat al-Islam* (dominance of Islam), not the caliphate. Al-Banna and Qutb laid the foundations not only for this legitimation of violence but also for transforming classical jihad, as a regular warfare conducted by the Islamic state, into terror waged by Islamist nonstate actors. This jihadism heralds much more than simple terrorism or insurgency. The new violence is no more than an instrument in the process of a remaking of the world according to the tenets of a reinvented shari'a. This context is largely absent from the mushrooming literature on jihad in the West, and also from U.S. policy, of both the Bush and the Obama administrations.

The Shari'atization of Islam

In this chapter and throughout this book I make frequent use of Eric Hobsbawm's concept of the invention of tradition. One of the key areas in which Islamism invents tradition is in its call for a "return" to shari'a law. Many scholars (including one of the academic reviewers of this book) will object that law has always been central to Islam, and thus Islamists' demand for a state legal order based on shari'a cannot be an "invention of tradition." Perhaps, they will argue, it may be described as an attempt to impose an old order that is at odds with modern realities, but surely I am wrong to call shari'a an invented tradition. I reply (and explain in detail in Chapter 6) that the Islamist understanding of shari'a is a fundamentally new one, which differs in crucial respects from the traditional or inherited shari'a. A shari'atized Islam is not traditional Islam but an invention of tradition.

Shari'a reflects a specific reasoning in Islam that has three different meanings. The first is scriptural: in the Qur'an (where the word appears but once, sure 45, verse 18), shari'a is a guide to moral conduct. The second meaning unfolded with the development of the Islamic legal tradition beginning in the eighth century. In this usage, shari'a was law for *mu'amalat* (roughly, civil law) and *ibadat* (cult rules), apart from the penal code of *hudud*. But as Joseph Schacht has argued in his authoritative *Introduction to Islamic Law,* in classical Islam there was always a clear line between shari'a and *siyasa* (politics).[48] This should not be confused with the modern separation of church and state— the caliph was expected to uphold shari'a law—but shari'a was not *identical* to the political order. Shari'a law never took the form of a uniform legal code: it consisted largely of individual judgments by Islamic jurists, the faqihs (*fuqaha'*), who were different from the theologians (*mutakalimun*).

The third meaning of shari'a is a new one that unfolded in the course of the politicization of Islam to Islamism. In this context, shari'a becomes a claim for a state law, to be written into national constitutions. Shari'a is supposed to be written into national constitutions and to direct the legal code passed by legislatures. This is an entirely new phenomenon within Islam, and the claim that it restores some historical institution is precisely an invention of tradition: an effort to inculcate certain behavioral values and norms by asserting continuity with imagined past practices. But it is a necessary invention. The claim to derive its laws not from human deliberation but from the will of God is central to Islamist ideology. This is what the Islamist shari'atization of Islam is all about.

How Authentic Is the Islamist Worldview?

Between the early nineteenth century and the middle of the twentieth century, a significant Westernization of the world of Islam took place under the name of modernization, but this model of development is now largely failed. These efforts nonetheless brought considerable modernization and secularization. Contemporary efforts at purification, which represent a backlash against this process, are undertaken in the name of authenticity. This is no retraditionalization, however, but another invention of tradition, as the claim to restore lost authenticity is imbued with modernity.

The West and Islam share a history not only of mutual conquest but of cultural borrowing. This positive legacy needs to be revived against those—Islamists and Westerners alike—obsessed with the rhetoric of a clash of civilizations. One is tempted to compare medieval Hellenization with modern Westernization. Medieval Islam's encounter with Hellenism led to a flowering of Islamic civilization. But with Islamic supremacy came the conquest of Constantinople, which ended the Byzantine Empire. Modern European expansion turned the tables and ended Islam's supremacy, but modern efforts at Westernization have been less successful than medieval Hellenization was. Islamism, which is clearly a reaction against the recent effects of Western globalization, confuses civilizational encounters and cultural borrowing with Western hegemony. The Islamist revolt against the West is partly a cultural uprising against Westernization. To the extent that it preserves and advances Islamic culture as a legitimate alternative to that of the West, this revolt would not be entirely a bad thing, if only it did not confuse cultural modernity with Western hegemony.

Why has the "revolt against the West" become a reflexive, antisemitic rejection of all things Western? Islamists like Anwar al-Jundi claim to see a Jewish conspiracy behind the *taghrib,* the "Western agenda of Westernization." The fight for authenticity is thus identified with an agenda of purification that combines anti-Americanism with antisemitism. The Islamization of antisemitism is a central segment in the story of Islamism. The Islamist mindset rejects the Islamic tradition of cross-civilizational fertilization and cultural borrowing. This history is not well known to most postmodernists, who praise cultural authenticity without necessarily being familiar with its substance. They do not understand how sharply Islamism differs from the classical heritage of Islam, which always displayed an open-minded spirit vis-à-vis the non-Muslim cultural other.

Islamism as Totalitarianism

This book's journey into the distinction between Islamism and Islam ends with an effort at defining Islamism as a new variety of totalitarianism. The political religion of Islamism does not, as some believe, provide a way forward for Islamic civilization in a time of crisis. Societies in crisis may go in many directions: they may democratize, or they may become susceptible to totalitarian ideologies. In Chapter 8 I argue that Islamism would move the world of Islam firmly in the latter direction.

Except for the Islamic Republic of Iran, the toppled Taliban regime in Afghanistan, Turkey under AKP rule, and the participation of Islamists in power in Iraq, Lebanon, and Palestine, Islamism is still part of the political opposition throughout the world of Islam—often the most significant part. In this book I focus on the Islamist movements seeking to establish a shari'a state. The study of their ideology does not support the view that Islamism is compatible with pluralist democracy and therefore I disagree with those commentators who would upgrade nonviolent Islamism to an engine of democratization. If we examine Islamism in light of Hannah Arendt's theoretical framework, we can see that it is the most recent variety of totalitarianism, not a force for democracy. The seizure of power by Islamists in any Middle Eastern state is therefore a disastrous outcome for that state. The slogan of the Islamists is *al-Islam huwa al-hall* (Islam is the solution). I argue that Islam is not the solution, at least not a political solution for the existing crisis of development and of political rule of authoritarian regimes. Islamists rightly refer to an existing crisis (in development, in economy, in the legitimacy of power, and in cultural alienation), but the solution they present, when it takes concrete form as the shari'a state, points to totalitarian rule. If they were to seize power, whether through jihad or through the ballot box, they would not be in position to solve the problems of Islamic societies. They can do no better than deliver stability—as in Iran—in a totalitarian context. Even in Iran we find the regime resorting to escalating levels of repression in order to maintain its rule. Also in Iran, which conducts formal but meaningless elections, the new totalitarianism rules, not "Islamic democracy."

True, the existing secular authoritarian regimes present an obstacle to development and to democratization. There is a need for an alternative, but Islamism is not the appropriate alternative. Replacing these regimes with a system based on religionized politics would amount to replacing one disease with another. Iraq is a case in point, and in no way a promising one. The second Bush administration once envisioned using Iraq as a model for democratization—not only throughout the Middle East but for the world of Islam at large. The lesson that experience should have taught them is this: do not bring Islamists to power in the name of democracy! The Bush "Middle East initiative," which tried to do precisely that, was a disaster. The distinction between Islamism and Islam that I present here is thus pertinent to American foreign policy under Barack Obama. But despite frequent references to rival American administrations, I hope to go beyond these topicalities and to provide a lasting assessment of Islamism, a phenomenon that seems likely to endure as long as Islam's predicament with modernity prevails.

Do the Media Help Us Think Usefully about Islamism?

I want to end this chapter with some comments about how the media portray this issue. I shall refer to a report about how a partly Muslim country,

Bosnia, has been hijacked by Islamists. The fate of Islam in Bosnia is a case in point for the Western response to Islamism.

Bosnia was once among those places that practiced a beautiful form of Islam—like the civil Islam of Indonesia or the Afro-Islam of Senegal—but this European Islam was largely killed off in the 1992–95 war. The killers were not only Serbians engaged in ethnic cleansing. The European Islam of Bosnia also fell victim to Arab-Muslim Islamists who ostensibly came to rescue their brothers in faith against "crusaders." Among these were jihadists known as Arab Afghans and Wahhabi Saudis who successfully replaced European Islam with their Salafist Wahhabism. Today the earlier open Islam survives in only a few places. Islamism and Wahhabism prevail in Bosnia and in Kosovo. Since 1995 Saudi Arabia has invested more than 500 million Euros to promote Wahhabi Islam in Bosnia. The greatest mosque in Sarajevo carries the name of the late Saudi king Fahd. Madrasa faith schools and kindergartens, all built after the war for indoctrination, are sprouting up throughout the country.

How do the Western media cover this process? Here is one example: an *International Herald Tribune* article in its weekend edition of December 27–28, 2008, carries the headline "Bosnia Experiencing an Islamic Revival." In the eyes of the *Herald Tribune,* the invention of tradition in an Islamization agenda equals an "Islamic revival." What does this revival look like? The article rightly gives this description: "Before the war, fully covered women and men with long beards were almost unheard of. Today, they are commonplace." Why? The article describes the "Muslim revival as a healthy assertion of identity." The reality is that it is the result of Islamization supported by Saudi Wahhabism. The *Herald Tribune* article trivializes this concern and quotes the Saudi-friendly Mufti of Bosnia, Mustafa Cerić, who "has played down worries about Islamic fundamentalism." The article goes a step further and cites "Muslim leaders and Western analysts" who dismiss concerns about an "Islamization of Bosnian culture and politics" as "an attempt by Serb nationalists to justify the brutal wartime subjugation of Muslims by both Serbs and Croats." The piece ends by quoting the defamatory slogan "Will You America Kill Muslims?"

This article—one of many I could have chosen—demonstrates how difficult it has become to speak plainly about Islamism and Islam in the current atmosphere of a "war of ideas." The Islamists have succeeded in defaming their critics as "Islamophobic" and pushing forward their narrative that Islam is under siege and Muslims are victims. This touches on Christian guilt, with the result that some Western scholars and opinion leaders, out of a general sympathy for victims, join in the defamation. Thus if you worry about the eradication of European Islam in Bosnia in favor of Wahhabism and Islamism, you risk being called an ally of the Serbian genocide.

Yet it is worth taking this risk. Beyond its iham (willful deception), Islamism precludes any dialogue with those outside its own circle of belief. Western critics are defamed as "crusaders," and Muslims who disagree are accused of committing kufr (unbelief). Undeniably, prejudice against Islam exists in the West and needs to be fought. Still, the notion of "Islamophobia" has become a weapon in the hands of Islamism and is no longer either useful in rational discourse or appropriate for fighting prejudice against Islam. I therefore propose to replace this charged notion with the term "Islam-bashing." To criticize Islamism is not to defame Islam. After all, non-Islamist Muslims are in a better position to understand political Islam and are among its staunchest critics.[49]

This book is an effort to help readers think properly about Islamism so that they will be better equipped to deal with this new totalitarianism. My intent is to discourage any engagement of Islamism that is based on false assumptions, in particular the assumption that there is a distinction between "moderate Islamists" and "terrorists." This mistaken idea must be replaced with a distinction between liberal-civil Islam and Islamism. Liberal and civil Islam is not "a small slice of Muslim societies," as an article in *Foreign Affairs* has suggested. Western analysts should beware of the Islamist game of iham and be extremely cautious about taking Islamists' words at face value. The West should engage in a dialogue with liberal Islam while emphasizing security in dealing with Islamists.

The Obama administration is to be congratulated for abandoning the rhetoric of the "war on terror," which too often became derailed into a war on Islam. That was exactly what Islamists hoped for, to help foster a perception of "Islam under siege." Yet while this administration appears to be more attentive to Muslim concerns, it seems to err in the opposite direction. The "sidelining of religious freedom"[50] aimed at appeasing Islamism in the guise of "moderate Islam" is no less damaging than the "war on terror." Thus it was reassuring to read in a *New York Times* op-ed piece by Patrick French the advice that President Obama should "recognize the real and immediate danger of the Islamist threat." French, who clearly has experience in the world of Islam, writes: "Millenarian Islamists are now seeking to destroy Pakistan as a nation-state, and realize that they have won a strategic victory. . . . President Obama's hope of weaning moderate elements in Afghanistan and Pakistan away from violence . . . is stymied by the fact that the Pakistani Taliban know they are winning. Making a real deal with them now is appeasement."[51] This statement could apply equally to all nation-states targeted by Islamism throughout the world of Islam.

The West's stance toward the world of Islam can be promising only if policymakers can pursue an engagement that does not succumb to the Islamist terms of discourse. No effort at building bridges between Islam and the West can succeed without an awareness of the distinction between Islam and Islamism.

Scholars as well as policymakers have been intimidated by Islamists who cry Islamophobia. Scholars protect themselves by pretending uncertainty. Richard Martin and Abbas Barzegar, the editors of *Islamism: Contested Perspectives on Political Islam,* write that their book does not "resolve the debate about Islamism" or take a stand in the controversy about "the usefulness of the term." Nonetheless, they have recruited two lead essayists who discard the notion of Islamism: Donald Emmerson, who labels the distinction between Islamism and Islam "invidious," and Daniel Varisco, who declares emphatically that "Islamism is a term we should abandon." The book provides evidence for the misgiving expressed in a most critical book on Islamism by Paul Berman: "The Islamist movement . . . has succeeded in imposing its own categories of analysis over how everyone else tends to think."[52]

2

Islamism and the Political Order

T HE FIRST STEP IN THE ISLAMIST invention of Islamic tradition is to establish a new understanding of Islam as din-wa-dawla: religion united with a state order.[1] When Islamists speak of *al-hall al-Islami* (Islamic solution), they mean not democracy but rather a remaking of the existing political order in pursuit of the Islamic shari'a state. It is this idea, not violence, that is the hallmark and *conditio sine qua non* of Islamism. It is no exaggeration to contend that Islamism puts the unity of religion and state[2] almost on an equal footing with shahadah (allegiance to Islam) as a test of how truly Islamic one is. Thus if you want to know whether a Muslim is an Islamist, ask him, "Is Islam for you a faith, or is it an order of the state?" Any Muslim who replies that "Islam is a state order" can be safely considered an Islamist. In my reading of American and European studies on political Islam, I have found that most analysts do not understand this dimension. Instead they reduce Islamism to the notion of "radical Islam" and overlook its quest for an Islamic order.[3] Not until the idea of the Islamic state is abandoned can one talk about "post-Islamism."

Our analysis of six basic features of Islamist ideology thus begins with the most important feature, the political order.

Islamism Is a Political Ideology of the Islamic State

Among the best sources for the study of Islamism is what former Islamists write. The British-Pakistani activist Maajid Nawaz not only was in the leadership of the Islamist Hizb ut-Tahrir (UT) but also spent four years in

Egyptian prison after the disclosure of his Islamist underground activities. Later Nawaz cofounded the Quilliam Foundation for the purpose of opposing Islamism. In his writings he contends that Islamism is about not theology but a political ideology. Islamists politicize Islam in "their desire for an Islamic state."[4]

The establishment of a *nizam Islami* (Islamic system) is meant to be the first step in an incremental process. What makes Islamism a global issue is the second part of this vision: the extension of the Islamic state to create a world order. The proclaimed Islamist world revolution not only aims to remake the political order of the territorial state, it is also directed toward a remaking of the world. Like Christianity, Islam is a religion with a universalist mission: it explicitly seeks to extend its doctrine throughout the world. Islamism transforms Islamic universalism into a political internationalism that seeks to replace the existing secular order of sovereign nation-states with an Islamist one. In this way Islamism resembles the communist doctrine. In place of the Marxist proletariat, which is expected to carry world revolution, Islamist internationalism offers an invented umma. This Islamist umma, unlike the traditional Islamic umma, is not a community of faith but a political movement whose members support the imposition of strict shari'a law by the state.

The terms used to describe this agenda do not occur in either the Qur'an or established classical sources. While the agenda is allegedly based on the Islamic shari'a,[5] closer scrutiny reveals that the envisioned remaking of state and world order is an invented tradition[6] with no precedent in the traditional shari'a of classical Islam.

Just as the secular sovereign state is the nucleus of the Westphalian order, the shari'a state is supposed to be the cornerstone of the Islamic order. These two world orders are mutually incompatible. It is a fallacy to believe that the Islamist vision of a new world order can be accommodated within a pluralist order, since Islamism explicitly rejects both other conceptions of the state and even the very idea of pluralism. It follows that Islamism, with its goal of replacing the current conception of the nation-state with a wholly different conception, constitutes an explicit threat to the existing world order. This threat is not a myth. True, Islamists lack the power to accomplish this goal, but they can destabilize many nations and thus generate disorder.[7]

The New Revolt

To understand the Islamist revolt one needs a correct grasp of the Westphalian order. According to the historian Charles Tilly, the Peace of Westphalia of 1648 changed the world and gave it a new shape. This treaty accomplished two things: it established the sovereign state as the fundamental unit of international relations, and it decoupled the religious establishments from the individual states. Sovereign states, as secular entities, were henceforth forbidden to go to war over religious differences. "Over the next three hundred years," Tilly writes in his 1975 book *The Formation of the National States in Western Europe,* "the Europeans and their descendents managed to impose that state system on the entire world." He goes on to say that "the recent wave of de-colonization has almost completed the mapping of the globe into that system."[8] In other words, almost the entire world is now the dominion of secular nation-states on the Westphalian model that originated in Europe. This is a political reality, not, as some Muslim scholars contend, a Eurocentric idea of international relations theory.

Islamists aim to overturn this world-historical reality.[9] The Islamist revolt against the secular nation-state, which began as a war within Islam, thus becomes a geo-civil war.[10] In a reversal of the "end of history"[11] prematurely pronounced by Francis Fukuyama at the end of the cold war, Islamists promote the return of history as a history of civilizations. This recourse to "civilizations" is an Islamist theme that has nothing to do with the late Samuel Huntington, whose book *The Clash of Civilizations* shows no familiarity with Islamist ideology. The clash of civilizations envisioned by Islamism, which predates Huntington's book, is not about the West and the rest but about Islam against the rest of the world, primarily the West. One can find this framework in Sayyid Qutb's writings, paraphrased most recently by his heir Yusuf al-Qaradawi.

The late Oxford scholar Hedley Bull described the rejection of the secular order of nation-states as a "revolt against the West." Unlike the earlier struggle against colonialism, the current revolt is not merely an upheaval against Western hegemony but also—and above all—"a revolt against Western values as such." Bull believed that this process was best "exemplified in Islamic fundamentalism,"[12] that is, the Islamist politicization of religion. The Islamist challenge to secularization and promotion of a return of the sacred, equally as a return of history, is a challenge to the basic foundations of the existing secular world order[13] based on the Westphalian synthesis.

If the return of religion in political form were limited to political ethics, there would be nothing wrong with it. But Islamism envisions a divine order for the state and for the world at large. This basic feature of Islamism is a major phenomenon in contemporary history, whose understanding calls for tremendous research. This collective task has been taken up by two separate research teams. One of them, assembled by the American Academy of Arts and Sciences under the title the Fundamentalism Project, consisted of an interdisciplinary group of scholars from all over the world and from diverse religious communities, engaged in thinking about the role of religion in politics and society. Their work resulted in an exceptional five-volume, jointly authored series, also entitled *The Fundamentalism Project*.[14] Unfortunately, despite the very strong scholarly credentials of the group and the high caliber of analysis provided by these volumes, their work has been largely ignored in the field of Islamic studies. The other research team, the Culture Matters Research Project (CMRP),[15] which brings "culture" into the study of development and politics, will be described later in this book.

Neither project has had the impact on scholarly debate that it deserves, in part because of confusion over the nature of the phenomenon. Some scholars argue that the term "fundamentalism" cannot be applied to Islam or to any other non-Western religion. To refute this, one can cite Hasan al-Hanafi, one of the international stars of the moderate branch of political Islam, who gave the title *al-usuliyya al-Islamiyya*—Islamic fundamentalism—to his influential book on the Islamist challenge. Hanafi, who embodies and promotes this challenge, does not hesitate to apply the Arabic term *usuliyya* (fundamentalism) to the Islamist movement when he writes in Arabic. Yet he polemicizes against this notion when he writes in English.[16]

Not only students of Islam but also others in the West need to understand the unusual nature of Islamism as a political religion. Unlike such secular ideologies as fascism and communism, which have often been viewed as political religions, Islamism is based on a real religious faith and a genuine conception of the divine. Thus the religious pronouncements of Islamists, unlike those of, say, fascists, do not reflect a purely instrumental use of religion. My research for the Fundamentalism Project,[17] which involved hundreds of informal interviews with Islamists, supports the conclusion that for them, religion is not instrumental. Islamists view themselves as true believers—and thus, in the most important sense, they are.

The study of political Islam is a study of conflict and tension.[18] For this reason I have taken in the past years an approach I call "Islamology," to distinguish it from standard Islamic studies. Islamology emulates the earlier model of Sovietology in dealing with Islamism as a source of global conflict. The underlying argument is that political, economic, and social concerns are articulated in terms of religious claims, thus heralding what I have termed the religionization of politics. The Islamists can legitimately be said to be engaged in a new cold war. Like the Soviets, they claim no more or less than a "remaking of the world." This "Islamic World Revolution" (as Sayyid Qutb calls it) has many different labels: the French call it *intégrisme*, others fundamentalism. All refer to the basic issue in the ideology of Islamism: the politicization of Islam in the pursuit of the shari'a state. This ideology is embraced by a transnational movement composed of nonstate actors. If one ignores these facts and restricts the issue to "radical Islam" and "moderate Islam," then "nonviolent Islamism" is not properly understood and one cannot grasp the general phenomenon of Islamism. It is more useful to distinguish between the institutional and jihadist Islamists. The former disavow the use of violence, play the game of democracy, and appear willing to work peacefully within existing institutions. The latter are explicitly committed to waging global jihad, which they understand as something akin to terrorism. But jihadism is more than simple terrorism. It is a new kind of warfare of irregular nonstate actors. Such jihadist movements as Hamas and Hezbollah also act as political parties and participate in elections even while they maintain their jihadist militias, which act parallel to their deputies in the elected parliament. This simultaneity creates great confusion unless one understands that these are simply two modes of operating in support of the same underlying ideology.

Islamism as the Pursuit of a Divine Political Order

To restate the issue: Islamism is not about violence but about political order. Violence is a marginal aspect even of the jihadist branch. Islamism speaks the language of religion, but its thinking revolves around questions of political rule and governance. The framework of a divine order is a basic feature of Islamism on all levels.

We should be skeptical, however, of the depiction of political Islam as a revival. Even though Islam has historically been a device for determining and asserting political legitimacy, Islamism is a novelty in this domain.

If Islamism is a political quest for a remaking of the world, it is wrong to look at it also as a religious awakening. The global phenomenon known as the "return of the sacred"—a notion coined by the sociologist Daniel Bell to contest Max Weber's assumption of a general secularization—takes a largely political shape. The politicization of religion does not come from nowhere; its roots are to be sought in a crisis generated by the encounter with modernity.[19]

One may draw a precarious parallel between European and Islamist totalitarianisms in that each emerged from a particular crisis. In the case of Islamism, the crisis arose from a failure of development in relation to the much more powerful West, a failure of both modernism and liberalism to strike roots in the Islamic world, and, as a more immediate precipitating event, a failure of secular leaders' legitimacy following the humiliating defeat by Israel in the 1967 war. In addition, Islamism shares with Nazism and communism the quality of being modern in the technological sense while vehemently rejecting the values and norms of cultural modernity. The historian Jeffrey Herf coined the term "reactionary modernism" to denote the Nazis' simultaneous embrace of modern technology and rejection of cultural modernity. I think the comparison is legitimate, but it should not be over-stretched. Germany under Hitler was one of the most industrially advanced countries in the world, while the present world of Islam consists of countries described (by, for instance, the Culture Matters Research Project) as societies based on "developing cultures."

The return of Islam in the shape of Islamism is not a return of faith but rather a return of the sacred with political claims. Islam never receded as a faith, but it no longer served as a vehicle of political legitimacy after the abolition of the caliphate in 1924 and the subsequent ascent of the secular nation-state throughout the Muslim world. Coming after a succession of failed religious and secular experiments, political Islam offers the formula *al-hall huwa al-Islam* (Islam is the solution). Like all of its predecessors, political Islam represents not an embrace of modernity but rather a defense against its values. Nonetheless, Islamists are not traditionalists, since they adopt modern instruments of science and technology, even though they combine this approach with a decisive rejection of modernity's values and rationalist worldview. This ambiguity is a major feature of all fundamentalisms.[20]

The notion of "the return of the sacred" rests on three contentions. Applied to Islam, these are:

> First, the religion of Islam is for ordinary Muslims not a *political* formula for a state order but a cult and cultural system that determines their worldview and way of life. It has been made abundantly clear that the Islamist formula din-wa-dawla (unity of religion and state) is not a feature of Islam itself but a marker of the key boundary between Islam and Islamism. It is this invented tradition, created in response to globalizing modernity, that is generated by the "crisis of modern Islam" prevalent throughout Islamic civilization. Without the crisis of the Weimar Republic in Germany there would have been no national socialism, and without the crisis in the world of Islam there probably would have been no Islamism.

> Second, as a variety of religious fundamentalism, Islamism is not simply another form of modernity, as some scholars who speak of "multiple modernities" contend. It is a totalitarian ideology, as is the movement it represents (a subject I will address in Chapter 8). The instrumental use of the forms of democratic civil society does not transform a totalitarian movement into a democratic one.

Third, the Islamization of democracy supposedly achieved in the context of shari'a only camouflages the agenda of a totalitarian order. The Islamist concept of divine order rejects not only popular sovereignty but any democratic pluralism that concedes a place to the political other. Islamists think in the binary code of true believers and unbelievers. Later in this book I will argue that Islamism is intrinsically incompatible with a liberal form of "open Islam." It lacks all of the ethical foundations for an embrace of democratic pluralism.[21]

Despite the controversy over the term "religious fundamentalism" in the study of political Islam, in this book I continue to employ the concept of fundamentalism as an analytical tool. The accusation that the term expresses Islamophobia is simply misguided: the Fundamentalism Project was based on an indiscriminate inquiry into the emergence of this phenomenon in all religions.

The Fundamentalism Project took the methodological approach of viewing religion as a social reality, not primarily as a set of beliefs. This understanding of religion as a *fait social* derives from Émile Durkheim's sociology of religion. The politicization of religion in this sense of social fact is what creates an ideology of religious fundamentalism. When defined in this way, and not simply used as a vague synonym for fervent, orthodox, or extremist belief, the term "fundamentalism" is not only useful but broadly applicable. One has to reiterate that the phenomenon is not restricted to Christianity but is found in all religions with a holy scripture, including Islam and Judaism. In all of these monotheisms there exists a clear distinction between religious orthodoxy and religious fundamentalism. The former is genuinely traditionalist, while the latter is a modern phenomenon that emerges in the context of exposure to a globalizing and universalizing modernity that consists of structures and instruments but is also based on cultural values. Islamists, like all fundamentalists, both contest modernity and are steeped in it: their claim of *al-sahwa al-Islamiyya* (Islamic awakening) is a dream of an Islamic modernity.

This "Islamic awakening" also relies on an invention of tradition. From the nineteenth century into the twentieth there existed in the Muslim world a cultural revivalism inspired by the pan-Islamic activist al-Afghani. The revivalist al-Afghani was by no means an Islamist. He had no ambition for a divinely based political order but simply sought the renewal of Islam in "response to imperialism" in the context of an anticolonial movement. Today, when Hasan al-Banna's grandson Tariq Ramadan asserts a continuity between al-Afghani and his grandfather,[22] he confuses the political religion of Islamism with Islamic revivalism. The Islamist al-Banna, on the other hand, was by no means a revivalist. Ramadan's effort to link the two not only is wrong but also has highly misleading implications.

Islamism is not religious revivalism. Its quest for a political order based on religion, which draws on the formula of din wa dawla, has no parallel in authoritative Islamic scripture. The term "dawla" (state) appears in neither the Qur'an nor the *hadith,* the canonical accounts of what the Prophet said and did. The same applies to the Islamist terms "nizam al-Islami" (Islamic system) and "hukuma Islamiyya" (Islamic government). They are not among the common terms employed in the Islamic tradition and its established scripture. Their coinage by adherents of Islamism is hard to square with the idea of revival of an older tradition. Here lies a key boundary between the revivalist al-Afghani and the Islamist al-Banna.

The Islamist claim for an "Islamic state" is given substance by the notion of *tatbiq al-shari'a* (implementation of shari'a). But it relies on a radically new interpretation of shari'a. In Islam, shari'a has a variety of meanings.[23] The term occurs only once in the text of the Qu'ran. In sure 45, verse 18, the Qu'ran prescribes shari'a in its literal meaning of a path leading to water, which implicitly means the right path. This "right path" means both correct ritual and moral conduct. In contrast, the Islamist shari'atization of Islam[24] results in political claims. The Islamists invent a shari'a tradition, specifically designed for a totalizing concept of law, that cannot be found in the text of the Qur'an. This represents neither a religious renaissance nor a revival of classical shari'a.

The Ideology of Islamism in a Global Context

It would be a mistake to look at any large movement only in terms of globalization while forgetting that it has local manifestations that are embedded in the global but that maintain their own dynamics. Islamic tradition is in fact many local traditions with a common theme. Islamism is an expression of a defensive culture that then becomes a mobilizing force in the shape of an activist revolutionary internationalism. There is an interplay between the local currents of tradition and the global Islamist movement. In addition, religion has meaning in its own right and is not just a reflection of a social reality, even though embedded in it. It is inappropriate to discard the ideology of Islamism as "un-Islamic," as is often done by those who would fully dissociate Islam from Islamism with the intention of contesting the use of the term "political Islam." It is a fact that Islamism is an ideology of Islamic fundamentalism.

The political agenda of Islamism envisions the mobilization of 1.7 billion Muslim people who live as a majority in fifty-seven states and as a minority all over the world. Most Muslims are not Islamists. For the non-Islamist Muslims, belonging to the umma of Islam means nothing more than being part of a "community of believers." In Chapter 1 I drew on the idea of an "imagined community" to conceptualize the Islamist perception of an umma. The worldview of Islamism politicizes this umma to promote the perception of a collective "we" against the rest of humanity. This identity politics shapes Islamism and contributes to conflicts on all levels, locally, regionally, and globally. The use of religion as identity marker by Islamism is associated with the contention that there is one monolithic Islam. This contention matters to the rest of the world. This Islamist identity politics serves polarization, not bridging.

One part of the Islamist invention of tradition is reflected in the effort to unite the entire umma into one polity that will lead humanity in an Islamic world order. The source of this vision is the work of Sayyid Qutb. Qutb, who was executed in 1966, did not live to see his vision become a mobilizing ideology. Now there is a dispute within Islamism over the means to be employed in the pursuit of this vision. Still, when the religious establishment and Salafists criticize the jihadists, they restrict their objections to the practices and exclude the worldview. As John Kelsay tells us in a recent book, "In broad outlines, the militant vision articulated by al-Zawahiri is also the vision of his critics. . . . They certainly argue that . . . the means . . .

are wrong . . . but they do not dissent from the judgment that . . . the cure . . . involves the establishment of Islamic governance. . . . The problem of militancy is not simply a matter of tactics. The problem is the very notion of Islamic governance."[25]

As in Islam, so in Islamism there exist commonalities and disagreements. It is therefore safe to speak of a "unity in diversity" when studying the politicization of Islam and the ideology of Islamism. The basic commonality is the notion of Islamic governance, and the disagreement, which is quite recent, relates to the use of violence. The founder of Islamism, Hasan al-Banna, never questioned the legitimacy of any resort to violence. He transformed classical jihad into jihadism,[26] but it is Sayyid Qutb, the *rector spiritus* of political Islam, who first interpreted jihad as an "Islamic world revolution" in the pursuit of an Islamic world order. The "Islamic state," which is only one step in this direction, is not restricted to the existing territories of the *dar al-Islam* but is ultimately applicable to the entire world in a challenge to secularism.[27]

In Islamist thinking, Europe is considered *dar al-shahadah,* an Islamic territoriality. Shahadah, the pronouncement of submission to Allah and allegiance to his Prophet Mohammed as a confession to Islam, is in Islamic faith not a political issue; it is the first of the five pillars of Islam. The revision of dar al-Islam to dar al-shahadah is a coinage by Tariq Ramadan. The term indicates an Islamic expansionism, and it envisions a mapping of Europe into the Islamist project.[28] By applying the phrase dar al-shahadah to Europe,[29] Ramadan proposes to establish an Islamic "counterculture" for the twenty-three million Muslim immigrants. This is not a project for the integration of Muslim immigrants to European citizenship, but rather an ethnicization of the Islamic diaspora.

The Islamist ideology essentializes Islam and is in conflict with the ideas of global pluralism and democratic peace. Its vision for the world includes the following characteristics:

- *Politically:* The concept of din wa dawla calls for interpreting Islam as a political religion that prescribes a divinely inspired order for the state.
- *Legally:* The concept of shari'a, as reinvented by Islamism, projects a new meaning into Islamic law. The Islamist shari'a goes beyond both the

Qur'anic meaning of morality and the traditional concept of Islamic law (divorce, inheritance, and so on). The shari'atization of Islamic politics (to be described in Chapter 6) happens in the pursuit of a divine state order. The new shari'a, unlike the decentralized classical one, is a totalizing state law.

- *Culturally:* The assumption that all Muslims constitute one monolithic umma reflects what Benedict Anderson has referred to (in the context of nationalism) as an "imagined community" that is supposed to share one culture. This invented culture underpins the ideology of Islamic internationalism.

- *Militarily:* The traditional Islamic concept of jihad, like the shari'a, is reinterpreted—again in an invention of tradition—beyond its original Qur'anic and traditional meaning. The new jihad is rather a *jihadiyya* (jihadism) that legitimates a war without rules. Violence in this ideology is not mere terror but rather a new kind of irregular warfare.

Again, the return of religion to the public sphere in a shape of religionized politics is not restricted to Islam but is a global phenomenon. Nonetheless, the ideology of political Islam matters to world politics more than does any other religious fundamentalism, because Islamism has been more aggressive than any other fundamentalism in translating traditional universalism into a new internationalism articulated on religious grounds. Islamists cannot be reduced to a "crazed gang," as the late Edward Said called them after 9/11. Islamism is not a rebellion against flawed Western policies in Palestine but a quest for a new world order. The phenomenon lies much deeper and is embedded in a structural and normative crisis in many Arab and other Islamic societies. An analysis of the Islamist ideology and its historical background helps us understand how the normative functions of religion as doctrine and meaning combine with its social aspects (religion as a *fait social*) to create a particular response to the crisis. Reductionist approaches do not help us understand this ideology. It is simply incorrect to argue that the Islamist is a "homo politicus" and thus a secular activist; or that Islamism is un-Islamic and uses religion only as a pretext for gaining power—as the British minister of the interior, Jacqui Smith, did in 2008 when, in a spasm of political correctness, she maintained that jihadists are "anti-Islamic." Nor can one derive Islamism merely from its social context. While it is surely

important to pay attention to the social environment, this is not the sole cause
of religionized politics. An analysis of political Islam based exclusively on sociological variables is misleading. Culture and religion and the ideologies and
worldviews to which they give rise cannot be reduced to social and economic
variables. It is no essentialization to argue that culture and religion matter on
their own terms. The religious and ideological background of Islamism must
lie therefore at the core of this analysis. It is to be repeated that "culture matters." When political and social grievances are expressed in religious and cultural terms, then these expressions matter too, on their own terms.

From its founding in 1928 to the execution of Sayyid Qutb in 1966 on
charges of plotting to assassinate Egyptian officials, political Islam unfolded
more or less as a fringe movement. (There is an exception, Islamism in Palestine, which I discuss in Chapter 3.) The watershed moment came in 1967,
with the defeat of Egypt, Jordan, and Syria in the Six-Day War against
Israel.[30] That defeat created a crisis of legitimacy in the Arab world and
marked the beginning of the decline of secularism and the concomitant
rise of the religionized politics of Islamism. Secular nationalists like Nasser
in Egypt and the Ba'thist leaders of Syria and Iraq found themselves in
retreat. They lost the admiration of their own people and came to be viewed
simply as tyrants.

Islamism first moved to the fore as a mobilizing power in its initial base
in Egypt.[31] From there its ideas disseminated throughout the Sunni world,
offering the al-hall al-Islami (Islamic solution) as the alternative to the *anzi-
mat al-hazima* (regimes of defeat, as the secular nationalists were branded).
This "solution" is meant not only for the Arab world but for the entire
world of Islam, and ultimately for the world at large. The new voice of an-
tisecularist Islamism[32] was again an Egyptian, Yusuf al-Qaradawi, the spiritual heir of Qutb. Today, in his role as a global television mufti, he enjoys
greater impact than he ever did. Westerners who classify Qaradawi as a
"moderate" are deceiving themselves. His trilogy *Hatmiyyat al-hall al-Islami*,
published in Cairo and Beirut, can be safely compared—in terms of impact—
with Qutb's *Signposts Along the Road*.

Some Western commentators (Olivier Roy comes to mind) argue that
the rejection of Western values by Islamists has nothing to do with Islam

but is merely a reflection of political and social problems related to globalization. This reflects a misunderstanding of the secular regimes' decline:
it was an integral part of a larger "revolt against the West"[33] and against
Western values. In the ideology of Islamism, toppling local secular regimes
is only the first step in a quest for a new world order. The larger goal for
Islamic fundamentalists is challenging the secular world order, and thus
the West itself. The pronouncements and deeds of al-Qaeda reveal a cosmic
worldview. Among Bin Laden's basic religious sources are Hasan al-Banna
and Sayyid Qutb. It was not the West that set "democracy" against "jihadism," as some contend. Political Islam launched its harb al-afkar (war of
ideas) on its own[34]—a global war, as Qutb puts it, of iman (belief) against
kufr (unbelief). This war of ideas is a global jihad not dependent on terrorist tactics.

Qutb makes this clear in *Ma'alim fi al-Tariq*. He first calls for a divine
order of hakimiyyat Allah throughout the dar al-Islam. This divine order
will then create an Islamic revolution designed to lead to world peace under
conditions of siyadat al-Islam (supremacy of Islam) over the entire globe. It
is a religious *farida* (obligation) to pursue jihad as a "world revolution of Islam" in order to overcome the *jahiliyya* (pre-Islamic ignorance, identical
with kufr, or unbelief) into which the world has fallen since the decline of
Islam and the rise of the West. This supremacist ideology underlies not
only Islamist internationalism but also its views on political order.[35]

Western readers may wonder how seriously such ideas are taken in the
Islamic world. This is not even a question for Muslims, because they know
how powerful Qutbism is. Roxanne Euben, an expert on Islamic fundamentalism, states: "Qutb's prominence seems an accepted fact. . . . [His]
influence is undisputed."[36] This influence is not restricted to jihadist groups
like al-Qaeda but extends also to institutional Islamist organizations such as
Turkey's AKP.[37] I have traveled throughout the world of Islam, far beyond
the Middle East (for example, West Africa, Central and Southeast Asia), and
live in Europe. In all of these places, one need only walk into any Islamic
bookstore to find Qutb's books on display—often one or two dozen titles. If
one can believe that the owners of these stores stock what they are most
likely to sell, Qutb is far from being marginal.

In short, the binary worldview of Islamist fundamentalist ideology (Muslims versus infidels) entails not only a struggle against perceived Western oppression but above all a remaking of the world in pursuit of a divinely ordained political order. This binary is characterized by an obsession with the West, which is clearly apparent in Islamist writing. We encounter this binary in the works of Qutb and al-Banna as well as Qaradawi. It is because it explicitly advocates a war of ideas between secular and religious concepts of order that the binary of political Islam is a concern for international security.[38] Given that this variety of religious fundamentalism claims universality for its political ideas, it puts the people of Islamic civilization in conflict with the rest of humanity. Non-Islamist Muslims are therefore challenged to join efforts at preventing the clash of civilizations[39] (as a famous book title has it) through bridging of the intercivilizational divides in a cross-cultural search for shared values.

The Westphalian Order versus the Internationalism of Political Islam

As a professor emeritus of international relations who spent his academic life teaching about the existing international system based on the Westphalian synthesis, I profess my preference for this secular system of sovereign nation-states but allow myself to question whether it is Eurocentric, even an expression of Orientalism, to do so. Why should the Westphalian synthesis be preferable to the world order envisioned by Islamism?

Why should one defend the secular world order against religionization? To answer these questions it seems prudent first to put the issue in a historical context. The competition between religious and secular worldviews is a contemporary issue, but its undercurrents are deeply rooted in history.

Islamic civilization dominated major parts of the world as a result of the successful jihad conquests from the seventh to the seventeenth centuries,[40] before its dominance was ended by the rise of the West. The West's "military revolution"[41] brought to a halt the Islamic project of expansion and replaced it with Europe's own. Modern science and technology, developed largely in the West, have meant that the current world order is shaped by Western standards. Most parts of Asia and Africa were colonized by European powers and then reemerged after World War II as sovereign states. But this sovereignty was often merely nominal. Former colonies ostensibly evolved into nation-states and were legally mapped into the modern international system. They then underwent "development," in which they were expected to modernize and nurture national (ideally democratic) institutions. This did not always work as planned. With a few successful exceptions such as India, the result has been a paired crisis: on the one hand a crisis of development and on the other a crisis of legitimacy for the secular nation-state.

Islamic civilization did not escape this process. In the course of its decolonization, the world of Islam made an effort to accommodate to the new international environment by joining the international system of nation-states. But the Western model of modernization did not work. The dar al-Islam, today no more than an imagined umma of 1.7 billion peoples, represents a historical memory of the old Islamic Empire now subdivided into nation-states. The crisis that evolved from this failed development has led to the return of the sacred in a political form. In presenting their agenda as the *hall* (solution) to these paired crises, Islamists construct collective memories about Islamic glory, claim that the return of history will be a return to that glory, and read modern history into the Islamic past with the argument that the new world order they envision will represent a restoration of the past. They talk about nizam (system), not, as some believe, about the caliphate. Now, why is it wrong for Islamists to want to reverse a historical development that has been detrimental to their civilization?

The anticolonial movements of Asia and Africa rightly defied Europe and European rule, but they also drew constructively on European political ideas of liberty and human dignity, based on what Habermas has called "cultural modernity,"[42] to justify their anticolonialism. The states that emerged from these former colonies have by and large accepted—if fitfully and often unsuccessfully—the fundamental tenets of the Westphalian order: the sovereignty of nations and the desirability of popular rule and market economies. In contrast, the Islamist revolt against the West rejects not only Western dominance but Western values. The Islamists deny that cultural modernity has any claim to universality that can be separated from Western hegemony—that it allows (at least in principle) for a global civil society that places all civilizations on an equal footing.[43]

The secular and rational principles of cultural modernity are potentially acceptable to all of humanity. Western hegemony, which ought to be criticized, should not be confused with the principles underlying the current world order. By contrast, the traditional universalism that political Islam translates into internationalism is not even shared by all Muslims. This internationalism simply aims to replace one type of hegemony with another. For non-Muslims, who are looked upon as intrinsically inferior *dhimmi,*[44] Islamic supremacy is by no means acceptable. The difference between modernity and hegemony can be demonstrated by a simple example: one can rationally criticize the use of human rights claims (even if they are to some extent justified) in hegemonic U.S. foreign policy without simultaneously rejecting the value of human rights as such. The abuse of rights by a particular U.S. policy is one thing, and the universality of rights quite another. But one cannot find a similar distinction between values and practices in Islamist ideology. The principle of siyadat al-Islam is unequivocal about the dominance of Islam. For Islamists this is the fundamental value.

Though many have disagreed with Samuel Huntington and his book *Clash of Civilizations,* he was right when he stated that "modern democracy . . . is democracy of the nation-state and its emergence is associated with the development of the nation-state."[45] When we promote this pattern of the democratic state, it is an endorsement of the universality of democracy and not—as some have suggested—an expression of "Orientalism." And it is this world order—an order that goes back to the Peace of Westphalia—that the Islamists reject. Earlier I quoted a 1975 book by the social historian Charles Tilly on the importance of this mapping of the world into the Westphalian system. In a book published two decades later, Tilly wrote, "Something has changed in the extension of the European state system to the rest of the earth."[46]

In the course of expansion, Europe created an international state system that has been able to dominate the entire globe—the system in which we live today. Yet the world outside Europe does not resemble Europe. It is

extremely relevant to understanding the Islamist challenge to the democratic
secular nation-state to grasp that this modern state pattern is not structurally and institutionally well established in most non-Western countries. Most
nation-states in the world of Islam are nominal states with quasi-sovereignty,
and most are only superficially democratic at best. It is a problem that the
current world order rests upon a pattern of the nation-state that lacks substance outside the West. The call for an Islamic state is aimed at toppling an
order of nominal nation-states that rest on weak foundations.[47]

The Arab state system was troubled from the beginning.[48] The Arab
nation-states designed along the Western model were first challenged by
pan-Arabism, the ideology of the secular Arab nationalists that led to the
creation of short-lived entities like the United Arab Republic, a three-year
merger of Egypt and Syria. These states have been plagued by two problems: firstly, the conflict between existing territorial states and the nationalist vision of a pan-Arab state, and second, the tensions related to universal
Islamism as well as pan-Islam (two phenomena that are often wrongly
equated).[49] Many of these nominal states lack most of the basic requirements for true nationhood: polity, civil society, citizenship, and a national
identity. It is this weakness that makes these states susceptible to the Islamist
drive to remake the world.[50]

To return to the question asked at the outset—why should we endorse
the Western idea of universality against the internationalism of political
Islam?—let us revisit the legitimacy of the Western-style nation-state. Yusuf
al-Qaradawi[51] addresses its shortcomings in *al-hall al-Islami* (The Islamic
solution). In line with the general ideology of Islamism, Qaradawi dismisses
everything coming from the West, including democracy, as *hulul mustawrada* (imported solutions) and argues for purity. His phrase "Islamist solutions versus imported solutions" serves as a convenient formula for blaming
the West for the ills of the Islamic world. (Edward Said does the same thing
with his accusation of "Orientalism.") Qaradawi argues that a wholesale de-
Westernization would purify Islam as a precondition for the Islamization of
the entire world. (It is surprising to find this TV mufti, who has a popular
program for incitement on Al Jazeera, listed under "Liberal Islam" and among
"moderate Muslims" in a reader on contemporary Islam.)[52]

Qaradawi's example serves as a reminder that arguments about the suitability of Western models are not carried out in a vacuum: one must also consider, should "Western solutions" be dispensed with, what would take their place. In a later chapter I will discuss the actual performance of Islamist groups in the few instances when they have taken power. Still, the ideological statements by themselves should make it clear that a democratic peace would be more promising for the future of Islamic civilization than any Islamist internationalism aimed at changing the international nation-state system. The Islamist agenda is intrinsically antithetical to pluralism, which is a better option for Muslims, as well as for the rest of humanity, than any form of religious absolutism. The internationalism promoted by Islamism creates a new cold war against the secular nation-state, with all the attendant tensions and conflicts. A preference for the Westphalian order—despite its shortcomings—is thus not an expression of Eurocentrism but is justified on universal humanist grounds.

The War of Collective Memories

John Kelsay is one of the few Western scholars who is deeply familiar with the tensions between Islamic and Western values. Kelsay describes the Islamists' "war of ideas" as a war of collective memories translated into world politics. Collective memories, he points out, are a source of contemporary Islamic nostalgia: they recall past Islamic glory, nurture outrage over the present order of the world, and underlie the Islamist claim of a "return of history." While specific memories are "constructed," history itself is not. Islamism has been able to revive memories of real history and use them to serve the illusion of establishing a new world order based on religion.

The collective memories constructed by Islamism concern Islam's imperial history, which begins long before the rise of the modern West. The expansion of Islamic civilization during the Middle Ages involved a kind of globalization, in the sense of an imposing of one's own political order, the "Islamicate," on the rest of the world. Islamic fundamentalism revives these memories of Islamic jihad wars.[53] This universal Islamicate came into being when Arab Muslims first engaged in wars of jihad[54] from the seventh century onward, with the proclaimed goal of expanding Islamic civilization everywhere. The result was that Islam became an "international civilization" with an "international order."[55] Though successful in medieval times, Arabs never fully succeeded in mapping the entire world into the globalization of the Islamicate. The Islamic caliphate did not become the dominant order of the world. After the Arabs went into decline, the ascending Turks continued the Islamic expansion until the seventeenth century, when the Industrial Revolution gave the West not only political and economic power but also "industrialized warfare."[56] This is the history now being revived by Islamism. Islamists blame not only Christianity and the West but also a "Jewish conspiracy" for the decline of the Islamic jihad. Sayyid Qutb called for a world revolution to create peace and prosperity under Islamic rule, a venture that is to include *ma'rakatuna ma'a al-yahud*[57] (our fight against the Jews). Qutb believed that the Jews, too, wanted to rule the world and were therefore in competition with Islam.[58]

To sum up, Islamism is not merely terrorist jihadism and it is not the religion of Islam, even though it emanates from Islam much as European totalitarianism emanates from the Enlightenment. The Islamist dream of a return of the history of civilizations represents a backlash against the ideologically driven repression of the history and the culture of the "other." In this regard Islam presents a greater challenge to the West than to India or China. Islamists construct collective memories in order to respond with contempt to Westerners who once looked at others as "people without history."[59] But in their revolt against such arrogance, Islamists also revolt against the West's positive contributions, such as the ideas of individual human rights and democracy. The pitfalls of anti-Westernism, anti-Americanism, and antisemitism are tremendous. Political religion and civilizational collective memories, when used as markers in identity politics, create barriers between the civilizations and serve as an Islamist instrument in the otherization of non-Muslims.

The Incorrect Notion of "the Decline of Islamism"

If you reduce Islamism to terror and associate it with violence, you may then—under certain circumstances—speak of "the decline of Islamism."

To do so, however, is to overlook the fundamental nature of Islamism as an ideology for the creation of a shari'a state and an Islamic world order. The peaceful and violent branches of political Islam differ over the means by which this "Islamic world revolution"—as advocated by Qutb—is to be brought about, but not over the goals. The rise of this ideology shows that Islamic civilization is at a crossroads: the choices are either to join the democratic peace under conditions of modernity and pluralism, or to endorse the call for the hall Islami (Islamic solution). The compassionate response of the West to the plight of Muslims after the tsunami of December 2004 compelled some Muslims to rethink their perception of Islam under siege. Many Muslims in Southeast Asia encountered the West as a helping partner, not as an enemy. At that time I was based in Singapore and observed these positive sentiments at first hand. Yet others, such as the Islamists of Aceh, took advantage of the tsunami to impose a local shari'a order. By and large the deplorable binary advanced by Islamism—a black-and-white choice of either Islam or the West—continues to prevail. The Islamist ambition of a "postsecular society," as part of a pattern of anti-Western development that gives religion a new role in world politics, is not abating in most of the Islamic world.

While the West (Europe in particular) has largely moved from universalist Christianity to post-Christianity and from secular modernity to the cultural relativism of postmodernity, the universalism of Islam is not only gathering force but changing in disturbing ways. The politicization of Islam transforms the relatively peaceful universalism of Islam into a call for world revolution. Fashionable forecasts of increasing moderation, such as Gilles Kepel's *fin de l'Islamisme* or Olivier Roy's "post-Islamism," have been repeatedly belied by events on the ground. While Islamist activists are a minority among Muslims, this vocal minority constitutes a powerful and highly appealing transnational movement. Islamist fundamentalists are active in the European diaspora, creating difficult choices there as well. Fukuyama, who recognized the power of diaspora Islamists and their identity politics, rightly speaks of Europe as "a battlefront of Islamism."[60] In this triangle comprising the world of Islam, the West at large, and the Islam diaspora in Europe, Islamism surely matters.

The study of Islamism faces a variety of obstacles. Islamists have been successful in stigmatizing their critics as xenophobes and Islamophobes, and in using the tools of propaganda to impose their own terms of analysis. In fact, neither Islamophobia nor "Orientalism" is at issue here. Few Western scholars are receptive to understanding Islamism as a variety of religious fundamentalism properly or are willing to criticize Islamist thinking as an expression of a totalitarian ideology. The late Ernest Gellner, a Jewish Holocaust survivor who understood fundamentalism, had the vision and courage to criticize Islamist fundamentalism in clear words. In Amsterdam in May 1994, I witnessed a head-on clash between Gellner and the anthropologist Clifford Geertz. Gellner called for reviving the ideals of the Enlightenment against the challenge of neo-absolutisms, among which he ranked Islamist fundamentalism at the top. He had written in his book *Religion and Postmodernism* that "religious fundamentalism . . . gives psychic satisfaction to many. . . . It is at present quite specifically persuasive and influential within one particular tradition, namely Islam."[61] In Amsterdam, he and Geertz engaged in a heated dispute between the universalism of Enlightenment (defamed most stupidly as "enlightenment fundamentalism") and the cultural relativism that Geertz favored.[62] In response to Geertz's argument that one needs to respect the "cultural peculiarity of the other," Gellner angrily stated "then one has to respect Hitlerism as 'the peculiarity of the Germans.'" Geertz disparaged this remark as unfair.[63]

The Gellner-Geertz controversy compels us to understand "the limits of pluralism" and Gellner's critique of cultural relativism. Islamism is absolutist. It will never accept a place as one among multiple modernities. Islamism has no commitment to democracy, it stands in opposition to civil Islam, and if it were to prevail, it would mark the beginning of a long era of darkness for the world of Islam, and for its diaspora in Europe. Gellner understood—as his opponents did not—that cultural relativism is an inadequate response to Islamist neo-absolutism.

The shari'a state envisioned by Islamism is not a political order that can be incorporated into the Westphalian system of sovereign states. To support this system against Islamist neo-absolutism is not necessarily an expression of Eurocentrism.[64] Legal scholars like Noah Feldman[65] view the shari'a state positively for its apparent acceptance of constitutionalism, but this is deceptive. Every expert who reads Arabic and is familiar with the literature Islamists produce knows that Islamists approve neither popular sovereignty nor the Westphalian synthesis that underlies the modern international system of sovereign states. The Islamist ideology of an Islamic shari'a state rests on the principle of hakimiyyat Allah (God's rule). Furthermore, this state is supposed to be the nucleus of an Islamic world order that will replace the existing Westphalian one. Given these facts, how can Islamism be accommodated? Some say that Islamists will change. If they ever did abandon the Islamist concept of order, this would be a positive sign—but they would no longer be Islamists.

3
Islamism and Antisemitism

S INCE THE HOLOCAUST, ANTISEMITISM has become a major humanitarian concern across cultures and civilizations.[1] The renunciation
and prevention of hatred of Jews and of the murderous practices
associated with it ranks today as a universal value, symbolic of the effort to
combat the dehumanization of any group of people in order to legitimate
their annihilation. In this chapter I draw on the work of the Holocaust survivor Hannah Arendt and her theory of totalitarianism. Arendt drew a
distinction between traditional Judeophobia, which is an evil, and antisemitism, a greater evil that advocates genocide. Antisemitism, she argued
in the preface to *The Origins of Totalitarianism,* "is not merely the hatred of
Jews." Much more than prejudice, it presents the Jews as an "evil" to be
eradicated. The distinction between Judeophobia and antisemitism is pertinent to the study of the place of Jews in Islam. In exploring this distinction
in this chapter, I also draw heavily on the groundbreaking work of the historian Bernard Lewis, as well as on more recent work by Jeffrey Herf that
relates the issue to contemporary Middle East politics.

Antisemitism, Judeophobia, and
Expressions of Grievances

In a *New York Times* review of two books on antisemitism, entitled "A Hatred That Resists Exorcism," Edward Rothstein begins by asking, "Is there
anything left to be said about Antisemitism?"[2] He then asks an even more
pertinent question: "Aren't those vulgar hatreds expressed by Muslim
protesters . . . just frustrated expressions of justifiable political grievances?"

He thus puts his finger on a key notion employed to deny the existence of a new antisemitism.

Antisemites do not view themselves as racists but instead see themselves as victims of a powerful Jewish conspiracy. As Rothstein puts it, "Antisemitism never sees itself as hatred; it views itself as a revelation. An attack on the Jew is never offensive, it is always defensive. This is precisely how the Nazis portrayed it. It is precisely how Islamist ideology does as well, evident, for example, in the principles and founding documents of Hamas and Hezbollah. . . . Nazi ideology bears many resemblances to that of contemporary Islamic extremism."[3] This is what sets antisemitism apart from prejudice.

Prejudice, often combined with the demonization of the cultural, religious, or ethnic other, is common in history and hardly restricted to anti-Jewish sentiments. It can be found in all cultures and levels of society. In any culture, prejudice can be expressed to the point of cruelty and can become a threat to its victims. Antisemitism is something else. It does not stop at the evil of prejudice and resentment but has a further agenda. Its victims are denied the right to exist. In an article in the *American Scholar,* Lewis writes:

> It is perfectly legitimate to criticize the action and policies of the state of Israel or the doctrines of Zionism without necessarily being motivated by antisemitism. . . . It is perfectly possible to hate and even persecute Jews without necessarily being antisemitic. . . . Antisemitism is something quite different. It is marked by two special features. . . . [First,] Jews are judged by a standard different from that applied to others. . . . The other special feature of antisemitism . . . is the accusation against Jews of cosmic evil. . . . This accusation of cosmic, satanic evil attributed to Jews . . . is what has come to be known in modern times as antisemitism.[4]

The attribution of cosmic evil is what justifies the call for annihilation and legitimates the genocidal agenda ultimately practiced by the Nazis in the Holocaust. Modern European antisemitism is thus far more perilous than any Judeophobia.

Judeophobia is not particular to German or European culture. As Lewis points out, it was present throughout Islamic history. Genocidal antisemitism, on the other hand, is a specifically European, primarily German, disease that never existed in Islam before the twentieth century. Its first appearance in the world of Islam was its adoption, more or less in its German form, by secular Arab nationalists in the 1930s. The more recent Islamization of antisemitism is a different and, I will argue, more dangerous phenomenon. While Islam, as a culture and a faith, is free of such hatred, this antisemitism is a basic feature of contemporary Islamism. Therefore the distinction between Islam and Islamism is—on all levels—pertinent to the relations of the world of Islam to Israel and to the Jews, as well as to the West in general.

In his anthology *The Legacy of Islamic Antisemitism,* Andrew Bostom makes the disturbing argument that there exists a "specific Islamic antisemitism"[5] that precludes any mutual recognition between Islam and Judaism. The inclusion of "legacy" in Bostom's title suggests that antisemitism is somehow traditional and essential to Islam. The jacket copy, which Bostom presumably approved, asserts that "Islamic antisemitism is as old as Islam itself," a contention supported within the book by Bostom's allegation that it is wrong "to assert that Muslim Jew-hatred is entirely a twentieth century phenomenon." As well as ignoring Hannah Arendt, this notion of "Islamic antisemitism" also ignores the historical facts presented by Lewis in his *Jews of Islam.* What Bostom repudiates is exactly what I state as the major premise of this chapter. Without denying or seeking to minimize traditional Islamic Judeophobia, I maintain that the attribution of a general and rampant phobia to all Muslims in their relation to Jews is not correct. There is no such thing as an "Islamic antisemitism."

I am not merely splitting hairs: the difference is important. The idea of Islamic antisemitism reinforces the artificial fault lines between Muslims and Jews at a time when we need to promote bridging between the groups. Any effort at a Jewish-Muslim dialogue to reach a shared understanding requires proper knowledge of the two distinctions central to this chapter: first, between Islam and Islamism, and second, between Judeophobia and antisemitism. In his address in Cairo on June 4, 2009, President Obama called for the unequivocal condemnation of antisemitism and of the Holocaust as well as Holocaust denial, and for mutual recognition of the right of both Jews and Palestinians to their own states. He described seven "sources of tension" between the peoples of Islamic civilization and the West, one of which is the conflict between Israel and Palestine, and in front of his Islamic audience he courageously deplored the suffering of Jews exposed to antisemitism.

The New Antisemitism

The notion of a "new antisemitism" became popular after Pope Benedict XVI used the phrase in a speech at the Cologne synagogue in August 2005.[6] Even though the pope did not specify what he was talking about and made no reference to Islamism, the setting was important: Cologne is among the strongholds of political Islam in Western Europe. Among the several varieties of the new antisemitism, the Islamized version is the most prominent. The phenomenon has five distinguishing features:

1. It is distinctly European and Christian in origin. European antisemitism, in particular its genocidal Nazi variety, was transmitted as an ideology to the Arab world in two stages and took root there. Its first advocates were Christian Arabs, followed by secular Muslims who embraced antisemitism as part of a secular pan-Arab nationalism.

2. The Islamization of this transplanted European antisemitism is a new phenomenon. It is a mistake to think that Islamist antisemitism emerges directly from secular Arab nationalism, and a worse mistake to confuse the two. At the same time, Islamism and secular pan-Arab nationalism, though mutually antagonistic, are related, and they borrow from each other. Political Islam gives antisemitism a religious imprint and aims to make it look like an authentic part of traditional Islam, not an import from the West.

3. The new antisemitism is thus no longer a mere adoption of the old European phenomenon, in either its Nazi or neo-Nazi form. As embraced by political Islam, it is strengthened by the cultural underpinning it acquires. Despite its claims of authenticity, most elements of the ideology of Islamism are based on an invention of tradition, but this invented tradition allows Islamist antisemitism to be articulated in culturally

familiar terms. Compared with secular Arab nationalism,[7] which was open about borrowing from Europe, at times even from Nazi ideology, religionized Islamist antisemitism is local and claims to be authentic, and is therefore more appealing. Religionized antisemitism is thus more dangerous.

4. The new antisemitism is often camouflaged as a variety of contemporary antiglobalization. This explains its appeal to the European left, which is thereby permitted to overlook the fact that Islamism is a right-wing ideology. Islamist antisemitism would presumably be condemned by the European left if it were not disguised as anti-Zionism, and if Islamist denunciations of Israel and the Jews as "evil" were not combined with anti-Americanism.[8] The anti-American component of Islamism is partly based on the conspiracy-driven belief that Jews rule the world[9] from New York and Washington, the twin headquarters of capitalist globalization. Antiglobalization thus shields political Islam from criticism by the European left.

5. Anti-Zionism serves as a cover for antisemitism. (This is not, I hasten to add, always true: the late French historian Maxime Rodinson made fair and reasonable criticisms of Zionism.)[10] While most in the West distinguish between anti-Zionism and antisemitism, this distinction does not exist in the Islamized variety of antisemitism. In Islamist thinking, Zionism is part of the Jews' master plan to establish their rule over the entire world. Islamists equate Jews with Zionists and view them as a threat to humanity. The implication is clear: they must be extinguished.

Two themes in Islamist ideology underlie its version of antisemitism. The first is the Islamist idea of "Islam under siege," and the second is the idea of a competition over the political order of the world. Islamists propagate the idea of a besieged Islam facing a *mu'amarah*[11] (conspiracy) devised by *al-yahud wa al-salibiyun* (Jews and crusaders), and they tamper with historical facts to present the Jews as the instigators of the Crusades, when in fact Jews were victims of the invaders as much as Muslims were. The second theme relates to the Islamist ideology of creating a new political order throughout the world. Islamists see themselves as competing against the Jews, who they believe are equally poised to shape the world order around

Jewish beliefs. These two strains of thought unite to create the vision of "cosmic, satanic evil" that underlies Islamist antisemitism.

The Arab nationalists' importation of antisemitism ignored a heritage of Jewish-Islamic amity that is well documented in historical records. Bernard Lewis describes the cultural life of Jews in medieval Andalusia, then part of the Islamic world, as a "Jewish-Islamic symbiosis."[12] With the decline of Islamic Spain, these Andalusian Jews were invited to relocate elsewhere in the Ottoman-Islamic Empire under the protection of Muslim sultans. Jews and Muslims defended Jerusalem shoulder to shoulder against the invading crusaders. Jewish historians contributed to discovering Islam and to upgrading it in Western scholarship to a world civilization[13]—and they did this, moreover, in the face of European prejudice against the civilization of Islam and its people. Today, Islamism is attempting to erase these positive records from our collective memory, and to make the world forget that antisemitism is itself a product of the modern era. In Islamist writing there is no mention of the positive place of Jews in Islamic history that we see in Lewis's work.

In the early decades of the nineteenth century, the Ottoman Empire found itself increasingly exposed to modernity. In the Arab parts of the empire, Arab Christians, strongly influenced by French culture and ideas, had a more important role in the Arab world than they have today. They were the proponents of Arab liberalism and also of secular nationalism. Neither these Arab Christians nor the Muslim secularists were anti-Western in their attitudes—quite the opposite. Their enthusiasm for the concept of the nation contributed to the dissolution of the Islam-based Ottoman order in 1923 and the abolition of the caliphate in 1924. The Republic of Turkey was not only the first secular state in the world of Islam but also the first Islamic country to recognize the Jewish state of Israel and to establish diplomatic relations with it. This amity has been eroding under the Islamist AKP. Since May 2010 the AKP has used the flotilla incident[14] to cool Turkish-Israeli relations. Turkish prime minister Recep Erdoğan has made many statements about both that incident and Israel itself that were seen as antisemitic.

This new antisemitism in the Middle East springs from developments after World War I that fed a transformation of the nationalist mood from liberal to populist. In 1916 France and Great Britain had made promises of independence to the nationalists in order to enlist the Arab support against the Ottoman Empire, but both countries reneged. After the empire was defeated, the French and British designed the Sykes-Picot plan to turn the former Ottoman Middle Eastern provinces into colonies. Thinking themselves victims of a Franco-British conspiracy, the Arab nationalists denounced their former allies, now their colonizers, and found a new ally, Germany. They nurtured a Germanophilia that included the illusion that Arabs were now dealing with a "clean" European state, not a colonial power.[15]

At first, the shift was primarily ideological and cultural. It later became political through cooperation with the Nazis. Largely Francophile before the First World War, the Arab nationalists turned increasingly Germanophile during the 1920s; and under the Third Reich, this Germanophilia created a susceptibility to antisemitic propaganda.[16] The German ideology of Volk had a formative influence on the Arab understanding of nation. Arab nationalists embraced the idea of an ethnic Kulturgemeinschaft in all of its exclusionary German implications. Some of these nationalists circulated the antisemitic *Protocols of the Elders of Zion* and shared an antisemitic perception of the Dreyfus affair in France.

When Arab nationalists approached the Nazis for help against their French and British colonizers, the Nazis were at first not interested. Lewis notes that they changed their minds "only when it became clear that Britain was an enemy, not a possible ally of the Nazis. . . . They used Arab nationalists not only against the Jews, but also against the British enemy."[17] In cooperating politically with Nazi Germany, the pan-Arab nationalists adopted its antisemitic ideology. This is how the totalitarian, genocidal form of antisemitism entered the world of Islam. Among the pan-Arab nationalists of that time were Rashid Ali Kailani, the leader of a Nazi-inspired coup in Iraq in 1941, and the Mufti of Jerusalem, Amin al-Husaini, the man seen as the "founder of national movement" in Palestine.[18] He met with Hitler on November 1941 and lived in Berlin from November 1941 until April 1945.

Mufti al-Husaini was a religious authority and, at the same time, an Arab nationalist. This fact confuses some scholars and induces them to identify him with political Islam. Even though he acted as a mufti, his ideas were rooted in Palestinian nationalism, not Islamism. Embracing Nazi ideology and submitting to its political leadership, as Husaini did, are things no modern Islamist would have done. Still, the distinction between pan-Arab secular and Islamist antisemitism is not absolute: it is important to acknowledge continuity next to the breaks, and, on these grounds, perhaps regard al-Husaini as a transitional figure between nationalism and Islamism. In Berlin in late 1937 he made explicitly Islamist arguments about Islam and the Jews, and he was one of the founders of the invented tradition of Islamist antisemitism.

Not only was Pan-Arab nationalism[19] a secular ideology, openly influenced by European ideas, it was also restricted to the Arab world. By the very concept of a secular Arab nation, the nationalists implicitly abandoned the idea of a universal umma as a political entity. They did so not for conspiratorial reasons, as the Islamists imagine, but as part of their embrace of the modern age. The pan-Arabists' vision of uniting all Arab peoples in one state, much like the United States of America, rests on national and ethnic foundations. They do not include non-Arab Muslims in their pan-Arabism because they are secular in their orientation. There is another distinction to be mentioned here, too. Unlike the pan-Arabists, the early pan-Islamists (such as al-Afghani) represented an ideology that aimed at uniting all Muslims in one imperial caliphate, but they did not seek to extend the caliphate beyond the confines of the umma. In this way pan-Islamism resembles pan-Arabism. As I argued in Chapter 2, the Islamist order of a nizam Islami is not the order of the caliphate, as often stated in the West, but something much broader and more modern.

The pan-Arab nationalists learned antisemitism in many ways from the Nazis, as Jeffrey Herf has shown in *Nazi Propaganda for the Arab World*. In a personal communication Bernard Lewis told me that the Nazis were most active in spreading antisemitic propaganda in the Middle East when Nazi Germany occupied France. He added that the Vichy regime opened such French colonies as Syria to Nazi penetration, giving a great boost to the propagation of Nazi doctrines into the Arab world.

The Islamization of Antisemitism

During this heyday of pan-Arab nationalism, Islamism existed on the fringe of society. Even though the Movement of the Muslim Brotherhood adopted the nationalists' antisemitic ideology, it rejected most of their other positions—and in fact turned its own antisemitism against the nationalists. In the ideology of Islamism, the introduction of the nation-state is perceived as a Jewish conspiracy to undermine Islam.[20] Islamists argue that Jews and Zionists instigated the abolition of the caliphate as the first step toward dividing the Muslim umma into small and weak nations. Nation building is therefore part of a Jewish master plan, carried out in conspiracy with non-Jewish enemies of Islam, to weaken the umma and destroy the Islamic polity. In this context, invented collective memories testify to the imagined alliance between the *salibiyyun* (crusaders) and the *yahud* (Jews) acting against Islam, an alliance that must be countered through global jihad. As we shall see, the only exception to the clear distinction between nationalism and Islamism is the case of Palestine.

If secular pan-Arab nationalism is a creation of "world Jewry," as Islamists contend, then Arab nationalists must be acting as agents of the Jews. In their adoption of the European idea of the nation and their abandonment of the umma, the secularists are helping to fulfill the *mukhatat yahudi* (Jewish master plan) to destroy Islam.[21] The restoration of the universal umma by political Islam is a strategy aimed at derailing this process of nation building. This is a major aspect of contemporary Islamist internationalism. Islamism aims to reverse the separation of religion and politics that has resulted from the conspiracy of "world Jewry" against Islam. The reversal is not only meant for the world of Islam: it includes global desecularization[22] in the pursuit of an Islamic world order.

The antisemitism of Islamism is thus distinct from both the old Islamic Judeophobia and modern pan-Arab nationalist antisemitism. The Islamist internationalist agenda, poised to undermine the "master plan of the Jews" who want to rule the world, is the substance of a religionized and powerful ideology. This is not well understood in the study of antisemitism.[23] Robert Wistrich, for instance, is a highly respected authority on antisemitism and one of the major sources of this study, but when he speaks of "Arab-Islamic antisemitism," he deplorably confuses Islamized antisemitism with the secular antisemitic ideas of some Arab nationalists.[24]

Sayyid Qutb's Struggle with the Jews

The significance of Qutb to Islamism is comparable to that of Marx to Marxism. He was never marginal, as some Western apologists of Islamist movements contend. No one wishing to study Islamism seriously can ignore Qutb's writings. His pamphleteering generated dozens of small books, which are translated into almost all the languages of the Islamic world. You can find his books in bookstores in Southeast Asia, Central Asia, and Europe, as well as, of course, throughout the Middle East. Millions of copies are in print. Qutb is also the mastermind of the antisemitism inherent in Islamist ideology. In *Ma'rakutna ma'a al-Yahud* (Our struggle with the Jews), he laid out all the essential features of the Islamization of antisemitism. Qutb's antisemitism thus merits some analysis.

Qutb is both the prime mover and the prime example of the sea change that occurred with the rise of political Islam. Egyptian Christian liberals such as Salamah Musah (1887–1958) were not antisemites in the genocidal sense in which I use the term. Others, such as the nineteenth-century Lebanese Christian Najib Azoury (d. 1916), did advocate European-style antisemitism—for instance in his book *Le Réveil de la nation arabe,* which clearly incited Jew hatred. But because he was essentially translating an ideology imported from elsewhere and had little to add, Azoury did not gain general appeal. His lack of popularity was due not to his being a Christian writing in French rather than Arabic but to the unintelligibility of his thoughts to an Arab and Muslim world whose local cultures were not yet familiar with this pattern of antisemitism.

The intellectual father of the Germanophile direction in pan-Arab nationalism, Sati al-Husri, also bears comparison with Sayyid Qutb. Husri himself never made any antisemitic statement, although his followers' cooperation with Nazi Germany in Iraq is well documented. The nationalists were willing to ally themselves with the Nazis—which is certainly despicable enough—but even so, antisemitism was never as central to their ideology as it is to that of the Islamists.

The great turning point in the shift from pan-Arab nationalism to Islamism was the shattering Arab military defeat by Israel in the Six-Day War of 1967, which delegitimized the defeated secular regimes. After decades as a fringe ideology, Islamism suddenly became powerful and appealing. Qutb himself did not live to see this. In 1966 he was executed in public, his hanging ordered by the hero of pan-Arabism, Egyptian president Gamal Abdel Nasser. But he had already laid the foundations for the Islamization of antisemitism.

In *Our Struggle with the Jews* Qutb describes the cosmic war the Muslim people are compelled to fight against the Jews and pays tribute to the youth who joins in that war "not for the sake of any material benefits, but simply to die and sacrifice one's own life." According to Qutb, Muslims have no choice but to fight, because the Jews themselves, whom he describes as the major enemy of Islam since the beginning of its history, want this war. They are accused of using their *la'ama* (wickedness) to destroy Islam. Qutb tells his readers that "this is an enduring war that will never end, because the Jews want no more and no less than to exterminate the religion of Islam. . . . Since Islam subdued them they are unforgiving and fight furiously through conspiracies, intrigues, and also through proxies who act in the darkness against all that Islam incorporates."[25]

This cosmic war against the Jews, Qutb writes, is not a military one, since Jews have no armed forces except in Israel. He argues, "The Jews do not fight in the battlefield with weapons. . . . They fight in a war of ideas through intrigues, suspicions, defamations, and maneuvering" and with their "wickedness and cunning."[26] Clearly the contemporary notion of a "war of ideas"[27] between democracy and global jihad is not solely an invention of Western commentators but an independent Islamist creation.

The claim of authenticity is pivotal. As we will see in Chapter 7, it constitutes one of Islamism's basic features. Nonetheless, Qutb does acknowledge a European source for his war of ideas when he quotes *The Protocols of the Elders of Zion* to support his allegations about the "evil" of the Jews. But he reads this antisemitism into Islamic history and gives it an Islamic shape. This is the Islamization of antisemitism. According to Qutb, the war of ideas begins with early Islam in 622 and continues unabated throughout all of Islamic history, from Medina to the present. Unlike the Arab Christians and the Muslim secular pan-Arabists, Qutb goes far beyond simply copying European antisemitic beliefs: he adds the original element of an invented history of Islamic antisemitism.

The Qur'an distinguishes between *ahl-al-kitab* (people of the book—that is, Jews and Christians), who are acknowledged as believers, and the kuffar (unbeliever). As an educated Muslim, Qutb was familiar with this distinction, yet he creates a new category of *al-kuffar al-yahud* (the Jewish unbeliever). He legitimates this deviation from the religious doctrine with the allegation that the Jews, "who were originally in fact included in the community, forfeited this right from the very beginning. . . . They committed unbelief and became herewith the worst enemies of believers." This enmity dates "from the very first moment, when an Islamic state was established at Medina, as it was opposed by the Jews, who acted against Muslims on the first day when those united themselves in one umma."[28] Qutb misrepresents the foundation of the polity of Medina when he speaks of a dawla (state). This term was never used in any of the Islamic sources in that time.

The war with the Jews continues throughout Islamic history. Qutb sums it up in a rhetorically memorable, thoroughly inaccurate, passage:

> Who tried to undermine the nascent Islamic state in Medina and who incited Quraish in Mecca, as well as other tribes against its foundation? It was a Jew. Who stood behind the *fitna*-war and the slaying of the third caliph Othman and all that followed hereafter as tragedies? It was a Jew. And who inflamed national divides against the last caliph and who stood behind the turmoil that ended with the abolition of shari'a? It was Ataturk, a Jew. The Jews always stood and continue to stand behind the war waged against Islam. Today, this war persists against the Islamic revival in all places on earth.[29]

In addition to inventing a history of Jews and of the interaction of Jews with Islam, Qutb also describes *simat al-yahud* (the basic traits of the Jews), which he articulates in unequivocally antisemitic jargon. Here we find the attribution of "cosmic, satanic evil" that Lewis identifies as an essential feature of antisemitism. The passage quoted above continues with a list of antisemitic tales, constructed in religious terms that serve to underpin the view that there can be no settlement, no reconciliation, and no compromise with Jews, ever. Qutb believed that the Jews "use all weapons and instruments and employ all their ingenious Jewish cunning"[30] in the pursuit of their malicious conspiracy. It is the Jews, he insists, not the Muslims, who in their evil wage this unending cosmic war.

One is inclined to ask Qutb why the Jews commit all these "assaults" against Islam. The answer is always "the Jewish character." Qutb believes that "the Jews" have never been other than "evil" and "wicked." He does not call for their annihilation, as the Nazis did, but the Holocaust is clearly implied in his writings. Qutb charges that the Jews "killed and massacred and even sawed the bodies of a number of their own prophets. . . . So what do you expect from people who do this to their prophets other than to be blood-letting and to target all of humanity?"[31] He adds a call to "free humanity" from this "evil." This is more than Judeophobia, it is a murderous ideology supported by the imagery of "the Jew" as a "wicked, bloodthirsty, inhuman" monster who is and does evil to all humanity and therefore should be exterminated. What makes this antisemitism more dangerous than its predecessors in the Arab world is that it is presented in specifically Islamized terms, as an expression of religionized politics.

This religionized antisemitism is then extended to a strategy to fight the alleged "Jewish-Christian" agenda that targets the entire Islamic umma. Christians act as salibiyyun (crusaders) in their capacity as proxies for the Jews, who are "the real instigators." Qutb maintains that "there is a crusader-Zionist *harban salibiyya-sahyuniyya* (war) against the roots of the religion of Islam." The interchangeability of "Zionist" for "Jewish" and "world Zionism" for "world Jewry" leads to the conclusion that for Qutb world Jewry and world Zionism are the same. He does not look at Zionism as a modern phenomenon but extends it back to the Crusades: "The Jews were the instigator from the very first moment. The Crusaders followed next."[32] The deep political implications of this equation are widely accepted by Islamists.

Qutb's reading of history provides an orientation with far-reaching consequences.

Today's Islamist anti-Americanism continues in the tradition of Qutb, who accused the United States of crusaderism. Historically, the crusaders were Europeans, but Islamists relocate them to America. The Islamist book by Salah A. al-Khalidi entitled *America Viewed from the Inside through the Lenses of Sayyid Qutb*[33] explicitly extends Qutb's antisemitism to implicate the United States. It describes the Jews as virtually ruling the world through their domination of the United States. Seen in this light, the perception of "Islam under siege" manages to unite anti-Americanism with the Islamization of antisemitism. The United States, as the major proxy of Zionists, becomes a key part of the zero-sum game Qutb has established. This connection between antisemitism and anti-Americanism is essential in the political thought of Islamism.

It is not only young Muslims who are susceptible to such indoctrination. The ideology also appeals to the European left, which celebrates Qutb's thought as a liberation theology. The danger for the European left in sympathizing with Islamist anti-Americanism is that antisemitism and anti-Americanism intermingle and at times become fused. Both ideologies indulge the perception that Jews steer American foreign policy through their lobby in Washington. The Jews are believed also to rule the United States indirectly from their strongholds on New York's Wall Street. This perception did not change with the election of an African-American as president of the United States.

Qutb's correlation of Islamist antisemitism with anti-Westernism underlies the anti-Zionism of Hamas as well as that of al-Qaeda. Hamas declares the Jews "an entity" inimical to Islam. In this thinking, local conflicts such as the one between Palestine and Israel become religionized and thus intractable. Islamists believe that peace with the Jews contradicts shari'a, which is nonnegotiable. When al-Qaeda was established 1998, it adopted a mission to "fight Jews and crusaders." Its founding statements make little distinction between Jews and *sahyuniyyun* (Zionists). Christians are called salibiyyun (crusaders). This again defies Islamic tradition, which qualifies Jews and Christians honorably as *dhimmi* (protected monotheist minorities). These are entitled not to equality but to protection. Self-congratulatory Muslims praise this as tolerance. I do not defend this ranking of faiths but nonetheless maintain that the classification is not, like the ideology of al-Qaeda, antisemitic. It is worth noting that after Barack Obama was elected president, al-Qaeda released a video in which Ayman al-Zawahiri, Osama Bin Laden's deputy, addressed Obama directly. Zawahiri said to him: "You were born to a Muslim father but chose to stand in the ranks of the enemies of the Muslims and pray the prayers of the Jews, although you claim to be Christian in order to climb the rungs of leadership in America."[34]

Obama's response was not only conciliatory to Muslims but perhaps frustratingly disarming to al-Qaeda. During his first state visit to a Muslim country, in April 2009, he said in front of the Turkish parliament, "The United States is not and will never be at war with Islam."[35] Neither in Ankara that April nor in Cairo two months later did Obama draw a distinction between Islam and Islamism, but he took a clear stand against antisemitism. Nonetheless, he demonstrated no awareness of the Islamization of antisemitism.

Zawahiri claims to speak in the name of Islam when he spreads his message of genocidal antisemitism. To understand that this message is alien to Islam, one needs to understand the distinction between Islam and Islamism.

As an import from Europe, Qutb's Islamized antisemitism must be understood in light of the historical fact noted by Walter Laqueur: "Traditionally Europe was the continent in which antisemitism has its strongest roots and most extreme manifestations." When this European antisemitism was transplanted to the world of Islam, new themes were introduced that are now returning to Europe. Laqueur tells us that today, "the revival of antisemitism in Europe is predominantly Muslim in character."[36] This new antisemitism is now spreading throughout the diasporic Islamic enclaves existing in most countries of the European Union. Muslim immigrants are mostly poor people who come to Europe because of its prosperity. Once there, they form an ethnic-religious underclass and often live in parallel societies separated from the mainstream by ethnic, cultural, language, and economic barriers. In their isolation in a process of self-ethnicization, many of these immigrants become susceptible to Islamist antisemitism. Qutb's *Our Struggle with the Jews* is read aloud in some mosques. Laqueur argues that "Islamist antisemites have collaborated with European antisemites of the left and with the fascist antisemites. . . . The main contribution of Islamism has been in the field of conspiracy theory."[37] In Europe, Qutb's worldview may spread beyond Islamists and propagate its obsession with a "Jewish conspiracy" outside the Muslim enclaves. Too often I had to listen to Muslim immigrants in Berlin as they told me that their troubles in the diaspora stemmed from the "fact" that the Zentralrat der Juden in Deutschland (the Central Council of Jews in Germany) is the nation's real government. When I asked about the source of this knowledge, it was always Qutb and the *Protocols*.

The Imagery of "Islam under Siege"

Everything is subject to change, and political Islam is no exception. Antisemitism is mutable as well; Laqueur rightly speaks of its "changing face." What changes could occur in Islamism and Islamized antisemitism? To identify the potential for change, one needs to consider three realms of analysis, not always consonant with one another: European (diaspora), Arabic (Middle East), and Islamic (Islamic civilization).

Globalization brings together people who not only do not share the same norms and values but also have different worldviews. Islamism turns this circumstance into the cultural perception of an imagined enemy, the West led by the conspiring Jew. Long before the expression "war of ideas"[38] was used in the West to describe the conflict between secular democracy and jihadism, Islamists and Salafists spoke of harb al-afkar against alleged victimization of the Muslim umma in a world-political circumstance of "Islam under siege."[39] The framework of this war is provided by the idea of *ghazu fikri* (intellectual invasion of the world of Islam), allegedly instigated by the Jews. One can find this perception in the work of the Islamists Ali Jarisha and Mohammed Zaibaq, two Saudi professors currently teaching at the Islamic University in Medina, who argue in their influential book *Asalib al-ghazu al-fikri lil alam al-Islami* that earlier patterns of "wars with weapons" have been mostly replaced by hurub al-afkar, wars of ideas. This new variety of war, they maintain, is more perilous to the Muslim umma.

Islamist antisemitism, with its imagery of "the Jew" designing a conspiracy against Islam, resorts to *The Protocols of the Elders of Zion* to support the perception of a Jewish master plan. The *Protocols* are, of course, a major source for modern antisemitism and the obsession with "Jewish conspiracies." Beyond remarking that no traditional Islamic document exists to serve this need, we should note how Islamism extends this conspiracy to include the West generally. Jarisha and Zaibaq continue Qutb's "reasoning" in this manner: "The West waves the flag of secularism . . . invades with its new values the society of Islam to replace the Islamic values by its own. . . . We shall talk about Zionism, or world Jewry, in order to address the related master plan pursued by the related secret societies for the destruction of the world."[40] Jarisha and Zaibaq thus endorse Qutb's allegations that Jews are evil and cowardly. According to Qutb, the Jews do not fight with "the sword and arrow in the battlefield, but rather with the diffusion of suspicions, defamations and through maneuvering."[41] This is a textbook example of antisemitism as a mindset that attributes to the Jews a universal conspiracy to destroy the world. The explicit Islamist equation of sahyuniyya (Zionism) with *al-yahudiyya al-'alamiyya* (world Jewry) belies the common Western misperception that "anti-Zionism is not antisemitism." Those who advance this argument help legitimate antisemitism by camouflaging it as political opposition to Zionism. Jarisha and Zaibaq make the equation even more explicit: "Zionism is an obnoxious evil, . . . but it is not a new one. It only became conspicuous under the name of world Jewry in the nineteenth century. In fact, Zionism is an old dogma that dominates the Jewish mind, and it exists since the early age of Judaism, transmitted by one generation to the other."[42] Such frankness is rare when Islamists address Western audiences. In these venues, anti-Zionism is presented strictly as a response to the grievances of the Israeli-Palestinian situation.

According to Jarisha and Zaibaq, the "perfidious plan" practiced by Jews has existed "since the Crusades." One may be confused to learn from these Saudi Islamists that the Jews were behind the Crusades. For the sake of clarification I should mention that not only did the Crusades predate Zionism and the conflict over Palestine by many centuries, they also were violently anti-Jewish. Nonetheless, undeterred by history, Jarisha and Zaibaq provide a nonsensical rationale for Jewish-Crusader conspiracy.

Here we have the invention not only of tradition but of history. Historical records support a distinction between Christian Europe and the secular West. The latter emerged along with humanism during the Renaissance.[43] This distinction is ignored in the Islamist invention of history. In the view of Jarisha and Zaibaq, secularity, "the idea of separating religion from the state, is a Jewish accomplishment as much as are the crusades and the two world wars. All are based on the work of Jews."[44] In real history, Jews fought side by side with Muslims to protect Jerusalem against the crusaders[45] and were punished heavily for it after the crusaders' victory: many were burned alive by Christians while hiding in their synagogue. Yet Jarisha and Zaibaq, in defiance of history, repeat throughout their book that "the Jews were the instigators of the crusades." The same antisemitic distortion can be found in dozens of other Islamist publications that invent history in order to demonize the Jews. Jarisha and Zaibaq and their nonsensical account are worth mentioning only because the narrative is so common.

As part of their war of ideas against Islam, the Jews are alleged to employ Islamic and Oriental studies, *al-istishraq,* to implement their "wicked master plan." Jarisha and Zaibaq believe that "Zionism entered Orientalism to use it for preventing Muslims from forming one united block that could powerfully resist world Jewry. . . . The Jewish Orientalist scholars were most active in this domain."[46] Again, the reality is different. European Jewish Orientalists contributed to a romanticization of Islam, in particular of Islamic rule in Spain. The distinguished political philosopher Shlomo Avineri told me, and has often said in public, that Jewish-European scholars presented "a beautiful Islam" in reaction to discrimination against Jews in Christian and secular Europe. As Bernard Lewis points out, Islamic Spain was for them the better model. Underlying this romanticization is what Martin Kramer identifies as the "Jewish discovery of Islam." This is a kind of an acknowledgment of the "Jewish-Islamic symbiosis" that thrived in Islamic Spain. Kramer cites the Jewish contribution to the study of Islam incorporated in Western scholarship.[47]

Islamists and Salafists, unfortunately joined by American followers of Edward Said, indict "Orientalism" as a major source of "distortion of Islam." One finds this accusation not only in Islamist books but also in many American works of Islamic studies. Western students of Islam who engage in the polemics of "Orientalism" seem not to know that the term is merely a translation of the Arabic al-istishraq. Today, the accusation of Orientalism can damage a young scholar's career, so many avoid speaking truths or offering candid opinions that have the potential to offend. This intimidation and self-censorship are practiced not by a totalitarian regime but by people who view themselves as scholars acting in an open society committed to academic freedom.

Long before Said published his famous book *Orientalism,* the Sheikh of al-Azhar, Muhammed al-Bahi,[48] published a huge volume dealing with the alleged war of ideas fought against Islam by "the Orientalists." The book contains a list of "orientalists" that includes mostly Jewish names. I cannot prove that Said adopted the term "Orientalism" from Bahi, but clearly the critique of Orientalism is not original to him. Still, unlike Bahi, Said must be acquitted of any profiling of Jews in his "Orientalism."

Let me say something positive about Said: despite the great disagreement that ultimately ended our friendship, I do not wish to vilify either his work or the man himself. Edward Said was an enlightened humanist, neither pro-Islamist nor an antisemite, who had a valid complaint against Eurocentrism in the study of Islam. But his critique of Orientalism became a cudgel in the hands of his followers, who today act as a kind of academic police force forbidding any criticism of political Islam.

Thus there is little complaint in the West when Jarisha and Zaibaq attempt to dismantle the secular idea of separation of church and state by writing that "secularity is the work of the Jews. . . . Fanaticist crusaderism and hateful Jewry introduced this idea of secularism which is alien to Islamic fiqh. . . . On these grounds, the hidden hand managed to destroy the Caliphate and it also was guided in this pursuit of the venture of the separation between religion and politics introduced by secular nationalism."[49]

Even the work of Kemal Atatürk, the founder of secular Turkey who abolished the caliphate, is described as "inner Orientalism." There are also some Western scholars who believe this.

The alliance of Jews and Western crusaders is often extended to Marx and Lenin, both of whom are identified as Jews embedded in the "master plan." Jarisha and Zaibaq present a more original interpretation. They concede the Jewish origins of Marxism but contend that the Jews engage in a superficial "Jewish propaganda war" against bolshevism in order "to scare non-Jews about communism" and thus deflect attention away from their own, far more insidious plans. This tale is meant to illustrate "how wicked" is the genius of the "Jewish conspiracy," which has created competing capitalism and communism and steered them both in a drive to rule the world by establishing a "world state dominated by the Jews."[50]

Beyond this spasm of creative paranoia, it makes no sense to delve further into the alleged Jewish conspiracy. Past this point Jarisha and Zaibaq mostly rephrase elements of *The Protocols of the Elders of Zion,* targeting all Muslims who do not share their views. Claiming to be more prudent and balanced than others, they do not rank all "Islamic reformers as agents of a Jewish conspiracy." Instead, they see in the work of liberal Muslim thinkers like Rifa'a Rafi' Tahtawi and Mohammed Abduh, who attempted to build bridges between Islam and the "Jewish dominated" West, mere ignorance and naïveté. "Reformist and rational Muslims," they write, fail to understand what they are "naïvely" doing. In the view of Jarisha and Zaibaq the business of bridging between civilizations is misguided because "the bridging between Islam, Christianity, and Judaism could only take place at the expense of Islam. Islam is the only true religion and any putting of Islam and other religions on an equal footing would only be detrimental to Islam."[51]

The dismissal of dialogue with other religions is driven by the Islamic claim of superiority in an Islamist ideology of supremacism. The dialogue is unveiled as an effort orchestrated by Freemasonry to undermine this claim. Here again one is confronted with "the hidden hand of the conspiring Jew," existing and acting everywhere. The Jews are supposed to rule the world with the assistance of their "secret societies," among which Freemasonry is believed to be the most prominent. The Freemasons are described

by Jarisha and Zaibaq as "one of the oldest Jewish organizations. A reference to The Protocols of the Elders of Zion suffices to provide an evidence
for the existing close ties between freemasonry and Judaism. These protocols are the Zionist constitution. . . . Freemasonry emanates from Jewish
religion."[52]

A few pages later they identify Freemasonry as a tool "in the pursuit of
the Jewish agenda." Muslims are expected not only to reject any dialogue
but to fight "jihad against the Jews" and their allies "the crusaders" in order
to thwart the "wicked plans" of Freemasonry.[53]

The imagery of the conspiring Jew unmasks the supposed distinction
in Islamism between anti-Zionism and antisemitism. The discourse of political Islam is dominated by a perception of an overall conspiracy that
targets Islam and its people. Islamic civilization is regarded as being under
siege, encircled by an imaginary Jewish evildoer who pulls the strings in all
wrongs to which Islam has been exposed since its history began in 622.
Hence the Islamist belief in a cosmic war between "Islam and world Jewry."
It follows that Islamist antisemitism does not emanate from the Middle
East conflict and will not subside after resolution of that conflict.

Unlike pan-Arab nationalist antisemitism, Islamist antisemitism claims
to be authentic. It contributes to a religionization of tensions that lead to
conflict.[54] One can point in particular to the Islamization of Palestinian
politics,[55] in which the secular PLO, though still in place, is challenged most
successfully by Hamas, in Gaza.

In his booklet "Why We Reject Peace with the Jews," written on behalf
of the Islamic Association of Palestinian Students in Kuwait, the Palestinian Islamist Muhsen Antabawi directly echoes Qutb's contention that "there
can be no peace between Muslims and Jews." Unlike the Iranian President
Mahmoud Ahmadinejad, who has taken pains to camouflage his antisemitism as anti-Zionism, al-Antawabi makes no distinction between al-yahud
(the Jews) and al-sahyuniyyun (the Zionists). He characterizes all Jews indiscriminately as "an anti-Islamic Zionist entity" permanently "conspiring"
in a cosmic war against Islam. Therefore, he concludes, "the solution for Palestine can only be brought by a generation mobilized against the Jews on

the grounds of a combination of the Qur'an with the gun."[56] This is not far from a call for annihilation.

As we have seen, Qutb was the Islamist thinker who laid the major foundations of this variety of antisemitism. It is a version that goes well beyond both European and pan-Arab nationalist antisemitism in religion-izing a political ideology based on cultural and historical perceptions. It has to be repeated: Qutb was at no point marginal. His views live on today in the charter of Hamas.

From Qutb to Hamas

Islamist antisemitism is not a frustrated expression of grievances. The ef-forts by some Europeans to reduce this cosmic war to political outrage ex-pressed as anti-Zionism unwittingly help camouflage an incipient crime against humanity. By viewing Hamas as a liberation movement, Europeans turn a blind eye to Islamist antisemitism. Humanist scholars like Matthias Küntzel, who break taboos by studying Islamist antisemitism, pay dearly for it even in Germany. Küntzel writes about the Hamas charter: "In every respect, Hamas' new document put the 1968 PLO charter in the shade. . . . The Hamas charter probably ranks as one of contemporary Islamism's most important programmatic documents and its significance goes far be-yond the Palestine conflict."[57] Hamas also revives the earlier conflation of nationalism and Islamism in Palestine. Its charter deserves scrutiny because it brings Islamized antisemitism into action.

The charter was issued in April 1988, but the movement was established on December 14, 1987.[58] The charter underlines Küntzel's point that its sig-nificance extends beyond the Palestine conflict. Article 2 identifies Hamas as an extension of the Movement of the Muslim Brotherhood, which represents the very origin of the Sunni version of Islamism and is today one of the major networks of internationalist Islamism. Article 32 identifies as Hamas's enemy not Israel but "world Zionism." Hamas perceives itself as a *ra's hurbah* (spear-head) in the war against world Zionism, specifically, as "the combatant arm of the Muslim Brotherhood for launching of a continuing jihad."[59]

According to the charter, the "Zionist master plan" knows no bound-aries; "today Palestine, tomorrow more expansion." The charter outlaws on religious grounds—that is, in the name of shari'a—all efforts by Muslims toward peaceful resolution of the conflict with Israel. This includes the Camp David Accord and all related efforts. Muslims who engage in peace-making are accused of *khiyana uzma* (great treason). A comparison of the charter with Qutb's pamphlet against the Jews reveals much borrowing of both ideas and rhetoric. Like other Islamist documents, the charter makes no distinction between Jews and Zionists; they are together the enemy. Article 22 views Jews as the source of all evil. Compare the following quotation with the one from Qutb's pamphlet quoted above:

> They stood behind the French and the communist revolutions . . . in the pursuit of the interests of Zionism. . . . They were behind the First World War that led to the abolition of the caliphate . . . to get the Balfour Declaration. . . . Then they established the League of Nations to rule the world through it, and hereafter they pulled the strings for the Second World War . . . to establish the state of Israel and to replace the League of Nations with the U.N. and its Security Council. They rule the world. . . . There is no single war that took place without the hidden hand of the Jews steering from behind.[60]

If this is not an expression of apocalyptic antisemitism, what is?

A few other questions come to mind. What is the distinction between Hamas's antisemitism and that of *The Protocols of the Elders of Zion*? Why is this more than an expression of Judeophobia? And foremost: what is au-thentically Islamic about Hamas?

Hamas is careful to identify itself as a religious organization and thus distinct from the secular PLO. Article 15 of the charter states that it is "im-perative to relate the issue of Palestine . . . to its religious character and to deal with it on these grounds." Article 27 goes farther: "Secular thought fully contradicts the religious idea. . . . We refuse the belittling of the place of religion in the Arab-Israel conflict and insist instead on the *Islamiyyat* (Is-lamicity) of Palestine. We cannot replace these claims with secular thoughts. The Islamicity of Palestine is part and parcel of our religion." This statement leaves no space for any conflict resolution based on compromise. It is God, not any secular power or worldly moral argument, who demands the destruction of Israel. This political goal is thus not negotiable. How could one ask God to compromise?

The charter of Hamas refers at its outset to the Qur'anic verse from Al Umran that qualifies Muslims as *khair umma* (chosen people), which it follows with a quotation from Hasan al-Banna, the founder of the Muslim Brotherhood: "Israel stands and shall continue to stand until Islam eradicates it, as it did unto earlier similar entities." Article 6 states that Hamas's goal is to "wave the flag of Allah over every inch in Palestine." The next article quotes a highly disputed hadith, or saying of Muhammad, that is alleged to have been transmitted from the Prophet by Buchari. This hadith refers to the day of resurrection that comes with a fight against the Jews. The battle ends with al-yahudi (the Jew) hiding behind a tree and a stone. The stone shouts: "Oh Muslim, oh server of Allah, a Jew is hidden behind me, come and kill him." But "the *gharqad* (tree) does not betray the hiding Jew, because it is Jewish." This hadith prescribes the "killing of the Jew" as "a religious obligation" and thus includes the most extreme implication of the religionization of antisemitism. Applied to Israel, it implies eradication. Again, the authenticity of this hadith is doubtful. Plenty of fake hadiths were posthumously attributed to the Prophet. But its quotation in the charter of Hamas is significant in itself.

Lest there be any doubt over the negotiability of the conflict with Israel, article 11 declares Palestine *waqf Islami,* that is, an nonnegotiable divinity. While acknowledging that Jerusalem was not an Islamic space before the Islamic *futuhat* wars, the charter claims that "the shari'a rules that every land conquered by Muslims is their property until the day of *qiyama* (resurrection)." Article 13 then adds: "Peaceful solutions contradict the commitment of Hamas to Islam. The abandonment of any piece of Palestine is an abandonment of the religion itself.... There is no real solution to the conflict over Palestine other than jihad.... Anything else is a waste of time."

Hamas resolves not only to fight Jews and crusaders with weapons but also to neutralize their intellectual impact. Article 35 asserts, "The lesson to learn is that the contemporary Zionist ghazu (invasion) was preceded by the crusaders of the West.... As Muslims defeated the earlier invasion they shall also manage with the new one. . . . Muslims learn from the past, and purify themselves from any ghazu fikri (intellectual invasion)." This theme of purification is not unique to Hamas but is central to the political thought of Islamism. It challenges not only Jews and Westerners but all other non-Muslims, for instance, in Southeast Asia.

There are two lessons to learn from the Hamas charter. First, by embracing religionized war, it makes killing a sacrament. Second, the rejection of Western ideas as an "intellectual invasion" is a rejection of the humanist agenda of the twenty-first century. One of that agenda's most fundamental elements is that the European Holocaust was an evil that must never be repeated. By abandoning the very core of the credibility and legitimacy of humanism, Hamas and other Islamists permit the return of genocidal thinking.

Let me reiterate that the "cosmic enmity" constructed by Hamas (following Qutb) between Jews and Muslims has no foundation in the history of Islam. It is not found in serious histories, only in the invented histories constructed by Islamists to justify their antisemitism.

That said, I remind the reader that everything changes, including Islamism. Has Hamas changed to the extent that we may count its anti-Western resistance as an expression of liberation? Many European leftists and liberals believe so. One of the journalists who make this argument, Paul McGough, met with the Hamas leader Khalid Mishal and asked for his views on an adjustment of the charter; McGough reports: "On the critical question of rewriting the charter, which calls for the destruction of Israel, . . . [Mishal] was unbending: 'not a chance.'"[61]

In the West most of those who approve of Hamas have never read its charter or thought very critically about the Islamist movement in general. Some of these people defend Hamas against criticism by arguing that the critics are defaming Islam—an argument that overlooks the crucial distinction between Islamism and Islam. Among the deplorable confusions, for instance, is the listing of the Egyptian Muslim Brother Yusuf al-Qaradawi as a "liberal" in Charles Kurzman's *Liberal Islam: A Sourcebook*. Qaradawi is the intellectual heir of Qutb and a source of Hamas's rejection of any borrowing as hulul mustawrada (imported solutions) from the *gharb salibi* (crusader West). Democracy is considered to be among these imports. In his highly popular trilogy *al-hall al-Islami*[62] (the Islamic solution), Qaradawi calls for a cosmic war of ideas against al-gharb al-salibi. He seems to apply this formula to all adoptions from the West except antisemitism. Laqueur quotes Qaradawi as saying on his weekly al-Jazeera program: "There is no dialogue between us and the Jews except the sword and the rifle."[63] This declaration of war recalls Qutb's *Struggle against the Jews* and justifies asking in what sense Qaradawi qualifies as a "liberal Muslim."

Hamas is listed by the United States as "terrorist organization," but it is courted not only by Turkey's Islamist AKP but also by the European left, which grants legitimacy to the increasing anti-Americanism and anti-Westernism in the world of Islam. In its indiscriminate "third-worldism," the left appears to view Islamism as an ally against capitalism.[64] Thus we get a marriage of convenience. The right-wing orientation of Islamism seems not to disturb European leftists, who share with Islamists the combination of anti-Americanism and antisemitism,[65] even if they do not want these sentiments clearly spelled out. Andrei Markovits does not buy into the left's denial of any such combination; in his book *Uncouth Nation: Why Europe Dislikes America,* he argues that antisemitism in Europe "has consistently been ... an integral part of anti-Americanism."[66] This mindset unites the antisemites of the European old right and those of the new left in an alliance with some leaders of Europe's Muslim immigrants, under the dual camouflage of anti-Zionism and anti-Americanism. Things become awkward, however, when the Islamists are not so careful to deny their antisemitism— when, for example, they deny the Holocaust. It is the peak of hypocrisy for antisemitic Islamists to present themselves as "the new Jews" and speak of a new Holocaust against Islam even while they assert that the actual Holocaust never happened.

Are Muslims in Europe "the New Jews"?

The process of ethnicization of the Islam diaspora in Europe[67] is only partly related to the discrimination and Islamophobic resentment Muslim immigrants encounter. These immigrants are unfortunately represented mostly by Islamist leaders, who do not have any right to declare themselves "the new Jews of Europe."[68] These leaders do not believe in an integration of Muslims into European citizenry but prefer to claim freedom of faith in order to establish an Islamic counterculture within European societies. If Islamists in Europe hate the Jews in this pursuit, why do they also steal the Holocaust and identify themselves with the Jews? Why do Europeans who discriminate against Muslims suddenly, on hearing them characterized as "the new Jews," become receptive to Islamist concerns? And finally: how does the distinction between Islamism and Islam apply to the Islamic diaspora in Europe? Markovits superbly helps us decipher the issue: "While these immigrants awakened first and foremost a nasty strain of xenophobia in all European countries against themselves, they also have triggered a massive, twofold reemergence of antisemitism: first, on the part of those who hate these newcomers and wish them ill, . . . second, on the part of those who are the targets of this hatred who happen to be from cultures where antisemitism has attained a major presence mainly—though not exclusively—by dint of the Arab-Israeli conflict." It is outrageous that European leftists, who were mostly silent when Serbian fascist groups massacred Bosnian Muslims in the Balkans, suddenly changed their attitudes and "raised their voices in the Bosnian war once the United States intervened."[69] Their opposition to the intervention was driven by anti-Americanism and not, apparently, by any humanistic opposition to war or the slaughter of innocents.

The concern of this chapter is not so much anti-Americanism per se but rather the antisemitism promoted by Islamism, for which anti-Zionism[70] and anti-Americanism provide a convenient camouflage. The Swiss daily *Neue Zürcher Zeitung* carried an article by a British Muslim democrat, Hanif Kureishi, who described his visits to several mosques in Great Britain: "The mosques which I visited were dominated by ardent and inflammatory preachers, one after the other agitating in an endless torrent. They were inciting against the West and the Jews. . . . This happens not only in mosques but also in most religious institutions, including the faith schools in which these ideas are disseminated."[71]

It's worth noting that multicultural Britain is quite different from France. Until the jihadist assaults of July 2005, the United Kingdom was open to Islamists and allowed them to operate openly in ways denied them elsewhere in Europe.[72] Some multiculturalists approved of this tolerant attitude, while others saw it as a cause of cultural fragmentation and a disuniting of Europe. This is a delicate area, and I hasten to add that I value cultural diversity and have no patience for European racism. My point is that even within the open atmosphere of London, the self-appointed spokesmen of the Islamic diaspora—most of whom hate the Jews—engage in cynical doublespeak. In their propaganda they condemn the Holocaust while also denying that it ever occurred, maintaining that the Muslims of Europe are as oppressed today as the Jews were under the (nonexistent) Holocaust.[73]

The spread of antisemitism among Muslims in Europe is a phenomenon to which Europeans turn a blind eye even as they are deaf to Islamist propaganda. This happens also in the United States. Some American commentators belittle the radicalization of Muslim youth in Western Europe. In a book on Islam in France, published by the Brookings Institution in 2006, one may find a chapter in which Jonathan Lawrence scandalously attempts to play down antisemitism by arguing that "in the overwhelming majority of cases antisemitic acts are not elaborate affairs."[74] This book carries a foreword by Olivier Roy, the French scholar who speaks of post-Islamism and dismisses the entire Islamist movement as "*takfiri* pockets of lost youngsters."

The issue here is not "pockets" but the return of antisemitism to its original home. The Jews are scapegoats for the failed integration of Muslim immigrants in European societies. Seyran Ateş, a Turkish lawyer who acts on behalf of Muslim women in Germany, has frequently criticized antisemitism in the Muslim diaspora. Ateş accuses multiculturalists of bigotry because they refuse to acknowledge Islamist antisemitism. In Berlin in 2007 she was fired upon, but she survived the assault and blamed antisemitic Turks in Berlin.[75]

At a symposium conducted at the Vidal Sassoon Center for the Study of Antisemitism at the Hebrew University in 2006, the interaction between Islamic fundamentalism and Western multiculturalism was one of the issues under debate. When multiculturalists romanticize non-European cultures, including Islam, they establish taboos against any criticism of these cultures as practiced by immigrants in Europe. The result is that Jew hatred in the diaspora of Islam in Europe is granted a degree of respectability as a form of outrage of the despised directed against oppressors. It does not matter that while Muslims in Europe are viewed as oppressed, the oppressors are not Jews in particular but rather Europeans at large. On a different occasion, Jeffrey Herf noted, "The unambiguous expressions of Jew-hatred from the Islamists have not aroused the same degree of moral revulsion that would be the case if the source was neo-Nazism in Europe."[76]

As I have argued throughout this chapter, antisemitism is a European disease that in the past generated the deadly racism that resulted in the Holocaust. Germans have laudably committed themselves to the idea that this crime must never be permitted again. They have established this as a basic element of their political culture. It is thus most perplexing to watch the same people remain silent about antisemitic Islamism or describe it as a legitimate response of the "oppressed." In a lecture on antisemitism delivered at Yale in March 2007 I felt I had more freedom to say this than at any time in Europe.

There is no denying the social marginalization of diaspora Muslims in Europe. Muslim immigrants exist as a poor ethnic underclass in European societies in a kind of segregation, partly imposed, partly self-chosen. When they express their resentment they do it through Islamist identity politics. It is unfortunate that these people turn their anger, which is largely justified, against the Jews. I do not like Islamist blame games, but I cannot refrain from ascribing their misery partly to Europeans. Even those Muslims in Europe who are privileged to be among the middle class feel the brunt of the ugly European exclusionary culture. Multiculturalism and cultural relativism exist side by side with this exclusionary racism and are not free of it. The majority of Muslims who make up the ethnic underclass in Europe are not educated and may not have even heard of multiculturalism, but they hear Europeans talk about tolerance of non-Western cultures while practicing exclusion. In Germany, for instance, the major application of affirmative action policies is to ensure the employment of (German) women, not to redress discrimination against Muslims. Jews pay for this European practice. In the agitprop of "Islam under siege," in which Islam is believed to be encircled by Jews and crusaders, Islamists project onto Jews the role of instigators.

Multiculturalism, meanwhile, presents itself as a postcolonial world-view poised to abandon the West's "mission civilisatrice" and its ugly Euro-centrism. This positive aspect seldom goes beyond rhetoric. Instead we get, in the name of cultural relativism, a new ideology that dismisses the universality of the values of humanism. Even the new antisemitism seems to be admissible as a view of the cultural other, granted respectability under the guise of anti-Zionism. Matthias Küntzel reports that after he wrote about his work on Islamist antisemitism, he was "excluded" by his peers. Jew hatred among Muslims in Europe is a taboo subject. The European left's view of Islamists as anti-imperialists and of their totalitarian movement as an antiglobalization effort legitimates the suppression of any critique of Islamism. Instead of Islamist antisemitism, one is encouraged to talk about Islamophobia.

This attitude explains situations in which the perpetrators of Jew hatred are tolerated when they are non-Western (for example, Islamic, especially Palestinian) immigrants. In the name of diversity, multiculturalism honors cultural difference indiscriminately. Recognition, elevated to a basic right, requires an unchecked toleration of the cultural views of others without any limitation. Thus as Herf rightly notes, antisemitism is condemned only when expressed by local Europeans. When it originates from other cultures, excuses are brought forward: it signifies the "outrage of an oppressed people" against Zionist atrocities in Palestine and the world.

For example, in the German cities of Essen and Düsseldorf some synagogues were desecrated in October 2000. Everyone assumed that the perpetrators were neo-Nazis. The chancellor at the time, Gerhard Schröder, responded with outrage, calling on all Germans to engage in an *Aufstand der Anständigen* (uprising of the decent people) against the new rise of antisemitism. Upon investigation, the German police found that the perpetrators were not German neo-Nazis but Arab Muslim immigrants. The outrage promptly subsided. It was transformed overnight into a multicultural understanding of the "oppressed" Palestinians. The desecration was no longer a disgrace but an expression of outrage over "the way Jews treat Arabs" in Palestine. The Jews were no longer victims but perpetrators, for some even "the new Nazis," and the vandals' hatred was no longer abhorrent antisemitism but laudable anti-Zionism. It is not known, of course, whether any of the congregants in these synagogues had ever mistreated a single Arab—and not relevant, for they too had been transformed, from individual Jews into "the Jews."

Following that incident I made an effort to launch a public debate about anti-Zionism and antisemitism. It was difficult to find an outlet for the article I wrote. At that time I was still a regular newspaper columnist, but my own publishers, *Frankfurter Allgemeine Zeitung* and *Der Spiegel,* would not print the piece, nor would any other German newspaper. In the end, the daily *Die Welt* ran it, but only after another assault: a Berlin Rabbi named Rothschild was beaten by an Arab-Islamist gang and had to be hospitalized.[77] What tolerance! What lessons learned from the Holocaust! Having lived in Germany from 1962 to 2009, I believe the Germans have in fact learned very little.

In the synagogue vandals' court trial, jurors were urged to understand their deeds as expressions of "legitimate outrage" against injustice in Palestine. The public's favorable attitude toward the perpetrators was reflected in the exceptionally light sentence they received. Had they been German, the sentence would have been much tougher and civil society would have been unanimously unforgiving.

In France assaults against Jews have become a daily business. The French police advise Jews to abandon all outward displays of their Jewishness as the best way to avoid assaults by young Muslims allegedly protesting Zionism or contesting their marginalization. The same happens in Scandinavia. Sweden hosts the antisemitic Radio Islam. Many European Jews living there describe a level of harassment sufficient to make them consider leaving, but which Scandinavians tolerate as "frustrated expressions of justifiable political grievances." Multiculturalism thus has become a cover for the return of antisemitism to Europe via Arab-Islamic migration. Among the so-called repentant Europeans, recognition of the right to cultural difference has been extended to enforced tolerance of Arab-Muslim antisemitism. Those who criticize this Islamist antisemitism are accused not only of Islamophobia—even if, like me, they are themselves Muslims—but also of creating tensions by offending Muslim immigrants.

Every analysis of diasporic cultures needs to deal with the invention and construction of cultural identity. This is especially relevant when the environment is perceived as hostile (such as Europe, seen as dar al-kuffar). Under Islamist influence, the underclass of the Islamic diaspora is constructing its cultural identity around an ideology of antisemitism. The Berlin newspaper *Tagesspiegel* reported that in some schools in predominantly Arab-Muslim districts (such as Neukölln), students underlined their Muslim identity in terms of antisemitic slogans such as *Hier kommt kein Jude rein* (no Jews are allowed to enter). Multiculturalism presently tolerates this variety of identity politics even as it decries identity politics of local people as "right-wing radicalism" and "anti-immigration." The equally radical right-wing Islamists are given a free pass.

The indiscriminate tolerance granted by European cultural relativists to Islamists takes identity politics to absurd levels. As a result of the Islamist indoctrination they receive in diaspora institutions—the scenes reported by Hanif Kureishi are hardly limited to London—young Muslims throughout Europe are radicalized from early childhood. The new antisemitism is part and parcel of this indoctrination. In this pursuit, Islamists make full use of civil rights. Invoking freedom of religion, they teach in faith schools an exclusive identity that denies the identity rights of non-Muslims and undermines efforts at integration of Muslims as citizens. While no balanced observer can overlook the way Muslims are treated in Europe, it is not only Europeans who are responsible for the failure of Muslims to integrate into European society. Muslims themselves are also to blame. Islamist leaders in Europe support not Europeanizing Islam but rather the Islamization of Europe.[78]

There is a proverb in German: *Angriff ist die beste Verteidigung* (attack is the best defense). If you accuse Islamists of spreading antisemitism, they call you an Islamophobe. Then they equate anti-Islamism with antisemitism and speak of a new Holocaust against Muslims. By this logic, those who advocate hatred are innocent, but those who object to hatred are promoting genocide. Tariq Ramadan defends himself against the accusation of doublespeak[79] by turning the tables in precisely this way. In an interview with *Der Spiegel* he declared, "I am a Muslim Jew." In view of his troubles with such French Jews as Alain Finkielkraut, this claim is little more than propaganda. Ramadan is mistrusted by Jewish intellectuals in France because they believe he profiles them in an antisemitic manner. In contrast, he has been celebrated in Oxford and in some circles in America as the voice of Islam in Europe.[80] I find nothing European in his Islamist thinking. In contrast there are truly European Muslims who take a clear stand against Tariq Ramadan.[81]

In an article in the *Frankfurter Allgemeine Zeitung* titled "Die falsche Parallele" (The false parallel), I disputed the equation of Muslim immigrants with Jews. As a Muslim immigrant, I can say from personal experience that Muslims in Europe today are discriminated against and socially marginalized. But we are not "the new Jews." We live in a democratic Europe and are by no means subjected to a Holocaust. Nowhere in the world of Islam do Islamists enjoy the degree of civil rights and freedom they have in Europe.[82]

One needs to deal honestly with the false comparison of antisemitism and anti-Islamism. In Europe one often hears Islamists speak of a new Holocaust that targets Muslims. As a Muslim humanist I fail to grasp how people who in fact despise Jews can take advantage of the very real suffering of the Holocaust to advance their political goals. Despite some wrongs done to Muslims, Europe is a democratic place. It grants Islamists political asylum and welfare payments when they flee persecution in the world of Islam. Any Muslim is much safer in Europe than in any Muslim country. The Islamists themselves are the foremost beneficiaries of the strict legal standards for civil rights in Europe. If there is a real Holocaust that targets Muslims in Europe, why do Islamists pour into Europe and continue to seek asylum there? Between 1950 and 2010 the Muslim diaspora in Western Europe grew from about 1 million to 23 million people.

The return of antisemitism to Europe via Islamic migrations happens in the context of the activities of diaspora Islamists who are at pains to hijack the Muslim diaspora in Europe and abuse it for their own purposes. They undermine integration and avert any criticism by hurling the stone of Islamophobia. The events in Essen in 2000 display the downgrading of the vice of antisemitism (which is real), and the upgrading of the allegation of Islamophobia (which is also real, but nonetheless highly exaggerated). In Islamist propaganda the two are equated. It bears repeating: Islamists enjoy more freedom and civil rights in Europe than in any place in the world of Islam except the countries where they are in charge. The ideologically biased environment of multiculturalism in Europe enforces a silence that benefits Islamists, who find in Europe a sanctuary from which to wage their war of ideas.

The multicultural tolerance extended to the Islamists of the diaspora creates a problem not only for European Jews but also for liberal Muslims, who flee Islamism at home only to find themselves exposed to it in Europe. Among the elements in the European ideology of antisemitism is the doctrine, much prized by the Nazis, of *Volk.* There is no similar concept in the original Islamic idea of umma. In its classical understanding the umma is fully inclusive: everyone can join by converting. In Chapter 1 I demonstrated that Islamism invents Islamic tradition by turning the Muslim umma into something like the Nazis' Volk: pure and exclusivist. Its foremost enemies are the Jews. Earlier I referred to the notion "ethnicity of fear" I coined to describe the process of mutual ethnicization now occurring between Muslims and Europeans. The constructed ethnicity of the restrictive Islamist umma reinforces the increasingly restrictive ethnicity of Europe. This is a fearful development by which European Jews are affected. The toleration of this trend serves to hide Europe's own antisemitism. Antisemitism is anathema to humanism. In its legacy Islam has a tradition of humanism[83] that includes a "Jewish-Islamic symbiosis."

An Exceptional Case: Islamism and "Nazi Palestine"

To the list of major distinctions I make in this book—between Islam and Islamism, for instance, and between the Judeophobia of traditional Islam and the modern form of genocidal antisemitism adopted from Europe—I add a smaller distinction between the antisemitism imported by secular pan-Arab nationalists and the religionized antisemitism later unfolded by Islamism. The historians Klaus-Michael Mallmann and Martin Cüppers, in their recent book *Nazi Palestine,*[84] and Jeffrey Herf, in his book *Nazi Propaganda for the Arab World,*[85] compel us to see an exception in Palestine. Though first established in 1928 with the foundation of the Movement of Muslim Brotherhood by Hasan al-Banna, Islamism thrived in most of the Middle East only after the Arab nationalists' defeat in the 1967 war with Israel. But it was successful in Palestine much earlier than elsewhere. There Islamist ideas entered the political theater during the 1930s and 1940s under the influence of Nazi Germany. Here was a conflation between national-ism (Palestinian nationalism was then still a part of secular pan-Arab nationalism) and Islamism. The ideas of Amin al-Husseini, the Mufti of Jerusalem, borrowed from those of al-Banna. It is among Herf's more significant findings that the two not only knew each other but were close, and shared an admiration of Hitler, approving his crimes against the Jews.[86]

Al-Husseini, it should be noted, was not an Islamist in the sense in which I use the term. Though a cleric and a religious authority, he was, rather, a Palestinian nationalist. He admired Hitler and invoked *The Pro-tocols of the Elders of Zion* to support his obsession with a "Jewish conspir-acy," which he believed also targeted Palestine. The Mufti enjoyed the support of the Muslim Brotherhood. Herf produces archival evidence of al-Banna's pro-Nazi orientation and shows that he "had made a careful study of the Nazi and Fascist organizations. Using them as a model, he had formed organizations of specially trained and trusted men." The Muslim Brotherhood was active not only in Egypt but also in Palestine, where Is-lamists "opened branches . . . in Nablus and Jaffa." Herf adds that "in the aftermath of World War II . . . Amin al-Husseini and Hasan al-Banna could point to Israel's emergence as a confirmation of Nazism's wartime predictions. . . . The Muslim Brotherhood, Hasan al-Banna, Sayyid Qutb . . . indicated continuity with the conspiracy theories that came daily from Radio Berlin extended beyond the Islamist fringe."[87]

Al-Husseini spent much of the war in Berlin in the service of Hitler; afterward he tried to flee but was arrested in France on suspicion of involve-ment in war crimes. The Muslim Brotherhood was one of the leading Arab-Muslim pressure groups that helped get him released. After al-Husseini's release, al-Banna issued this statement: "Al-Ikhwan al-Muslimin . . . declares that the Mufti is welcome to stay in any Arab country. . . . The lion is at last free. . . . Oh, Amin, what a great, stubborn terrific wonderful man you are. . . . Hitler and Mussolini's defeat did not frighten you . . . a hero who . . . fought Zionism."[88] Herf comments: "A plausible reading of al-Banna's statement would be that Husseini was continuing the same struggle that Hitler and Germany—and Husseini himself—had been waging during the war. . . . Having sided with Germany and Hitler . . . brought admiration for Husseini's wartime activities."[89]

Second and more horrible is the finding by Mallmann and Cüppers that there existed a plan to orchestrate a Holocaust against the Jews in Palestine. This was to be a cooperative effort between the Nazis and their Arab-Muslim allies. It was already well known that Husseini had created a Muslim extension of the Waffen SS in the Balkans. But Mallmann and Cüppers have discovered a plan to implement the Eastern European Nazi experience of the Einsatzkommando in Palestine. In Eastern Europe, non-German collaborators had killed Jews on behalf of German Nazi troops. "The example of the Einsatzgruppen in Eastern Europe," the authors write, "shows that the mass murders initiated by the Germans . . . were supported by local collaborators and were smoothly implemented with only minimal guidance." This example served as the model for what was to happen in Palestine. "A vast number of Arabs, in some cases already well-organized, were ready to serve as willing accomplices of the Germans in the Middle East. . . . The central task of Rauff's Einsatzkommando was the implementation of the Holocaust in Palestine . . . with the help of those collaborators." This collaboration for the annihilation of the Jews would have proceeded smoothly had there been no "friction"—to borrow a term from Carl von Clausewitz. The plan for a Holocaust in Palestine, with Islamist collaboration, had to be deferred after the German defeat at El Alamein and other losses on the Eastern Front. Eventually, all that "Hitler had planned in 1941 against the British positions in the Arab world . . . had to be definitely abandoned."[90]

Other German mainstream scholars, by contrast, are sympathetic even to Jihadist Islamists in Palestine—for instance, the anti-Zionist terrorist Izz al-Din al-Qassam, who worked closely with al-Husseini. Mallmann and

Cüppers express wonder "that such a terrorist, even after September 11, 2001, could still be labeled in Western scholarly literature as martyr who bore witness to his faith and the Palestinian cause." This remark refers to the misrepresentation of al-Qassam in the work of Gudrun Krämer, who teaches Islamic studies at the Free University of Berlin. It is worth noting that Hamas names the missiles it fires at the civil Israeli population Qassam Missiles. Mallmann and Cüppers do not accuse mainstream scholars of anti-semitism, but they take issue with those who limit critical scholarship about other cultures in the name of respect. To do this "amounts to a form of censorship against any kind of thinking," and they remind readers of the need for "the acceptance of the universal values of all human beings beyond the limits of religion, economic growth, or gender. . . . It is precisely because of the universality of the human condition that no one can be released from such responsibility."[91]

The authors detect in Western third-worldism "a mixture of blindness and infatuation." Scholars like Krämer defend "prejudiced-based ideologies, such as . . . anti-Zionism and Antisemitism" as frustrated expressions of grievance. Mallmann and Cüppers deplore the loss of "the difference between enlightened thinking and the alternative road to barbarism." They conclude, "The full awareness of crimes against humanity resides precisely in this ability to differentiate, which should be defended at all costs."[92]

The Pillars of Islamist Antisemitism

The reality of a politically motivated but religionized antisemitism spreading throughout the world of Islam should remind us that antisemitism in Europe led to the ugliest crimes in the history of humanity. The study of anti-semitism in Islam is thus a project for prevention of future crimes.

This is why it is important that modern Islamist antisemitism be distinguished from traditional Judeophobia. Although Islam honors Jews as believers and classifies them as ahl-al-kitab, people of the book, prejudice against Jews has long existed in the Islamic world.[93] While conceding the traditional Islamic tolerance that in medieval times allowed subject Jews to practice their religion—and while acknowledging that this tolerance was laudable compared with the butchering of Jews by medieval Christians—we must also note the obvious fact that this standard of "tolerance" no longer suffices.[94] No Jew today would agree to be ranked as dhimmi, part of a protected minority of second-class believers.[95] By modern standards this is simply discrimination. Therefore it is understandable that Israeli Jews reject the idea, promoted by some so-called moderate members of Hamas, of providing Jews peace within the framework of dhimmi status in an Islamic shari'a state in Palestine that would replace Israel. This proposal contradicts all standards of civil society.[96]

When Islamists accuse secular Arab and Turkish nationalists of acting as proxies for the Jews in a conspiracy to undermine the Islamic order, they ignore the fact that secular nationalists also engage in antisemitism. But unlike the secular nationalists, the Islamists give this ideology a religious garb. The Islamization of antisemitism, the foundations of which were laid by Sayyid Qutb and which continues today in the doctrines of organizations like Hamas, invokes a false tradition of unending, intrinsic hatred between Jews and Islam. The pillars of Islamized antisemitism can be summed up by a series of allegations:

- that a Jewish conspiracy against Islam has existed since 622;
- that Jews want to rule the world and thus deprive Islam of its own claim to rule the world;
- that Jews employ a variety of "secret" forces (such as Freemasonry) to further their goal of world domination, the chief of these being Zionism;
- that since the Crusades, Jews have used Christians as their proxies; and
- that America is today ruled by Jews.

These beliefs make Islamist antisemitism inseparable from Islamist anti-Zionism and anti-Americanism. Those in the West who argue that Jew hatred in the world of Islam is not antisemitism but rather is based in anti-Zionism or opposition to Israel's policies must contend with the Islamists' own statements to the contrary.[97]

Let me conclude with three observations:

1. Belief in the "cosmic, satanic evil" of Jews is tantamount to approval of a new Holocaust. Creatures of such evil could not be human, and their

extermination would be not only logical but necessary. To state it thus, of course, makes the absurdity of the belief immediately obvious. This kind of thinking never existed in Islam until the emergence of Islamism.

2. The Islamization of antisemitism by Sayyid Qutb and the Muslim Brothers (who are seen by some policymakers as "moderate Islamists") is a new development. The new religionized antisemitism is significantly different from "racial" Arab national antisemitism.

3. This Islamized, religionized antisemitism is more dangerous than racial antisemitism because it claims *asalah* (authenticity) as something native to Islam and is in this way more appealing to Islamic people.

How, then, can the West face this new form of the antisemitic disease without alienating itself from the world of Islam? The best way to counter Islamized antisemitism is on its own terms: to delegitimate it as foreign to Islamic thought and tradition and to deny it authenticity. Liberal Muslims who are aware of the cordial Jewish-Muslim relations in Muslim Spain and of the Muslim Ibn Rushd's congeniality with the Jewish philosopher Maimonides must enlighten their fellow Muslims about this history. The historical relationship between Muslims and Jews is far from ideal, but it is very far from a state of constant (let alone cosmic) war. The better side of this tradition should be revived in modern Jewish-Islamic cooperation against the Islamist agenda. It is important for the world to understand that antisemitism lies at the core of the ideology of Islamism. The alternative to Islamism is a revival of the buried tradition of Islamic humanism that unites prominent Jewish and Muslim philosophers like Maimonides and Ibn Rushd in a cultural symbiosis abhorrent to Islamism.

This positive tradition is still alive in Morocco, the only Arab-Islamic country I know that outlaws Jew hatred. In July 2009 I was in the Moroccan city of Fez attending a Congrès Mondial sur Multiculturalisme et Pluralisme and was pleased to hear local politicians and scholars publicly exchanging their views in a context of pluralism and diversity. "The Jewish sources of Morrocan culture" were openly acknowledged. In an interview with Moroccan National Radio I voiced my admiration for the nation's culture of civil Islam and called it a model for other Arabs and Muslims. Such an interview would be unthinkable in Egypt, Syria, or anywhere else

in the Middle East. Antisemitism in those countries is so strong that object-
ing to it is a subversive act. Unlike the earlier variety of pan-Arab antisemitism, which was restricted to the elites, the new Islamist antisemitism is
represented by popular mass movements. It has gained roots and has been
elevated to a public choice. It is in no way an expression of Islamophobia to
outlaw this new Islamist antisemitism. On the contrary, this outlawing is
in line with the mindset of the tradition of "Jewish-Islamic Symbiosis" that
flourished in medieval Islamic humanism.

I conclude this chapter by asking: Is the Arab Spring of 2011 inspired
by this Islamic humanism? The downfall of authoritarian regimes and the
subsequent emergence of new freedoms in the course of the Arab Spring
did not unleash only positive sentiments. Some of the demonstrating masses
in Tahrir Square in Cairo in mid-September 2011 found their way to the
Israeli embassy to translate antisemitic sentiments into assault and destruction. This happened a week after AKP-Islamist Turkey expelled the Israeli
ambassador. Then the Islamist Turkish prime minister came to Cairo to let
himself be celebrated as the leader of the Muslims against the Jews. He did
not engage in antisemitic slogans, but he exploited the anti-Israel card. Michael Borgstede, the German Middle East correspondent of the German
daily *Die Welt,* wrote: "Since the fall of Mubarak Egyptian people speak
out freely what is on their mind. A part of this freedom of expression is a
tremendous amount of antisemitism and Jew-hatred."[98] If one accepts Hannah Arendt's view as articulated in this chapter—namely, that any antisemitism is totalitarian—then the likelihood of the Arab Spring serving to elevate
Islamists neither promises democracy nor reflects a mindset of Islamic humanism.

4

Islamism and Democracy

Is islamism compatible with democracy? This question has aroused
a heated debate among supporters and critics of Islamism.[1] The analysis
of Islamist antisemitism provided in the preceding chapter offers little
cause for hope. If one accepts Hannah Arendt's reasoning in *The Origins of
Totalitarianism* that any ideology that includes antisemitism is totalitarian,
then Islamism clearly qualifies as a totalitarian, hence undemocratic, ideology.[2] But this formulation is indirect. In this chapter we will listen directly
to the founders of Islamist ideology and their heirs to hear what they say
about democracy. It is important to read the major writings of Islamist
leaders in their own language. Scholars who fail to do so cannot distinguish
between statements made for convenience, intended for Western audiences,
and those that express what Islamists really think.

The relation of Islamism to democracy has sparked some heated debates. One of these appeared in 2008 in the *Journal of Democracy,* to which
I contributed an essay subtitled "Why They Can't Be Democratic."[3] Among
the chief opponents of such a view are Andrew March, who advocates accommodation of peaceful Islamists "who are motivated by explicit religious
faith," and Marc Lynch, who writes that if one doubts the Islamist commitment to democracy, then one risks being accused of "a profound insult" to
the "faith and identity" of Muslims.[4] As I have emphasized, these positions
overlook the distinction between Islamism and Islam. The dispute is not
about faith but about religionized politics.

Part of the debate centers on the difference between institutional and
jihadist Islamists. Let us set aside, for the moment, how porous the boundary is between these two groups. While it is not difficult to label the latter

undemocratic, the former pose a challenge because they frequently advocate and participate in democratic processes. Even though I mistrust the honesty of Islamists who declare support of democracy, I approve the politics of engagement and oppose outlawing nonviolent Islamists. But the distinction between engagement and empowerment, always highly pertinent, has become critical with the recent uprisings across the Middle East and North Africa. I shall return to this issue later in this chapter.

In a review in *Foreign Affairs* of Paul Berman's book on Islamism *The Flight of the Intellectuals,* Lynch characterizes any linkage of the institutional and jihadist strains of Islamism as "lumping Islamist groups together." He is aware of the problem posed by nonviolent Islamists: these movements "are committed to working within democratic institutions, but promote values at odds with progressive standards of freedom, equality, and tolerance."[5] How are democrats to deal with this dilemma? Having been active in debates on this subject in both the Western[6] and Arab Muslim worlds,[7] I argue that democracy is based on two pillars: first, the values and the political culture of democracy, and second, electoral politics. You cannot separate the two—yet this is what Lynch seems to want to do. He argues that though the Islamist vision of democracy "may not be a classically liberal one, it is a fully legitimate guide for how Muslims . . . can participate in a liberal and democratic system." This separation allows Lynch to describe the Islamist leader Yusef al-Qaradawi as "a fierce advocate of democratic participation . . . an icon to mainstream non-violent Islamists."[8]

There is no disputing that Qaradawi is an "icon" of Islamism.[9] The question is whether being such an icon, or a follower of one, is in any way compatible with a commitment to democracy.

Three Islamist Authorities and Three Western Confusions

The best place to begin is with Sayyid Qutb's most influential book, *Ma'alim fi al-tariq* (Signposts along the road). Here Qutb diagnoses why the "sick West" is falling apart along with its democracy. The West is to be replaced by an imagined Islamic power that will take over the world in a "return of history" that is synonymous with a return of Muslim glory. Such thinking is manifest in most Islamist writings. Qutb writes: "Humanity is at the brink . . . most clearly in the West itself . . . after the *bankruptcy of democracy, which is finished* . . . the rule of the Western man is about to break down. . . . It is only Islam that possesses the needed values and method. . . . It is now the turn of Islam and its umma community in the most tense time to take over."[10] This is the hall Islami, the Islamic solution, that Qaradawi preaches as well.

Second to Qutb among the founding fathers of Islamism, but of much the same caliber, is the Indian Muslim Abu al-A'la al-Mawdudi, who articulates his rejection of democracy in much stronger words: "I tell you Muslim brothers in all frankness that democracy . . . stands in contrast to what you embrace as religion and its dogma. *The Islam that you believe in* and according to which you identify yourself as Muslims differs in its substance from this hateful system [of democracy]. . . . *Where this system of democracy prevails Islam is in absence,* and where Islam prevails there is no place [*la makan*] for this system of democracy.[11]

Qutb was executed in public in 1966, and Mawdudi died a decade later. The foremost Islamist alive today, in terms of impact, is Yusuf al-Qaradawi, widely considered the heir of Qutb. Al-Jazeera television so extends his reach that he has been nicknamed "the global Mufti." Qaradawi first became known after the devastating Arab defeat in the Six-Day War of 1967; his writings contributed to the delegitimation of secular regimes. His book *al-Hall al-Islami wa al-hulul al-mustawradah* (The Islamic solutions and the imported solutions) is the first volume of a trilogy advocating the rejection of Western values for "Islamic" ones. Qaradawi issues all kinds of *fatwas,* which make a great impact. (A fatwa is simply a legal judgment that includes teachings and instructions for right behavior. It is not, as has been widely believed in the West since the Salman Rushdie affair, a death sentence.) Qaradawi dismisses and even ridicules all cultural borrowings, including democracy, as "imported solutions." In one of his fatwas, Qaradawi writes that "the term liberal democracy reflects its European origin. . . . Liberal democratic thought entered into the life of Muslims through colonization. . . . What looms behind this thought is the wicked colonial notion that religion is to be separated from politics and from the state." Behind this wickedness are the familiar villains: "The colonial crusaders and world Jewry are the instigators of this *fitna* within Islam." [12] There is a double meaning involved in the notion of fitna: literally, the word means sexual danger, but it is also used by Muslims to connote violent fighting among Muslims (fitna wars), with the implication that the fighting has been instigated by a non-Muslim.

In Qaradawi's view, Islam presents "shari'a as the alternative to the imported solutions." The Islamist shari'a state must replace "liberal democracy [which] failed in the world of Islam" because the latter is imported and "alien to Islam." Like all other Islamists, Qaradawi does not speak like this when he visits Europe and talks to Westerners. There he voices approval of democracy. This Islamist double-speak is a great obstacle to the West's understanding of Islamism.

If we take these statements by the three foremost authorities of political Islam at face value, we may conclude without further discussion that Islamism, by its own declaration, is not compatible with democracy. Why, then, am I writing this chapter?

Despite the evidence, the job is not that easy. Many Western scholars quote and take at face value different Islamist pronouncements about democracy—those specifically designed for Western ears—and on these grounds reach different conclusions. [13] The major source of their confusion is the missing distinction between Islam and Islamism. Islam itself, as a faith and system of religious ethics, could be made compatible with democracy if combined with the will to religious reform. The Koranic term "shura" means in Arabic "consultation," not democracy. However, one can refer today to shura in the course of helping to resolve the Islamic predicament with cultural modernity [14] and introducing democracy to Islam, and thus view shura in a new interpretation as a democratic ethics.

A second source of Western confusion is the postmodern objection to the universalization of modernity. From this comes the view that Islamism is a kind of "other modernity" whose relation to democracy will necessarily be different from what Westerners expect. In practice, this amounts to an apology for political Islam's use of the ballot box solely to seize power and its renunciation of democratic principles once that goal is achieved. Such an instrumental use of democratic forms—with none of their substance—grows increasingly likely as the Islamist movement gains appeal and its ideology becomes elevated to a public choice. Today, no Middle Eastern democracy can afford to exclude Islamism without sliding into authoritarian rule. But since Islamism is not compatible with democracy, its participation in democratic institutions raises a dilemma.[15]

The final source of confusion comprises American policymakers who today are attempting to democratize the Middle East with Islamists as allies. They have apparently never learned from the past. American support of the Afghan-Islamist mujahidin against the Soviet invasion in the 1980s was a grave error that gave rise to the Taliban.[16] After 9/11, the Bush administration's disastrous "war on terror," conducted against these same Islamists, succeeded in alienating all Muslims suspected of supporting jihadist terror but failed to deter jihadism. Then followed a bit of pure madness sold to the public as "the politics of democratization," which brought Islamists to power in Iraq and Palestine and may soon do so in Egypt. Those efforts at "regime change" have utterly failed to bring democracy. Why? The ignorance of Western policymakers about Islam and its civilization has certainly been a major factor. While the Obama administration has pursued a markedly different and more conciliatory approach, it, too, has demonstrated no clear understanding of democracy and democratization in the Arab world, and no proper assessment of Islamism. Islamist parties are presented by Islamists and their Western apologists as comparable to the Christian Democratic parties of Western Europe, but this is utterly wrong. Unlike those parties, the Islamist parties are not secular—they have, in fact, an agenda of desecularization—and their commitment to democratization ends with the ballot box. In this upside-down world, speaking the truth about Islamism is a Sisyphean task.

Two Cases of Institutional Islamism: AKP and the Muslim Brothers

The current politics of democratization depends on the entirely fictitious concept of "moderate Islamists," coined by policymakers and some scholars to justify a changed assessment of institutional Islamism. There has been a shift from a rejection of "radical Islam" to an excessively positive sentiment toward those Islamists who forgo terror and pay lip service to democracy. The notion of "moderate Islamists" entertains the illusion that any Islamist leader who is not openly jihadist is a potential democrat. Such Islamists are approved as replacements for ruling autocrats and their authoritarian regimes. In Iraq, the Sunni Ba'thists who supported Saddam Hussein have been replaced by Shi'ite Islamists, who have conspicuously failed to become paragons of democracy. In this section I shall focus on the Turkish AKP and on Egypt's Muslim Brothers, the latter said to represent "Islam without fear,"[17] because they are ready to take over political power since the fall of Hosni Mubarak. Not surprisingly, this takeover may take place with the blessing of American policymakers who imagine that the Brothers' rule over Egypt will resemble that of Turkey under the AKP, itself a regime idealized by some in the West.

Among the Americans supporting Turkey as a "moderate Islamic republic" one finds Stephen Larrabee of the Rand Corporation, who argues that "under the AKP, Turkey has emerged as an important actor in the region. . . . [The] banning of the party could undercut efforts to promote reform and democracy."[18] Such a ban, on grounds that the AKP threatened to undermine the secular constitution, was considered by Turkey's Constitutional Court in July 2008 but ultimately not imposed. Nonetheless, Larrabee is concerned that if the court succeeded in abolishing the AKP, "the United States would lose an important partner." This is an example of an unexamined assumption posing as news analysis. The real foreign policy of AKP-ruled Turkey belies this assessment. A more knowledgeable account comes from the Turkish-American analyst Zeyno Baran, who documents the "creeping Islamization" of Turkey, an ongoing desecularization disguised as democratization. Baran writes:

> Increasing evidence suggests that AKP leaders . . . use state institutions to shape public opinion in favour of Islamism. . . . Statistics showing declines in gender equality and respect for religious and ethnic minorities seem to corroborate the Kemalists' fears about the erosion of the boundary between religion and public life—and with it, the weakening of secular democracy.

Such statistics counter the AKP's insistence that it is simply implementing reforms and other domestic policies that reflect the will of the Turkish voter.[19]

Events since the publication of this book support Baran's warnings on the Islamization of the secular Turkish state. With the referendum of September 12, 2010, which approved a change of Turkey's secular constitution, the AKP has successfully launched an initiative that promises to weaken the secular pillars of the republic, in particular the judiciary, which a *New York Times* article described as "the traditional safeguard of a staunchly secular state," and the Western-trained and -educated military. President Obama praised the referendum as a sign of a "vibrant" democracy, but critics—as the *New York Times* piece notes—"have considered this referendum as the latest round in a power struggle" between the AKP Islamists and the Turkish secular elite.[20] The revamping of the constitutional court and the restructuring of the Supreme Board of Judges and Prosecutors are, says the *Times,* efforts "to undermine the independence of the judiciary and to install (AKP) supporters in senior judicial posts, as a part of a long-term strategy to roll back secularism in Turkey."[21] These changes reflect an orchestrated power grab aimed at undermining the secular order established by the republic's founder, Mustafa Kemal Atatürk, in 1923. This process of desecularization and de-Westernization of the Kemalist republic is occurring in a country that not only is a NATO member but also has noncombat troops in Afghanistan and hopes to join the European Union.

The increasing closeness of AKP, and thus Turkey, to Iran, Hamas, and Hezbollah calls its commitment to the West into question. One is inclined to credit the *Times* for identifying the AKP as a party that leads "the Islamist-rooted government" of Turkey, thus acknowledging the distinction between what is Islamic and what is Islamist. In contrast, the European press, for instance *Frankfurter Allgemeine Zeitung,* prefers self-deception: it labels the AKP "Islamic-conservative." But by laying the groundwork for a "whole new constitution," the AKP is working toward bringing secular institutions under Islamist control. Equally disturbing is "the rising number of prosecutions against journalists" cited by the European Union, which sharply criticized Turkey for its "attack on Turkey's press freedom."[22] These policies do not indicate a democratic mindset.

The view that the AKP is not an Islamic-conservative but rather an Islamist party seems to be shared by many American diplomats. Following the release of masses of U.S. State Department cables by the internet organization WikiLeaks in late 2010, the German news magazine *Der Spiegel* published a special issue devoted to the disclosures. Since Turkey's proposed entry into the European Union is a major topic of discussion in Europe, the issue included an article on these diplomats' views about the AKP.[23]

The cables revealed an intriguing contradiction between official U.S. statements on Turkey and what its closest observers reported. Both the Bush and Obama administrations have described the AKP as committed to democracy and have supported the admission of Turkey under AKP rule to the EU. But U.S. diplomats based in Ankara have been highly critical. According to the documents published in *Der Spiegel*, "AKP politicians are favourable to Turkey's entry to the European Union . . . because they believe Turkey should spread Islam in Europe." One AKP politician is quoted as saying, "We want al-Andalus [Islamic Spain] back, and we are going to take revenge for the defeat in Vienna 1683." (The European Balkans were occupied by the Islamic Ottoman Empire for about five centuries. In 1683 Ottoman troops were repulsed in an effort to take over and Islamize Vienna.) The documents refer to what is called the "Davutoğlu approach," after the Turkish minister for foreign affairs, the Islamist Ahmed Davutoğlu, who also has a great influence on Erdoğan's foreign policy views. They quote Davutoğlu as saying: "We shall restore the Ottoman Balkans." The *Der Spiegel* reporter comments, "This neo-Ottoman approach of Davutoğlu is a worrying concern for the United States," a concern expressed in several reports from Ankara in which "the Islamist impact of Davutoğlu on Erdoğan" is made clear. According to *Der Spiegel*, "These documents include assessments that stand fully in contradiction to all the U.S. administration statements in public about Turkey . . . and above all its prime minister Erdoğan." In one report from the U.S. embassy in Ankara, Erdoğan is said to "get[] his information almost exclusively from Islamist newspapers" and from a small circle of Islamist advisers identified as "stubborn, arrogant and subordinate to Erdoğan." The leader of the AKP is quoted as saying, "Democracy is like a train: we take a ride in it and we get off when we reach the station of our destination."[24] The reader should be reminded that with the exception of Morocco, all Arab lands—both in the Middle East and in North Africa—were subdued for many centuries under Turkish Ottoman rule. Neo-Ottomanism aims to revive this tradition. In his "Muslime an die Front" the Instanbul-based German journalist Michael Martens reported in *Frankfurter Allgemeine Zeitung* of August 26, 2011, a Turkish AKP plan that demonstrates Turkey's claim to be—in a neo-Ottoman mindset—the new regional power of the Middle East. The AKP is using the power vacuum caused by the Arab Spring to support the bid for Turkish leadership. The plan is not only political but also military. The Islamist AKP government makes an arbitrary comparison between the Arab Middle East—in particular Libya—and Bosnia: if "Muslim troops" had replaced the international ones in Bosnia in 1995, the AKP argues, the massacre in Srebrenica could have been averted. Martens reports that "Turkey views itself as a regional power. . . . In this context the formula of Muslim peace troops is reinforced. . . . Some not only see these not being complementary to the U.N. but rather as a substitute to international peace troops."[25] Islamist neo-Ottomanism thus evolves from political ideology to military state strategy: to support the rising Islamist movements in the transition from opposition to political rule.

In January 2011 the global edition of the *New York Times/International Herald Tribune* published a front-page article in which the "Davutoğlu approach" is described in some detail. According to the *Times* reporter, "Mr. Davutoğlu has shaped Turkey's ambitious foreign policy," and "Mr. Erdoğan and Mr. Davutoğlu share a grand vision of a renascent Turkey, expanding to fill a bygone Ottoman imperial space." This is not a vision of ordinary nationhood but rather one of imperial ambition. The AKP's Neo-Ottomanism is a curious mix of Turkish Nationalism with Islamist internationalism. As we shall see, the links between the AKP and the Muslim Brothers support this assessment.

One is inclined to ask why President Obama chose AKP-led Turkey as the first place from which he addressed the world of Islam in his pursuit of intercivilizational bridging. Had he been briefed on his diplomats' opinions? One must also question the suitability of institutional Islamism as a partner for the West. Turkey is a member of NATO and wants U.S. support for becoming a full member of the EU, but its foreign policy is at the same time drifting away from compatibility with the West. Some blame the EU's reluctance to admit Turkey for this shift, but the WikiLeaks cables raise the possibility that the AKP's attitude is more a reflection of the "Davutoğlu approach" than the policy of a disappointed would-be ally.

In the face of a popular uprising in early 2011, Egyptian president Hosni Mubarak ceded power to his vice president, Omar Suleiman.[26] The military took effective control of the country, and as this book goes to press, Egypt's future remains uncertain, but one can safely assume that any honest election in Egypt will hand over considerable power, and possibly a ruling majority, to the Muslim Brothers.[27] This will not, however, bring the democratization Egypt has awaited for so long. Islamist rule will not involve any power sharing, only the replacement of secular authoritarianism with religious totalitarianism. Unlike their predecessors at the party's founding in 1928, the Muslim Brothers of today pay lip service to democracy and present their Islamism as a version of "moderate Islam" willing to coexist in a context of alleged multiple modernities. Is this simply an expression of iham (deception) or does it truly represent a new mindset? What actions of the Muslim Brothers suggest that their ideology is now compatible with the civic culture of democracy? Well-informed observers know of the growing connections between the Muslim Brothers and the AKP, as Turkish-Islamists claim a neo-Ottoman leadership of the Middle East. The Muslim Brothers are also growing outside of Egypt, including in the United States[28] and Europe,[29] thus becoming a transnational movement.

Recently, a team of experts studied this movement and published a volume, edited by Barry Rubin, entitled *The Muslim Brotherhood: The Organization and Policies of a Global Islamist Movement.*[30] In their case studies, the authors present strong evidence that the Muslim Brotherhood is not a democratic movement. In his study of the group's activities in the United Kingdom, David Rich argues that "Tariq Ramadan is one of the most influential Islamist voices in Britain."[31] Ramadan, he writes, was not successful in his native Switzerland and left in search of a venue where he could be more influential. In France he failed too, due to the more powerful liberal French Islam represented by the imam of the Grand Mosque of Paris, Dalil Bouba-kir. Finally he moved to the United Kingdom, where, according to Rich, "The Muslim Brotherhood propagates heresies against liberal democracy; its entire ideology is a rejection of fundamental liberal values."[32] (Another author in the volume, Ana B. Soage, describes the leading Muslim Brother Yusuf al-Qaradawi as a "Favorite Ideological Guide" for the diaspora Islamists.[33] Ramadan has high regard for Qaradawi: Paul Berman calls him "Ramadan's admired hero.") Ramadan's institutional Islamism pays lip service to democracy and forgoes violence, but his vision of European inclu-sion does not mean that Muslim immigrants should become "European citizens of the heart." Instead, Ramadan wants, as Berman rightly states, a "Muslim counterculture in the West to assume a shape of its own, under the name of Western Islam."[34] Liberal Muslims refuse to join forces in this venture, which looks very much like a politics of Islamization. There are two competing options: the Islamization of Europe, or a Europeanizing of Islam.[35] The extension of the Muslim Brotherhood into Europe portends the former.

One may argue that institutional Islamism treats Western Europe as an Islamist asylum. Islamists enjoy in Europe the civil rights denied to them in the world of Islam itself. In a recent study based on fieldwork in several Eu-ropean countries, Lorenzo Vidino provides strong evidence for the power the Movement of the Muslim Brothers has obtained in Europe. He cites critics of institutional Islamism who see the Muslim Brothers as "deceitful actors seeking to destroy the very same freedoms that have allowed them to flourish." Vidino agrees, but opposes a politics that would outlaw the Mus-lim Brotherhood. On the one hand his study presents "ample evidence showing that the aims of the New Western Brothers do not necessarily cor-respond to those publically stated in dialogues with Western establishments." On the other hand, these "nonviolent Islamists are a reality that cannot be ignored."[36] How should democracy respond to this challenge? I share Vidino's view that no democrat would deny nonviolent Islamists the right of engagement. But the difference between engagement and empowerment has to be kept in mind when democracies develop an approach for dealing with institutional Islamism, whether in the world of Islam or in its diaspora in Europe and the United States.

These insights are most pertinent for Egypt after Mubarak. A seizure of power by the Muslim Brothers, whether by election or other means, would create an Islamist regime. The alternative order is the civil Islam of Indonesia.[37]

The Islamist Use of Democracy

"Moderate Islamism" is a delusion based on the assumption that institutional Islamism is a pro-democracy movement. There would be no contradiction, and hence no delusion, if Islamism were rooted in Islamic ethics,[38] which, if combined with religious reforms, actually could make Islam compatible with democracy. But the political ideology of Islamism does not operate on either Islamic ethics or the democratic values of pluralism and power sharing. The major political concern of Islamism is to establish the nizam-Islami, the Islamic system.

Today, one of the greatest problems of Islamic civilization, particularly in its Middle Eastern core, is the lack of democracy and individual human rights. As the Egyptian liberal Muslim Saad Eddin Ibrahim has put it, "we are twisted between ruling autocrats and the theocrats opposing them."[39] The implication is that Islamism is not the needed alternative to authoritarian and despotic regimes in the Middle East: Islamists would merely replace one malaise with another. For expressing such thoughts, Ibrahim was prosecuted and jailed in his own country and lives today in exile. But his remark requires us to question the unproven assumption that institutional Islamism is compatible with the political culture of democracy.

The distinction made earlier between institutional Islamism and jihadism provides a far more informative set of categories than the standard distinction between "radical" and "moderate" Islam or Islamism. When paired with "Islam," the political terms "radical" and "moderate" are largely meaningless; when paired with "Islamism" they suggest doctrinal differences that simply do not exist. It is also wrong to reserve the term "Islamism" for "radicals," "fanatics," or "extremists." "Radical" implies a minority acting on the fringes. The reality is that Islamism is the most popular public choice in the world of Islam. Organized Islamists are a minority in numbers, but they receive financial support from wealthy Gulf donors and have considerable facilities at their disposal. The difference between institutional and jihadist Islamists is a difference in tactics, not in doctrines or fundamental goals concerning Islamist governance.[40]

Institutional Islamists do not engage in the violence of jihadism but instead play the game of democracy and agree to go to the ballot box. They still share the common goal of the Islamist movement, to establish al-nizam al-Islami, the shari'a-based Islamic order. The Islamist worldview includes a belief in siyadat al-Islam (supremacy of Islam) based on a universal *rabbaniyya* (theocentrism). Islamist religion-based internationalism stands in sharp contrast to a pluralist democracy and to power sharing.

If democracy were merely a voting procedure, then no one would have a reason to object when totalitarian movements use the ballot box as an instrument for the soft seizure of power. But it is more than this. There is a political culture of democracy in which civic pluralism and power sharing in society and state are essential. No democracy, of course, can exist without voting, but equally no democracy can prevail if the necessary political culture and public institutions are not in place. Thus the norm of diversity applies to democracy, but only up to a point. Despite the many variations in democratic practice, democracy, like human rights, has a certain irreducible universality. Liberal Arab democrats approve in their reasoning the core values of democracy.[41]

It is abundantly clear that Islamism is a political opposition in the world of Islam that no one can afford to overlook. Islamist movements are not only a potent opposition to existing autocratic rulers but also the only ones ready to take over. In many places the question is not whether Islamists will come to power but what they will bring to it. The opinion expressed in the *Financial Times* that "the participation [of Islamists] in the political process remains the best hope of moderating their often radical views"[42] represents established wisdom in the West. But putting Islamists in charge will not give rise to a new politics of inclusion in a participatory democracy. Hamas, for instance, came to power through election in 2006 and soon put all its PLO opponents in jail without trial. One year later, Hamas followed its electoral victory with a military coup.

The test of Islamism's compatibility with democracy rests on the Islamist idea of nizam Islami (Islamic system of government) based on hakimiyyat Allah (God's rule). The core contention of Islamist ideology is that only God, not man, is entitled to rule the world. Can this truly be reconciled with the popular sovereignty of secular democracy? How can democracy grow out of a commitment to the shari'atization of politics?

Throughout the world of Islam, conflicts occur not only between authoritarian regimes and Islamist opposition but also between Islamism and liberal democracy. In what follows I shall focus on Sunni Islam, because the terms of the debate over Islamism and democracy are often set by Arab Sunni thinkers. Political Islam first flourished in the Arab Middle East and rippled outward from there.

A look at the practices of Hezbollah in Lebanon, Hamas in Palestine, and the Islamist parties in Iraq does not offer reassurance that the inclusion of Islamists in government tends to moderate them. In all three places, political Islamist parties are represented in the elected parliament and in the government, yet maintain their terrorist militias and nonstate military networks, which are often used to intimidate opponents of Islamism. There is little evidence that Islamists' electoral victories are transforming them into moderate democratic parties.

In Iraq the Islamist Da'wa party reflects an institutional variety of Islamism. It rules the country in coalition with two Shi'ite jihadist movements: the Supreme Islamic Iraqi Council (SIIC, earlier SCIRI), whose military wing is the Failaq Badr or Badr Brigade, and the faction allied with Muqtada Sadr and his equally jihadist al-Mahdi army. The line in Iraq between institutional Islamism and jihadism is blurred. The "U.S.-led liberation" that brought the Shi'ite majority to power has been described as the "foreigner's gift."[43] It brought liberation from the tyranny of the Sunni minority, but it replaced Saddam's dictatorship with a tyranny of the Shi'a parties, which came from their exile in Iran. This is not democratization. One can hardly proclaim democracy when the Mahdi army forbids posting the pictures of parliamentary candidates competing against the Sadrists.

The Palestinian Hamas[44] movement won an absolute majority in the elections of February 2006. In a *Financial Times* commentary, Carl Bildt and Anna Palacio, respectively the foreign minister of Sweden and the former foreign minister of Spain, applauded this as a democratic result.

The behavior of the Hamas Islamists, who ousted the autocratic secular Fatah and its Palestinian National Authority in Gaza, shows no evidence of a willingness to share power. This stance deepened the existing tensions between Islamist and secularist Palestinians in the occupied territories,[45] with the result that Fatah, fearing a repeat of what happened in Gaza, now resists joint rule with Hamas in the West Bank. In Gaza, Hamas went to the ballot box while continuing its terrorist assaults against civilians, both Israeli and Palestinian. A year after the election Hamas used its militias to seize full power in Gaza through a military coup. It is considered a "terrorist" movement by both the United States and the European Union, and the free election did not transform it into a democratic party. Hamas has abolished the constitutional court created by the PNA and routinely jails political opponents without trial.

The Islamist AKP in Turkey is free of bullets (it has no private militia, though it does control the oppressive local police), but it was the first government to receive a delegation from Hamas after the 2006 election and to support it in the Gaza war of 2008–9. Only Iran followed its example. None of the Arab states did. The AKP has resisted establishing freedom of faith and freedom of expression in the Turkish constitution and continually replaces secular judges and university presidents with Islamist ones from its party ranks.

In Lebanon, Hezbollah[46] as of this writing controls 14 of the 128 seats in the parliament and 11 of 30 cabinet posts, but it continues to maintain its own irregular army, which acts as a militia in Hezbollah-controlled territories. In July and August 2006, the Israeli Defense Force could not dislodge this militia; in fact, Hezbollah received a great boost from the war with Israel.[47] The Lebanese air force is not allowed to fly over the military zones controlled by Hezbollah, nor is the Lebanese army permitted to enter.

These zones constitute a state within the state. The question is: is Hezbollah now a democratic power or a jihadist movement?

What conclusions are to be drawn? This depends on where you stand. All of these parties participate in elections (at least until they gain power), but none is practicing democracy as it is commonly understood or, I would argue, as it must be understood in order to mean anything at all.

There is no doubt that democracy and democratization offer the best promise for a better future in the world of Islam. But given the *azmat al-democratiyya* (crisis of democracy) in the Arab world, the best examples of Islamic democracy are to be found outside the Middle East. In the past three decades, I have had the chance to study Islam and democracy not only in the Arab Middle East but also outside of it,[48] and thus escape the confines of its Arabocentrism. Living, pursuing research, and teaching in several countries in West Africa and in Southeast Asia, I encountered a "civil Islam" that belies the common contention that Islam and democracy "meet in Europe."[49] The Islamic diaspora in the West is caught up in a culture of apology and defensiveness, the hallmark of identity politics in a gated community. Other sources of Islamic democracy are, unfortunately, not gaining but losing influence.

The civil Islam of Indonesia, for example, is highly favorable to democracy, but this country has never affected thinking in the Arab world. I have lived and worked in Indonesia and have seen Arab preachers (some with American Ph.D.'s) teaching Indonesians that their version of Islam is based on incorrect views. But I have never met a single Indonesian Muslim preaching civil Islam in the Middle East. At al-Azhar University in Cairo, I met Indonesians learning Salafi Islam with the intention of bringing it home, to the detriment of civil Islam.

The Paradox of Democratic Shari'a

Is there a specific Arab or an Islamic democracy? Perhaps Western patterns of democracy cannot succeed or be properly applied in the world of Islam, and despite its universal roots, democracy must adopt some authentic Arab and Islamic features. Is shari'a perhaps *necessary* to the success of democracy in the Islamic world? Is it necessary that the political order of that world comes not from the outside but from within? I shall address these issues more fully in Chapter 6, but for now it is important to understand that the Islamist shari'a is not the classical version, but rather an invention of tradition. The Islamist shari'a is a totalitarian concept rather than an Islamic adoption of democracy.

Postmodernism and cultural relativism put aside the political culture of democracy, focus on the ballot box, and suggest a positive assessment of Islamism and its ideology of an Islamic state based on the shari'a. Democracy, one might argue, is understood by the Islamists in a different way, and it would be both futile and patronizing to impose specific Western ideas onto Muslim cultures. Enlightened Muslims[50] answer that despite different understandings of the concept of democracy, there must remain a distinction between democracy and its opposite. The Islamist shari'a state is that opposite.

One of the three Islamist voices with which this chapter opened was that of Yusuf al-Qaradawi; he rightly notes that secularism, democracy, and cultural modernity entered the world of Islam in a civilizational encounter with the West shaped by power and hegemony, but he then draws the wrong conclusions. His ideology of "Islam under siege" forces one to ask why India, despite its colonial past, succeeded in becoming a democratic state and rising power, while Arab and Muslim states that were never colonies (such as Yemen, Saudi Arabia, and Afghanistan) have never managed to do so. Islamists have no satisfactory explanation. Instead, they argue that the introduction of democracy to the Arab world was doomed to failure because democracy, like secularization, is alien to the world of Islam. This assertion would elevate Islam's resistance to external ideas from a normative principle to a sociological fact: that Islam, uniquely among all the world's civilizations, is somehow immune to outside influence. Like so many other Islamist ideas, this one relies on an invention of history.

In fact, democratization is not a recent issue in the civilizational interaction of Muslims with Europe. In a positive kind of cultural borrowing, the adoption of democracy was often on the agenda. Islamic civilization not

only absorbed Hellenic thought long before Europe rediscovered it but adopted its legacy into the Islamic heritage and acted as a mediator in passing
this legacy on to the West. The historian of civilizations Leslie Lipson
writes that "Aristotle crept back into Europe by the side door. His return
was due to the Arabs, who had become acquainted with Greek thinkers."[51]
In the classical heritage of Islam one finds a rich historical record of this
cultural borrowing. Hellenist philosophy became an essential part of the
classical Islamic *falsafa* (rationalism) as opposed to the *fiqh* (orthodoxy). (I
address this issue further in Chapter 7.)

The adoption of a kind of democracy suitable to the Middle East was a
major concern of early Arab liberalism.[52] Nineteenth-century Arab-Muslim
liberals who went to Europe were impressed by French democracy. The first
was the reformer Rifa'a al-Tahtawi; he lived in Paris and advocated cultural
borrowing from the West, provided that it did not contradict Islamic law.[53]
The Arab Muslims who followed were not only liberal but also secular. Convinced that democracy and shari'a are not compatible, they abandoned shari'a
altogether.

Decolonization during the mid-twentieth century, the period of nation-
state formation in the world of Islam,[54] was followed by efforts at democratic rule. Arab-Muslim elites in Egypt, Syria, and Iraq faced the challenge
of modernity, despite having been exposed to it in a colonial context, by
setting up systems of parliamentary democracy. The only remnant of this
democratic tradition is Lebanon, where democracy is now threatened by
the Islamist party Hezbollah. Everywhere else, these infant democracies
failed to take root and quickly gave way to praetorian nationalist military
regimes like that of Nasser in Egypt and the Ba'thists in Syria and Iraq.
The pan-Arab nationalists appealed to populist sentiments but abandoned
democracy on the pretext that it is alien to the Arab people. Populist rule by
the military[55] was presented as a remedy for the corruption of democratic
multiparty systems. The secular ideology of pan-Arab populist nationalism
emphasized the unity of the nation against both pluralism and multiparty
democracy, which were seen as divisive and thus as promoting the fragmentation of the Arab nation. Those who did not openly reject democracy

advocated a specific Arab democracy based on unity. But this was a deception offered in the name of Arab authenticity.

It is important to note that the failure of democracy was not due to a
conspiracy by Westerners but rather was a consequence of underdevelopment.
Development is not merely a matter of economics; it has to include institutional and cultural development. The concept of "developing cultures"[56] is
critical to establishing democracy in the world of Islam. The Muslim liberals failed to establish a culture of democracy and individual human rights.
Qaradawi points at this failure not only to shift responsibility for failed development onto outside powers and paint the Arab nations as victims, but
also to discard democracy itself.

The secular nationalists are now being replaced by Islamists whose
goal (in, for instance, Iraq and Palestine) is to bring back the shari'a in the
name of democratization. As I have noted, the humiliation of the secular
nationalist regimes in the Six-Day War of 1967 created a crisis of confidence
throughout the Arab world. One consequence was an opening for an "enlightenment" launched by disillusioned Arab intellectuals, who engaged in
a process of self-criticism that was unprecedented for Arabs,[57] who tend to
equate criticism with disparagement. This effort did not last long. What
Qaradawi named al hall al-Islami, the Islamic solution, became the mobilizing ideology, poisoning the seeds of the intellectuals' enlightenment. Political Islam is today the foremost political power in the Arab world, even
where it is not yet in power.

The American invasion of Iraq in 2003 removed the most powerful of
the remaining secular nationalist regimes. With the ensuing experiment in
democratization, Islamist movements began to adopt the institutional
way to power. In Iraq it became clear that regime change did not equal
democratization. Democracy might be universal, but still one cannot escape
local constraints and cultural peculiarities. By contesting the universality of
democratic values, the Islamists end up legitimating particularism as an expression of Arab authenticity. The notion of asalah (authenticity) as a cultural
underpinning for purity serves as an excuse to discard the liberal experiment.
The next step is then to argue that the shari'a must be reintroduced in the
name of democracy. This is done in the service of establishing the Islamist

dawla Islamiyya (Islamic state),[58] a state order not at all consonant with democracy and individual human rights.

The new Iraqi constitution does not mention shari'a by name, but it contains the rule (as paraphrased in the *Wall Street Journal*) that "no laws may contradict the fixed principles of Islam.... A supreme court is to be created, composed of experts in Islamic law, that will have the power to strike laws down as unconstitutional."[59] A similar provision exists in the Afghani constitution, written, like the Iraqi document, with American advice. There are many fine-sounding guarantees of rights and freedoms in these constitutions, but should these be alleged to contradict Islamic law, it will be up to a court to decide which provisions shall prevail. This is a model not for democratization but for the shari'atization of the state, a prospect that threatens not only Iraq and Afghanistan but many Islamic countries, above all Egypt if the Muslim Brothers come to power. With the intensification of the "Arab predicament" after the 1967 war, one of the factors in the rise of political Islam has been its opposition to all *al-hulul al-mustawradah* (imports from the West). Secular democracy is at the top of the list of such "imports." All Islamist parties—like Turkey's AKP—use democracy as their access to power. As Zeyno Baran notes, "Democratic elections ... [have] proven to be the easiest and most legitimate path to power."[60] Islamists accept the procedure as a way of legitimating their rule but reject the pluralist culture of democracy. In their propaganda the nonviolent Islamists approve democracy, but among themselves, they refer to democracy's ancient Greek origins to show that it is among the hulul mustawradah (imported solutions) that must be rejected. Instead they propagate the formula al-hall huwa al-Islam—Islam is the solution—except that by Islam they mean the Islamic shari'a state, based on the principle of hakimiyyat Allah, God's rule. This is anything but democracy.

Given the long history of Islamic engagement with Western ideas, why couldn't Muslims today adopt the heritage of democracy as an outcome of cultural modernity, much as their ancestors were able to adopt the accomplishments of Hellenism? Democracy's claim to universality is acceptable to those Muslims who subscribe to a civil Islam, but a genuine embrace of its spirit would require cultural reforms that are in opposition to the agenda of

Islamism. The lip service Islamists pay to democracy is both recent and instrumental; it does not reflect a shift of mindset. Hamas[61] went to the ballot box and won an election, but the political system it represents does not conform to any understanding of democracy, "Arab" or otherwise.

The Illusion of Multiple Democracies

By now it should be clear that Islamism is not an achiever in the field of democracy and that mere opposition to existing autocratic regimes does not qualify it as a pro-democracy movement. The politicization and shari'atization of Islam are not compatible with democracy. On the other hand, Islam—given certain reforms—could be made a source of democratic legitimacy. Thus my criticism in this chapter of political Islam and its agenda of an Islamic state based on shari'a is not a judgment about Islam itself.

In civil society, the rule of law is an essential part of democracy, but there are ideological and civilizational differences in the understanding of law. Hence the idea of multiple democracies has arisen alongside that of multiple modernities. Can shari'a law provide the basis for a democratic order? Let us put aside for a moment the tensions within Islam, particularly those between Sunna and Shi'a, who have different views about shari'a law, and focus more abstractly on the concept of shari'a law, which Islamists view as the basis of the Islamic state. Is the envisioned shari'a state just an expression of cultural differences, or is it a constructed civilizational ideology incompatible with democracy? In the West, such a question creates two opposing camps: the universalists and the cultural relativists. Neither side, however, has much feel for non-Western cultures.

The particular features of Middle Eastern life and custom are partly determined by Islam in its manifestation in local cultures. Some of these create obstacles to the acceptance of democracy. One may argue that those particularities need to be limited, even though one has to consider cultural differences seriously. But these differences must first be identified and discussed freely. The core question is to what extent Islam is to be democratized through reform and to what extent democracy is to be adjusted to an Islamic environment. It is not an either/or question. Given the prevalence of Sunni

Islam, Arab debates on these issues are highly influential in determining what forms democracy might take in the Islamic world, and whether shari'a can really be viewed as constitutional law.

To understand the issues that underlie the lack of political freedom in Arab societies, it is important to move beyond ideological contentions, attitudes of victimization, and ritual accusations of the West. In this venture, some Arab debates that took place more than a quarter of a century ago are worth reviewing. In October 1980 a group of Arab intellectuals assembled in Tunis to address the future of their region, including the options for democracy. The occasion was titled *Les Arabes face à leur destin,* or Arabs face their future.[62] The major question related to whether Arabs would act with a sense of responsibility or engage in self-congratulation while blaming others for their misfortunes. (Edward Said's "Orientalism" had helped feed the latter sentiment.) The participants were unanimous on two points: there was no political freedom in the majority of Arab countries, and creating such freedom would require cultural change. Two decades later, in 2002, this self-critical observation was restated less rhetorically in a report completed by Arab experts for the United Nations Development Program.[63] The same lack of freedom prevents Arab intellectuals from expressing their commitment to liberty or working openly to establish any authentic framework for democracy in their own countries. Most fear imprisonment if they reveal their pro-democracy political commitments. Those who are not imprisoned are often denied access to the means of cultural and political expression. The system of surveillance by the state allows freedom of action only to mercenary intellectuals. The Islamic Middle East exists in a system of homemade neopatriarchy.[64] What President Obama told Africans in July 2009 applies to Arabs as well: "The legacy of colonialism is not an excuse for failing to build . . . democratic societies." Obama compared the country his father came from, Kenya, with South Korea, pointing out that while both had colonial legacies, they had very different records of accomplishment.

Does contemporary Islamism, as the only visible opposition to authoritarian repression, provide the needed alternative? Or, to repeat the formula of Saad Eddin Ibrahim, are we entangled between autocracy and theocracy? The autocrats say that democracy is alien to Arabs, and the Islamists

say that democracy is alien to Islam. The political order envisioned by the
Islamists is by no means a democracy and cannot be considered a remedy
for the existing malaise. Yet there is a need for a change. The complete failure of the Bush administration's "regime change" in Iraq, an effort to create
a democratic culture by military force, led some to speak of an incompatibility between Islam and democracy. One cannot simply dismiss such specu-
lations as "Orientalism." Even some Arabs entertained these thoughts, earning
criticism from Sadik al-Azm for practicing "Orientalism in reverse."[65]

The lack of democracy in the world of Islam cannot be explained
by reference to imperialism and its colonial legacy, or by the imagery of a
mu'amarah (conspiracy).[66] Such ideas lead nowhere, but they have to be
taken into consideration because they are powerful. The bottom line is that
political Islam's insistence on presenting shari'a as constitutional law is a
symptom of a larger issue. The invention of tradition, the use of a distorted
or even imaginary history to justify present political ambitions, is a wide-
spread practice. What Muslims need instead is Islamic rationalism, an hon-
orable if neglected part of Islamic tradition. The Hellenization of Islamic
civilization under the rationalists' influence during the Middle Ages was an
extensive cultural borrowing that led to significant advances. Muslim societies need to borrow from the West again to create the structural and institutional underpinnings of democracy. Human rights as well as the freedoms
of expression and assembly can exist only if guaranteed by both cultural
and legal safeguards. Muslims must recognize that these are not Western
impositions but universal goods.

Civic pluralism is the criterion for determining what is democratic and
what is not. The compatibility of Islamism and democracy falters on the
Islamists' rejection of democratic pluralism as a part of their general rejection of Western values. Pluralism cannot be reconciled with the religionization of politics: the universality of democracy conflicts with the authenticity
of the "Islamic solution." For Islamists, democracy is not universal but only
a source of tactics; its European origin serves to legitimate their limiting
its role to *shura* (consultation) and the adoption of certain procedures.
The institutional safeguards that underpin democracy are reduced to an

institutional control mechanism that must be in compliance with shari'a. This is done in the name of authenticity. The obstacles to the establishment of democracy in Islam are different from those in the West, where the issue was largely the painful expansion of participation to previously excluded social groups. The denial of equal protection under the law to different social groups and classes is not the problem with shari'a. The problem is rather twofold: first, there is no single comprehensive shari'a. Reference to it is always arbitrary, though done in the name of God. Second, because it denies equality between Muslims and non-Muslims, shari'a lacks religious pluralism.

In a democracy, power is depersonalized: it resides in institutions, such as courts and legislatures, not in specific individuals. In Islamic tradition, the imam embodies a personalized authority. The late Majid Khadduri, a U.S.-based Iraqi-born scholar, published many books in which Arab politics is reduced to the biographies of Arab politicians. Though this approach is methodologically flawed, I believe Khadduri had a point; power in Arab politics is personalized, not based in institutions. This does not mean, of course, that there are no structures underlying Arab politics. In my study of the Islamic intellectual history, I repeatedly encountered the traditional question asked by the jurists: "who is the *imam fadil*," the true Imam?[67] Legal issues were resolved on the basis of personal authority. Only rarely were proper and just institutions a relevant issue in the jurists' reasoning.

There were exceptions. Among them one finds al-Farabi's classical work *al-Madina al-Fadila*,[68] in which he discussed the proper order of society and state, leaning on ancient Greek philosophy and its adoption into an Islamic tradition of rationalism. Clearly, some universal standards can be usefully accepted by people of different cultures.

In short, institutions matter to democracy. With this in mind, it is helpful to consult Barrington Moore's classic *The Social Origins of Dictatorship and Democracy*,[69] which provides a comparative analysis of Western and non-Western political development and shows that those European societies that were able to develop a pattern of democracy did so on the basis of some comparatively autonomous medieval institutions. Moore concludes that these institutions contributed to strengthening the civil society vis-à-vis the state. A working democracy presupposes the existence of institutions of a civil state and a civil society, not only an *Imam adil* (just Imam). In this regard there can be no "multiple democracies." The Islamist argument that Western patterns of democracy do not apply to Islam is a mere ploy to prevent any democratization that goes beyond the ballot box. Islamist thinking also prevents the expansion of political participation and equal protection to non-Muslims that is possible under institutionalized law. Shari'a is interpretative, not legislative, and thus cannot be institutionalized.

The anti-Western argument also ignores the cultural heritage of Islam. Learning from others within the framework of cultural borrowing not only is not alien to the Arab-Islamic heritage, it is most pertinent to the present. Democracy's Greek origin does not make it alien to Islam. Hellenism is a part of the Islamic legacy. Of course there are different varieties of democracy—every democratic rule is adjusted to local conditions—but these varieties, to be considered democracies, must all satisfy certain universal conditions.

There is no reason these conditions cannot be made to harmonize with authenticity and identity politics, but this is not what the Islamists have in mind. The successes of Hamas in Palestine, SIIC in Iraq, Hezbollah in Lebanon, the Muslim Brothers (earlier disguised as the Wasat Party) in Egypt, al-Nahada in Tunisia, the Islamic Action Front in Jordan, and FIS in Algeria are signs not of democracy on the rise but rather of the seizure of power by Islamism wearing democratic camouflage. I say this not as a rebuke of the current "Islamic revival," but rather to point out that democracy requires something other than a revival of shari'a in an Islamist shape. This path is a dead end.

One may argue for an Islam in line with liberal democracy in the Arab world, as the famous liberal Lebanese professor Hassan Sa'b did in an important book in which he called for a "pro-democracy Islam" as opposed to an "Islam of despotism."[70] Sa'b argues that a "comprehensive spiritual revolution in the soul of Muslims" is needed to foster the cultural change required for achieving democracy in the Arab world. This position acknowledges that culture matters for the introduction of democratic traditions. Liberal Islamic thinkers like Sa'b who are committed to democracy in this ethical understanding are rare. The Islamists, with their return of the sacred, are interested not in ethics or in a postsecular renaissance of religion as a cultural meaning, but rather in the politics of an Islamic order [71] based on the din-wa-dawla (unity of state and religion) that they present as the substance of Islam.

Despite the incompatibility of Islamism with democratic pluralism, we are compelled to ponder ways to include the institutional Islamists in the game of democracy, because this is imperative if democracy is to take hold. Yet we must be vigilant to ensure that no undermining of democratization happens in the name of democracy. The American debate on Islam and democracy confuses these imperatives. The problem is the conspicuous lack of knowledge even among those who offer themselves as pundits. One of the few well-informed observers is Zeyno Baran, who writes that Turkey's AKP pays lip service to democracy while it promotes a creeping Islamization.[72] But others, like Voll and Esposito, write books on Islam and democracy that not only overlook basic original sources but also conflate Islam and Islamism, with the result that they end up watering down the meaning of democracy itself.

What Are We Talking About?

With its growing appeal, political Islam is gaining the power to mobilize whole societies. At the same time, Western scholars and policymakers are seeking ways to include "moderate" Islamism in democratic processes. This is a risky strategy. Western assessments of institutional Islamism are often based on poorly defined terms. Research on political Islam needs to be based on clear thinking about the compatibility of both Islam and Islamism with democracy. To reiterate, I have no doubts about the compatibility of a reformed Islam, as a political ethics, with democracy. Islamism is another matter.

Lip service to democracy does not suffice to establish commitment. My interest, as an Arab-Muslim pro-democracy theorist and practitioner, is to establish secular democracy in the Islamic world. Except as it informs a society's ethics, religion cannot be the basis of a democracy. The foregoing inquiry has made use of secular notions and social-science concepts to advance five major ideas. To review, these are:

1. The pertinence of a well-informed analysis of political Islam. In general, one has to understand what Islamism is all about before one can say anything useful about its relation to democracy. This is both an academic and a political concern. Academic analysis exists to help guide policy. Western responses to Islamism have been faulty because policymakers lacked basic information and their actions did not rest on well-founded assessments. Therefore, the first step is to clarify the nature of Islamism.

2. The varied nature of Islam. It is not monolithic, any more than Christianity is. On all levels, as a faith, local culture, and cross-cultural civilization, Islam is characterized by diversity and change. Though it is not by nature a political religion, throughout its history Islam has been embedded into politics in the sense that it was used—always post eventum—to legitimate the authority and actions of the ruling imam-caliph. Today, however, Islamism uses the tradition of shari'a reasoning[73] as a "precedent" (in John Kelsay's formulation) to legitimate novelties. Islamists would use this combination of religion and politics to create a monolithic Islam that did not exist in the past.

3. Islam versus Islamism. It is highly misleading—and a great service to the Islamists—to blur the terms "Islam" and "Islamism," to use them interchangeably, or to assume that Islamism is simply a more fervent or extreme variety of Islam, as Voll, Esposito, and others assert. Thus even though I endorse most of his analysis of the shari'a reasoning in Islam, I disagree with Kelsay when he writes that Hasan al-Banna's Muslim Brothers are an "embodiment of the clerical shari'a vision."[74] Islamists camouflage themselves as the "true Muslims," but there is ample reason to doubt this self-description. When we speak of compatibility with democracy, therefore, we are in fact asking two different questions of two different objects. To the first question, about Islam's compatibility with democracy, we can answer yes, conditional to religious reform (Salafist Islam is not compatible). For instance, the Nahdatul Ulama in Indonesia is an Islamic—not an Islamist—party, and it qualifies as a democratic institution that represents a civil Islam. In contrast, the Islamist Muslim Brotherhood in

Egypt—as well as its offspring such as Hamas—is not democratic but rather totalitarian in its outlook. It is a serious mistake to speak of this movement with the formula "Islam without fear."

4. "Moderation." Related to the distinction between Islam as a faith and Islamism as a religionized ideology is the distinction between peaceful and violent Islamists. The latter enact jihad to pursue their political agenda, whereas peaceful Islamists forgo violence for tactical reasons. In short, jihadist Islamism differs from institutional Islamism in means, not in goals. Kelsay is completely right in stating that even though "moderates" and "militants" disagree over practices, they share the same vision:[75] the shari'a-based order of nizam Islami. As Baran puts it, the "moderates" consent "instrumentally to democratic elections . . . the easiest path to power," forgoing violent "Islamization . . . in favor of a gradual bottom-up policy." Despite the occasional resort to legitimate elections, this "creeping Islamization"[76] is not democratization.

5. Elections versus democracy. In assessing Islam's and Islamism's compatibility with democracy, we must bear in mind a further distinction within democracy itself. Democracy is based institutionally on an electoral procedure, but it is much more than balloting. It is above all a political culture of pluralism and tolerance for reasonable disagreement, based on core values combined with the acceptance of diversity. The procedure of elections and the establishment of this political culture are two parts of the same system and cannot be separated. When institutional Islamists try to separate them, they only substitute bottom-up Islamization for violent top-down Islamization. They agree to balloting but not to the pluralist political culture of democratic civil society. This distinction is lost on pundits who reject as "secular fundamentalism" an insistence on the pluralist civic culture of democracy.

Institutional Islamists and Democracy

In this chapter I have raised four broad issues:

Unity and diversity in Islam and Islamism. Diversity within a category does not mean a lack of all commonalities—otherwise there could be no categories. In Islam, there is a core set of tenets—a worldview, a faith, and a set of ethical teachings—that all Muslims share. In my thirty years of research in some twenty Islamic countries in Africa and Asia, I have seen countless examples of both commonalities and differences. The same applies to Islamism. All Islamists have in common that they shari'atize Islam and flatly ignore the fact that the term "shari'a" occurs only once in the Qur'an, where it refers to morality, not law. All Islamists share an agenda of establishing an Islamic state order, or nizam Islami—not the "global caliphate" as many self-pronounced experts maintain. Neither "dawla" (state) nor "nizam"—both of which are pivotal in the shari'a reasoning of the Islamists—occurs in the Qur'an. What all Islamists share, therefore, is a modern religionized political ideology geared to a remaking of the world on the basis of an inverted tradition of shari'a. All Muslims who subscribe to this agenda can be identified as Islamists. Faithful Muslims with a spiritual understanding of Islam, who do not subscribe to this agenda, are not Islamists. The term "post-Islamism," which refers to Islamist renunciation of jihadism in favor of democratic participation, makes no sense. How can Islamists be "post-Islamists" if they still aspire to create an "Islamist order"? Only if this goal is abandoned may one talk of post-Islamism. I do not know a single Islamist movement that has abandoned this Islamist agenda. Some parties, such as Turkey's AKP, deny their Islamism to avoid constitutional banning. This is by no means a sign of post-Islamism.

In any case, the distinction between institutional and jihadist Islamists is often blurred. Several Islamist parties agree to go to the ballot box but retain their militias. Hamas, Hezbollah, and SIIC all want to have it both ways: they claim legitimacy through their elected representation in the parliament but continue the practice of terror.

"Genuine commitment to democracy." The word "genuine" in this context denotes a liberal understanding based on democratic pluralism. Study of the ideology of Islamism and of its pillars does not support a belief in any such commitment. The nizam Islami is a totalitarian order. One could argue that a change could happen through shifts in the thinking and cultural values of Islamists themselves. In my study of political Islam I have yet to see any such shift. There has been a rhetorical and strategic adjust-

ment to democracy. In all cases, this adjustment happens merely for in-strumental reasons, to avoid proscription or, in the case of the Muslim Brothers in Egypt, to avoid prosecution. Of course, there may be individu-als who have undergone such a shift.[77] One can say that these persons have abandoned Islamism altogether. Neither the AKP nor the Muslim Broth-erhood has done this.

The compatibility of Islamist ideology with democracy. The Islamist reli-gionization of politics leaves no room for negotiation, since the sacred is not negotiable. Disagreement is heresy. Pluralism and tolerance of diversity, essential elements of democracy, are rejected as "divisive." Participation in elections and the ambiguous renunciation of violence are by themselves not indications that Islamists are becoming genuinely democratic. Islamist move-ments reject power sharing with secular parties or with non-Muslim mi-norities in the name of shari'a. They admit only what they believe that their totalitarian shari'a allows. Despite the claim of shari'a as constitutional law, constitutionalism and shari'a are completely at odds.[78]

Inclusion versus exclusion. Despite the incompatibility of the Islamist state order with democracy, no democratic government can ignore the Islamist movements, which represent the major opposition throughout most of the world of Islam. So what can we do? Two approaches exist, one inclusionary, represented by the model of Turkey, and the other exclusion-ary, represented by Algeria, where Islamist parties are banned outright. I confess that I prefer the Turkish example.

Not that Turkey's experience with the AKP is reassuring. It has re-sulted in "a creeping Islamization" at the expense of democratic pluralism. The AKP is an Islamist party, not, as it pretends, an Islamic-conservative party comparable to the German Christian Democrats. It is intolerant of secularists, which it calls *dönme* (hidden Jews), and of ethnic and religious minorities, like Kurds and Allawis. The politics of inclusion has given power to a party of exclusion.[79] The AKP has successfully used elections as the "most legitimate path to power" and has been able "to reshape the republic, chiefly along Islamist lines,"[80] but not in the direction of demo-cratization.

The unequivocal conclusion is that Islamism and democracy are deeply at odds. We should never forget that democracy is a novel cultural concept in the world of Islam. Can this introduction be successful as part of a global democratization?[81] The introduction of democracy needs institutional and cultural underpinnings, which every civilization develops according to its own calendar. The claim that democracy is universal is questioned not only by Western cultural relativists but also by non-Westerners as a European invention. Yusuf al-Qaradawi describes "secular democracy" as one of the *hulul mustawradah* (imported solutions) that Islam must reject. Other Islamists play at democracy in a superficial and halfhearted way. There is little sign that Islamists want to (or can) reconcile the universality of secular democracy with their "Islamic solution" of a shari'a order.

All of the civil foundations for democracy are missing in the world of Islam. The only working institution is the *mukhabarat,* the secret police guaranteeing the oppressive surveillance of the entire population in a culture of fear. Even though Islamists are themselves victims of this oppressive institution, we can be sure that they would continue this system if they came to power. The chief evidence is the Islamic Republic of Iran. Gaza under the rule of Hamas and Turkey under the AKP are not reassuring either.

If Islamists honestly engaged in a shift of mindset and accepted democracy as a political culture, they really would become post-Islamists. But doing so would require them to renounce the core of their political/religious beliefs. The central tenets of political Islam—the belief in an organic entity named din-wa-dawla, unity of state and religion, the concept of a "shari'a state"[82] that does not exist in the Qur'an, and, for jihadists, and "Islamic world revolution" that is for them the only means of politics—are all at war with the ideas and political culture of democracy.[83]

Arab Spring, Democracy, and Islamism

The breathtaking events in the Middle East in the spring and summer of 2011, just as this book was in the final stages of editing, demand some comment even though the dramatic evolution that started then is far from completed. On February 11, President Obama rightly spoke of the "blinding pace" of events. Both Turkey and Iran have presented themselves as models for post-Mubarak Egypt.

So far the "Arab Spring" has brought the unseating of rulers in Tunisia (Ben Ali), in Egypt (Mubarak), and in Libya (Qadhafi) and ongoing uprisings in three countries: Syria, Yemen, and Bahrain. The stalemates in Egypt and Tunisia and the bloodshed and unrestrained violence in Libya and Syria dismissed the naïve Western expectation of a swift turn from authoritarianism to democracy. One of the most insightful Western commentators, Thomas Friedman, has described the situation aptly:

> There's one big problem: The Tahrir Square revolution was a largely spontaneous, bottom-up affair. It was not led by any particular party or leader. Parties are just now being formed. If elections . . . are held in September, the only group in Egypt with a real party network ready to roll is the one that has been living underground and is now suddenly legal: the Islamist Muslim Brotherhood. Liberal people are feeling some concerns that they made the revolution and the Muslim Brotherhood can now take it.[84]

Another perceptive Western reporter wrote a late-summer account of this great world-historical event:

> The idealism of the revolts in Egypt and Tunisia . . . revived an Arab world anticipating change. But Libya's unfinished revolution . . . illustrates how perilous that change has become. . . . The intentions and influence of Islamists in their ranks are uncertain. . . . Libya's complexities suggest[] that the prolonged transition of Arab countries to a new order may prove as tumultuous to the region as Egypt's moment was stirring. . . . Uncertainty is far more pronounced today [in] power vacuums. . . . In Yemen, militant Islamists have found a haven. . . . Islamists . . . have emerged as a force in Egypt, Libya, Syria and elsewhere.[85]

These events turn the page, but the new page is blank. Who is going to fill it? A liberal Islamic opposition, or the Islamists? It is fair to say that the road is rocky for all parties. For the Middle East, as the core of Islamic civilization, the events of February 2011 reflect a change of a world-historical significance that is most pertinent to the theme of this book. Therefore, a proper understanding of the watershed is highly imperative.

The point of departure is the fact that the Middle East stood outside history following the breakdown of communism beginning in 1989 and the ensuing global democratization. All Arab states were ruled, with varying degrees of oppression, by authoritarian regimes. In January 2011 this changed. In the Tunisian city Sidi Bouzaid, a street vendor publicly burned himself to protest the arbitrary confiscation of his business. This individual protest triggered a mass upheaval that ultimately compelled the dictator Ben Ali to flee to Saudi Arabia after ten days of mass protest. In the same month, the successful Tunisian protest spilled over to Algeria, Jordan, Yemen, and Syria, and most significantly to Egypt, the hub of the Middle East. Mass protests for eighteen days—January 25 to February 11—ended President Mubarak's three decades of rule. By the time you read this, the leadership of that part of the world is likely to look very different.

These events put the central subject of this chapter—the depth of the Islamists' commitment to democracy—into a much different and starker context. The rise to power of Islamist parties in several additional countries has evolved from a theoretical future eventuality to a very near-term prospect. The core of the world of Islam is attempting to move from authoritarianism to democratic rule, and it is therefore imperative to assess the place of Islamist movements in this process.

Three points need to guide our analysis. First, the removal of an authoritarian government will not necessarily lead to democracy, as happened in much of postcommunist Europe after 1989. In Iran, the tyranny of the shah was replaced after 1979 by the tyranny of the Islamist ayatollahs. Second, Islamism has become a transnational movement. The Egyptian Muslim Brothers and Turkish AKP, for instance, are well connected. The *International Herald Tribune* global edition of the *New York Times* reported that "Erdoğan's party has already established ties to the Muslim Brotherhood in Egypt—as a result of Mr. Erdoğan's longstanding and successful campaign to present himself as a dominant and increasingly anti-Israel voice in the Middle East. . . . Three members of the Egyptian Muslim Brotherhood . . . were on the Turkish-sponsored ship . . . that was attacked by Israeli soldiers"[86] in May 2010. Third, authoritarian regimes in the Middle East have always presented themselves as secular bulwarks against Islamism. The Mubarak regime was no exception. The effect has been to create a smoke screen in the assessment of Islamism. In 2011 there has been a strong trend in the West to idealize Islamism as a force for democratization. A *Times* global edition report on the Muslim Brotherhood acknowledges that "among specialists, the degree of uncertainty about the Brotherhood's future is striking." This uncertainty extends to the degree of moderation in the movement, which "may prove to have been a convenient false front to be cast off if the group achieved real power."[87]

Let us start by noting that the upheavals in the Middle East were not engineered by Islamists and their supporters; they are spontaneous expressions of anger by people who not only endure political suppression but also suffer economically. The Tunisian street vendor burned himself not for democracy but to protest his economic repression. The Islamists step into this amalgam of all kinds of opposition that relates to all walks of life. Could they prevail? Could they hijack the revolt? And how should they be dealt with as a political reality? If nothing else, it is clear that no politics can be designed in the Arab–Middle Eastern part of the world of Islam without engaging the existing Islamist movements. Moreover, no democratic participatory government can specifically exclude these movements and be true to democratic principles. Despite their undemocratic ideology, there is no alternative to engaging those Islamists who forgo violence. Still, engagement and empowerment are distinctly different issues. To engage Islamism is not to empower it, let alone hand over power to Islamists in the name of democracy, as has happened and is happening in Lebanon, Gaza, Iraq, and even Turkey. The Islamists must be opposed by a counterweight of truly democratic forces, to try to move the transitions in a more liberal direction.

Whatever happens in Egypt in the post-Mubarak era will be more important than what happened in Iran after the toppling of the shah in 1979.

Iran is the center of Shi'a Islam, and Egypt is the center of Sunni Islam. The difference is that Sunni Muslims make up 90 percent of the worldwide umma. It seems useful, therefore, to cite two contrasting outlooks that were published in the same edition of the *Financial Times* of January 31, 2011, at the height of the uprising in Egypt. Emile Nakleh, a former director of the CIA Political Islam Strategic Analysis Program, believes that "a new government can be formed uniting seculars and Islamists. . . . The Brotherhood has already participated in elections and it is willing to work with other groups." He concludes that "there are no ayatollahs waiting in the wings to take over."[88] This statement is literally true because there are no ayatollahs in Sunni Islam. The Sunni clergy is based at al-Azhar, in Cairo, and the Muslim Brotherhood did not come from there—unlike the ayatollahs, who emerge from Iran's Shi'ite equivalent, Qum. Most Sunni Islamist movements are composed of laymen.

The other *Financial Times* piece is a report by Roula Khalaf acknowledging that the Muslim Brotherhood "has a big head start on anyone else in terms of organization and it can count on what remains a very potent mobilizing tool—religion." Khalaf is not silent about the Muslim Brothers' participation in the 2005 elections (they won 20 percent of the seats in the parliament), but she adds this information: the Muslim Brothers "two years later attempted to draft a proper political agenda. The proposed program, however, caused a stir by calling for a ban on women and non-Muslims becoming head of state and creation of a religious council to vet governmental decisions."[89] While the Muslim Brotherhood shelved these demands in the face of public opposition, it never abandoned its Islamist agenda. That agenda raises the likelihood that the Muslim Brotherhood will make pro-democratic noises but, if it gains power, will practice the kind of "Islamic democracy" seen in Gaza and Iran. A hasty election in the post-Mubarak era could therefore be highly damaging. What Egypt needs most is a careful institutional preparation of a transition from authoritarianism to some kind of democracy. At present, all of the democratic institutions needed for the implementation of Western democracy in the Middle East are missing.

In some of the most recent contributions to political theory it is acknowledged that underdevelopment is no longer restricted to underdeveloped economic structures. The low standard of institution building is a basic feature of underdevelopment. Authoritarian rulers in the Middle East have undermined institution building in favor of personal rule. The fall of dictators creates under these conditions a political vacuum that only Islamists can fill, because they are the only opposition that has successfully maintained underground networks stretching beyond the Middle East to become transnational. Liberal-democratic opposition needs time to build its institutions to be able to compete with the Islamists. Thomas Friedman writes that if an early election takes place in the name of democratization, and if the Muslim Brothers win, their movement

> could have an inordinate impact on writing Egypt's first truly free Constitution and could inject restrictions on women, alcohol, dress and the relations between mosque and state. "You will have an unrepresentative Parliament writing an unrepresentative Constitution," argued Mohammed El Baradei, the former international atomic energy czar who is running for president on a reform platform. "Because the Muslim Brotherhood is ready, they want elections first," adds Osama Ghazali Harb, another reform party leader. "We as secular forces prefer to have some time to consolidate our parties."[90]

To understand these complexities one has to keep in mind that democracy is not merely about elections; it is a culture of pluralism and a philosophy for civil society. The Islamists want "elections now," but are against the values of democratic pluralism and the lifestyle of civil society.[91]

The Egyptian revolution was broad-based. Non-Islamist people flooded the streets to demonstrate against three evils of the Mubarak regime: poor development policies, increasing unemployment and poverty, and repression by the ruling secret police. These added up to a deepening lack of legitimacy. Despite what the contested regimes themselves contend, the common view among experts is that the Islamists did not instigate the uprising. On the contrary, in both Tunisia and Egypt the Islamists were taken by surprise. But while no specific movement engineered the outbreaks, which were truly spontaneous, it is also a fact that there is no well-organized opposition able to lead the uprising—with one exception: the Islamist movements. In Egypt this means, of course, the Muslim Brotherhood, and in Tunisia it is al-Nahda, built up by Rashid Gannouchi since 1981 in emulation of the Muslim Brotherhood. The authoritarian regimes' relentless destruction of any viable opposition has left Islamism, with its efficient networks—particularly political asylum in Europe—as the only organized outside political group to survive the oppression.

No one can say what is going to happen in Egypt, but better knowledge about the country would help establish some clarity. Among the dozens of articles and commentaries I have read in the Western press, a piece by Bret Stephens in the *Wall Street Journal* strikes me as the most insightful. Stephens writes: "If the Brotherhood has its way, Egypt will become a Sunni theocracy modelled on Iran." This Islamist goal, as Stephens knows, is not yet within reach, but he sketches a scenario that could lead there: "a weak parliamentary system, incapable of exercising authority over the army and a cat's paw for a Brotherhood . . . especially since Mr. El Baradei, imagining he has the upper hand, stumbled into a political alliance with the Brotherhood."[92] Mohamed El-Baradei is a respected Egyptian and former United Nations official who has spent most of his professional life in New York and Vienna. He returned to Cairo to become the self-appointed leader of the leaderless opposition. He is not a politician and does not have a constituent base from which to unite the numerous competing groups. Except to call for democracy, he has no clear agenda. Unlike El-Baradei and most of the protestors, the Muslim Brotherhood has both a following and an agenda. In the short run it will—and should—participate in the transition to a democratic Egypt. But the transition from authoritarianism to democracy is not the agenda of Islamism. Though I have little regard for Ayan Hirsi Ali's views about Islam, she is right when she asks, "Why are the secular democratic forces in Egypt so much weaker than the Muslim Brothers?" For the most part, the non-Islamist protesters are "an amalgam of very diverse elements . . . and lack common ideological glue" beyond the immediate goal (now achieved) of removing Mubarak. In contrast, Hirsi Ali rightly states, the Muslim Brothers "have a political program and a vision not only until the next election, but in their view, until the Hereafter. . . . The Muslim Brotherhood whose aim is to install the shari'a . . . will insist that a vote for them is a vote for Allah's law. . . . Without effective organization, the secular democratic forces that have swept one tyranny aside could easily succumb to another."[93] To avoid this scenario one needs to learn from what happened in Iran in 1979. There, the Islamists filled the void, even though the people of Iran, not the Ayatollah, toppled the tyranny. The transition from authoritarianism to democratic rule cannot exclude the Muslim Brotherhood, but it has to be protected from their agenda through democratic measures. Above all, this means building democratic institutions. Democracy in Egypt must not be reduced to mere voting with no underlying democratic political culture. Though the Muslim Brothers cannot be excluded from the democratization process, their vision for the future of Egypt should be countered by all democratic means.

In a telling demonstration of the deceptive pro-democracy "New Islamism," the general secretary of the Muslim Brothers, Hussein Mahmoud, in an interview with the German newspaper *Frankfurter Allgemeine Zeitung,* expressed approval of a democratic system for Egypt and did not deny that the Muslim Brothers did not comprise the majority of people rebelling on the street.[94] He supported the participation of the Muslim Brothers in a pluralist national government. But he unwittingly confirmed Hirsi Ali's misgivings when he said—responding to the question, Are you going to establish a shari'a state?—"Yes, because the Islamic shari'a law grants all rights and freedom. . . . Shari'a maintains the security of the people . . . and it provides the state with the general framework needed for a civilized and happy society. . . . Egypt is an Islamic state in which Muslims are the majority. . . . Shari'a is the way of life for Muslims. . . . Egypt should never be allowed to become a secular state, because this would mean to take the country out of its history and its civilization." Not only is this view not compatible with democracy, it is—as I will explain in Chapter 6—not true to Egyptian history and tradition. The state order of shari'a that Islamism seeks to impose is not the shari'a of traditional Islam.

There is another dimension of the contemporary events, namely regional peace in the Middle East. The Israeli strategist Yossi K. Halevi wrote in the *Times* global edition about "the grim assumption that it is just a matter of time before the only real opposition group in Egypt, the Islamist Muslim Brotherhood takes power. . . . [The] result would be the end of Israel's most important relationship in the Arab World. The Muslim Brotherhood has long stated its opposition to peace with Israel and has pledged to revoke the 1979 Egyptian-Israeli peace treaty if it comes to power."[95] The *New York Times* columnist Thomas Friedman knows this well, but in an insightful commentary in the same edition, he observes that "Mubarak deserves all the wrath directed at him." He adds that the post-Mubarak "time is perilous for Israel and its anxiety is understandable," but Mubarak and Israel itself share in the responsibility for this peril. Mubarak never tried "to fill the void between his authoritarian state and the Muslim Brotherhood." For his part, Israeli prime minister Netanyahu—today and during his earlier rule in the late 1990s—"has found every excuse for not putting a peace plan on the table," thus "becoming the Mubarak of the peace process."[96] In these troubled waters the Muslim Brotherhood finds a favorable environment for successful action in the post-Mubarak Middle East. Israel would be as accountable for this as it is for creating the conditions for the Hamas take-over in Gaza.

Finally, the "shari'a state" is not the democracy that the people who flooded the streets in Cairo and Tunis have been yearning for. The unseated authoritarian rulers—and the others still in charge—who falsely legitimated themselves as the only secular alternative to Islamism foisted a distortion on the world of Islam. It is another distortion when Islamists reverse the argument with their slogan: "Islam [by which they mean Islamism] is the solution." For non-Islamist Muslims, democratic freedom, and not Islamism, is the alternative.

Thus the future of the Middle East is far from certain. It is only Western wishful thinking that predicts a swift transition from authoritarianism to democracy. The participation of Islamist movements in the governments—whatever they are—that succeed the authoritarian rulers only makes democracy more uncertain. The legitimate uprising started in Tunisia and Egypt as a promising Arab Spring, which, however, turned in Libya to a Blazing Summer and to mass murders by the tanks of the Syrian army. The revolt might become a dark Arab Winter by the end of 2011 if Islamists come to power and if the Syrian Ba'th regime turns Syria into a mass grave.

By the fall of 2011 the Arab Spring had taken a distinctly Islamist turn. Local Islamist movements were gaining power. A Libyan democrat quoted in the *New York Times* said: "The Islamists . . . seem more influential than their real weight. . . . Most Libyans are not strongly Islamic, but the Islamists are strongly organized and that's the problem."[97] In the same story, the *Times* reported the preeminent influence in politics of the Islamist leader Sheik Ali Salabi and in the military of the jihadist Abdul Hakim Belhaj, commander of the rebel Tripoli Brigade. In Egypt and Tunisia, too, well-organized Islamist groups have come to the fore.

Regionally, Turkey has championed the Arab Spring. The first states-man to visit all three countries that by late 2011 had overthrown dictators—Egypt, Libya, and Tunisia—was Turkish Prime Minister Erdoğan. Before the trip, Erdoğan blasted Israel in a television interview, then expelled the Israeli ambassador. He consequently was welcomed as a "hero" by the Muslim Brotherhood in Cairo. A news analysis provided this assessment: "Erdoğan has sought to leverage the Arab uprisings into greater influence for Turkey in a region where, as the seat of the Ottoman Empire, it once ruled for centuries."[98] Another analyst argued that Turkey "meant to promote itself as a political power in the Arab region and spread its influence."[99]

Is there a democracy at the end of this tunnel? The major Islamist movements claim to have abandoned jihadism in favor of a democratic shari'a state. But their understanding of the concept is shallow at best. Anthony Shadid quoted the following comment from a 26-year-old Islamist in Cairo, Mohammed Nadi: "Is democracy the voice of the majority? We as Islamists are the majority. Why do they want to impose on us the views of the minorities—the liberals and the secularists?"[100] Far from the pluralist ideal of democracy, the Islamist version evokes what John Stuart Mill called "the tyranny of the majority."[101] And the Islamists may not even be a majority.

5

Islamism and Violence
The New World Disorder

JIHADISM IS NOT SIMPLE TERRORISM, nor is it insurgency. It is, first, a new warfare, and second, a political agenda for fighting a nonstate war described by Sayyid Qutb as an "Islamic world revolution." The idea of remaking the world through militancy provides the overarching context of Islamism and violence.[1] The founder of Islamism, Hasan al-Banna, argued that jihad is the means by which Islamism would establish an Islamic order for the world. In so doing, al-Banna transformed the traditional Islamic notion of jihad into something new. Put differently, just as political Islam grows out of Islam but is a significantly different phenomenon, modern jihadism grows out of classical jihad.[2]

Understanding Jihad and Jihadism

In 2005 I published an article in the *International Herald Tribune* headlined "Jihadism's Roots in Political Islam" and was amazed to find that some people were unaware of these shared roots. The militants and the so-called moderates are two branches of the same tree, two sides of the same coin. This insight was not welcomed, especially by those who look to the institutional Islamists to bring democracy to the Middle East. As we saw in the last chapter, that is unlikely to happen. In this chapter I deal with the other side of the coin, the Islamists who reinvent jihad and turn it into jihadism.[3] (We can add to this book's list of important distinctions the one between classical jihad and contemporary jihadism.) Given that jihadism is an important direction in Islamism, one needs to look at it seriously, not merely in terms of radicalism or terrorism. Despite its significance, however, jihadism is not the mainstream of Islamism. Violence is not inherent in Islamism, since the core concern is the order of the state and of the world. Islamists resort to violence only in pursuit of their goal of a shari'a state. The American debate on Islamism almost always misses this point.

In classical and traditional Islam, jihad can mean either self-exertion (*jihad al-nafs*) or physical fighting (qital). The two definitions are, however, inseparable.[4] Muslims fought the jihad wars of the *futuhat* from the seventh through the seventeenth centuries in order to extend dar al-Islam (the world of Islam) throughout their known world. These wars were in line with the Qu'ranic concept of jihad as war, not terror. Long before Carl Clausewitz formulated his theory of war, Muslims abided by rules and a code of conduct that limited targets in line with humanitarian standards. Although these rules fell far short of the practices prescribed by the Geneva Conventions, they still constituted a regulated system by which jihad would be conducted by regular armies. The practices of modern jihadism as a pattern of an irregular war waged by nonstate actors clearly do not conform to these standards.

The question is how well Western scholars and policymakers[5] understand the difference between classical jihad and modern jihadism.[6] In June 2010, while I was in Washington, D.C., in the final stages of revising this manuscript, I encountered the thinking of John Brennan, the top counterterrorism adviser to President Obama, who gave a speech at the Center for Strategic and International Studies. The speech was covered by the Associated Press and is also accessible on the internet, from which I quote this passage:

> As the President's principal advisor on homeland security and counterterrorism, I want to address how this national security strategy is guiding our efforts to secure our homeland. . . . Our enemy is not "terrorism" because terrorism is but a tactic. Our enemy is not "terror" because terror is a state of mind. . . . Nor do we describe our enemy as "jihadists" or "Islamists" because jihad is a holy struggle, a legitimate tenet of Islam, meaning to purify oneself or one's community, and there is nothing holy or legitimate or Islamic about murdering innocent men, women and children. . . . Describing our enemy in religious terms would lend credence to the lie—propagated by al Qaeda and its affiliates to justify terrorism—that the United States is somehow at war against Islam. . . . Our enemy is al Qaeda and its terrorist affiliates. . . . We will take the fight to al Qaeda and its extremist affiliates.[7]

Brennan, speaking for the Obama administration, abandons altogether the terms "Islamism" and "jihadism" and reduces "al-Qaeda and its affiliates" to violent extremists who have nothing to do with Islam and Islamism. This is an improvement over the previous administration's "war on terror," but in reacting to that doctrine Brennan rejects too much.

This issue resembles in a way the distinction between Judeophobia and antisemitism that I discussed in Chapter 3. I began that chapter by asking whether Islamist Jew hatred might not be, rather than antisemitism, a "frustrated expression of justifiable political grievances"—that is, something completely unrelated to Islam and Islamism. In the analysis I showed that this is not the case. Similarly, we may ask here what jihadist terrorism is and how to fight it in a way that does not alienate the West from ordinary Muslims. Brennan believes that "addressing the political, economic, and social forces that can make some people fall victim to the cancer of violent extremism" would help, and he adds, "We seek to show that legitimate grievances can be resolved peacefully through democratic institutions and dialogue." In line with my reasoning in Chapter 3, I consider jihadist Islamism not merely a tactic chosen to effect the redress of particular grievances, which can be abandoned once the jihadists become convinced that equally effective but less costly tactics are available. Instead, it is an interpretation of Islam in which Islamic tradition undergoes an invention that results in the religious legitimation of violence.

Like the scholar Daniel Varisco, Brennan not only misses the distinction between Islam and Islamism, he also accepts a definition of Islamism as inherently violent. These two confusions lead him to assume that to say that one is fighting Islamism is tantamount to declaring all of Islam a violent enemy. Like Varisco, he would abolish all of these terms and insist that the enemy is specifically, and only, al-Qaeda, which is artificially disconnected from Islam, Islamism, and jihadism. This is far too reductive. There are other ways to exonerate Islam from violence—and to protect Muslims from prejudice—than by denying the obvious. We can understand these phenomena only when we dissociate not just Islam but also the contemporary phenomenon of Islamism from violence.

Of course, this hardly means that all Islamist movements are nonviolent. One faction within Islamism is committed to violence, and this branch is identified in this chapter as jihadist Islamism. To be sure, jihadism does not stand outside Islam: it bases all of its actions on religionized politics. Islamists who are prone to violence also engage in shari'a reasoning. There is in Islam a tradition that revolves around the legitimization of just war, as shown by John Kelsay in *Arguing the Just War in Islam*.[8] But for Islamists, these arguments take place within a wholly novel interpretation of jihad.[9] One cannot repeat enough that Islamist violence is not mere terror. It is, to paraphrase Clausewitz, a pursuit of politics by other means.

How Not to Win Friends

Some in the West have an image of Islam as a "religion of the sword."[10] This distorted view—supported by such examples as the Saudi Arabian flag and the name of Muammar Qadhafi's son, Saif-ul-Islam, which means "Sword of Islam"—represents a misperception of Islam that affects any inquiry into jihadism. The idea that religiously inspired violence is historically central to Islam encourages the conflation of modern jihadism with traditional jihad. Not even the pope seems quite sure of the difference. In a September 2006 lecture at Regensburg University entitled "Religion, Reason, and the University—Memories and Reflections,"[11] Pope Benedict attempted to raise the theme of violence as a subject for discussion between Islam and the West by quoting the Byzantine emperor Manuel II, Paleologus, a Christian, who in 1392 criticized Islam's tolerance of violence for the spread of religion. Unlike professional politicians, Benedict refuses to employ a speechwriter. He writes his speeches alone, as if he were a scholar who seeks no advice, and this habit sometimes gets him into trouble. In his lecture the pope quoted the following line from Manuel's *Dialogue Held with a Certain Persian:* "Show me just what Muhammad brought that was new and there you will find things only evil and inhuman, such as his command to spread by the sword the faith he preached." This is undeniably a clumsy way to raise any issue with followers of the Prophet, especially when one represents the church that brought us the Crusades and the Inquisition. Still, the underlying message was entirely reasonable: the pope wished to engage the Islamic world in a discussion of whether it is ever legitimate to use violence to spread faith. It is not the request that was wrong but the way he made it. The response, largely orchestrated by Islamists, was worldwide Muslim outrage.

I have no doubt that the pope's intentions were benign. I do not buy into the suspicion that he was driven by Islamophobia and instead believe that he intended to involve Muslims in an honest dialogue between civilizations in which violence is supposed to be outlawed. Why is the request to dissociate religion from violent proselytization a problem? Why the outrage and the accusations of Islamophobia? Was it the single reference that struck a raw nerve, or the larger issue of religious violence? Deplorably, not only Islamists but also ordinary Muslim opinion leaders seemed to seize on the excuse of outrage to distance themselves from this proposed dialogue. Most Muslims believe that the expansion of Islam was well served by jihad, which they see as a peaceful pursuit that has nothing to do with war. The historical facts do not support this contention.

The image Muslims have of themselves as people of a peaceful religion must be contrasted with the undisputed historical fact that the pursuit of *da'wa* (proselytization) was combined with jihad wars. Nonetheless, it is taboo for Muslims to associate da'wa with violence, because they contend that jihad is peaceful. The literal meaning of jihad is self-exertion. Muslims may use violence in the expansion of their religion, but only in self-defense, when "unbelievers" prevent them from spreading Islam. This contention notwithstanding, it is a fact that the Byzantine Empire was brought down in 1453 by Islamic conquest, which was by no means an act of self-defense but rather one of military aggression preceded by years of jihad wars. Constantinople was conquered by force and the son of Manuel II was killed. The city, transformed into Islamic Istanbul, became the capital of the last imperial order of Islam. The earlier conquest of Spain was a similar action of violence, not peaceful proselytization, and not in any way "self-defense." Jihad means self-exertion, but it also means qital, or war. Still, classical jihad was warfare, never terrorism.

The pope's intention in his Regensburg lecture, as he reiterated in his subsequent public apology to Muslims, was to argue that "the genuine dialogue of cultures and religions is . . . urgently needed today." [12] To this legitimate point I would add that the dialogue needs also to be honest. Both sides must candidly address the relationship of violence and religion. The terror attacks in the United States in 2001 and in Europe between 2004 and 2006 were committed in the name of Islam and had no other legitimation than jihad. These assaults continue to give rise to problems that cannot be ignored. The rising Muslim immigration in Europe is an issue as well. The lack of integration of this diaspora contributes to the narrative of "Islam under siege" and legitimates recruitment for jihadism.

Thus we have within Islam an impasse characterized by self-deception on both sides. Ordinary Muslims wish to ignore the violent jihad of the past, while jihadists wish to pretend that their very different form of violence continues an ancient and honored tradition. The true relation of jihadism to jihad is more nuanced than either side acknowledges. Traditional jihad includes violence, but it is regular warfare, not terror. Jihadism is a contemporary phenomenon rooted in political Islam. The purpose of this chapter is to relate violence in Islam to the contemporary context of jihadism pursued by Islamists. I do this not merely to make subtle academic points but because a proper understanding of this relationship has implications for national and international policies. To understand how jihad has been reinvented by Islamism into an instrument of terror, one first needs some basic knowledge about the doctrine of jihad and its history. [13]

Classical Jihad

The history of jihad begins not in Mecca, with the commencement of Islamic revelation in 610, but rather with the establishment of the new Islamic polity in Medina in 622—the polity that modern Islamists, in an invention of tradition, have upgraded to an "Islamic state." In the Islamic calendar following the hijra, the migration of the Prophet, this is the Year One. After 622, and in particular after 632—in the aftermath of the death of the Prophet—the new religion was spread by a combination of peaceful proselytization, trade, and jihad wars. Various Islamic empires based in the Middle East gained control over North Africa, the Indian subcontinent, the Iberian Peninsula, and the Balkans.[14] Muslims grew convinced of their superiority over their infidel enemies, who were to be subdued by jihad. This imperial expansion took place from the seventh century to the seventeenth, in the context of jihad wars.

Medieval faqihs, Islamic jurists, dealt with non-Muslims only when the cultural other was seen as a threat, defined in terms of "the house of war," or in a context of submission through conversion and acceptance of dhimmi (protected minority) status.[15] These fiqh jurists were powerful opinion leaders in Islam because they acted at the same time as *ulema* (men of knowledge) equipped with the religious authority to determine what is right and what is wrong. Authoritative faqihs conceded a temporary cessation of hostilities only in the emergency case of Islamic weakness. In general, Islam is viewed by its believers as a religious mission designed for all humanity. Muslims are religiously obliged to disseminate the Islamic faith throughout the world. The Qur'an says in sure 34, verse 28: "We have sent you forth to all mankind." Muslims believe that spreading the Islamic faith is not an act of aggression but rather a fulfillment of that Qur'anic commandment. They resort to violence only to subdue those who resist this mission of da'wa, and they see this not as aggression but as a defensive act against the enemies of Islam. If non-Muslims refuse the option of peaceful submission, then Muslims are obliged to wage war against the unbelievers. They argue that if non-Muslims were to submit to the call of da'wa through either conversion or subjugation, there would be no violence, which is thus the fault of the infidels. Peace requires that non-Muslims accept the status of dhimmi and pay a *jizya* (tax). World peace, the final stage of da'wa, can be reached only when all of humankind has converted or submitted to Islam. Thus the literal translation of da'wa as "invitation" is not quite correct. One can turn down this invitation, but only at the price of being subject to violent jihad.

In Islamic belief, the resort to force to disseminate Islam is not *harb* (war)—a word used only to describe the use of force by non-Muslims—but jihad. Islamic conquests are not *hurub* (the plural of *harb*) but *futuhat* (opening). They open the world to the entrance of Islam. Jihad is the instrument of futuhat expansion. Relations between dar al-Islam, the abode of peace, and dar al-harb, the world of unbelievers, thus remain, by both doctrine and history, in a state of war.

In short, jihad is understood by Muslims as a religious duty, a defensive war to break resistance to Islam's mission of expansion. I know of no Muslim who has the courage to reform this unacceptable and illogical belief. Add to this the Islamic doctrine that admits no perpetual peace with non-Muslims. Only *hudna,* temporary peace, is allowed with unbelievers. This hudna, an intermediate state between war and peace, is a standard condition for relations between Muslims and non-Muslim: all treaties between Muslim and non-Muslim powers are considered temporary. Islamic jurists differ on what length of time counts as "temporary." In the authoritative commentaries, the length of this hudna is, on average, ten years. Israeli students of Islam thus wonder when the peace of Camp David, accomplished with the mediation of President Carter in 1979, shall expire. If we could apply to Islamic tradition the European distinction between just and unjust wars (a concept that is foreign to the Islamic fiqh doctrine), we might say that when Muslims wage war for the dissemination of Islam, it is a just war (futuhat), and when non-Muslims attack Muslims or resist their jihad, it is an unjust war (*'idwan*). But the application of the just war concept to jihad would be a Western reading, not the way Muslims themselves view the issue.

From Traditional Jihad to Jihadism

Traditional jihad was a war carried out by the Islamic Empire and symbolically led by the ruling caliph in his capacity as imam of all Muslims. The caliph acted as head of state, and the jihad war he led was subject to rules regarding tactics and legitimate targets.[16] Jihadism is a reinterpretation of jihad, much as Islamism is a political reinvention of Islam. It is not simply terror practiced by mavericks creating havoc but a variety of "irregular warfare."[17] This new jihadist pattern of warfare is waged by nonstate actors with no recognition of previously accepted rules or limits on targets. The schism within Islam between Sunna and Shi'a also matters to jihadism.[18] My research on this new warfare aligns me with scholars like Martin van Creveld in his study of "low intensity war" and Kalevi Holsti in his description of "war of the third kind." Jihadism is a religionized ideology that legitimates this form of irregular warfare by pairing it with harb al-afkar (war of ideas). Jihadist war is presented as a just war of the oppressed against their oppressors. Nazis and communists also joined violence with propaganda in a way that resembles the Islamists' war of ideas.

The jihadist war articulates what the late Hedley Bull once described as "the revolt against the West." This revolt contests the hegemony of the West, but it also assumes a cultural dimension: it is directed against "Western values as such,"[19] including the secularism of the Westphalian synthesis on which the international system rests.[20] The Peace of Westphalia, two treaties signed in 1648, not only recognized the sovereignty of states but established certain freedoms of (Christian) religion and prohibited nations from interfering with one another's religious establishments. This is the secularism that Islamists reject. They would reinsert religion into world politics, not so much as a faith and a cultural system but as a politicized ideology.

The new revolt also legitimates the violence practiced by nonstate actors. Jihadist Islamists see themselves as warriors, not criminals. They view their resort to violence as "terror in the mind of God,"[21] as Mark Juergensmeyer aptly titles his book on jihadism. Islamism is religionized politics and jihadism is religionized war. I mean this not in the traditional sense of a "religious war," or a European-style war over religion, but in the sense of the return of the sacred: the articulation and legitimation of warfare in religious terms. Jihadism is a divine war, a "global jihad," in which violence is only an element. Hezbollah, for instance, views the outcome of its war with Israel in July and August 2006 as a "divine victory."[22] Its jihadists employed violence not as "criminals," as a prominent student of war put it at a major international security meeting, but as true believers fulfilling a *farida ghaibah* (neglected duty) by purifying the world of its sins and Western vices. The lack of respect for rules—Hezbollah, for instance, used the population of south Lebanon as a shield, leading to many civilian deaths—grows out of their war's divine status. What do international conventions matter when the stakes are cosmic?

Another essential part of the agenda is the radicalization and indoctrination of young Muslims in order to recruit them as loyal and obedient soldiers of jihadist Islamism. This again is a common feature of totalitarian movements. The collective memories of imperial Islamic conquests as futuhat, and the traditional view of jihad as defensive, are revived by the Islamist movement in the notion of "Islam under siege." This justifies jihadist irregular warfare anywhere in the world as a defensive action.

It has become risky to engage in the study of jihadism because such study is regarded even by some Western scholars as an indication of Islamophobia. The impulse is to minimize the jihadists' importance and pretend to do so out of sensitivity to Muslim feelings. The result is to deny the connection between jihadism and terror as well as the phenomenon's roots in political Islam. Too few Western scholars are willing to contest the jihadists' claim to be the spokesmen of the umma and, as "true believers," the legitimate representatives of Islam.

The warriors of the new irregular war represent a complex issue in international relations.[23] Islamist jihadism is the ideology of many transnational movements, all legitimated by politicized religion and embedded in global networks. To understand this phenomenon one has to free oneself from the logic of interstate war. Traditional international relations scholars, though well aware of the decline of interstate war and the rise of nonstate actors, tend to overlook two basic aspects of the problem. First, the need to come to terms with changed patterns of violence and war is undermined by a lack of knowledge in strategic studies about culture, religion, and history. Without this, no grasp of jihadism is possible. Second, the terrorists act within networks of transnational religion. They are not criminals but warriors waging a new kind of cosmic war in the name of God. Their concept of jihadist violence is rooted in an ideology[24] that religionizes existing conflicts.

The West and the New Proletariat

Any analysis of jihad and jihadism risks offending Muslims, especially when the issues are addressed frankly. Islamists take advantage of this sensitivity;

they use the accusation of Islamophobia to mobilize their followers and silence their critics. They also seize any pretext to prevent vigorous and candid
debate about jihadism and its roots in political Islam. This is what happened
to the pope, and it will continue to happen. In short, complaints of Western
Islamophobia have been a most useful instrument in the hands of the Islamists and a basic part of their war of ideas. Jihadists defame any linking of
Islamism with terrorism as a "war on Islam." It is unfortunate that there are
serious Muslims—not only Islamists—who voice this perception.

The birth of jihadism coincides with the birth of Islamism. The founder
of the Movement of the Muslim Brotherhood, Hasan al-Banna, set out all
of jihadism's essential features.[25] The claim of a return of history, the religionization of politics and the politicization of religion, the use of collective
memories of early Islamic conquests[26] to revive the Islamic dream of a
"remaking of the world"[27] through jihad, and the claim that Islamist doctrine represents the authentic jihad can all be found in al-Banna's writings.
His decisive 1930 publication *Risalat al-Djihad* laid the foundations for the
jihadist-Islamist ideology. Moreover, al-Banna practiced what he preached.
Today, there is a part of the Muslim Brotherhood that pretends to have
abandoned jihadist warfare and instead engages in the more promising war
of ideas. This venture, which has proved more successful than the resort to
violence, blurs the distinction between jihadism and institutional Islamism.

None of these issues are well understood in the West, which explains
the lack of appropriate policies for dealing with Islamism. This will have to
change. Recently, in a development most Europeans ignore or deny, Europe
has also seen a religionization of social conflicts. Peter Neumann writes
that the connection between jihad and jihadism matters to the rising and
intensifying Muslim immigration to Europe.[28] The Muslim Brothers have
established a following among the European diaspora of Islam.

Western politicians need to avoid the mistakes of the second Bush administration and of American conservatives in the post-Bush era, and must
beware of raising general suspicions against Muslims. Disregarding the difference between Islamism and Islam only validates the followers of the
jihadist ideology in their allegation that Islam and its people are being

targeted by the West. This is why a successful strategy against terrorism requires Muslim-Western cooperation.

Unfortunately, one of the least helpful groups in this regard has been the political left. If jihadism is a revolutionary ideology of the religious right, why does the left support it? It is not possible to prove that the founders of Islamist ideology have ever read Marx or Lenin, but a close reading of the Islamists' prose strongly suggests some level of familiarity. The Islamist use of Marxist-Leninist terms shows an acquaintance with the vocabulary of Marxist secular internationalism, even if Islamist internationalism is religious and emerges from a politicization of traditional Islamic universalism. One may read Sayyid Qutb as having adopted the Marxist-Leninist idea of world revolution and applied it to jihad. Qutb writes: "Islam pursues a complete and comprehensive *thawrah* (revolution). . . . Jihad is an obligation of Muslims to carry out this revolution to establish hakimiyyat Allah (God's rule on the entire globe). . . . It follows that jihad is an idea of *thawrah alamiyyah* (world revolution). . . . In this understanding, Islam is a permanent jihad for a remaking of the world along the *nizam salih* (just system).[29]

In Marxist thought the vehicle of revolution is the proletariat. This revolution did not happen during Marx's lifetime. Lenin replaced the proletariat with the party of revolutionary cadres. Al-Banna and Qutb also speak of a permanent revolution that will realize Islamist goals. Unlike the futuristic Marxist utopia of a classless free society, the Islamist utopia is backward-oriented: it first constructs an imaginary "Islamic state" and projects it, in a new reading of Islamic history, into the past. In this reading the first Islamic state was allegedly established in Medina 622. But the Prophet in his hadiths never used the term "dawla" (state). Second, the restoration of this "Islamic state" (despite some Western misconceptions, Islamists do not speak of a restoration of the caliphate) is to be accomplished by a revolution that restores Islam's historic glory. This vision is constructed out of collective memories and identity politics. The Islamist internationalism it reflects could be a religious version of secular Marxist internationalism. Islamists argue that Muslims have fallen into *jahilliyya,* ignorance, and lack political consciousness and so need a surrogate to act on behalf of the besieged and oppressed umma: these are the jihadist revolutionaries. Their role is that of the Leninist party which speaks on behalf of the dormant proletariat. They act in the belief that they are "the true believers."[30]

Pax Islamica

Despite the outpouring that has swamped the book market since 9/11, the place of jihadism[31] in political Islam is not well analyzed in the Western literature on Islamic politics.[32] Many of these books employ the old language of "holy terror." Some equate the origins of jihadism with the rise of Osama bin Laden. I repeat that jihadism is historically rooted in the twentieth-century phenomenon of political Islam and predates bin Laden by many decades. Islamism is something other than what is described as "Islamic politics."

Qutb's concept of "jihad as a permanent Islamic world revolution" is an advance over the simple thinking of al-Banna, who lacked Qutb's intelligence. The overarching goal of jihadism is to establish hakimiyyat Allah, God's rule, as a political order, first in the world of Islam and then in the world at large. This new order would replace the Western secular Westphalian system with an Islamic one. This political goal is common to both jihadism and institutional Islamism.

The only difference is that jihadism[33] adds a new concept of war. This is not well understood by such Western experts as Marc Sageman,[34] who focuses on terror and overlooks the ideological dimensions of jihadism. To deal with jihadism as pure terror[35] is to miss the point. A cultural and religious underpinning serves to legitimate global jihad and keep it rooted in political Islam. Terror is simply a means to achieve the vision of a pax Islamica, the world order that is to emerge after jihad has toppled the international Westphalian order of secular states and that is the endpoint of the Islamic world revolution. These are the ideological foundations of terrorism. We lack a strategy for dealing with them. It is most disturbing to see "scholarly" publications attacking analyses of these foundations and accusing their authors of Islamophobia.

Jihadist Islamists cultivate an Islamic nostalgia[36] with their claims of a "return of history" and a return to the Islamic glory of the past. But their terrorism lacks authenticity: it is based on an invention of tradition. The Islamist visions are strictly modern, embedded not in the mythic past but in the postbipolar twenty-first-century world. The return of the sacred, the ascendance of nonstate actors in world politics, and the emergence of transnational movements that act globally do not represent the return of any known history. The transformation of classical jihad[37] from a holy war for the spread of Islam—subject to rules—into an irregular war without rules, carried out as an Islamist world revolution, is likewise a modern invention. All of these things occur in a world-political context that originates in the nostalgia of political Islam but is new.

This novelty compels us to abandon traditional wisdom and engage in new reasoning to understand how the rise of politicized religion has become one of the major issues of international affairs. This political religion that legitimates jihad in the path of God articulates an intercivilizational conflict that is not about terror but about the order of the world.[38] The Kantian concept of world peace based on secular, democratic nation-states is challenged by Qutb's vision of an Islamic peace[39] achieved by jihad through a world revolution.

The West as a Competing Civilization and the New World Disorder

The political agenda of the jihadist branch of Islamism is articulated in cultural terms as a war against a competing civilization. It is essential to understand that the cause of antagonism is not only the outsize political power that underpins Western hegemony but Western values and knowledge. Islamists view Cartesian rationalism as an expression of "epistemological imperialism." The intellectual undercurrent of jihadism is a de-Westernization of the world. Alongside their concept of world order, the Islamists would impose a new cultural narrative.

To explain this issue I draw on the tradition of Hedley Bull, as well as Stanley Hofmann's idea of an emerging "world disorder."[40] The Islamist threat is neutralized by Islamists' inability to create the order they envision. They resort to violence but lack the power to accomplish what they pronounce. Nonetheless, jihadism does not remain idle. The result is international destabilization: the irregular war of jihadism helps Islamists compensate for their enemy's technological superiority, but this asymmetrical warfare cannot take them beyond destabilization and disorder. The envisioned order of "God's rule," despite its ability to mobilize followers, will always remain a mirage. Nonetheless, the Islamist internationalism of global jihad has to be taken most seriously as an ideology and movement of world revolution in postbipolar politics.

Thus the issue with, for example, al-Qaeda[41] relates to more than mere terrorism. Al-Qaeda is engaged in a civilizational competition between two concepts of order. This is not Samuel Huntington's "clash of civilizations," which in any case he saw as impending and unpreventable. The return of religion to world politics has already happened, and it presents a most pertinent and urgent problem for international security. There is a need for new approaches in the study of international relations to account for politicized religion as one of the major sources of the current crisis of order.

To properly understand the ongoing competition between civilizations over the order of the world, Western experts must realize that structural globalization does not bring any automatic universalization of Western values. On the contrary, development generates a crisis of meaning that results in the emergence of a great variety of non-Western defensive cultures. Globalization of structures without Westernization of values has been occurring worldwide. Seen in this context, the return of the sacred in a political shape must be viewed as an effort at de-Westernization. This novelty is not properly understood in the West. Western cultural relativism is not the solution but rather a dead end that exacerbates the incomprehension. Postmodern cultural relativists seem unable to comprehend that Islamism is an absolutist ideology that never compromises. In an encounter of relativism and absolutism, the cultural relativists are the losers.

For a proper understanding of contemporary international affairs, the work of Raymond Aron and Hedley Bull is more promising. The Islamist revival's civilizational challenge to the existing world order embraces political, cultural, and religious issues alike. Perceiving a "Judeo-Christian conspiracy"[42] directed against Islam, jihadist Islamists think their "revolt against the West"—captured well in Bull's essay on the subject—is the right resort. They mobilize their jihad in pursuit of de-Westernization. The implication is that there can be no world peace without a change in the Islamist worldview.

Raymond Aron notes that throughout the history of humankind there has been a heterogeneity of civilizations. The ideological commitment of persons like bin Laden and globally networked movements like al-Qaeda to the Islamist order of pax Islamica ignores this civilizational diversity. The Islamist, in challenging the existing world order, creates dividing lines that would separate Muslims from the rest of humanity. This is the context in which relations between Islam and the West are now developing. The trenches are being dug deeper every day.

Here I am compelled once again to invoke the precursor and foremost thinker of contemporary political Islam, Sayyid Qutb. Perceiving a deep civilizational crisis of the West, he challenged the existing world order in cultural terms. Only the competing civilization of Islam, he believed, could resolve this crisis, and it had to do so by establishing Islamic dominance. In his pamphleteering, in particular *Signposts along the Road* and *World Peace and Islam,* Qutb proposed that only Islam was in a position to overcome the global crisis and rescue humanity. To reiterate: this is the source of the worldview of bin Laden and of all the al-Qaeda jihad fighters. It is not the view of a "crazed gang" or of criminals but the authoritative expression of mainstream jihadist Islamism. The rejection of the Westphalian order in world politics and its replacement by an Islamic order is shared by all branches of Islamism, peaceful and jihadist.

Hedley Bull never read Qutb, but he was aware that the civilizational "revolt against the West" is best "exemplified in Islamic fundamentalism."[43] With the postbipolar crisis of international order, Qutb's ideas have become widely disseminated in the world of Islam. By articulating a new role for Islam, they give the Islamists great appeal. The fact that political Islam can be traced back to 1928 and the founding of the Society of Muslim Brothers shows clearly that it predates the end (and even the beginning) of the cold war. Yet for much of its history political Islam could not mobilize much popular support. What Aron called the "heterogeneity of civilizations" was veiled by the bipolar world order. Today, this veil is gone. Heterogeneity, re-emergent, is underpinned by politicized religion.

That the civilizational project of an Islamist order is unlikely to succeed does not mean that its chief target, the Westphalian order, is safe. One may ask, are we heading "beyond Westphalia"?

There is nothing sacred about the Westphalian order. It is fully legitimate to question its existence and attempt to renegotiate its foundations under conditions of a changed world. Still, neither the violence of jihadist Islamism nor the ideology of hakimiyyat Allah, divine rule, offers a promising alternative. These options are not even approved by all Muslims, because Islamism is not Islam. I doubt that non-Muslims and democratic Muslims would accept the Islamist concept of order. However deep the crisis of the secular nation-state may grow, for a religiously diverse humanity, no alternative based on a particular religion can be admitted. Why?

On the state level, the nizam Islami (Islamic system)[44] is a totalitarian political pronouncement that is not acceptable to anyone, Muslim or non-Muslim, who is committed to freedom and democracy. Experts familiar with the original literary sources of Islamism know well that Islamists talk about this nizam, not about the restoration of the traditional order of the caliphate of Sunni Islam, because the caliphate is not acceptable to the Shi'a. The ecumenical-minded ideologues of political Islam prefer to unite the umma under the nonsectarian banner of an overall Islam directed against non-Muslims. We can conclude that the Islamist is a political man of action first, and simultaneously a man of religion by worldview. Therefore one can speak, as Jansen does, of "the dual nature of Islamic fundamentalism."[45] Religion, ethnicity, and culture are all sources of conflict between Islam and the West. In the case of jihadism, intercivilizational competition is the motive for violence. It is foolish to consider Islamist jihadism a passing phenomenon or a reaction to current events. In Chapter 1 I took issue with Gilles Kepel, who predicts the end not only of jihadism but of Islamism altogether. This is a grave mistake. Jihadist Islamism is much more than terrorism, and it needs to be understood in a way that moves beyond the facile rhetoric of a "clash of civilizations" or the obsessions of a "war on terror."

Civilizations Do Not Fight Wars, but Jihadist Warriors Do

The first suggestion of an approach to understanding the new challenges to world order was presented by Barry Buzan in his 1991 book *People, States, and Fear,*[46] which addressed the problem in a way that went beyond conventional military wisdom and interstate relations. A decade later, the 9/11 attacks reminded everyone that security studies will have to deal with a new pattern of war: the irregular war of jihadism. But while the violence of terrorism needs to be understood from a new perspective, we have not traveled very far down this road. The complexity of the war in Afghanistan against jihadism remains poorly understood by most analysts. The change of administrations from Bush to Obama has brought no change in the level of understanding. Commentators and policymakers alike reduce the new warfare to an "insurgency" and pay too little attention to religion and culture. The new American military strategy in Afghanistan relies heavily on counterinsurgency tactics developed during the Iraq War. These tactics are better than sending columns of tanks, but they address only part of the problem—and not the most important part. To be sure, the war is not between the civilizations of Islam and the West, but jihadism is warfare fought by violent Islamists. They are warriors, not "criminal extremists."

Statistically oriented political scientists like Robert Pape,[47] who argues in his 2005 book *Dying to Win* that jihadism is a social movement that has little to do with religion, fail to understand jihadism or the religious ideology that underpins it. The concept of a politicized world religion cannot be grasped properly with quantitative tools. To understand how a religious formula can mobilize a vision of world revolution, one needs to grasp how Islam is addressed as one invented umma and how this imagined community is mobilized against the West. Can political Islam succeed in turning the imagined Islamic umma to the service of its jihadist ideology of irregular war? No quantitative method could ever answer this question.

Islamists who refer to religion in the pursuit of nonreligious ends constitute a minority of the Islamic umma, but they are well organized and well equipped, and their message is appealing to many. Their small numbers matter less than the efficiency of their global networks and their ability to mobilize. These groups are very capable of creating disorder through irregular war. How can this warfare be contained?

I have raised many fundamental distinctions in this book: between Islamism and Islam; between jihadism and classical jihad.[48] Along with these there are the more familiar differences within Islam between Sunnite and Shi'ite Muslims,[49] exemplified by the Shi'i-Sunni conflict in Iraq. In fact there exists within Islam a greater religious diversity that can be politicized. This politicization is generating violence within the umma itself among Islam's many divergent denominations and sects. The African varieties of Islam are entirely different from the pattern that prevails in Southeast Asia. Islam on the Indian subcontinent is a case in itself. Of course, the original Arab pattern of Islam is supposed to stand above religious and cultural diversity. Nevertheless, there is no monolithic Islamism.

Though it originated as a Sunni ideology, Islamist jihadism denies Islamic diversity and claims to unite all Muslim believers as soldiers of jihad. In this guise it is capable of borrowing ideas from other sects. The Muslim Brotherhood in its early years did not practice suicide terrorism, which is alien to Sunni Islam. It is a recent Shi'i innovation that has been adopted by Sunni Islamists. The Shi'i concept of taqiyya (dissimulation) has also been adopted by Sunni Islamists and given the new shape of iham (deception). Despite its sectarian mentality, Sunni Islamist movements lean on Shi'i martyrdom and borrow its legitimation of terror as *tadhiya* (sacrifice). What matters is that Islamist nonstate actors speak religionized politics in the language of multiple cultures. Long before Huntington, Islamists had developed their rhetoric of a "clash of civilizations." The field of international relations needs to follow the Islamists' lead and focus less on the state and more on religion, culture, ethnicity, and civilizations.

Yet civilizations cannot function as actors in world politics. Samuel Huntington was aware of this problem, and he believed he could bypass it by stating that each civilization can be led by a "core state." He failed to see that this construct does not hold for Islam, for the simple reason that none of the fifty-six nominally Islamic nation-states is in a position to lead the entire umma. In addition, even though this group includes some rogue states, none of them is the central cause of jihadism in world politics. Iran's state-sponsored jihadism comes the closest, but jihadism would thrive without it.[50]

The jihadist movements that constituted a threat in the "war on terror" are all nonstate actors. It is unfortunate that the American occupation of Iraq has inadvertently strengthened jihadism and the popular Muslim support for it and also provided Iran with a new venue in which to support Islamist groups. The war removed an ugly dictatorship but introduced new problems. The power vacuum created by the fall of Saddam Hussein was filled by Iran, which has become a regional superpower.[51]

Iran now claims to lead the Islamist "revolt against the West." This notion turns an intercivilizational conflict into an international conflict[52] and makes abundantly clear the importance of civilizational worldviews in world politics. In professional international relations and political science, with rare exceptions such as the enlightening article by Daniel Philpott published in the influential international relations journal *World Politics* in 2002, this issue is not yet part of the research agenda.

One can rightly criticize the American presence in Afghanistan and Iraq as a military occupation. But to speak of "crusaders," as some U.S. scholars do, is to take sides in the propaganda war. Conflicting worldviews are involved. The conflict of worldviews and of different sets of norms and values has to find its place in the analysis of security. After all, the idea of order is always based on civilizational values, and intercivilizational conflict revolves around normatively different understandings of the state, law, religion, war and peace, and knowledge. In my 1995 book *War of Civilizations,* I do not deal at all with the military but rather focus on conflicting concepts of world order. One may argue that value-related conflicts have nothing to do with military capabilities, because civilizations have no armies.

This is true, but values contribute to the emergence of real conflicts in a "war of civilizations." The Islamists, whose military capabilities are not institutionalized, explicitly conceive their global jihad as such a war of ideas and worldviews.

The war of ideas was clearly an essential part of Hezbollah's jihadist warfare in Lebanon in July–August 2006, and of Hamas's in 2008–9. In neither case was the issue restricted to a movement fighting alone in an irregular war. The front was civilizational. On the state level Shi'ite Iran has become—thanks to the American invasion of Iraq—a regional power igniting conflicts that cannot be settled by military means. Neither the American superpower nor the mighty Israeli Defense Force could tame with their conventional means the irregular power of the Islamists. These believe they are involved in a cosmic war in the "mind of God"—a belief that is echoed in the global support these movements enjoy. Civilizational perception matters, as do facts on the ground. In world politics, perception is reality.

The attacks of September 11 and jihadist assaults elsewhere have demonstrated how closely values and worldviews are related to material violence. The Islamists committing these assaults were not acting as a "crazed gang," but within the irregular war of jihadism. Their terrorism was the actualization of a conflict over civilizational worldviews—the fight over "what world order" in military form. Gangs do not involve themselves in this business. Gangsters take risks for material benefits, but they never sacrifice their lives for mere values. In this understanding, the Taliban and other jihadists are not "criminal extremists," as criminals do not "die to win." They are irregulars in a new pattern of warfare.

In this new pattern of war, jihadists use their bodies as bombs to assail persons and target infrastructure but also to attack the "cosmic enemy." The major target of this *action directe* (to employ Georges Sorel's term) is the order of the secular nation-state. The combination of a war of ideas and jihadism is meant to demoralize the enemy and make him uncertain. Under conditions of the new warfare no one knows what lies ahead. The objects of terror are not only what the Islamists label as "Jews and crusaders" but also, as we saw in Algeria and since 2003 in Iraq, ordinary Muslims who do not cooperate.

John Kelsay writes that "in encounters between the West and Islam, the struggle is over who will provide the primary definition to the world order." He continues: "Will it be the West, with its notions of territorial boundaries, market economies, private religiosity, and the priority of individual rights? Or will it be Islam, with its emphasis on the universal mission of a transtribal community called to build a social order founded on pure monotheism natural to humanity?"[53]

For Islamists, of course, the answer is clear, readily found in the work of Sayyid Qutb, who writes in *Signposts along the Road* that only Islam is designed to lead all of humanity in a world order.

The atmosphere of the new cold war comes down to a confrontation of secular and religious worldviews. The issue is not simply a state of mind, a dispute over differences, or a matter of "freedom of faith," as some Western apologists of Islamism contend. If this were the case, then one might prescribe tolerance. The issue is life and death in a practice of violence as terror.

The Findings

The analysis provided in this chapter can be summed up in three central statements:

The problem of order. Islamist fundamentalism is not merely an expression of existing cultural differences between Islam and the West. It expresses a civilizational disagreement over the world order. The jihadists' irregular war is the articulation of this disagreement, and as such it cannot be countered by state armies. The new strategy that is required should be neither fixated on the state nor dominated by conventional military thinking.

Holy terror and irregular war. Jihadism is a variety of what Mark Juergensmeyer identified as "terror in the mind of God." The fact and methods of terrorism are inextricable from its legitimation as "holy terror" practiced as irregular war.

Religious fundamentalism as a security issue. The existence of global jihad shows that the study of Islamism belongs to the field of security studies as part of the "new frontiers of security."[54] The traditional concept of security must expand to include religion and culture in order to deal with the challenge of irregular warfare.

The commitment to violence is among the basic features of jihadist Islamism. But violence is a means, not a goal in itself. The goal is the Islamic order. Jihadism operates on a religious legitimation for an irregular war presented as a true jihad. In reality, jihadist violence is a variety of terrorism and therefore not consistent with the ethics of classical jihad. Sadly, the religious institutions of the Islamic establishment fail to make a clear-cut condemnation of jihadist fundamentalists to help distinguish between them and ordinary, peaceful Muslims. The reluctance to do so arises from opportunism and fear. The unconvincing argument is put forward that there is no such a thing as jihadism and the terrorists have nothing to do with Islam.

Jihadist Islamism is highly appealing to young, socially marginalized Muslims in the Islamic diaspora. They are susceptible to recruitment, not so much because they like jihadism but because it provides comfort and meaning in a dreadful situation of hopelessness. In this regard, there exist other options: in Europe, either Europeanizing Islam or an Islamization of Europe.[55] This issue does not sit well with Europeans, who in their inaction and indifference confuse freedom of faith and jihadist warfare, and thus unwittingly support jihadist internationalism. In the triangle formed by the world of Islam, the West, and the Muslim diasporic culture in Europe, the blurring of the lines between Islam and Islamism becomes highly consequential.

Some European states (such as Germany) limit the culture of citizenship to granting Muslim immigrants passports without ever allowing them to become true members of the community. Even those who are privileged to be a part of the middle class never succeed in being treated as equals; they remain "guest workers." In my own case, which is by no means unique, I never escaped discrimination in my academic career and never became a member of the community of ethnic Germans. In ethnic Europe[56] I failed to become in substance a German citizen, beyond legally holding a German passport. Living in Germany for five decades and writing twenty-eight books in German made no difference. My education and my knowledge of Islam help me to be immune to the anti-Western appeal of jihadist ideologues. But for ordinary Muslim immigrants who do not have the privilege of a higher education, Islamist activism in the diaspora[57] and European racism conspire to make the idea of becoming a soldier of al-Qaeda very attractive. One result was recently noted in a *New York Times* article that described young Muslims born in Germany who journeyed to Afghanistan to join jihadist groups.[58] The "othering" of Muslims in European societies creates fertile ground for the recruitment of jihadist Islamists.[59] In the world of Islam itself it is becoming increasingly difficult to counter the appeal of jihadism among young people. Existing patterns of education in those mosques not controlled by the state do not undermine the jihadist ideology but rather promote it, and the traditional security approach of policing is unable to suppress it.[60] The life of young Muslims has to be improved. Simple preservation of the status quo is not enough to defend freedom and democracy. Democratization in the world of Islam, better development policies, and institutions that build the principles of civil society against the authoritarian state are better means of dealing with jihadist Islamism in Islamic civilization. To accomplish this, however, will require cultural changes both in the world of Islam and in the West.

6

Islamism and Law
Shari'atization as an Invention of Tradition

L AW HAS ALWAYS BEEN CENTRAL to Islamic thought. The foremost
authority on shari'a, Joseph Schacht, states on the first page of his
Introduction to Islamic Law that "Islamic law is the epitome of Islamic
thought. . . . It is impossible to understand Islam without understanding
Islamic law." [1] John Kelsay, in *Arguing the Just War in Islam,* depicts the entire intellectual history of Islam in terms of different ways of "shari'a reasoning." [2] It is this central role that Islamists invoke when they call for tatbiq
al-shari'a, the implementation of shari'a, as the governing law in Islamic
lands. If Islamists are explicitly attempting to restore a past order, why do I
call this effort an invention of tradition?

While shari'a reasoning has always assumed a central place in Islam, it
has always had diverse meanings, determined by different historical developments. The combination of centrality, diversity, and historicity within
shari'a is confusing for some, to the point that many people fail to understand how shari'a is today torn between Islam and Islamism. Mahmoud
Zaqzuq, the Egyptian minister of *awqaf* (religious affairs) and a former
dean of the shari'a faculty at Cairo's al-Azhar University, the world's oldest
and most authoritative Sunni institution, once shared with me his anger at
an Islamist call for tatbiq al-shari'a as part of an agenda for an "Islamic
state." In his introduction to Islam, one finds chapters on Islamic spirituality, ethics, human rights, diversity, and justice, but no chapter on a shari'a-based
political order. [3] "This call to implement shari'a," Zaqzuq told me rather
heatedly, "denies how central the shari'a is for us. It is not only at the basis
of our constitution, but also our ethical way of life." [4] In fact, since the time of
Anwar Sadat the Egyptian constitution has mandated shari'a as the source

of all lawmaking.[5] But this does not satisfy the Islamists because their understanding of shari'a is very different from Zaqzuq's.

The heir of Sayyid Qutb and the foremost authority of contemporary Islamism, Yusuf al-Qaradawi, who coined the formula al-hall al-Islami ("the Islamic solution," meaning the Islamist solution), declares shari'a as the basic feature of this solution: "The Western crusader colonialism invaded the abode of Islam and changed its way of life ... in politics and law. ... Shari'a receded to a personal law. ... Therefore the Islamic solution aims to restore the shari'a. ... The constitution [of the Islamic state] has to provision shari'a in all its entirety and all of its sources. ... Legislated law that deviates from the absolute divine texts [*al-nusus al-qat'iyya*] is doomed to invalidity [*butlan*]."[6]

This suggests a confusion of traditional shari'a with the order of a totalitarian state. To understand the difference between the political shari'a of Islamism and traditional shari'a,[7] one first needs a few pertinent facts.

Shari'a Politics in Islam

Despite al-Qaradawi's reference to "absolute divine text," the fact is that the term "shari'a" occurs only once in the Qur'an, in sura 45, verse 18: *thumma ja'alnaka ala shari'a min al-amr fa attabi'uha* (We have set you on the right path. Follow it). In this verse the Qur'an mandates the moral conduct of *al-amr bi al-ma'ruf wa an-nahi 'an al-munkar* (enjoining the good and forbidding the evil). "The Qur'an contains ... prescriptions for the life of the community of Muslims. They were elaborated ... in later times to constitute what is now known as Islamic law, or the shari'a."[8] Basically these rules refer to the five pillars of Islam: (1) submission to Allah, (2) prayer, (3) legal alms or poor tax, (4) the fast of Ramadan, and (5) the pilgrimage to Mecca.

All other uses of the term are post-Qur'anic constructions. In the early 700s, about a century after the death of the Prophet, Muslim scribes, or fiqh jurists, began to establish the *madhahib* as competing schools of law.[9] In Sunni Islam there were four such schools: the Hannafi, Shafi'i, Maliki, and Hanbali law schools. Their mission was to establish legal rules based on interpretation of the Qur'an, and the canonical records of the Prophet (the hadith). In classical shari'a, these rules revolved around two areas: on one hand, the ibadat (cult) and mu'amalat (civil law such as marriage and divorce, inheritance, and other miscellaneous regulations) and on the other, the *hudud*[10] (penal code), which provides physical punishments. Even though the caliph was expected to guarantee the practice of shari'a by his office—an office that does not exist in the Qur'an, which prescribes no particular system of government—he acted as a secular ruler. The ulema legitimated what he did, always post eventum, with a reference to the shari'a.[11] Thus in the classical caliphate there existed a separation between siyasa (state administration or politics) and shari'a (divine guidance). Joseph Schacht argues in *Introduction to Islamic Law* that the Muslim ruler pretended "to apply and to complete the sacred law . . . [but] in practice . . . regulate[d] by virtually independent legislation matters of police, taxation, justice, all of which had escaped the control of the Kadi"—that is, the judge in charge of the shari'a. These latter areas were designated siyasa. The result, Schacht writes, was "a double administration . . . one religious . . . on the basis of shari'a, the other secular exercised by political authorities on the basis of . . . —sometimes— arbitrariness of governmental regulation."[12]

Another authority on Muslim law, also Oxford-based, was the late Iranian-born Hamid Enayat. Two statements from his book *Modern Islamic Political Thought* are worth quoting. First, he says of the shari'a doctrine that "there is no such thing as a unified Islamic system, enshrined in integrated codes and accepted and acknowledged unquestionably by all Muslims." Later he adds that the classical shari'a itself does "not form any rigid code of laws." Second, he says of shari'a's place in Islamic history that it "was never implemented as an integral system, and the bulk of its provisions remained as legal fictions."[13]

Thus the Islamist attempt to impose monolithic "shari'a" in the form of a rigid code that will be implemented as an integral system has no basis in history. The claim that such a shari'a existed in the past is the epitome of an invented tradition.

In their invention of a nonexistent Islamic tradition of law, Islamists reinterpret all of the facts reviewed above. Mohammed Said al-Ashmawi, the former highest judge of the Egyptian legal system and the author of

Usul al-shari'a (The origins of shari'a),[14] states in his book *al-Islam al-Siyasi* (Political Islam) that the shari'atized Islam of Islamism is not consonant with traditional Islamic tenets, in particular with the classic shari'a.[15] Islamists do to shari'a what they do to classical jihad: they create a thoroughly modern practice and claim continuity with ancient tradition. In their invention of an Islamic legal system, shari'a becomes a state law, something it never was under the caliphs. Some Western pundits classify this political shari'a as "constitutionalism," but this is utterly wrong.[16]

Instead, we must locate this invention of tradition within the overall phenomenon of the return of the sacred to politics, which in turn is a product of the contemporary crisis of modernity. These developments challenge Weber's assumptions about secularization as a continuing "disenchantment of the world."[17] We are in fact seeing the reverse, a desecularization[18] in which shari'a in its invented new shape assumes a central place. This is not an Islamic variety of constitutionalism. The Islamic political revival, of which the shari'atization[19] of Islam is a part, is nothing else than a variety of religious fundamentalism. This is a major issue in the distinction between Islamism and Islam.

The Muslim legal scholar Abdullahi an-Na'im notes that "the Qur'an does not mention constitutionalism." Thus the Islamist claim for an Islamic constitutional law is another invention of tradition. It is clearly an instance of post-Qur'anic thinking, even though it claims to be divine and therefore unquestionable. An-Na'im argues that democratic constitutionalism "is unattainable under shari'a" and emphasizes that "only two options [are] open to modern Muslims: either abandon the public law of shari'a or disregard constitutionalism."[20]

In this chapter we will look at the Islamist program for the shari'atization of politics in Islam[21] and see how it relates to shari'a, old and new.[22]

Desecularization and the Quest for a Divine Political Order

Since the end of the cold war, competition between the religious and secular visions for the order of the world has moved to center stage. The U.S.

scholar Mark Juergensmeyer uses the phrase "the new cold war"[23] to describe postbipolar politics. In this formulation, Islam has replaced communism as the West's chief opponent. Why? On the left it was suggested that having lost an intimate enemy that ensured the unity of its civilization, the West was moved to find a "new enemy" in Islam. Islamophobia is thus a substitute for anticommunism in a new war of ideas. This analysis is entirely ethnocentric: it is focused solely on political rivalries within the West and makes Islam itself almost irrelevant. One must go beyond these parochial obsessions to see the real issue, which is the challenge to modernity posed by the return of the sacred within Islamic civilization.[24]

During the era of European expansion, Islam functioned as an anticolonial, defensive-cultural ideology in which jihad was seen as a response to Western imperialism.[25] Today it claims more: leadership of the world. In Sayyid Qutb's writings of the late 1950s and early 1960s, humanity is seen as on the *hafat al-hawiya* (brink), mired in "a crisis of the West and the bankruptcy of its democracy" out of which "only Islam is eligible to lead humanity."[26] In a later book, *World Peace and Islam,* Qutb argues that only Islamic dominance can guarantee world peace; to achieve it he suggests reinterpreting jihad as "a permanent comprehensive world revolution in order to establish God's rule for saving all humanity [hakimiyyat Allah]."[27] The new shari'a is the overall framework for the transformation of Qutb's rhetorical salvation into a mobilizing ideology. Islamist political internationalism, which is based on an imagined transnational umma, not only requires a shari'a state but also a desecularized world order based on the shari'a.

As I argue throughout this book, Islamism and its shari'atization project are the result of the failed introduction of modernity and an unsuccessful secularization, paired with the developmental crisis of the Islamic nation-state. Earlier gains are being reversed: the Islamic world is moving from acculturation to deacculturation, from modernization to retraditionalization, from Westernization to de-Westernization and, above all, from secularization to desecularization. The de-Westernization of knowledge has reached the point of questioning rationalism itself;[28] Weber's once universally accepted (albeit culturally limited) notion of secularization as rationalization is now under dispute. The challenge to the secular nation-state arises even in the West. The Islamists' idea of shari'a must be viewed in the context of their ambition to replace the secular order of the world with a divine one based on Islamic tenets. The invented tradition of shari'a provides the primary definition to this world order.[29]

Classical shari'a has concepts for peace, order, and justice, but in the contemporary "competition between cultural traditions," the conflict between shari'a and democratic constitutionalism assumes a new meaning. In Islamic theology, the Qur'an itself is divine, the word of God, but post-Quranic thought is of human origin and thus susceptible to dispute, modification, and accommodation with the secular in a way that the words of the Qur'an are not. The classical development of the shari'a legal system by the four madhahib schools was a post-Quranic enterprise undertaken by the ulema and fuqaha'. Later, with the influential work of Ibn Taymiyyah (1263–1328), shari'a was associated with siyyasa, or state administration.[30] But this adaptability does not serve the needs of contemporary Islamism. To underpin an irreconcilably anti-Western state order, invented shari'a law must claim divine origin.

The invention of shari'a[31] in its new meaning heralds a new project. The rival agendas of secularization and desecularization do not divide entirely along civilizational lines. Secular thought is not exclusively European: it also has roots in medieval Islam. As we shall see in Chapter 7, Averroism, a variety of rationalism[32] based on the Hellenization of Islam, led to the acceptance of the primacy of reason in the medieval Islamic world. For a variety of reasons, however, this rationalist school of thought faded from Islamic civilization. In contrast, rationalist, Enlightenment views became a permanent part of European culture. This thinking has also influenced the rest of the world in the course of the globalization of European structures and the universalization of European ideas dismissed today as Westernization.[33] Western-educated elites emerged in non-Western cultures, but in the Islamic world they have so far failed to strike deep cultural roots and instead have begun to give way to a new nativism.[34] The shari'atization of politics in contemporary Islam is about nativism, not about "postsecular society."[35]

The return of shari'a in a new political shape is embedded in the phenomenon of the return of the sacred. The Islamist response to the crisis of modernity is not a spiritually driven religious renaissance but a religionization of politics and a politicization of religion, which together have contributed to a culturalization of conflict.[36] The shari'atization of Islam becomes a part of the problem.

Islamic Shari'a and Its Claim to Be a Constitutional Law

The claim of a divine Islamic law that covers all areas, including constitutional law, is a legal novelty. When various parties in Iraq after the liberation from Saddam's dictatorship were discussing a new constitution, the Committee of Islamic Ulema, a major group of clerics active in Iraqi politics, issued a pronouncement demanding that any such constitution be based on Islamic shari'a law. The speaker of the committee, the Islamic scribe Adbulsalam al-Kubaisi, said: "We do not care for a referendum, but insist that Islamic law should be the major source [*al-masdar al-asasi*] of the constitution."[37]

This insistence on an Islamic state gives rise to a question: is a state based on a shari'a-inspired constitution the necessary democratic alternative to Saddam's "republic of fear"? As I write this, Sunni and Shi'ite Iraqis are killing each other daily in their dispute over what precisely is meant by a constitutional legal system based on shari'a. Though the so-called democratization of Iraq has brought with it an imposed constitution in which, at American insistence, the term "shari'a" does not appear, shari'a is nonetheless established under a different name: "Islamic ruling." Everyone understands this except, apparently, the U.S. military and the U.S. State Department. Thus the project of democratization faces the competing project of an Islamization of law. Despite all claims to the contrary, it is well established that the post-Qur'anic shari'a rules are not consonant with individual human rights[38] but contradict them on all counts.

Do not be mistaken: I am not against shari'a in its moral meaning as set forth in the Qur'an. But I am dubious, to put it charitably, about any *lex divina* or sacral law of Islam established as shari'a by humans who are not favorable to secular democracy. We must keep in mind the post-Qur'anic—human-constructed—character of the shari'a. The four madhahib of Islamic law that created the medieval shari'a based their ideas on diverse interpretations of the Qur'an. In addition, this Islamic law was never codified: there were no written statutes of shari'a. Shari'a remained an interpretative law, mostly restricted to civil law and a penal code, based entirely on an accumulating body of individual judgments in particular cases. Today's call for shari'a, by contrast, is a demand to construct an Islamic state with an alleged shari'a as its constitution. If we set aside the question of invented tradition, this is on its face no more absurd than the creation of the U.S. Constitution out of the whole cloth of English common law, Enlightenment political philosophy, and the immediate political situation in 1780s America. The important questions are whether shari'a could really function as a constitutional law and how consonant the related call for Islamization would be with the vision of democracy for the world of Islam.

The return of the sacred in the guise of shari'a, or the shari'atization of Islamic politics,[39] is a setback for Islamic civilization. What Islamism presents to Muslims is not a solution; it is rather the problem and one of the sources of their crisis. The reason relates to the interplay of religion and politics. In support of this contention I offer three points:

First, law in Islam is shari'a, but there is no common understanding among Muslims of what shari'a precisely means. This dispute is at once scholarly, religious, and political.

Second, the term *dustur,* or constitution, and the perception of shari'a as constitutional law, are recent additions to Islamic thought.

Third, individual human rights, including freedom of faith, are also—despite claims to the contrary—recent additions to Islam. This subject has generated a great deal of dispute among Muslims. Some Egyptian Muslims—close to the Muslim Brotherhood, like the late Mohammed al-Ghazali and Mohammed Imara—claim that the very origin of the ideal of human rights lies in Islam.[40] Others, like the Sudanese Islamist Hasan Turabi, argue that human rights are alien to Islam and that "we do not need them." Meanwhile, Muslim secular scholars like An Nai'im call for legal reforms in contemporary Islamic civilization.[41] The shari'atization of Islamic politics tends to distract from reforms, obstructing their adoption and creating limits to the freedom of faith.

The distinction between scriptural and historical Islam is pertinent for discussing shari'a and the freedom of faith in Islam. Islamic tradition recognizes three levels of non-Islams. In descending order:

Non-Muslim monotheists (Jews and Christians) are dhimmi,[42] people who are allowed to retain their religious beliefs under Islamic rule and under certain restrictions but are not considered equal to Muslims.

Followers of nonmonotheistic religions (all others besides Judaism, Christianity, and Islam) are considered to be in a state of kufr (unbelief) and are to be fought on terms specified by Qur'anic provisions. The only Islamic country that acknowledges these religions in a mindset of pluralism is Indonesia.

Muslims who either leave Islamic belief through conversion or choose not to believe (atheists or agnostics) are considered to commit either *riddah* (apostasy) or heresy and are to be punished as unbelievers. The riddah doctrine legitimates the slaying of ex-Muslims or those subjected to takfir.

Already, these three levels portend a conflict between shari'atization and democratic constitutionalism. Some argue that the noncodified nature of shari'a makes it a highly flexible legal system. This may be true of classical shari'a, but the dogmatic form embraced by Islamism today is a very rigid code. For instance, the three levels described above are largely collapsed into one. Islamists classify everyone who disagrees with them, including other Muslims, as *kafirun,* or infidels,[43] and call for tatbiq al-shari'a, implementation of shari'a, against them. The politicization of shari'a and its elevation to dustur, constitutional law, thus legitimates a new civilizational project.[44] The Islamist refers in this project to "law" not in the democratic meaning of "rule of law," but as a "law of movement" in the understanding of Hannah Arendt. One may write anything at all into a constitution, of course, but it seems clear that shari'a is in conflict with modern legal standards. This is acknowledged by enlightened Muslims.[45]

Of course, Islamists are not alone in the field. There are Muslim scribes who view the shari'a as a "holy given," and though they never subject it to scrutiny, are willing to adapt it at least somewhat. There are also a few Muslim scholars who go beyond this,[46] as did Najib Armanazi in his 1930 book on international law in Islam and, more recently, Mohammed Said al-Ashmawi. Then there exist Islamic writings that are in one way or another reasonable. Among these one finds a shari'a book by the slain Subhi al-Salih of Lebanon, who received his Ph.D. in Paris at the Sorbonne. He allowed rational reasoning about the shari'a. But by and large, the view of shari'a that prevails in today's Islam is the one reinvented by Islamism in the contemporary "shari'a reasoning."

The Islamist denial of pluralism even occurs within Islam. Given that there exists no codified shari'a law, nor any understanding of the shari'a that is universal among Muslims, one is inclined to ask the Islamists who demand shari'a law, "*Which* shari'a do you mean?" Shari'atization opens the door for arbitrary politics in the guise of divine law. Islamism implements the law of its totalitarian movement as law in general. In contrast to the flexible interpretative law—shari'a was always subject both to individual and to madhahib (legal school) interpretations of the Qur'an and of the hadith—contemporary shari'atization prescribes the conduct of politics in a totalitarian manner. It proposes a remaking of Islam with regard to law and order. In the past, the role of shari'a in politics was limited to providing the caliphs post eventum with legal legitimacy, amounting to a declaration that the rulers' political deeds were in line with shari'a. The faqihs were never independent in their rulings and had no reason to venture into the domain of constitutional law. When I ask Islamists which shari'a they have in mind, I remind them of the three different understandings of the term, restated systematically in the following historical order:

First, one cannot repeat often enough that the sole Qur'anic verse in which shari'a appears reads: *thumma ja'alnaka ala shari'a min al-amr fa attabi'uha* (We have set you on the right path [shari'a]. Follow it). Again, the traditional understanding of this shari'a is as morality, not law. As phrased in the Qur'an the provision reads: *al-amr bi al-ma'ruf wa al-nahi an al-munkar* (to enjoin the good and forbid the evil). In short, this shari'a is a morality of conduct, a summum bonum, and clearly not a legal system. Muslim scholars need to revive this understanding, to refute, in Islamic terms, the popular call for the shari'atization of law in Islamist politics, and to contain any arbitrary legal system that violates human rights.

Second, in the eighth century four Muslim scribes, Abu Hanifa, Ibn Hanbal, al-Shafi'i, and Malik bin Anas, established the four legal schools of

Sunni Islam that carry their names. They were and continue to be restricted to civil law, but they also cover matters of liturgy. With regard to
freedom of faith of non-Muslims, Islamic law recognizes only monotheists
(Jews and Christians) and grants them a limited restricted degree of freedom as dhimmitude living under Islamic rule.

Third, with the rise of Islamism in the twentieth century, shari'a obtained a political dimension as the legal basis of a state order. This vision of
shari'a has no basis in Islamic history. As an ideology, as I will show in Chapter
8, it legitimates a clearly totalitarian rule.

Shari'atization and the Universality of Law

In today's international society,[47] in our state of simultaneous globalization
and cultural fragmentation,[48] there is a need for civilizational bridging.
The return of the sacred should not prevent us from defending the universality of secular law and making it acceptable to Muslims. Shari'a has
always been a pendulum between ethics and politics. Ethically, the Qur'an
includes some opening for freedom of faith. We read the provision *la ikraha
fi al-din* ("no compulsion in religion," sure 2, verse 256), and elsewhere the
Qur'an teaches believers to say to others: *lakum dinakum wa liya din* ("You
have your religion and I have mine," sure 109, verse 6). A problem in Islam
is that all issues are subject to regulation by shari'a, which is identified as
divine law. Unlike other religions, whose religious scholars are basically theologians, in Islam we find learned men of religion (ulema, or scribes) acting
as sacral jurists or faqihs, not as mutakallimun, theologians. Medieval Islam
did contain a religious tradition of *kalam* (theology). There were Mutazilite
theologians who were "defenders of reason," but they never succeeded in
becoming mainstream. The fiqh (Islamic sacral jurisprudence) has always
possessed a monopoly over the interpretation of religious affairs in Islam.
For these jurists a legal claim to freedom of faith does not exist, because this
contradicts their reading of the Qur'an. It is a historical reality that shari'a
law does not recognize freedom of faith. It considers any deviation by a
Muslim to be apostasy subject to the penal code. The punishment is death.
For non-Muslims the lack of freedom of faith is even tougher. Muslims

are challenged to accept the pluralism of religions, but the shari'atization of Islam makes pluralism impossible. The universality of reason, to act as a bridge between faiths, has to be secular.

In fact, there is no globally accepted universal law. Humanity is divided into a number of religion-based civilizations, each with its own distinct legal traditions. Civilizations comprise a great diversity of local cultures. Yet we now live in a global system with an international law based on one legal tradition that claims to be universal and to merit general acceptance. Though international law originates in a Western legal tradition, it is worth maintaining as a secular law in this age of the return of the sacred. If each civilization were to revive its legal traditions on the basis of its own religion and to perceive international law as "alien legal instructions," as happens now in Islamic civilization with Saudi-Wahhabi promotion,[49] then the world would fragment into warring camps. As it is, the Islamists propose a binary system. They regard their shari'a as universal, as Westerners regard their secular law, and thus create mutually exclusive universalisms.

As a Muslim immigrant in the West, I have seldom heard a Western legal scholar question the universal character of European law. When the term "law" is employed in any law school, it means the tradition that evolved within Europe based on Roman origins. Culturally, this understanding of law prevails only in the Western hemisphere. Although the world is determined by a global system and its inherent international structures, and although Article 1 of the U.N. Charter rules that international disputes are to be settled by peaceful—legal—means supposedly valid for all people and states, there are no grounds for assuming the existence of a universally accepted notion of law. The United Nations is a worldwide organization of peoples, but international law is basically European law. It does not enjoy universal recognition in non-Western civilizations. This is the background of our simultaneous structural globalization and cultural fragmentation. In contrast, an international society presupposes a cross-cultural consensus on basic values. The late Oxford International Relations scholar Hedley Bull introduced the systematic distinction between an international system based on interaction and an international society based on shared values. In Bull's understanding law is based on cultural values. Cultural diversity, legal particularisms, and fragmentation act as impediments to establishing a universality of law on which an international society could rest.

Although there is formally only one international law, the diversity of legal systems parallels the diversity of cultures and regional civilizations. It is most perplexing to see in this context how Salafi Muslims and Islamists, who generally reject Western political concepts, apply the Western notion of dustur to the Qur'an in order to advocate an Islamic constitution that supports their claim for Islamic universalism. Shari'a is to be valid for all humanity. To understand this situation I turn to the Oxford jurist H. L. A. Hart. Hart shows how European-structured law becomes international law that binds new states, including those of Islamic civilization. "It has never been doubted," he writes, "that when a new, independent state emerges into existence . . . it is bound by the general obligations of international law. . . . Here the attempt to rest the new state's international obligations on a 'tacit' or 'inferred' consent seems wholly threadbare."[50]

At present, Islamism remains a movement within a religion-based civilization whose worldviews and cultural attitudes are committed to legal traditions. But despite local variations, the context of its action is global. The basic change in international relations brought about by the end of bipolarity is the rise of nonstate actors, including Islamist movements. The conflict is thus between European legislative law and the traditional concept of sacred interpretative law, both existing in the same time and place but not consonant with each other. In modern democracies lawmakers are elected parliamentarians who act in legislative institutions. But in Islam, unelected ulema have the authority to act as interpreters of scripture. They behave not as legal scholars but rather as people who claim to know the law revealed by Allah. Thus we may contrast two competing legal traditions: legislative democratic law versus interpretative authoritarian law. Islamism complicates the issue by introducing two novelties: first, we are exposed to a new shari'a that translates traditional Islamic universalism into an activist political internationalism; and second, this shari'atization agenda is represented not by a state but by nonstate actors organized in transnational movements.[51] Islamism, with its shari'a universalism, thus presents a great stumbling block to postbipolar peace based on the Western concept of an international society.

Every legal tradition entails a distinction between philosophy and practice. At the level of legal practice, one encounters many similarities between sacral shari'a law and some traditions of Western secular law. Both traditions involve interpretation of a text, whether the Qur'an or the code of positive law, by some authoritative figure. The difference, however, is that the shari'a has been neither codified nor endowed with any legal institution independent of the ruler. Given this lack of autonomy, there is great room for arbitrary lawmaking, often *post eventum* in the service of the ruler, in the guise of interpretation of God's revelation.

The incompatibility of shari'a law with a diversity of belief systems shows the need for the universality of law. Could Muslims combine their commitment to shari'a with an engagement in an "Islamic reformation"[52] that provides appropriate legal interpretations and does not lead them to adopt a version of law that legitimizes de-Westernization? Law is one of the basic three issues that underlie Islam's predicament with modernity.[53]

Can There Be Shari'a without a Shari'atization of the State?

In the preceding section we looked at some major disadvantages to the Islamist version of shari'a. To readers still unconvinced of the distinction between Islamism and Islam or between classical and Islamist shari'a, I offer the following deliberation.

In Islam there is supposed to be only one caliph-state, but at times—such as the tenth century—there existed three caliphates (in Baghdad, Cairo, and Córdoba) at war with one another. Nowhere in Islamic society was there any cultural concept of separation of church and state, nor was the mosque an institution of its own like the Christian Church. The founder of historical sociology, Barrington Moore, wrote in *The Social Origins of Dictatorship and Democracy* that feudal Europe accommodated autonomous institutions in a kind of preexisting separation of church and state that facilitated secularization in the West. There is no such thing in Islam. In fact, Islam throughout history has been more than a state religion in the modern European sense, in that it affects not only rulers but everyday life. Thus law and shari'a—understood as "way of life"—were essentially synonymous. Still, many points distinguish classical shari'a from the contemporary shari'a of Islamism. Practically, as Joseph Schacht has argued, there was a separation between shari'a and siyasa, politics. In addition, classical Islam proceeded from moral teachings and matters of ritual, and the judges who administered local law were expected to use these moral teachings independently to arrive at resolutions within a body of accepted precedents and traditions. In contrast, Islamism creates a rigid exclusionary behavioral code with the intent of coercing people into compliance (just as Hannah Arendt understood the relation between indoctrination and coercion), not using shari'a as "law" but declaring the law of the movement to be shari'a. This coercion is a totalitarian feature that never existed in traditional Islam.

At this point we are compelled to ask, given the public popularity of shari'a, whether there are any grounds for moderation. Can shari'a be reformed or reduced to ethics, rather than abandoned altogether in an age of globalization? This is not only a most delicate issue but also a highly pertinent one, given that the return of the sacred is powerfully combined with the revival in non-Western civilizations of their cultural and legal traditions—however invented they may be. In Islamic societies with advanced legal systems, such as Turkey, this revival creates conflict between Islamists and secular modernists, who refuse shari'a altogether.

To cope with this situation, one needs to revive traditions of cross-cultural international ethics. This is more promising than the contradictory proposition of Abdullahi An-Na'im, who was a reformer, but recently underwent a sea change; he wants to have his cake and eat it. In *Islam and the Secular State,* in which he discusses "the future of shari'a," An-Na'im combines his approval of shari'a, which he calls "a source of liberation and self-realization," with a plea for a "secular state." Unbelievably, he believes that this is consonant with a rejection of "the secularization of society."[54] More consistent is the approach of the German legal philosopher Theodor Viehweg, who argues that "[European] legal terminology prefers the assertive to the instructive form of expression for constructing a legal reality of its own."[55] Islamic legal terminology, on the other hand, constantly uses the instructive form: interpretations of the Qur'an, the primary source of Islamic law, expressly articulate what is *halal* and *haram,* what is permitted and what is forbidden. Despite these differences, however, similarities exist in the way both traditions handle legal text. These similarities are important if an international society based on common norms, values, and laws is to be realized and civilizations with divergent legal traditions are to be prevented from drifting apart in an intensifying process of cultural fragmentation.

The Kantian idea of democratic peace based on common constitutional standards offers a platform for culturally establishing an international, legally anchored consensus among civilizations. Such a platform would materially substantiate the principles contained in the U.N. Charter but would not prematurely integrate new states into an international legal order they had no part in creating. Moreover, such a cross-cultural international morality[56] must be disassociated as much as possible from the premise of Eurocentric Westernization. Universal values—or the values we wish to make universal—cannot be imposed on non-Western cultures but instead need to be harmonized with them.

This is not always so easy. How can we establish the constitutional norm of freedom of faith in Islamic terms? Doing so will require a rethinking of Islam through legal reform, so that law forms the basis for a local cultural underpinning of universal legal values. The tradition that might enable such a rethinking exists within Islam, if it can be reawakened. Only a reformed shari'a, restricted to ethics and based on the tradition of Islamic medieval humanism, can be consonant with the idea of religious freedom that abandons the binary of believers versus unbelievers in the classic dichotomy of war and peace.[57] A tradition of Islamic humanism exists in contrast to this binary.[58]

Islamism would take us in the other direction. Far from committing itself to plurality amid diversity combined with a consensus over core values, Islamism contests cultural diversity even within Islam itself. The Islamist politics of shari'atization dismisses cultural and religious pluralism as divisive and also revives the dichotomy between the dar al-Islam, the house of

Islam (literally, of peace), and the dar al-harb, the house of war, a concept that contradicts all norms of religious and cultural pluralism. We need an Islamic reformation.

Shari'a and Fiqh

Allow me to introduce one more distinction. Shari'a and fiqh are often confused, sometimes deliberately. In the history of law in Islam, the scribes who kept and transmitted sacral knowledge were interchangeably addressed either as faqihs or as ulema. They confused fiqh, sacred jurisprudence pursued by human beings, with shari'a, God's commandment.[59] This confusion affects the unity of religion and law.[60] As I have mentioned, Islam differs from Christianity in that there exists no church hierarchy. It is an organic rather than an ecclesiastical religious system.[61] This also explains why fiqh or orthodoxy is more central to Islam than a theology of kalam, theology.

The Qur'an,[62] revealed between A.D. 610 and 632, stands, for most Muslims, above time and space.[63] It constitutes the first primary source of Islamic law. The second primary source is the *sunna* (the tradition of the Prophet), based on the hadith (canonical records of the Prophet). Shari'a could be derived from these two primary sources. But two further components of Islamic law are acknowledged as secondary sources: *ijma'* (consensus doctorum) and *qiyas* (conclusion by analogy). This is fiqh, and it is pursued by humans. It follows that fiqh is not sacral. Progressive Muslims also allow the tradition of *ijtihad* (free reasoning) as a source of lawmaking. The Islamic faqihs who dismiss the ijtihad and confuse fiqh with shari'a arrive at the position that Islamic law is both eternal and immutable; its jurisdiction is unlimited. This absolutism, related in traditional Islam to despotism, should not be confused with the present shari'atization, which is related to modern totalitarianism. These are politically two different types of rule.

The late British scholar N. J. Coulson divides the history of Islamic law into three phases.[64] The first phase comprises post-Qur'anic development up to the ninth century, during which an Islamic legal system was developed. In the second phase, which lasted from the tenth century to the twentieth, this law grew increasingly rigid, until it was thought to constitute divine truth, valid for all times and in no way modifiable by history. The twentieth century, after the introduction of the European institution of the secular nation-state into the world of Islam, marks a third phase, in which modern states have been unable to maintain their regimes while relying on classical Islamic law. This form of law does not meet the requirements of the modern world, and this has been an element of Islam's predicament with modernity. I would argue that the Islamic world has now entered a fourth phase, marked by a de-Westernization of law as political Islam pursues its program of ideological shari'atization of Islam with the aim of tatbiq al-shari'a, implementing the law of the Islamist movement on state and society. The Islamist society that would result bears none of the features of an open civil society.

Shari'a and Freedom

Under the flag of Islamism, classical shari'a has been developed into the idea of shari'atization of the state. This is much more than a defensive cultural response to the challenge of modernity.[65] Islamism projects into the text of the Qur'an a new meaning in which politics has been religionized with a totalizing shari'a. The door for reform[66] that Islamic modernists once opened has been closed, along with the Islamic mind. Will this continue to determine the future?

Under the old Islamic tradition, accommodation to altered conditions was feasible, and Muslims today need to emulate their ancestors in learning from others. Fiqh orthodoxy does not admit a concept of cultural change and religious reform.[67] Yet what is missing in the scholastic fiqh tradition appears in the Qur'an. Sure 13, verse 11, tells us, "Allah does not change people, unless they change themselves by themselves."

Against the Islamist shari'atization project, this chapter proposes an alternative project that would enormously enrich Islamic law, promote flexibility, and enable cultural innovation.[68] Shari'a should not be abandoned altogether but should be restricted to religious ethics. The obstacles to this approach are, however, tremendous. The first victim of shari'atization is the

concept of individual rights, including freedom of faith. The suppression of
political and religious dissent, of course, makes reform much more difficult—
that is its purpose. Traditional shari'a, as a morality that was developed into
a kind of divine civil law and a system of *faraid* (duty), never became the
totalizing law envisioned by the Islamists. The Islamization of law violates
the rights of non-Muslims, of women, of intellectuals, of Sunnis in Shi'ite
areas and Shi'a in Sunni areas, of Muslim followers of other sects such as
Baha'i or Ahmadiyya—and ultimately of everyone outside the ruling elite.

In shari'atized Islam there is no place for the topical discourse or an acceptance of an Islamic legal philosophy. Islamists fight a war of ideas against
any attempt to engage in a cultural transformation of Islam. Religious reform and cultural change are being undermined, while shari'atization pro-
gresses. The Islamist call for tatbiq al-shari'a is not an indication of a return
to the tradition and does not portend a religious renaissance. The unprecedented Islamist ideology of an "Islamic state" based on shari'a is becoming
the foremost mobilizing force in the world of Islam. This process does not
feature a revival of anything but is a step toward a violent and oppressive
future in a totalitarian state. To criticize the Islamist project of a shari'a state
and to identify it as totalitarian is by no means "a profound insult" to Muslims
or to "their faith and identity," as the political scientist Marc Lynch contends
in his article "Veiled Truths," published in *Foreign Affairs*. On the contrary,
this criticism is rather a defense for a civil Islam against shari'atization.

7
Islamism, Purity, and Authenticity

AMONG THE BASIC FEATURES of Islamism is the aspiration for purity, put forward as a claim of authenticity.[1] Religious fundamentalism is in all cases a response to the challenge of cultural modernity, and the specific case of Islamism emerges from a modernization[2] that has largely failed. A generation ago, American scholars looked at modernization in non-Western societies as Westernization, which was conceived in wholly secular terms. Today, no one can speak of "Westernization" in academic circles and emerge unscathed. Not only has the linkage the term suggests generally been discarded, the very concept of evolutionary modernization has become suspect. In dissociating themselves from this thinking, some U.S. scholars go to the opposite extreme and tend to view Islamism as a legitimate opposition to Westernization, arguing that it presents an alternative model of development. The Islamist venture is seen as a legitimate response to the crisis of modernity. This includes a search for authenticity that draws on Islamic tradition. In fact, the Islamist authenticity project is based on an agenda of cultural purification. This agenda is alien to the classical heritage of an open Islam enriched by cultural borrowing from the non-Muslim other.

In fact, Islamism is neither traditional nor authentic. The Islamist is a thoroughly modern male, yet a deeply conflicted one: his "modernity" is really a semimodernity, which approves the adoption of scientific and technological tools (such as e-jihad) while firmly rejecting the cultural values that gave rise to them.

Max Weber understood modernization as the adoption of rational, secular ways of thinking. In rejecting the Weberian frame of reference, cultural relativist postmodernism finds itself navigating the same waters as neoabsolutist political Islam. Islamism aims at a desecularization understood as purification, while postmodernists speak of postsecular development and of multiple modernities. Of course, the incentives vary, but the targets resemble each other.

This chapter relates to Chapter 3, as one aspect of the search for authenticity includes the Islamization of antisemitism. Islamists want to purify Islam of "Jewish influence." The idea of a pure and "uncontaminated" Islam is recent. It can be traced back, once again, to the work of Sayyid Qutb and is expressed in the clearest terms by his current heir, the Egyptian Muslim Brother Yusuf al-Qaradawi. Qaradawi challenges any cultural borrowing from the non-Muslim other; Western-educated Muslim liberal elites are vilified in the third volume of his trilogy *al-hall Islami* (The Islamic solution) as *mustaghribun* (Westernized).[3] They are described as infected by an alien virus and thus no longer authentic Muslims.

This rejection of Western ideas is one of the things that separates the two varieties of Middle Eastern antisemitism. Pan-Arab nationalists openly adopted their antisemitism from Europe. Islamism, which renounces cultural imports, must pretend not to simply copy from Europe as the secularists did and therefore engages in a cultural authentification that depicts a war with the Jews as an essential element of the entire history of Islam. Antisemitism thus becomes an expression of cultural and religious purity.

Among my arguments in this book is that the crisis of modern Islam is exacerbated by a predicament with modernity as well as by a crisis of development related to the Arab world's unsuccessful modernization. The resulting woes are seen by the Islamists as stemming from a so-called conspiracy of taghrib, Westernization. They wish to go back to their roots: they answer the crisis of modernity with a return of the sacred. Any secularization of society is thus questioned in the name of purity and condemned as a Westernization aimed at destroying Islam. The search for authenticity pits itself against all that is secular and all that has been adopted from the West.

With the exception of Europe, the retreat from secularism is global. However, Islamic migration to the West brings religion and the related conflicts back to Europe. Europeans fail to understand this. Religious fundamentalism characterized by purity and desecularization is a hallmark of our age, and it thrives in the Islam diaspora in the West. Is this the "postsecular society" Habermas proclaims? Support for the retreat from secularism in the name of purity and authenticity is often accompanied by no proper knowledge of the Islamist agenda of authenticity. Islamists understand their jihad against the "wicked master plans of the Jews" as a defensive fight for purity against a Jewish conspiracy to undermine the umma. Part of this "Jewish master plan" is an agenda of secularization meant to discredit Islam by depriving it of authenticity, thus steering people away from God. Islamists believe that "Jewish genius" is a "hidden hand" acting "in the dark," by proxy. In the past, the proxy was the "European crusaders"; at present it is the United States, allied with the Westernized Muslim elites. This conspiracy-driven narrative may be found in dozens of widely disseminated books by major Islamists, who propose an agenda to thwart this "devilish Jewish plan" aimed at secularizing Islam. In their venture the Islamists claim to purify the religion of Islam by casting out all "inauthentic" ideas and influences. They believe that the ghazu fikri (intellectual invasion) is the source of this contamination of the world of Islam in modern times.

I begin this chapter by addressing the Islamist view of secularity as an assault on authentic Islam. In their belief that Islam is din wa dawla, a concept of political order, Islamists maintain that Islam does not separate religion from politics. Purity lies in a divine order. Then I show how Islamists employ the concept of authenticity in the realm of cultural purification. I look at Islamic history to reveal that the truth is exactly opposite to the Islamist agenda: cultural borrowing not only happened in medieval Islam but was a driver for the glory of Islamic civilization at its height. Cross-cultural fertilization enriched Islam to the point that it has become an essential part of its heritage. On the basis of this history I argue that the classical heritage of Islam is more authentic than is the contemporary purification agenda of Islamism. This contrast reveals how different the Islamist mindset is from that of genuine Islam.

The Islamist Meaning of Authenticity

In his depiction of modernity, Weber equated secularization and rationality. Both contribute to *Entzauberung* (disenchantment). Islamists reject this understanding in favor of a sentiment of self-victimization. They accuse Europeans of launching a program of global secularization. It is ironic that in the face of these attacks, Europeans seem uninterested in defending the core values and accomplishments of cultural modernity. It is most perplexing when Christian guilt seems to succumb to the Islamist claim to authenticity and to support its opposition to secularity—for instance, when a Swedish foundation sponsors a symposium under the title "The Secular State and Society" and invites Tariq Ramadan to lecture the Swedes about "The Islamic Mission in Europe." This mission seems to be based on proselytizing Islam as the solution to Europe's crisis of secularism.

One of the Islamists who leads the debate on Islam and secularism is Faruq Abdul-Salam. In an influential book entitled *Political Parties and the Separation between Religion and Politics* he states that the Jews stand behind "secularism, rationalism and Macchiavellianism." These "Jewish" pursuits are supposed to be "the goals of a Zionist movement." Secularism, Abdul-Salam argues, is a means to weaken other religions in order to promote Jewish world rule. Furthermore, "documents and serious studies disclose the hidden Jewish hand that generated the separation between religion and politics."[4] These alleged documents provide evidence of the *takhtit al-yahudi al-alami* (Jewish world master plan) to extend "the principle of the separation of religion and the state." One page later, Abdul-Salam refers to a book by another prominent Islamist, Anwar al-Jundi, who in *Al-Mukhatatat al-Talmudiyya al-Sahyuniyya al-Yahudiyya* (The Talmud-based Jewish-Zionist master plans) claims to present "evidence" for a conspiracy that justifies cultural purification.

Despite their professed regard for authenticity, Jundi and other Islamists support their views by quoting at length from *The Protocols of the*

Elders of Zion. One is entitled to wonder what is authentic about this, and where the claimed purity lies.

Let us for a moment return to Abdul-Salam, who prides himself on "uncovering" the "Jewish-Zionist master-plan of secularization." It is puzzling to encounter his additional argument that the Jews invented individual human rights. Why did they do that? Abdul-Salam explains:

> In addition to the secularization agenda, which is the foremost destructive innovation [*bid'a*] of modern times, the Jews invented human rights. The rationale is that the Jews claim human rights to put themselves on equal footing with non-Jews with regard to civil and political rights. In so doing, they make instrumental use of human rights, employ them as a ladder to claim to high positions in society. In this manner, they have been able to position themselves in a place from which they infiltrate society in order to implement their secret plans. These are listed in the Zionist Protocols. Their pursuit is the establishment of the Jewish world government imposed by themselves on others in the belief to be the chosen people by God. They thrive to achieve this goal after the vanishing of all other religions.[5]

I am discussing secularization and desecularization in a chapter on authenticity and purity because Islamists themselves pair these two themes. For them, secularization is a "Jewish master plan" to be countered by Islamization. We can best look at the Islamist strategy of authenticity, *al-asalah,*[6] through the eyes of the foremost ideologue of these themes, the Egyptian Anwar al-Jundi. In unequivocal language he insists on the purity and the supremacy of Islam and rejects any dialogue with non-Muslims, let alone cultural borrowing from the non-Muslim other. Jundi wrote dozens of books, which continue to be influential. I will mention just three of them, published in the late 1980s and early 1990s, because this author is highly repetitive and tends to fill his books with the same ideas, rehashed over and over. The first is *Min al-tabai'iyya ila al-asalah* (From dependency to authenticity), in which Jundi argues against interfaith dialogue: "In the past years many events were organized in Beirut, Tunis, and Cordoba, etc., to promote an approach of rapprochement between religions. . . . The underlying assumption of this venture is that Islam is only a faith, with no ties to society, law, and the system of governance. Any pursuit in this direction is to inject a poison, a most killing one, into the world of Islam. Behind the plan for an interfaith dialogue lies an agenda of proselytization and Westernization."[7]

Two pages later, "efforts at a Christian proselytization" are disclosed as the *hisab* (agenda) of *al-sahyuniyya al-alamiyya* (world Zionism). The book ends with the warning: "The efforts of rapprochement and dialogue are clearly . . . a master-plan of world Zionism." To counter this "conspiracy," Jundi recommends to his fellow Islamists the politics of authenticity.

The purification agenda of this politics discloses what "authenticity" really means. In a nutshell, every thought in the purity debate revolves around the "Jewish-Zionist master plan." In his second book, *Ahdaf al-taghrib* (The goal of Westernization) Jundi claims to have uncovered a conspiracy of "Westernization" embedded in the overall "Jewish conspiracy."[8]

The Islamist notion of authenticity is often referred to positively by scholars who do not read Arabic and thus lack the ability to see how this notion is actually used by Islamists when they are not speaking for Western ears. Some of these people think my reading of Islamist writers on al-asalah, or authenticity, is based on the work of "marginal authors." This idea may be refuted by a quick look in any Arabic-language bookstore. Jundi, for instance, is anything but marginal.

In the first book of three cited above, Jundi presents asalah as the proper response to cultural and economic dependency. A closer look at his use of "asalah" reveals unambiguously that this concept is based on cultural purification. The Jews are singled out and held responsible for all the wrongs that happened to Islam in its civilizational exposure to the West. In general one finds in Islamist writings that the Westernizing of Muslims and their civilization is identified as ghazu fikri (intellectual invasion).[9] As I have said, we find here the Islamist idea of authenticity viewed as an instrument to purify Islam from the "poisonous Jewish influences"—thus the combination of authenticity and purity. Jundi equates the opening of one's mind to other cultures with "opening the door to world Zionism as happened in Palestine." Muslims who engage in a dialogue with non-Muslims submit to "this master plan, which is of the making of world Zionism."

Again, this purification agenda is an Islamist invention and it is alien to the classical heritage of Islam.

A third book by Jundi is *al-Mu'asarah fi itar al-asalah* (Modernity in the framework of authenticity). Here he acknowledges that modernity is based on the Enlightenment, but asserts that "the word *Enlightenment* itself is a Jewish vocabulary. It intends to lead the West away from Christianity to secularism and thus consequently to atheism. . . . This is a Jewish conspiracy against the entire humanity as is made clear in *The Protocols of the Elders of Zion*. . . . The venture ends up in putting forward the claims of the Jews to Palestine."[10] He adds that a *mu'amarat al-istishraq* (conspiracy of Orientalism) is at work.

The supposed Jewish roots of the Enlightenment are emphasized again and again. The Jewish plan has three faces: one is liberal, another is Marxist, and the third is Zionist. All are designed "by the conspiring Jews as disclosed in the protocols" and disguised as "modernity" and "secularity." The sahwa (awakening) of Islam is aimed at defeating this Jewish conspiracy. Jundi tells his readers, "There is only one way to avert and to beat the conspiracy of Jews. It is the path of Islam." To be sure, when Jundi speaks of Islam, it is to be read as "political Islam," or Islamism. Islam as a faith and a culture is limited to spirituality. The "Islam" of Jundi is based above all on the concept of a nizam siyasi, a political system of governance. The attentive reader knows already that this view reflects precisely the basic feature of Islamism that distinguishes it from the faith of Islam.

The politics of authenticity targets not only the "Jewish master plan of Westernization" but also the great nineteenth- and twentieth-century thinkers who produced the thought and literature of the Arab-Muslim liberal age.[11] These great minds are all referred to by name in Jundi's book, in an inventory reminiscent of a secret police dossier of wanted dissidents. The docket includes Tawfiq al-Hakim, Ihsan Abdul Qaddus, Anis Mansur, Zaki Najib Mahmud, and the first and so far only Arab-Muslim Nobel laureate, Najib Mahfuz. For a Muslim such as myself who lives in Germany, this Islamist list is reminiscent of the Nazi culture of purification. In those days all German scholars and intellectuals who were found to be *undeutsch* (un-German) were eliminated. One of them was Einstein, the incomparable originator of "Jewish physics" (that is, relativity), who rightly ridiculed the attenuated "German physics" that resulted from the purge of Jews from German universities. Today, for an Islamist to call another Muslim un-Islamic because of "infection" by a foreign virus invokes the Nazi mindset of purification. What would remain in the Arab-Muslim world if this purification were to happen is only the rubble on which totalitarianism is built.

The Nazis, in purifying German culture of un-German influences, targeted not only Jews but all elements of the Enlightenment. The de-Nazification of Germany after 1945 was therefore a kind of re-Westernization. Similarly, the victims of the Islamist purification are not only Jews but all enlightened and democracy-loving Muslims. Why are the parallels not understood in the West? Those Westerners who benignly praise Islamist authenticity seem either not to know what they are talking about or not to be informed about what happens in the world of Islam. I assume that most of these liberal scholars would reconsider their endorsement if they became familiar with what this notion really means in Islamist writings.

Was Islamic *Falsafa* Rationalism Authentic?

The Islamic cultural legacy that exists in a heritage of Islamic rationalism is a historical fact. I refer to it as *falsafa* rationalism. This tradition was explicitly based on cross-cultural fertilization. A conflict emerged within classical Islamic civilization between falsafa (rational philosophy) and fiqh (orthodoxy).[12] I translate fiqh in a free way as "orthodoxy," knowing that it rather means in Arabic (sacral) jurisprudence. This tradition in Islam reflects, however, orthodoxy. Based on a decade of studying this conflict, which seems to be poorly known in Western Islamic studies, if one can judge by the occasionally bizarre comments of peer reviewers, I maintain a conflict between falsafa and fiqh as two rival traditions in Islam.

In the aftermath of the death of the Prophet in 632, Muslim scribes were at pains to transform Islamic faith into a ritual legal and cultural system. In the course of this development, four madhahib (schools) of shari'a emerged. This term is understood today as a religious equivalent to Western law, but this is not quite right. Shari'a is not law but a system that regulates ibadat (cult) and mu'amalat (interaction, but restricted to inheritance, marriage, and divorce). In classical Islam this system was named fiqh (proper knowledge). The scribes constituted the fiqh orthodoxy. A sociologist of religion would think of these scribes as clergy, even though Islam claims to not have any clergy. But in the institutional reality of Sunni Islam (for example, the position of mufti) and Shi'ite Islam (ayatollahs) these scribes constitute a de facto clergy.

Starting in the ninth century, a rival tradition to this scriptural Islam emerged through a process of Hellenization. This new tradition was falsafa (rationalism), based on cultural borrowing and on the primacy of reason. Falsafa and fiqh have been at odds ever since.

Which of these two traditions is really authentic in Islam? Is it scriptural orthodoxy, or the rationalism of Avicenna and Averroës?[13] On which of these traditions does identity politics[14] in Islam rest today? If we assert that one is "authentic," does that mean that the other is not?

And is it permissible today to learn from the non-Muslim cultural other? Let me briefly leave off bashing the left and devote some attention to the right. There are (genuinely) Islamophobic Westerners who respond to the irrational thinking of Islamism by asserting that "Islam has no tradition of any enlightenment." Most authors of this caliber confuse the unenlightened attitudes and irrational behavior of Islamists with Islam itself. They obviously do not know that the classical heritage of Islam contained the seeds of an enlightenment that resembles European cultural modernity.[15] I am inclined to qualify this as an Islamic "Enlightenment."[16] The seeds of this rationalism were suppressed by the Islamic fiqh orthodoxy but are nonetheless entitled to be viewed as authentic and deserve to be revived. The late Moroccan philosopher Mohammed al-Jabri believes that cultural modernity is in line with that earlier Islamic tradition. I would argue that the Islamic tradition of rationalism[17] is fully consonant with cultural modernity as summarized by Habermas: "In modernity . . .

religious life, state and society, as well as science and morality . . . are transformed . . . as abstract subjectivity in Descartes' *cogito ergo sum*. . . . Kant carried out this approach . . . [and] installed reason in the supreme seat of judgement before which anything that made a claim to validity has to be justified." [18]

Could this European notion of modernity apply today to Islam? Islamists refer to an invented Islamic authenticity to defame this understanding of modernity as a Jewish master plan directed against Islam. Unlike medieval Muslim rationalists, who revered the non-Muslims Plato and Aristotle, today's Islamists embrace an identity politics that requires the creation of fault lines between cultures. In contrast, Jabri refers to the Islamic rationalism of Averroës to argue that modernity is authentic for Muslims. Western theorists of politics of authenticity who reject Weber's and Habermas's approach to cultural modernity and instead support the Islamist claimants of authenticity presumably don't know of this ideology's "purification" agenda. Robert Lee, for instance, writes that "modernity has eroded cultures, values and identities . . . [which] the advocates of authenticity would attempt to repair." [19] Such views, which are standard in U.S. Islamic studies, end up—wittingly or unwittingly—legitimating the Islamist agenda. It is a great mistake to view Islamism as a liberation theology characterized by an "attempt to repair." No, it is an agenda of cultural-totalitarian purification.

The project of enlightenment, understood as recognition of the primacy of reason, is universal and thus accessible to all cultures, including those of Islamic civilization. It runs counter to any purification. Al-Jabri argues that such enlightenment existed in medieval Islam. It follows that rationalism was authentically Islamic and constitutes a part of the classical heritage of Islam. For a few hundred years—between the ninth and twelfth centuries—there was an ongoing tradition of Muslim reasoning based on cultural borrowings from Hellenism and the acceptance of the primacy of reason. It is perfectly "authentic" to learn, like great Muslim minds in the past, from non-Islamic sources.

It would be dishonest to depict Islamic rationalism as the prevailing tradition in its time. It was not. It was relatively short-lived, eradicated by the Muslim orthodoxy of fiqh scribes. There were seeds of enlightenment, but the Islamic *Aufklärer* (enlightened thinkers) failed to generate a wide-scale Enlightenment in their civilization. Still, there is a precedent worth emulating, and it is more authentic than the tradition invented by contemporary Islamism.

Moreover, even if the Muslim rationalists were not able to shape the worldview of the entire Islamic civilization, they were not wholly ineffectual. Much as Europe had its Descartes and Kant, Islam had its Farabi, Ibn Sina (Avicenna), and Ibn Rushd (Averroës). Not only were they rationalists, but intellectually they were of the same caliber as their European peers. In Europe, however, the thinking of Descartes was institutionalized and built upon, both philosophically and mathematically. A reason-based (*res cogito*) philosophy had been able to shape the prevailing European worldview. In contrast, Muslim rationalists were denied the opportunity to shape the course of Islamic civilization and its worldview, as George Makdisi tells us. Enlightened rationalism in classical Islam was not included in the curriculum of the *madrasa* ("Muslim college"). Its impact was therefore confined to these philosophers' private circles.[20] Some of them managed to enter the court of the caliph and exert some influence. But lacking institutional continuity and the support of the wealthy and powerful, the Golden Age of Islamic learning petered out. The last great mind of the era of Islamic rationalism was Ibn Khaldun, who died in 1406. Why did Islamic civilization not produce a single thinker of great caliber after that?

Great Muslim thinkers of the late nineteenth century and the first half of the twentieth century were aware of this long lapse. Therefore they undertook efforts to revive the tradition of Islamic rationalism.[21] These efforts were undertaken by Muslim liberals against the fiqh orthodoxy in a cultural development that lasted until the rise of political Islam. At the moment they appear to have failed. Yet despite the odds, Jabri has given his fellow Muslims a wake-up call: "A better future of Islam can only be Averroist."[22] If Islamic civilization fails to follow the Averroist rationalist path, he believes, then the alternative is a resumption of the age of darkness. Certainly the flat-earth epistemology of Islamism suggests a bleak future.

If contemporary Islamism and Salafism were to prevail, their agenda of purification would set the people of Islam back centuries. The rationalism of Avicenna, Averroës, and al-Farabi[23] is a better choice. The classical heritage of Islam is intrinsically more authentic than the invention of tradition being promoted by the followers of Sayyid Qutb.

Islamist Purity and the Exclusion of the Non-Muslim Other

The rich cultural heritage and precious accomplishments of Islamic rationalism are based on borrowing from classical Hellenism. If this were left behind it would be unimaginable for Islamic civilization to flourish. The lesson to learn today is that we must not overlook the vastly different historical contexts. Hellenization in medieval times was the appropriation of the treasures of a weaker civilization by a more powerful Islamic one. Still, the attitude of learning from the cultural other need not depend on context. The Muslim modernizers of the liberal age also learned from the cultural other. But there is a difference. The medieval Islamic rationalists rethought and extended what they borrowed. The Muslim liberals basically copied items from modernity without really accommodating its rationality in their culture. They did not change their worldview. This did not, however, let them escape the Islamist accusation of cultural treason.

Despite their propensity to culturally exclude the non-Islamic cultural other, Islamists—their xenophobia not withstanding—have a valid point in their complaints about the harm European civilization did to Islam. The problem is that they draw the wrong conclusions. Ignorant of Islamic history, they fail to realize that Islamic rationalism competed with, and lost out to, fiqh orthodoxy. Science and philosophy flourished in Islamic civilization in spite of this orthodoxy. The Islamists fall into the trap of contradiction when they boast that Europe owes a great deal of its Renaissance to cultural borrowing from Islam while at the same time ignoring and trying to obliterate what the West adopted from Islamic tradition. In fact, pre-Renaissance Europe adopted from medieval Islam the tradition of Islamized

Hellenism, which is the one but definitely not the pure fiqh tradition. Ideologically blinkered Islamists reveal not only that they are ignorant of the real history but that they are selective about what they do choose to know.

Despite their purist rejection of any learning from the contemporary West, Islamists do not hesitate to adopt modern instruments of science and technology.[24] For this mindset I have coined the term "semimodernity." Islamists divide modernity into two parts: the instruments to be adopted and the values to be vehemently rejected. The traditional fiqh orthodoxy does not share this semimodernity. Contemporary Islamists[25] pair modern politics with medieval fiqh. They are products of modernization who, reacting against their failure to accommodate modernizing development, invent tradition in a search for authenticity and in fact engage in cultural purification.

Can the purifying agenda of the "Islamic solution" ever achieve anything like actual authenticity? Could it ever be the expression of a purely (even if incomplete and selective) Islamic tradition and no other? Probably not. Robert Lee, who did important research on this subject, writes: "The quest for authenticity requires a scale of politics that conforms to what is legitimately ours rather than theirs." He adds: "The search for authenticity is a search for foundations."[26] Now: what are these foundations?

In the Arabic language, the word for "foundations" is *usul*. *Usuliyya* in modern Arabic means fundamentalism. The competition in medieval Islamic civilization between falsafa (rationalism) and fiqh (orthodoxy) was also a fight over what is specifically Islamic and what is not. To be sure, the term asalah (authenticity) is itself a modern addition to the Arab language. It refers to what is to be recognized as "foundation" and harks back to the earlier battle between falsafa and fiqh. In the search for authentic foundations, the local and the global mix in an odd way. Cosmopolitan world citizenship and ethnicity mingle with identity politics in a way that, on the one hand, precludes learning from the cultural other, but on the other is fully imbued with modernity. In this context the "foundations" are blurred. There is a kind of authenticity that elevates what Lee calls "irrationalities of condition." Despite my criticisms of Lee, I join him in "mistrusting proclamations of difference and otherness whether they come from Orientalists or Islamic militants."[27] In fact, as Lee points out, "the search for authenticity founders" on the rock of reality.

In the established meaning of authenticity, which focuses on divisions between the self and the other, the polarizing effects of an exclusive mindset are often overlooked. Why can't we, instead, give the term a different meaning and say that to be authentic is to maintain the self while borrowing or learning from the cultural other? Islamic falsafa would then be its most authentically Islamic tradition. Cultural learning from Western theories would become legitimate, and no longer "inauthentic," as postmodernists and Islamists—despite their different mindsets of cultural relativism and neoabsolutism—come together to argue. If this proposition is accepted and cross-cultural fertilization is permitted, then one can revive the tradition of Muslim rationalists and dissociate authenticity from the Islamist agenda of "cultural purification."

With the exception of fiqh orthodoxy, in classical Islam there existed no fault lines between the "self" and the "cultural other." The conflict between rational knowledge and fiqh jurisprudence over what is authentically Islam took place within Islamic civilization. Today's conflict is different: it revolves around the exposure of Muslims to a modernity that exerts its pressure from outside the umma. Since the nineteenth century this exposure has triggered a variety of responses, none adequate to the challenge. Islamists today are compelled to live with this legacy. Escaping cultural modernity is not really an option.

The contemporary exclusionary and purist Islamist mindset did not exist in early Islamic modernism. The first Muslim imam to go to Paris, Rifa'a Rafi' al-Tahtawi, lived there from 1826 to 1831, and he opened his mind to the non-Muslim other: to Europe and to modernity. He was amazed to find that when Europeans talked about science, knowledge, and scholars, they meant something different from what Muslims meant. In Arabic, the term *alim* (plural: ulema) means scholar, but it refers to a cleric, a man of religion. In French, the same vocabulary points to a different meaning. Tahtawi wrote in his *Paris Diary*[28] that secular knowledge, not religion, is the concern of a European scholar. In Islamic scholarship, which consists of "commentaries and supercommentaries" for the interpretation of the Qur'an, an alim is a person who has a mastery of religion and is thus a cleric. The Islamic identification of knowledge with religion was gradually abandoned, but the Islamic view of the world changed only slightly, with the result that Islam suffered an intensifying predicament with cultural modernity.[29]

Unlike Tahtawi, who acknowledged that Muslims needed to learn from others, contemporary Islamists have chosen to close their minds and engage in cultural purification. Earlier in this book I took issue with Tariq Ramadan's claim that his grandfather Hasan al-Banna, the founder of Islamism, was an intellectual descendant of the nineteenth-century revivalist al-Afghani. This alleged continuity never existed: the comparison between al-Afghani and al-Banna is baseless. Afghani was open-minded; he related the decay of Islamic civilization to the "ignorance" of Muslims. The rise of the West and its colonial rule over others, Afghani acknowledged, relates to the superiority of their scientific knowledge over that of non-Europeans. He specifically described the Muslims of his time as *juhala'* (ignorants)[30]—which is pretty strong language. In Islam, *jahl* (ignorance) is associated with unbelief, and jahilliyya is used to describe the Arab world's pre-Islamic state of ignorance. Afghani's usage, then, was roughly similar to an Englishman's describing his countrymen as "heathen" or "savages" and recommending that they absorb the values of another culture. The Islamist al-Banna, with his agenda of cultural purification, takes the exact opposite view.[31]

Islamism considers the superiority of Islam to be beyond question and takes it as grounds for the claim to purity. Islamists are reluctant to acknowledge that Muslims today lag not only behind "Western science" but also behind the earlier standards reached by their own civilization.[32] A complacent sense of superiority and consequent reluctance to learn from the cultural other is a hazard for any civilization; but it has reached new highs in the recent Islamist agenda of the cultural purification of knowledge. The need of a "knowledge society" is not on the Islamist agenda.

I have repeatedly drawn on Hedley Bull's idea of a "revolt against the West." This is not only about contesting Western hegemony. The revolt is also directed against "Western values as such," including the idea of a continuous advancement of knowledge. De-Westernization thus includes purification against science. This antiscience[33] attitude is combined with the instrumental adoption of science and technology. This happens in a mindset of semimodernity, which means to adopt the instruments and reject the underlying values. This mindset prevents Muslims from developing their own science and would keep them forever borrowing technologies from the cultural other. This flaw is combined with all of the unpredictable cultural effects that new technologies create. The need for ever more stringent forms of purification would be never-ending. Muslims would remain trapped in their predicament with cultural modernity.

The discourse of Islamic civilization in its high days was determined not by the search for purity, but by openness to learning. Unlike the Muslim rationalists of the past, today's Islamists engage in a politics that generates ever-increasing cultural tensions emanating from the Islamist purification agenda based on fault lines between the self and the cultural other. This drive is detrimental to the future of Islamic civilization. Muslims, rather, need a way to open themselves to the cultural other without abandoning their own authenticity. They need to revive the legacy of their medieval Islamic heritage for promoting cultural change. The tradition of Islamic rationalism is in line with modern science and with Max Weber's "disenchantment of the world."[34] It offers the way out of the predicament with modernity.

I have often been accused of Orientalism (or, given my background, "self-Orientalization") simply because I take a Weberian approach in my study of Islam. There are, of course, pitfalls to Orientalism, but one must also beware of Orientalism in reverse. Postmodernists tend to promote antisecular and antiscience views in the name of authenticity. But today Muslims need science. One may respect cultural particularisms, and also authenticity, and yet set limits and subscribe to a universal thinking based on humanism. I contend that this humanism existed in the Islam of Averroës and Ibn Khaldun. These men were not only universal rationalists but authentic Muslims who, if they lived today, might also find themselves condemned by Westerners for "self-Orientalization." It is not Orientalism to oppose the Islamist antiscience position.

Bringing Back the Humanism of Islamic Rationalism

Given that the purity ideology of political Islam not only lacks authenticity but is also detrimental to Muslims, a revival of Islamic rationalism is a far better option. In their own interest, Muslims need to engage in creating a new tradition that includes interaction with other cultures. There is a lesson to be learned from the Islamic past: Muslims cannot both have their cake and eat it. A new tradition cannot succeed without a clear and unequivocal stand against fiqh orthodoxy and Islamism.

The process of Hellenization was initiated by the Christian Nestorian translators in the late eighth century and lasted from the ninth through the twelfth centuries. These translations made Greek writings available in Arabic. In *The Beginnings of Western Science,* the historian David Lindberg tells us: "By the year 1000 A.D. almost the entire corpus of Greek medicine, natural philosophy, and mathematical science has been rendered into usable Arabic versions." Then Lindberg asks: "Was there a religious price that had to be paid for the acceptance of Greek science?"[35] The answer is that Islamic rationalists had fallen under the illusion that they could come to terms with the fiqh orthodoxy, and they paid dearly for this belief: accused of damaging the purity of Islam, they were excommunicated from the umma. Their mistake was that they did not take a clear stand and did not defend their school of thought. Their conciliatory attitude did not pay off; their books were burned in public.

The purity argument revolves around what is acceptable as a cultural source of knowledge. In the Salafist Islamic orthodoxy tradition, the foremost knowledge is that which is transmitted through revelation as fixed in the Qur'an. The acceptance of Greek science suggested a competing view: a pattern of knowledge based on human reason and also acquired from non-Islamic sources. The resulting clash between fiqh and falsafa led to a continuing rivalry between Islamic orthodoxy and reason-based Muslim thinkers. There are Muslims who open their minds to the cultural other and those who close their minds in the name of authenticity of knowledge. The competing options are articulated in the classical formula *bi al-wahi aw bi al-'aql* (either by revelation or by reason). One or the other is supposed to be the sole source of valid knowledge. This dichotomy stands in contrast to Averroës's *haqiqa muzdawaja* (double truth), advanced by Muslim rationalists in an effort to honor the divine while recognizing a separation between knowledge based on the religious worldview and rational knowledge that emanates from human reason. Each has its own domain. Today, the source of knowledge is the central issue in Islam's predicament with modernity.[36]

It is difficult for a Muslim like myself to conceive that there are Muslim scholars teaching at Western universities (for instance, the British-Muslim professor Ziauddin Sardar)[37] who disparage Cartesianism, the rationalism of cultural modernity, as "epistemological imperialism." In Islam, there were once better times. During the Abbasid period, under caliphs like the great Harun al-Rashid and his son al-Ma'mun, philosophers were honored and promoted. The caliphs "cultivated a religious climate that was relatively intellectual, secularized, and tolerant,"[38] and also supported the Mu'tazilites as "defenders of reason."[39] Other centers for these cultural borrowings and their integration into Islam were in Córdoba and Toledo in Islamic Spain. Unlike Mawardi,[40] who put *wahi* (revelation) above *aql* (reason)—and unlike the vigorous philosophers of the French Enlightenment—Islamic rationalists compromised in an attempt to avoid conflict. In arguing that revelation and reason could coexist, they believed that they had solved the problem. Unlike Voltaire, they refrained from applying their rationalist ideas to a rethinking of religious doctrine.

It is a sad fact that knowledge in Islamic civilization has been primarily determined by the ulema orthodoxy and its establishment. These clerics succeeded in undermining the development launched by the Hellenization of Islam. The ulema also established a hostile distinction between "alien sciences" or "sciences of the ancients" (the Greeks, the *qudama'*) and Islamic sciences. The first were reason-based, while the latter were related to the study of religious doctrine, primarily the exegesis of Qur'an and hadith. These "Islamic sciences" also include shari'a learning, as well as the philological disciplines required for dealing with the divine texts. The fiqh scholars insisted on the holistic validity of revelation as the sole and unrestricted source of true knowledge in all realms. Even though the caliph al-Ma'mun established the dar al-hikma (house of wisdom) as a kind of Islamic academy of sciences, this vision was never realized. The major institutions of Islamic learning remained exclusively in the hands of the ulema. As George Makdisi writes in *The Rise of the Colleges,* Islamic orthodoxy controlled the madrasa as the Islamic institution of higher learning and maintained its purity against the impact of the alien *ulum al-qudama'* (science of the ancients). Lindberg tells us, "Greek learning never found a secure institutional home in Islam. . . . Islamic schools would never develop a curriculum that systematically taught the foreign sciences. . . . From the middle of the ninth century until well into the thirteenth, we find impressive scientific work in all the main branches of Greek science being carried forward throughout the Islamic world . . . but during the thirteenth and fourteenth centuries, Islamic sciences went into decline, and by the fifteenth century, little was left."[41]

Thus if we wish to know why rational and scientific thought in Islam did not gain a permanent foothold, the historical record helps us eliminate two proposed answers. Rationalism did not fail because it was an alien system of thought imposed on Islam by Jews and crusaders: Hellenism flourished well before either group was in a position to force anything upon the Islamic world. Nor did it fail because the Muslim scholars were simply translators who added nothing to the Greek learning they appropriated, as alleged by certain racist German Orientalists. (Despite my reservations about the Saidist cult of Orientalism, the accusation fits those who advance this prejudice.) There is no doubt that Islamic scholars did a great deal to develop their adopted Greek legacy. Historians of science agree that Muslim civilization in the medieval age had the most advanced science in the world.[42] The reason for its decline lies elsewhere. In *Meaning and Moral Order,* Robert Wuthnow argues that the institutionalization of knowledge is most essential for the maintenance of science.[43]

Systematically excluded from institutions of education, scientific thought could not be successfully diffused into the Islamic worldview. It could not strike roots. In a needless war between rationalism and faith, rationalism lost out, and the tradition of science in Islamic civilization failed to give birth to modern science.

It would be wrong to infer from this that the sciences were marginal in Islam. Naturalization, if not partial assimilation, took place to a certain extent. But it was undermined by the orthodoxy. The control of the educational system allowed fiqh orthodoxy to prevent the spread of scientific thought and thwarted the efforts of Islamic rationalists. The inherited religious conception of the world's divine order continued to prevail in Islamic civilization.

The absence of a rationalist view of the world, of humanity, and of nature has had enduring and detrimental effects. The cultural and institutional drive toward purity created by fiqh orthodoxy that ruined Islamic civilization in the past continues to burden the present. It was not "a conspiracy hatched by Jews and crusaders against the world of Islam" that caused the decline of Islamic civilization but rather the very insistence on purity that fiqh orthodoxy by then imposed and Islamists of today wish to reclaim. Only in the most ironic sense can Islamism be termed an "Islamic revival," as a revival of this fiqh tradition. Yet the contemporary Islamist agenda of purification is quite recent and in this shape unprecedented in Islamic history.

The cultural and epistemological agenda of Islamism heralds a setback into an age of flat-earthism. That agenda is formulated by the Saudi-funded International Institute of Islamic Thought as follows: "The pursuit of knowledge in Islam is not an end in itself; it is only a means of acquiring an understanding of God. . . . Reason and the pursuit of knowledge . . . are subservient to Qur'anic values. . . . In this framework reason and revelation go hand in hand. Modern science, on the other hand, considers reason to be supreme."[44]

The Islamist alternative to modern science employs an epistemology that would purify Islamic thinking and alienate Islamic civilization from modern scientific knowledge. Epistemologically, Islamism fails to meet the requirements for a "knowledge society."[45] Politically and historically it falls back behind the accomplishments of Islamic heritage, in particular with regard to a rational thinking about the proper polity.[46]

The Futility of Dogma

The phrase "Islamic revival" is widely misused in the West; already I have questioned this formula. The foremost Muslim thinker of the nineteenth century, Afghani, was a genuine revivalist, but contemporary Islamists are clearly not. Afghani argued that the European powers were able to colonize the Islamic Middle East through their superior knowledge of the world. The Islamist slogan al-hall huwa al-Islam (Islam is the solution) advocates lesser knowledge of the world. Afghani believed that the dominance of Europe over the world of Islam reflected "the hegemony of states and peoples, who have science and thus are able to dominate over those who are weak. . . . In other words, power and science enable [one] to rule over weakness and ignorance. This is a cosmic law."[47] The only similarity between Afghani and the Islamists is that both related modernity to instruments and not to a rational worldview. The reform Afghani envisioned failed because he was not poised to change the Islamic worldview.

Afghani was keen to see himself as the Martin Luther of Islam. But because he lacked the courage, or perhaps the will, to introduce to Islam the religious reform and related cultural change that Luther had introduced to Christianity, Afghani remained a lesser figure. The comparison between them is not only presumptuous but baseless. Nonetheless, Afghani was better than the Islamists, because he was sincere about the adoption of modernity and never engaged in a fake authenticity based on a fictitious and fickle ideology. But his revivalism had a limited scope, and his attempted religious reform failed.

If a religious reform is established on the grounds of a religious dogma that remains unquestioned, then this way of thinking presents insurmountable obstacles to modernization. The sociologist of religion Niklas Luhmann, commenting on the social function of a religious dogma that seeks to answer all cosmic questions, observed that "religious dogma departs from

unanalyzed abstractions and thus . . . it does not consciously reflect on its
social function but rather understands itself, its concept of dogma, dog-
matically. . . . On the other hand, it rests on a universal and contextless
applicability, hence on a certain disregard of the bonds it interprets."[48]

Despite their great differences, Islamists and revivalists share a similar
understanding of the religious dogma in that they fail to rethink, or even
question, the validity of dogma itself. But while nineteenth-century Islamic
modernism remained basically scripturalist, acting exclusively within dogmatic confines, Islamism engages in an invention of tradition that is imbued with modernity. Islamism engages in an instrumental adjustment to
modernity but resists any effort at cultural modernization.

The Islamist project of "semimodernity"[49] attempts to separate modern instruments from cultural values and as a result leads to an impasse.
The commitment of Islamists to authenticity based on a purification agenda
is a venture that leads nowhere. In this sense early Muslim modernists were
better off, because they were more open minded.[50] On the model of Karl
Popper's "open society," I have coined the notion of "open Islam" to denote
a tradition from others and thus navigators in different waters from those
of Islamist purification.

The futility of religious dogma in Islam can be illustrated on the bulk
of the contemporary literary production in Arabic. This literature is quan-
titatively enormous but mostly poor in substance. Among the hundreds of
thousands of books written by Muslims in the recent past one seldom encounters as courageous a book as *Critique of Religious Thought*[51] by the
Yale-educated Muslim philosopher Sadik Jalal al-Azm. It was not a surprise to see that his thinking was not welcomed. After the book's publication, al-Azm was hounded by the state, by the fiqh orthodoxy, and of
course by Islamists. His Yale education was invoked to support an accusation of lack of purity. He was accused of kufr (unbelief or heresy), an ugly
weapon employed by Islamists. The Islamist takfir—that is, the classification of a Muslim as having "become an unbeliever"—is not idle, since it
could legitimate an assassination as a divine execution. In dogmatic Islam,
there is no liberty of conscience. Talk about purity and authenticity does
not resemble a free academic debate in which disagreement is supposed to

be tolerated. Powerful scholars in a free society have many ways to undermine unwelcome knowledge, but they cannot execute their foes.

Free debate on Islam's predicament with modernity exists neither in the world of Islam nor in the West. There are not only threats and repression but also sanctions by those who do not admit that there is any such predicament. Most fearful are the accusations of heresy or cultural treason made in the name of protecting authenticity, whether by Islamists or by authorities intent on safeguarding a politically correct academic culture. It is sad to see how some liberal Europeans and Americans not only embrace Islamism but also dismiss any distinction between Islam and Islamism.

Mohammed al-Jabri and I are both Muslims who believe that the future can only be Averroist. Al-Jabri writes that "the survival of philosophical tradition is likely to contribute to our time. . . . The Averroist spirit is adoptable to our era, because it agrees with it on more than one point: rationalism, realism, axiomatic method, and critical approach."[52] In the name of the authentic Islamization of knowledge, Islamists promote a competing agenda. The International Institute of Islamic Thought summarizes it this way: "*Fiqh, usul al-fiqh,* and *shari'a* are the greatest expression of Islamic spirit, it is absolutely necessary to make these contents readily available to the research school in each of the specific disciplines of modern times. . . . *Fiqh* and *shari'a* are the quintessence."[53]

The old conflict within medieval Islam between the fiqh orthodoxy and falsafa rationalism is inflamed again, but under different names and circumstances. There is once again a fight between scientific thought of a rationalist worldview and the divine, but this time it is presented as a conflict between Islam and the West. In fact one can find advocates on both sides in both civilizations.

It is amazing to see these similarities between the past and the present. Today, Islamists argue that all scientific findings should be subjected to shari'a. Like proponents of the medieval fiqh orthodoxy, they check the compatibility of modern thinking with Islam and only on these grounds admit its validity. When I read what David Lindberg writes about that past, I am reminded of the present on all counts: "Conservative religious forces made themselves increasingly felt. . . . Science became naturalized in

Islam—losing its alien quality and finally becoming Islamic science, instead of Greek science . . . —by accepting a greatly restricted hand-maiden role. This meant a loss of attention to many problems."[54]

A similar Islamization of knowledge is taking place today in the name of authenticity and purity. The result is a general Islamist purification not recognized in the U.S. academy, where scholars are obsessed with upgrading the instrumental adoption of science in a mindset of religious orthodoxy to an "other modernity." As a Muslim political scientist I fail to see in this semimodernity an authentic "other modernity." Its flat-earthist epistemology reminds me of the disastrous past when the Islamic fiqh orthodoxy ended the tradition of rational science in Islam.[55] The inference is clear: Islamism is neither a postmodernity nor the other modernity.

If Islamism prevails, then the loser is Islamic civilization in its predicament with modernity. The only U.S. political scientist known to me who masters Arabic like a native-speaker, John Waterbury, shares this assessment. Waterbury, who was professor at Princeton University before he assumed the presidency of the American University of Beirut, 1998–2008, knows intimately the world of Islam. Waterbury believes that if Islamization of knowledge succeeds, then "a new era of flatearthism" would be the outcome. In his view a kind of epistemological authenticity "may emerge in the Middle East in which the epistemology underlying social inquiry will be rejected as a culturally alien importation, a tool of the adversaries of Arabs and Islam."[56] Waterbury wrote this forecast in a chapter to the 1988 book *The Next Arab Decade,* edited by the late Palestinian Muslim historian Hisham Sharabi. As described in this chapter, that era has come to pass, just as the present book sees light, a sad reality for Arabs and Muslims. Waterbury is also the coauthor of the authoritative book *Political Economy of the Middle East.* There he begins one chapter with the question "Is Islam the Solution?"—an allusion to a major Islamist slogan. He ends the chapter: "The answer to the question at the beginning of this chapter is no."[57] Since I couldn't agree more, I have nothing to add.

8

Islamism and Totalitarianism

ISLAMISM IS A POLITICAL RELIGION;[1] it does not fall from heaven. It originated in 1928 and became a powerful force thanks to two watershed moments: first, the crushing Arab defeat in the 1967 war, which uncovered a deep crisis related to the lack of democracy combined with unsuccessful development, both attributed to the ruling authoritarian regimes; and second, the end of the cold war. This smoothed the way for what Raymond Aron described as "unveiling the heterogeneity of civilizations."[2] The West, however, was not prepared for any such unveiling. With the demise of totalitarian communism, the West assumed that its own values would prevail and that global democratization would proceed unhindered. Francis Fukuyama famously declared "the end of history."[3] This forecast did not take into account the rising challenge of Islamism. The new global conflict over civilizational values then just beginning to emerge was utterly overlooked. Even today, many continue to deny that this conflict exists.

To this intercivilizational conflict (which, as I explain below, is not to be confused with Samuel Huntington's "clash of civilizations")[4] add the situation within Islamic civilization, which is at war with itself. The conflict has partly to do with the lack of democracy: the record of democratization in the world of Islam is extremely poor. With few exceptions, such as the pre-AKP Kemalist government in Turkey and civil Islam in Indonesia after the fall of Suharto, most Islamic states are ruled by authoritarian regimes. This is not the only way in which Islamic civilization has underachieved. Failed democratization coexists with unsuccessful development.[5] The two shortcomings reinforce each other, creating a deep crisis that leads some scholars to speak of Islam's civil war.[6] Islamism emerges out of these two levels of conflict and it makes this "war" a geopolitical one.

Lawrence Harrison argues that we should enhance the concept of structural development (economics and politics) to speak also of developing cultures.[7] The inference is that one has to include value systems and the related worldviews in analyzing development and world politics. Values are as subject to change as structures are.

The Attraction of Islamism

The crisis of Islam[8] is structurally determined, but it is also normative and related to values and identity politics.[9] Islamism not only emerges from this crisis but presents itself as the exit strategy. Its appeal stems from its dual nature: it promises to provide both a political-social solution and also religious salvation. Religion provides meaning,[10] and if we attempt to consider it reductively, as another form of economic consideration, we can never understand the issues surrounding Islamism. Political Islam is a totalitarian ideology that presents itself as the proper vehicle for implementing al-hall al-Islami,[11] the Islamic solution, a kind of magic answer for all of the problems—global and local, socioeconomic or value-related—in the crisis-ridden world of Islam. The Islamist flag attracts a growing constituency; what was a trend has become a mass movement thriving especially after the Arab Spring of 2011.

In a spirit of self-victimization, Islamism discards all other options as hulul mustawradah (imported solutions) and holds the cultural other responsible for all of the misfortunes that have befallen the world of Islam.[12] But the expectation of salvation that Islamism raises has gone entirely unfulfilled in Iran under the mullahs and in Afghanistan under the Taliban.[13] Sudan came under Islamist rule when the current dictator, General Omar al-Bashir, made an alliance with the Sudanese Muslim Brothers under the leadership of Hasan al-Turabi. Turabi was later put in jail, but the regime's Islamist perspective was not abandoned. In Iraq and in Palestine, Islamists killed more Muslims than non-Muslims ever did. None of these varieties of Islamism has delivered either democracy or development. Nor has Hamas in Gaza. In many other countries, the political organizations of the Islamist movement are still in opposition, waiting to seize power to establish the envisioned shari'a state. By the time this book is published they may already have done so in Egypt and elsewhere in the context of the Arab Spring.

In the West, a proper response to failed development and the lack of democracy requires that we critically assess the feasibility of the Islamist promise of an "Islamic solution." It is important to understand how much Islamic civilization matters to the West since the breakdown of the Soviet Union and the return of Islam to world politics. It matters especially to Europe. The lack of democracy and flawed development in the world of Islam have caused massive numbers of Muslims to migrate to Europe in the hope of a better life. Today this diaspora amounts, according to an unofficial estimate, to 23 million people, most of whom are unintegrated and living on welfare, in ethnicized enclaves of parallel societies that carry great potential for conflict.[14] The assessment of a successful "integrating of Islam" in Europe runs so strongly counter to the facts[15] that it amounts to self-delusion. Because of its inability—and unwillingness—to integrate its Muslim immigrants, Europe today courts serious trouble, but it is a trouble Europeans are reluctant to acknowledge. The lack of integration contributes to a process of ethnicization of the Islamic diaspora and to making young European-born Muslims highly susceptible to Islamism with the potential of an "ethnicity of fear."[16] Those who speak of post-Islamism seem not to know what they are talking about. How can a phenomenon subside if all of the forces that gave rise to it remain powerfully in place?

Let us return to the crucial distinction between Islam and Islamism. This distinction is not recognized, for instance, by the legal scholar Noah Feldman, who in *The Fall and Rise of the Islamic State* weighs the options and concludes that a shari'a state, as envisioned by Islamists, could be "the most promising development in Islamic law," but that it also could be "a disaster waiting to happen." Yet on balance, and even though he is knowledgeable enough to concede other possibilities, Feldman seems to believe in the viability of the Islamist option. He speaks of the "Islamist promise of the rule of law" without spelling out what law the Islamists are promising. He also seems to accept the "compatibility of shari'a and democracy"[17] and endorses the shari'a as "Islamic constitutionalism."

There are a number of flaws in any thinking that would ally Islamism with constitutionalism. Feldman, who seems not to understand the Islamist claim to supremacy (siyadat al-Islam), apparently believes that once you get past the specifics of the legal code (Islamists endorse the severing of thieves' hands, lashing of suspects and stoning; democracies don't), one legal system is much like another. This is a misconception. In Chapter 6 we saw that historically, shari'a has three different meanings: it is morality as revealed in the Qur'an; it was traditionally interpreted by the faqihs as the cult rules and civil code of ibadat and mu'amalat, and the penal code of hudud; and under Islamist ideology it would become a state order. To which of these does Feldman refer? He confuses all these levels of meaning.

The same criticism applies to his use of the concept of democracy. Is democracy a mere procedure of the ballot box, or does it relate elections to a civic culture of pluralism? Nothing is spelled out. Let Islamists come to power, Feldman seems to say, and then we shall see. My prediction is that the crisis of derailed democratization and flawed development will intensify. This ongoing crisis promotes Islamist movements but cannot be solved by Islamism. We have seen what Islamism has delivered in Iran: the ballot manipulation practiced under Islamist rule in 2009, when Ahmadinejad was "reelected" in a fraudulent procedure. The mass upheaval of young Iranians against the rule of Islamism, and the bloody crackdown that followed, illustrate the extent of the Islamists' commitment to democracy: it is a mechanism for getting and keeping power.[18] Iran is a Shi'ite state, but any Sunni Islamist movement that comes to power is unlikely to behave differently.

The results of Feldman's wait-and-see attitude are likely to be apparent elsewhere soon enough. There are two Sunni states in the world of Islam where the record for the future will be set—where we will find out once and for all whether the Islamist solution actually solves anything. One can state with certainty that Shi'ite Iran will not be the model for Islamists elsewhere to emulate. Ninety percent of the world's Muslims (1.7 billion) are Sunni. The Shi'a are the majority in Iran and Iraq but a minority in most other places. Sunni Muslims are highly prejudiced against the Shi'a and do not trust Shi'ites. Sunnis would never accept Shi'ite leadership. Apart from

Iran, Iraq, Gaza under Hamas, and the earlier Taliban state in Afghanistan, Sunni Islamists do not rule but are in opposition. The countries that matter most as potential models of Islamist rule are the Sunni states Saudi Arabia and Egypt.

Let us begin with Saudi Arabia. Despite all odds, and despite the troubled waters in which the Saudi dynasty navigates, the Wahhabi regime of this tribal kingdom remains stable for the present.[19] Saudi Arabia is a traditional tribal monarchy, not an Islamist state, though it uses Islam as a source of legitimacy. Wahhabism is a variety of Salafism (orthodox, traditional Islam), not Islamism. Even though the Saudi monarchy continues to support Islamist movements—mostly for expediency—the Islamists do not hide their desire to replace the Wahhabi order of Saudi Arabia with their nizam Islami. This, however, is not likely to happen very soon. Major Islamist leaders are pragmatic; they know that Saudi Arabia needs their blessing and is willing to pay for it most generously. It appears that the Muslim Brothers have traded their agenda for Saudi funds, which buy their silence about Wahhabism, at least in Saudi Arabia and probably in the Islam diaspora in Europe.

The other country that matters, Egypt, is a different case. Egyptian Islamists could come to power soon, possibly with American assistance. Could Egypt under the Muslim Brothers, who have been upgraded to the "new Islamists," become a model for Islamist democracy and development? Will Islamists become moderate? These questions matter far beyond Egypt. The forecast of a "democratic" Islamist shari'a state in Egypt stands in contradiction to the totalitarian order I describe later in this chapter.

John Waterbury of Princeton University has provided the best account of the political economy of development in postcolonial Egypt.[20] This distinguished former president of the American University of Beirut describes how the Egyptian experiment of development ended in a failure that was inherited by the Mubarak regime, which followed Anwar Sadat's assassination in 1981 and fell in 2011. Islamists are today close to attaining their goal of seizing power via the ballot box, most disturbingly with American and European support. This happened under different conditions in Turkey, which has been ruled since 2002 by the Islamist AKP. As shown in Chapter 4, the AKP curtails civil freedoms, including that of the press, and undermines the Kemalist secular accomplishment while the Western press remains silent about what Zeyno Baran has called Turkey's "creeping Islamization." Most of the Western media accept the AKP's self-description as "Islamic-conservative" and view the plan for a new constitution[21] approved in September 2010 as "democratization" even while it tightens the AKP's grip on Turkey's secular institutions.

To be sure, Turkey and Egypt are different cases. Turkey retains a strong secular elite and a strong secular army. Both are pillars of declining Kemalism and are opposed to Islamism. Turkey is not yet an Islamist state, even though it is changing under AKP rule. In a "Letter from Istanbul," the *New York Times* columnist Thomas Friedman wrote, "Turkey's Islamist government seemingly focused not on joining the European Union but the Arab-League—no, scratch that, on joining the Hamas-Hezbollah-Iran resistance front against Israel." Moreover, though it is geopolitically important for Europe, Turkey does not have Egypt's religious weight. Egypt is not only geographically central, it hosts the most authoritative religious institution in Sunni Islam, al-Azhar University. It is second only to Saudi Arabia—with its two major mosques—in being at the cultural center of the Sunni-Muslim world. The sheikh of al-Azhar is the authority who issues fatwas valid for all Sunni Muslims. Egypt matters more for the future of the world of Islam than Turkey ever will.

Today in Egypt, the Islamists have become the most powerful political opposition group. Since the death of Gamal Abdel Nasser 1971, and in particular since the 1980s, the Movement of the Muslim Brotherhood has penetrated most professional institutions and associations of Egyptian society.[22] The prospects for a regime change that brings Islamists to power after the fall of Mubarak in Egypt would have ripple effects throughout Islamic civilization that far exceed those of the 1979 Islamic revolution in Iran. Of course, the army is poised to prevent this, even after the Arab Spring. The Muslim Brothers, misidentified as "moderate Islamists," could receive U.S. blessing. A reliable source tells me that among the audience at President

Obama's June 2009 speech in Cairo were fifteen high-ranking leaders of the Muslim Brotherhood. According to Egyptian sources, they were invited with Obama's consent. Another source reports back-channel communications between the thriving Muslim Brothers and the European Union. These hints of Western acceptance, while unconfirmed, are worrisome.

Decision makers in Washington are often blamed for failing to learn from their mistakes. In the 1980s they supported the mujahidin in Afghanistan against the Soviet Union without inquiring into the nature of their ally.[23] Years later they were shocked to find the jihadists they once supported attacking them through their proxies in Europe and the United States. During the summer of 2010 the *New York Times* frequently reported that the Taliban were fighting American troops in Afghanistan with weapons the United States had supplied in their war against the Soviet occupation in the 1980s. When al-Qaeda cells that originated in Germany struck in the United States on September 11, 2001,[24] one might have expected that the American decision makers would have learned a lesson. But they seem to have learned the wrong one, because they still fail to distinguish between Islam and Islamism. Instead they see a difference between "moderate Islam" and a terrorism they are now reluctant even to call "jihadist." U.S. policymakers fail to distinguish between method and ideology: some of the parties they support as "moderate" have very immoderate ideas. The huge mistake made by President George W. Bush following 9/11, when he employed the term "crusade" to announce his determination to defeat Islamic jihad, is being addressed by an Obama administration that abandons the terms "jihad" and "jihadism" altogether. This is not moderation but a move from one extreme to the other.

A serious Egyptian scholar, Emad El Din Shahin, believes the prediction of disaster in Egypt should the toppled Mubarak's rule be followed by that of the Muslim Brothers is exaggerated. In a paper written for the European Union think tank CEPS, he first makes the following realistic statement: "The ability of the Muslim Brotherhood to organize . . . demonstrations despite government harassment attests to its organizational skills and popular influence."[25] In a way Shahin is right to say that the political success of the

Muslim Brothers justifies their inclusion in a democratic system. Not only the Islamists' considerable popularity but also democratic principles demand this. Moreover, he is aware that the inclusion of the Islamist movement in the political process has to be combined with "institutional guarantees and strong safeguards that would prevent any force—radical Islamic, etc.— . . . from sabotaging any future democratic gains."[26] Shahin recognizes that democracy is based on pluralism that allows "different visions and perspectives." But he does not take the next step and ask what are the Islamist visions and perspectives. Are they consonant with secular, pluralist democracy? Have the Muslim Brothers abandoned the concept of shari'a as a divine order? Shahin speaks of "change" within the movement but adds no further specification. The Muslim Brothers also claim to have changed, but do not specify what this change consists of. They forgo violence, but a commitment to democracy requires much more. There is no evidence that their assurances are anything other than iham, deception. The movement's positions on Israel and the Jews, its support for Hamas, its efforts to highjack the Muslim diaspora in Europe, and its use of Islamist education as indoctrination have not changed.

Still, Robert Leiken and Steven Brooke of the Nixon Center state their approval of the Muslim Brothers in an assessment published in the influential policy journal *Foreign Affairs*.[27] Though Leiken is not considered a scholarly authority on the Middle East (his Web page lists his areas of expertise as European Muslims, immigration and integration, terrorism, and Latin America), his opinion is in line with those expressed by other scholars in Middle Eastern Studies, such as Raymond Baker and Bruce Rutherford, and more recently by Marc Lynch (also published in *Foreign Affairs*).[28] These scholars seem to believe that Islamists are the only political power eligible to replace the corrupt authoritarianism of the Mubarak regime with a promise for a better future. This assessment ignores the fact that the Muslim Brothers endorse regime change but not the values of democratic pluralism. A post-Mubarak Egypt ruled by the Muslim Brothers would be a disaster for the country and the region. Egypt would incrementally become a Sunni version of Iran, but all the more dangerous because it would appeal to the Sunni majority of the Islamic umma. The first policy measure of a

Muslim Brotherhood regime in Egypt would be to vacate the Camp David peace with Israel and throw the country's support to Hamas. This prospect has become most likely after the Arab Spring.

Hannah Arendt and Islamism

The German *Kaiserreich* was abolished in the aftermath of the First World War, not long before the last Islamic order of the caliphate also fell. In Germany, the failure of development and democratization[29] in the 1920s, followed by a worldwide depression in the early 1930s, helped Hitler's National Socialist Party come to power on the ruins of the Weimar Republic. Could something similar happen if Islamists were to come to power on the ruins of the authoritarian secular regimes now falling one after the other in the world of Islam? In this chapter I not only draw on the work of Hannah Arendt to compare the two histories but also make predictions while knowing that people "ignore predictions they dislike."[30]

Let me pause here to review some things the Islamic state order, al-Nizam al-Islami, is not. We have seen that almost no Islamists advocate the restoration of the Caliphate that was abolished in 1924 when Kemal Atatürk came to power and established modern Turkey as a secular state. Neither is it "Oriental despotism," a formula coined by Karl Wittfogel in a book of that title.[31] Islamist rule, real or envisioned, cannot be properly described as traditional despotism. Finally, under the Bush administration, the notion of "Islamofascism" was introduced and used interchangeably with "radical Islam," but it was rightly rebuffed. While other critics of Islamism not allied with that administration have since employed the term, I disagree with its usage. Paul Berman and Jeffrey Herf,[32] on whose research Berman draws, both disclose Islamist-fascist connections. Still, I'm not fully convinced that the phenomenon of Islamism can be adequately conceptualized as fascism. I prefer the concept of totalitarianism.

In previous chapters I stated that the political order of nizam Islami in Islamist thinking is a religionized politics and that the notion of din-wa-dawla, unity of religion and politics, is an expression of a totalitarian ideology. If Islamists were to abandon this ideology, one might then speak of "post-Islamism." In that case they would no longer be Islamists and might even become liberal Muslims. But no such development is in sight. There is also no such thing as "democratic Islamism," any more than there is a "democratic totalitarianism." The interpretation of Islamism as a totalitarian ideology poised to establish a totalitarian state leans on the theory put forward by Hannah Arendt in *The Origins of Totalitarianism*. In this seminal study, Arendt argues that any regime that emanates from a failure of democracy and development, as the Nazi regime did, and is in addition antisemitic, can be viewed as totalitarian.[33] The basic feature of totalitarian ideologies is that they regulate every aspect of human life and leave no free space for the individual. Adorno's and Horkheimer's *Dialectics of Enlightenment* explains how enlightenment turns into its reverse in a crisis-ridden situation. In Chapter 1 I touched on the pertinence of this idea to the unfolding of Islamism from Islam, but here I shall confine myself to examining the validity of Arendt's approach to the study of Islamism.

In addition to the Nazi regime, Arendt also studied communist totalitarianism in an effort to compare the two. My study of Islamism follows the tradition of comparative political theory she established. Just as Arendt does not lump together Nazism and Stalinism, I do not lump jihadist and nonviolent Islamists together when I argue that both are totalitarian. One may ask whether Arendt still matters, or whether her theory of totalitarianism was too rooted in the specifics of her own time to offer much guidance on the very different political realities of our own era.[34]

While pondering this question I discovered a book by a former student of Arendt's, Elisabeth Young-Bruehl,[35] who had had the privilege of completing her Ph.D. under Arendt's supervision and later became her biographer. The book's title, *Why Hannah Arendt Matters,* suggested that Young-Bruehl was wrestling with similar questions. It turned out that some of her concerns were not merely similar to mine but identical. It is true, she writes, that Arendt dealt with secular totalitarian ideologies, not with religion. Nonetheless, national socialism and Stalinism functioned as political religions.[36] Some of today's intrinsically religious ideologies, Young-Bruehl argues, are directly comparable with the earlier two secular totalitarianisms. In her view, "religious ideologies both grow from and foster the kind of supersense that had characterized the totalitarian ideologies. For those who subscribe to them, religious ideologies have an irrefutable logic."[37]

In view of this interrelation between politicized religion and totalitarian ideologies, I maintain that contemporary Islamism is the most prominent case of a political religion. It can be interpreted with the assistance of Hannah Arendt's work as a new kind of totalitarianism. As I stated earlier, I limit my reference to Arendt's first two levels: ideology and movement. I leave aside the applicability of the third level, political rule. As a prominent example that supports this contention, I refer to the Islamist movement of the United Islamic Front, established by Osama bin Laden "as a kind of imperialism or a kind of totalitarianism." The pronouncements made by this movement are not new; Young-Bruehl is aware that the roots of bin-Ladenism go back to "the Muslim Brotherhood led by the Egyptian Hasan al-Banna." The historian Jeffrey Herf has recently shown that Banna made highly favorable statements about Hitler. One is amazed to learn that the movement Banna established enjoyed the support of the Eisenhower administration in its fight against communism. Today, American pundits praise the movement as the "moderate Muslim Brotherhood," but Young-Bruehl does not buy into this; she states that U.S. support for Islamism represents "one of the most threatening ways that adopting totalitarian methods to fight totalitarianism helped shape the current world order. [This] was in practice adopted by U.S. governments."[38]

Yet Young-Bruehl, like the American decision makers she rightly criticizes, does not distinguish Islamism as something separate from Islam. Only on the grounds of this distinction is it possible to argue that Islamist thinking—whether institutional or jihadist—is a totalitarian ideology while Islam is not. This new ideology is not merely a political religion as earlier secular ideologies were. It claims to rest on the salvation of real religion. Applying Arendt's ideas to Islamism decouples the issue from the unhelpful notion of "radical Islam" and the preoccupation with "terrorism," a preoccupation that leads to shortsighted analysis and leaves us incapable of grasping the political religion of Islamism. The attacks of 9/11 charged the study of Islamism with a persistent focus on jihadist terrorism that has been detrimental to both scholarship and politics. The myopic obsession with terror leads analysts to ignore the substance of the phenomenon and to forget that terrorists do not grow on trees. Neither world poverty and globalization nor the Palestine conflict can ever convincingly explain the phenomenon of Islamism. Even worse is the explanation of jihadist Islamism as a criminal activity whose perpetrators should be dealt with through law enforcement and the courts. This only leads to cowboy-style efforts to chase down jihadists and kill them, as American armed forces did with al-Zarqawi.[39] More recently, the Obama administration succeeded via a covert action in Pakistan in executing bin Laden instead of bringing him to a court. Obama's promise that the world is safer after the death of bin Laden reflects an uninformed view, for two reasons. First, even before bin Laden was killed, the jihadist branch of Islamism had been declining in influence relative to institutional Islamism, a development utterly misconceived by some and viewed wrongly as post-Islamism. Second, after 9/11 and the ensuing war in Afghanistan, a development occurred that has been described as "leaderless jihad"; as a result, al-Qaeda lost its function and its central command even while bin Laden was alive and hiding. In short, the impact of killing bin Laden is not as great as Obama suggests. The movement is still alive.

Daniel Benjamin and Steven Simon, in an *International Herald Tribune* article entitled "Zarqawi's Life and Death," remarked that "the jihadists comprise a social movement, not just a cluster of terrorist organizations."[40] To this astute warning against reductionism one needs to add that Islamist movements religionize politics and social issues. The term "social movement," if not specified, is still misleading. When Hamas, for instance, is praised as a social movement, it constitutes a healthy recognition that jihadists are not simply a bunch of terrorists, but it ignores their role within a transnational political movement in which religion plays a key mobilizing function.[41]

In short, Islamism is neither "the other modernity," "radical reform," a "liberation theology," nor a "movement of resistance," as some of its spokesmen persuade people to believe. We need Arendt's guidance to see past these deceptions. *The Origins of Totalitarianism* was written in the years following the Second World War and was completed in autumn 1949. Nazi Germany had been destroyed, but Stalinism, and Stalin himself, still ruled the

Soviet Union. In making it clear that "totalitarianism is not merely dictatorship," Arendt sets out three levels of analysis: the ideology, the movement, and the rule. As I have stated, I limit my discussion to the first two levels, ideology and movement, and leave aside the applicability of the third level, political rule. The most important feature of any totalitarianism, Arendt writes, is "the permanent domination of each single individual in each and every sphere of life." Later she adds that "totalitarian movements can command the same total loyalty in life and death."[42] This is the same loyalty that all Islamist movements demand from their followers. It is more than mere submission to a dictatorship.

The question arises of why totalitarianisms *need* antisemitism. The need for loyalty and obedience at the extreme level demands that a totalitarian movement construct an enemy with certain characteristics, the most basic of which is what Bernard Lewis described as "cosmic, satanic evil" (see Chapter 3). The enemy must exist within the society even while its loyalties are outside the society. The constructed enemy must be *absolutely* evil. Its battle against good must have a cosmic dimension. The ideology of antisemitism fulfills this need. The constructed "world Jewry" functions as the ultimate evil that affects humanity's ultimate fate. This enemy need not be the Jews. But Islamism has adopted from Nazism the view of the Jews as a "cancer on society," as Hitler put it, whose complete annihilation is required before humanity can fulfill its destiny.

In general, totalitarian movements "aim at and succeed in organizing masses, not classes." Like the masses Arendt described, the politicized umma that Islamism aims to mobilize against the kuffar (unbelievers) is subjected to "adherence to a fictitious world." The Islamists argue that Islam is "under siege" by an imaginary enemy, "Jews and crusaders." Here again we must appreciate the distinction between Islam and Islamism. Islam is a monotheist world religion that acknowledges Judaism as a monotheist world religion. Islamism adopts from Nazi ideology the idea that "the Jews" present an existential threat, and like the Nazis they employ *The Protocols of the Elders of Zion* to support this view. The imagery of antisemitism is at the center of Arendt's book. She writes: "The motive of a global conspiracy in the Protocols . . . appeals most to the masses."[43] This pattern of antisemitism is at the core of any totalitarian ideology. Though Islamist ideology insists on purity and authenticity, the fraudulent *Protocols* are extensively cited in most Islamist pronouncements.

The threat of "world Jewry," as depicted in the *Protocols,* must be impressed on the movement's followers. Indoctrination is essential inside the movement when it is still in opposition, but when the movement takes over and possesses control of government institutions, indoctrination becomes official policy and gains effect throughout society. It functions not only to control and discipline followers but to sustain their loyalty. This feature is characteristic of totalitarian movements, which demand total, unrestricted, unconditional, and unalterable loyalty and in which indoctrination is combined with terror to prevent deviance. The movement equates deviation with treason. All followers who fail to comply are punished with execution. During the occupation by the Israeli Defense Force, Hamas[44] killed more Palestinians in Gaza than Israeli soldiers ever did.

Another area for comparison is the use of democracy. The Nazis had as much contempt for democracy as do today's Islamists. Nonetheless, they did not mind taking advantage of the ballot box. Arendt wrote that "totalitarian movements use and abuse democratic freedoms to abolish them."[45] As the Nazis did, Hamas and Hezbollah use democratic institutions in order to seize power. Following the elections of 2006, Hamas abandoned democracy; a year later it arrested all the leaders of the opposition. Some 450 members of the Palestinian Liberation Organization were jailed without trial, ending this organization's effectiveness as a political force. The movement denounces the American prison at Guantánamo Bay while employing the same tactics. This is the Hamas variety of Islamist democracy. Western media rightly publish disclosures about Guantánamo, but they are silent about Hamas prisons in Gaza. The same applies to Turkey under AKP rule.[46]

In Lebanon, Hezbollah plays the same game under much tougher constraints. Hezbollah is represented in the Lebanese parliament and government, but unlike Hamas it is not yet in a position to seize full power. Nonetheless, Hezbollah is powerful enough to forbid the Lebanese air force to fly over its territory. In 2008 the air force violated this restriction, and one of its fighters was shot down. The air force took no action, allowing Hezbollah to set a precedent. Is this the sort of organization one can trust to remain committed to a democratic system?

Arendt writes that on all three levels, ideology, movement, and political rule, totalitarian systems deny the separation between the private and the public spheres. Islamism is no exception. Islamist ideology subordinates society to a comprehensive state apparatus designed along shari'a-based rules. The Islamist idea of the shari'a-based "Islamic state" clearly reflects a totalitarian order. This vision is not yet a reality, but what we can see of it is not at all promising. The Sunni Islamic state of Hamas in Gaza, the former Taliban in Afghanistan, and the current de facto one in the Swat Valley of Pakistan, as well as the Shi'ite Islamic Republic of Iran, do not give a favorable taste of this state order. Anything identified by the totalitarian Islamism as "un-Islamic" is to be eradicated, so this kind of order leaves no space for pluralism and diversity. Among the Taliban, the control of individual behavior extends to forbidding literacy among women and even controlling personal dress and facial hair. These are taken as outward signs of a loyalty that one is expected to internalize completely and absolutely.

As opposition, the Islamist ideology promises to provide salvation, but once in power it fails to deliver anything positive. As Arendt writes, "Practically speaking . . . totalitarianism in power is not an unmixed blessing for a totalitarian movement. Its disregard for facts, its strict adherence to the rules of a fictitious world, becomes steadily more difficult to sustain, yet remains as essential as it was before."[47]

Arendt's analysis of violence as a practice of terror has some relevance to the Islamist movement, but her focus is on the state. I shall leave this aside, but note that it is necessary to modify her ideas somewhat. In Islamism the jihadization of Islam is pursued by nonstate actors, not by a state. The pattern of an irregular warfare is conducted in anticipation of establishing the totalitarian order. This happens in an invention of tradition. In Arendt's terms, "The pronounced activism of the totalitarian movements, their preference for terrorism ranks over all other forms of political activity."[48] In the process of shari'atization of politics, Islamist movements establish their own law in the name of God. The Islamist shari'a to which these movements refer does not exist in the Qur'an in the meaning they employ. Nor can one find the Islamist shari'a in the canonical accounts of the Prophet or any other authoritative sources. Islamist shari'a is an example of what Arendt identifies as the arbitrary understanding of law practiced in totalitarian movements.

When Islamists execute their opponents, they do this as an act of law. This terror is for them "the realization of the law of movement," as Arendt argues, adding that "terror as the execution of a law of movement . . . eliminates individuals for the sake of the species, sacrifices the parts for the sake of the whole."[49] This insight explains how "true believers"[50] sacrifice their lives in suicide missions to advance the good of the umma. In so doing they combine the shari'a law of the movement, which has little to do with traditional shari'a, with jihadist terror, which also barely resembles classical jihad.

In their fight against an imagined enemy, totalitarian movements combine terror with a war of propaganda. This is, in Islamist terms, a war of ideas, harb al-afkar.[51] They enact a law of tadhiya (sacrifice) embedded in a combination of indoctrination and propaganda war. The invented shari'a law of the movement prescribes sacrifice, not "dying to win."[52] The only thing the true believers hope for when they die as *shahdid* (martyrs) is to enjoy the comfort of salvation, not "virgins" in paradise as the sexual-Orientalist fantasies of some Western writers suggest. This is the nature of totalitarianism, which demands from its followers total submission and upgrades this expectation to a religious duty.

The Roots of Totalitarian Islamism

In this book I have argued against, among other things, the work of John Esposito, Raymond Baker, Robert Leiken, Marc Lynch, and many similar-minded Western writers. Unlike those who express various shades of approval of Islamism, I argue that the Muslim Brotherhood and all of its offshoots—even the so-called moderate branches[53]—are best viewed as totalitarian Islamism.[54] To be sure, Islam is compatible with democracy, but Islamism is not. My critique of Islamism is also in the interest of Muslims who wish to protect Islam from abuse by a totalitarian ideology that distorts its tolerant spirit.

Yet instead of enlightening people about the distinction between Islamism and Islam, many scholars are doing the opposite. Major Islamists like Qaradawi and Ghannouchi are introduced to Western audiences as voices of "liberal Islam."[55] This does a great disservice to true civil and liberal Islam. If academic freedom means anything, one has to be permitted to identify Islamism as a totalitarian movement, and to support this assertion with the relevant arguments, without being defamed as "bashing Islam." This happens equally in the United States and in Europe, where such arguments risk being labeled Islamophobic. That Europe is becoming not only a shelter but also a battleground for Islamism[56] is well known to the intelligence community but disregarded by politicians who want to avoid controversy.

On the rare occasions when commentators recognize the undemocratic nature of Islamism, it is dismissed as a trend restricted to a minority of extremists. Yet the two great totalitarian ideologies of the twentieth century, Nazism and Leninism, also began as minority movements. Islamists have successfully used madrasas and faith schools, both in the world of Islam and in Europe, to spread their ideology in a deliberate policy of recruitment and indoctrination. The Muslim Brotherhood has been able to win the hearts and minds of many young Muslims for its war of ideas. Arendt describes how the dissemination of a totalitarian ideology through propaganda and indoctrination happens on all levels. In the case of Islamism, it takes the form of an invention of tradition in the course of a reinterpretation of Islamic doctrines such as jihad and shari'a. The work of Sayyid Qutb serves as a foundation for this ideologization of Islam.

While pondering the roots of Islamism, we need to acknowledge the return of religion and ask whether the process of global desecularization that coincided with the end of bipolarity is really a religious renaissance. With 9/11, the debate over the return of the sacred turned to the world of Islam. On one side of this debate one finds Jürgen Habermas, who speaks in a benign manner of a "postsecular society"[57] and thus demonstrates his failure to understand what Islamism is all about. In *Glauben und Wissen* (Faith and knowledge), Habermas seems to abandon the commitment to the cultural secular order of the world. I contend that Hannah Arendt's theory of totalitarianism is more helpful for understanding religionized politics than is Habermas's "postsecular society."

Beyond this, however, we should also incorporate Hedley Bull's idea of "political order," because Islamism is about a remaking of the state and the world. Bull understands order as the pivotal subject of world politics.[58] An order can be democratic, dictatorial, despotic, or totalitarian. It is difficult to imagine a composite of the four. The order the Movement of the Muslim Brotherhood envisions—that is, the order of a nizam Islami based on a political shari'a invented by Islamism—bears no democratic features whatsoever. The remaking of the state and the world to reorder it along the tenets of the shari'a as constructed by Sayyid Qutb is in no way a politics of democratization. After a closer look, the Islamist order can be unraveled as a totalitarian system.

Since Samuel Huntington's controversial article "The Clash of Civilizations?" appeared in *Foreign Affairs* in 1993, there has been a heated debate about the post–cold war "remaking of world order." In this debate it has been overlooked that this point is correct, but the problem is the use of the term "clash" and not "intercivilizational conflict." These terms refer to different issues. Before Huntington, Sayyid Qutb, in *al-Islam wa mushkilat al-hadarah* (Islam and the problems of civilizations), posited "a clash" between Islam and its enemies, "the Zionists and the crusaders." The idea of hakimiyyat Allah, God's rule, based on "shari'a, the Islamic way of life and its worldview,"[59] was presented as the Islamist alternative to Western-secular concepts of order. If the issue were to be addressed in terms of conflict, then negotiation would probably replace the polarization implied by "clash."

Stated in a nutshell: the agenda of a *pax Islamica* pursued by the Muslim Brotherhood reflects a totalitarian ideology; the Islamist variety of religious fundamentalism in the pursuit of a remaking of the world to conform to hakimiyyat Allah. This new totalitarianism does not restrict its goals to the abode of Islam but is designed for the world at large. The "moderate" (institutional Islamist) Muslim Brotherhood is, like the jihadist al-Qaeda, a movement based on internationalism in the Marxist sense.

The two elements in Hannah Arendt's theory, movement and ideology, are applicable for understanding contemporary Islamism as a combination of "medieval theology and modern politics."[60] While this ideology draws on Islamic tenets and claims authenticity to justify its politics of purification, the reference to Islamic tradition not only is highly selective but also heralds an invention of tradition. There remains the third issue in Arendt's theory, the political rule. Why is the envisioned Islamist shari'a state a totalitarian rule?

Islamism, Not Islam, Is the New Totalitarianism

The return of the sacred reaches Europe via migration and the related transnational religion,[61] but the distinction between Islamism and Islam draws attention to the order of hakimiyyat Allah, God's rule,[62] envisioned by Islamism, and contrasts it to a liberal-civil Islam compatible with democracy and civil society. The example of a progressive Islam is also an argument against people like Bruce Bawer (whose book *Surrender* I discussed in Chapter 1), who confuse ordinary Muslims with Islamists. It is true, both in the world of Islam and in the diaspora, Islamism threatens the open society, but Islam does not.

With that said, one can safely and without prejudice examine the claim of Islamism to present a political order. Qutb writes: "The overall and comprehensive revolution of Islam prescribes fighting jihad as a duty on all Muslims for establishing the centrality of Allah [rabbaniyya] and his rule [hakimiyya] on all earth. . . . Therefore, jihad is an idea of world revolution [thawrah alamiyyah]. . . . In Islam jihad is a permanent fight."[63] This is an agenda for the remaking of the world. It is neither "radical" nor "fanatic" Islam but a new phenomenon. Isn't it legitimate to counter this agenda, as Jean Bethke Elshtain[64] proposes, in defense of open society?

The novelty of Islamism is supported by the fact that orthodox religious doctrines in Islam make no mention of either "revolution" or hakimiyyat

Allah. Nor do they mention the jihadist pattern of irregular war as a means of "remaking the world." These are all inventions of tradition, yet they bring with them the sincere belief that the tradition is authentic, combined with a nostalgic notion of civilizational awakening in a "revolt against the West."[65] Again, however, this is not an instrumental use of religion: the people contesting secular values honestly are "true believers." The invented connection between religion and civilization becomes pertinent to the study of international relations because Islamism opposes on civilizational grounds the secular international system as well.[66]

In this civilizational revolt against the West, cultural fragmentation assumes a totalitarian shape. The civilizational rejectionists dismiss the notion of universally valid and accepted norms and values, including those of democracy and human rights. For nonstate actors aiming at a general de-Westernization and purification, above all in the field of knowledge, religion helps legitimate the political order envisioned by Islamism. Nazism, too, wanted to purify German culture by de-Westernizing Germany.

When religion is politicized in the "revolt against the West," political Islam becomes the frame of reference for all relations to the West. This venture ends up in a call for a totalitarian order, hakimiyyat Allah. Democracy is depicted as popular sovereignty that replaces the sovereignty of Allah, something that cannot be permitted. Establishing democracy thus becomes a most difficult undertaking in an age of Islamism.

The conflict between secular democracy and the hakimiyyat Allah leads to a conflict that Mark Juergensmeyer has labeled the "new cold war." The differing views about secularization and desecularization become elements of conflicting world political visions. I use the term "inter-civilizational conflict"[67] to conceptualize the tensions that result from the combination of value conflict and competition between two orders. Following Qutb and Mawdudi, the contemporary Islamist Yusuf al-Qaradawi argues against "liberal Islam" and dismisses democracy as hall mustawrad (an imported solution) alien to Islam. It is perplexing to see Qaradawi included in a U.S. reader on "liberal Islam."

It is a rhetorical strategy of some leaders of Islamist movements to make use of democracy for their own ends. Here again one can draw on

Hannah Arendt's insight that totalitarian movements exploit and abuse democracy. Despite their deep contempt for liberal democracy, institutional Islamists employ Western democratic and civil rights to establish their movements. They have had some success in the United States and Western Europe, and are also drawing American support in the world of Islam. Will the United States support institutional Islamism (for example, the Muslim Brothers in Egypt) in the misguided belief that it offers a pathway to democratization in the context of the Arab Spring?

Islamism reimagines the Islamic umma and aims to mobilize this imagined community through the use of identity politics. Constructed memories of past Islamic glory are revived in a hopeless dream of the return of a nonexistent history. At the same time, Islamists are embroiled in a worldtime determined by Western civilization. The term "worldtime," coined by Theda Skocpol of Harvard, refers to the fact that each civilization has its own calendar. The European calendar underpins today's worldtime. Islamists try to reverse this process in reviving the Islamic hijra calendar. In this pursuit they aim to mobilize the umma as an imagined community.[68] There is no distinction between jihadist and institutional Islamists when it comes to creating trenches between "we" (the umma) and "they" (the West of "crusaders and Jews"). But despite its rhetoric of unity, Islamist internationalism is divided along the sectarian lines of Sunna and Shi'a. Iran's failure to export its "Islamic revolution" was determined by this sectarian divide. The totalitarian Islamist state in Iran motivated a few scholars to study Islam in terms of a foreign policy[69] legitimated by a politicized transnational religion, but this approach faltered in the face of reality: Islamism is largely a Sunni phenomenon of nonstate actors that resemble one another but are not united in one movement under a single leadership.

The Islamic State and the Rhetoric of the Clash of Civilizations

If the Islamist ideology is totalitarian, it follows that Islamism is not an Islamic variety of constitutionalism. John Kelsay phrases the crucial question posed by institutional Islamism as "Who will provide the primary definition to world order? Will it be the West or will it be Islam . . . with its emphasis on the universal mission of a transnational community?"[70] This defines the competition over the design of world order as a political conflict between religious and secular views. For the time being, Islamists are not in a position to deliver their envisioned order. They are, however, in a position to generate international destabilization. They can employ the tactics of asymmetrical war to compensate for the West's technological superiority and create international disorder.[71]

In addition to the accusations of Orientalism and Islamophobia, another of the conversation killers one encounters in contemporary scholarship is the inclination to associate every scholar who studies Islamist internationalism with the rhetoric of the late Samuel P. Huntington's "clash of civilizations." Among the flaws in Huntington's work, besides his missing the distinction between Islam and Islamism, is his failure to grasp the "defensive culture" in which Islamism politicizes the intercivilizational conflict of values. Still, despite my disagreements with him, I must acknowledge that Huntington at least made the debate on civilizations a legitimate topic in international studies. Even though he has contaminated the term "civilization" in his contentious book on this subject, it is utterly wrong to defame him as a cold war ideologue attempting to find in Islam a "substitute to the Soviet Union" as the "needed enemy of the West." The most important aspect of the Huntington story is its use in silencing those who forecast scenarios of conflict between values and worldviews of competing civilizations. This happened again in the damaging reviews of Paul Berman's book *The Flight of the Intellectuals,* in which he not only criticizes Islamism but also deplores Islamists' success in "imposing" their "own categories of analysis over how everyone else tends to think" about Islamism.[72]

It is more useful to relate Islamism to the developmental crisis of the nominal secular nation-states in the Middle East and to deal with the challenge of the new interpretation of Islam as din-wa-dawla—a unity of religion and state used as an ideological device to legitimate an "Islamic state." Islamism challenges the validity of the secular democratic nation-state to the world of Islam and promotes the alternative of hakimiyyat Allah, God's rule. As I argued in Chapter 2, this drive for an Islamic state is what Islamism is all about. This concept of Islamic government is a construction of a to-talitarian Islamist "we" against "they" within an internationalism based on Islamist ideology. The Islamist concern is neither faith nor democracy but the nizam Islami, the Islamic system.[73]

Islamism admits only its own law. This is not the vision of an innocent political opposition participating in a pluralistic democracy. To understand the Islamist threat to security we need an approach that goes beyond the state and beyond conventional military wisdom. Islamism is not under-stood well by experts in security studies, who still operate in old paradigms that cannot deal adequately with politicized religion practiced by nonstate actors in well-organized totalitarian movements.

Islamist movements draw on shari'a law not in the sense of modern constitutionalism, as Noah Feldman suggests, but to justify their drive for power. In this pursuit they see their violent acts not as mere terrorism but as jihad war on the existing order of the world. They wage war not only with arms but with propaganda, and camouflaged as "democrats," they also act within institutions.

The agenda of Islamism is to mobilize the Islamic umma in order to establish the totalitarian order called nizam Islami. Jihadist violence is only a means toward this end. But given the cultural and religious diversity within Islamic civilization, including the difference between Sunni and Shi'ite Mus-lims, this order could never comprise the single entity that Islamists envision. This entity exists in the minds of the Islamists, who, in an echo of "clash of civilizations" rhetoric, imagine an Islamic collectivity acting as a monolith that rules the world.

In assessing the Islamist "revolt against the West," one has to concede that if the movement were politically restricted to contesting the excessive power of the West and resisting cultural Eurocentrism, it might legitimately deserve endorsement. But the vilification of "crusaderism" as a power act-ing in alliance with a demonized Jewish conspiracy is something from which every non-Islamist Muslim should dissociate himself. This Islamist mindset inflames its adherents against the values of liberal democracy and secular humanism. It is not "Islam-bashing" to oppose this mindset. I see in the heritage of Islam not only the seeds of enlightenment but also the "grammar of an Islamic humanism"[74] with the potential to be revived in opposition to Islamism. The Islamist worldview is one of counterenlightenment and totalitarian ideology, not the ethic of a legitimate resistance movement.

Islamism fights a war of ideas over normatively different understandings of five issue areas: the state, law, religion, war and peace, and knowledge. The absence of intercivilizational consensus on these issues can, if politicized, generate conflict. The resulting "war of civilizations" has little to do with the strategic or economic concerns that usually generate wars in the West; it is a war over values and worldviews.[75] The conflict happens on three levels, domestic, regional, and international. At present, it revolves around the question "What world order?" Will it be the liberal one or the totalitarian order of hakimmiyyat Allah—God's rule as envisioned by Islamism? One of the reasons the conflict is so intractable is that the two notions of world order are based in entirely different kinds of ideas. The Western definition, as John Kelsay writes, relies on the "notions of territorial boundaries, market economies, private religiosity, and the priority of individual rights," while the Islamist hakimiyyat Allah is based on the "universal mission of a transtribal community called to build a social order founded on pure monotheism natural to humanity."[76] There seems to be no ground for compromise between these fundamentally different ideas. Some argue it is about a cultural misunderstanding, while in reality it is about a real conflict.

The dialogue that is needed between Islam and the West is one between liberal Islam and liberal democracy in the Kantian mindset of democratic peace.[77] Between Islamists and those security obsessed Westerners who believe in an appeasement of Islamism, there can be no satisfactory discussion or mutual understanding. The West's true partners are "the other Muslims, moderate and secular."[78] Only with them can there be a dialogue free of the extremes of both Islamophobia and islamophile apologetics. The honest dialogue has to take place within a mindset of bridging with a goal of conflict resolution.[79]

9
Civil Islam as an Alternative to Islamism

I N THIS BOOK I have made an effort to describe the ideology of Islamism to Western readers and to dissociate it from the faith of Islam. I have argued that Islamism is not the heritage of Islam but is a contemporary political interpretation of Islam based on an invention of tradition. Among the themes running throughout this book is the tension within Islamic civilization. As in the past, when Islamic rationalist philosophers—from al-Fatabi to Ibn Rushd (Averroës)—stood against the fiqh orthodoxy, liberal Muslims today stand against Islamism. Islamism is not Islam, but neither does Islamism stand outside of Islam. The stereotype of a monolithic Islam must be done away with. Both the Islamists and (genuinely) Islamophobic Western writers argue in a simplistic manner—of course with different intentions—that there is only "one Islam." In fact one encounters in both Islam and Islamism simultaneous unity and diversity.

Why Is Islamism Not Islam?

The major argument of this book can be rephrased as follows: In a time of both normative and structural crises, some Muslim political activists have reinvented Islamic traditions to produce something new, called Islamism. These figures included Hasan al-Banna, Sayyid Qutb, Abu al A'la al-Mawdudi, and various successors such as Yusuf al-Qaradawi. A marginal tradition from 1928 to 1967, Islamism became a major current in the Sunni Arab world in the aftermath of the Arab defeat in the Six-Day War of 1967. Islamism is an example of an invented tradition which brings previously marginal elements of Islam, especially its anti-Jewish currents, to the center.

This is done by selectively choosing passages from the Qu'ran and the commentaries on it, the hadith, and taking them out of their context. The result is an antidemocratic, totalitarian vision that aims at reshaping the order of the state and subsequently the entire system of world politics. Islamism seeks to replace the existing system of sovereign states that emerged following the Peace of Westphalia in 1648 with an order of the state centered on a conception of divine law. Following the French Revolution and the European expansion, the international system created under the Peace of Westphalia spread around the world. The doctrines of Islamism envision a reversal of this historical process. Islamism is at its core a form of Jew hatred because it believes that "the Jews" rule the world and hence are in conflict with Islam. Islamism also rejects democracy, a branch of it justifies violence, and it has no objection in principle to the use of terror. The advocacy of shari'a law, which it represents as a return to traditional practice, is a modern invention. Islamism subjects the individual to an all-encompassing ideology that is a new form of totalitarianism. It is the Islamists' ability to evoke the traditions of Islam, however distorted or inaccurate, and their claim to Islamic authenticity that accounts for their ability to reach a broad audience of Muslim populations. Western writers who belittle Islamism as marginal, or who view it as a secular cover for social concerns such as the expression of grievances, fail to understand how an invented tradition becomes appealing and powerful via a selective reading of the much larger traditions of Islam itself.

In this book I take issue, first, with the Islamists themselves, deconstructing their claim to be the correct interpreters of Islam; second, with those in the West who wrongly believe that Islamism is the logical outgrowth of the religion of Islam; and third, with those in the West who are favorable to Muslims—sometimes in the name of realism—but embrace those Islamists labeled "moderate Muslims" because they reject terrorism. None of these three groups of people seem to grasp what Islamism is. I analyze each of the six historically specific, distinctive features of Islamism in a separate chapter. In Chapter 8 I find in Islamism a new totalitarianism.

Why do I believe this book is urgently needed? Why did I write it as the last work of my academic career? I wrote this book as a social scientist in an effort to describe and explain a new phenomenon; the politicization of the religion of Islam to a concept of state order. The basic distinction between Islam and Islamism is a means by which to elucidate the related issues. While in substance this book is an academic inquiry, I have repeatedly professed two other leading concerns. First, I hope to defend Islam against Islamism (and against defamation through its association with terror); and second, I hope to contribute to the bridging of the divides between the civilizations of the West and of Islam. Neither of these goals is realistic without first establishing the distinction between Islam and Islamism.

World events wait for no author. While I was writing, for example, a controversy arose over a proposal to build an Islamic center, including a mosque, near the site of the 9/11 attacks in New York City. Without engaging in a comprehensive analysis of this debate, I find in the controversy relevance to the theme of this book. As the *New York Times* reported on August 8, 2010, "While a high profile battle rages . . . in Manhattan, heated confrontations have also broken out . . . across the country." The *Times* added that "in all of the recent conflicts opponents have said their problem is Islam itself." One finds the same view expressed in many other influential publications. For instance, a former federal prosecutor, Andrew McCarthy, writes in *The Grand Jihad,* "I'm not a Muslim, and I appreciate that there is a plethora of Islamic forms. . . . Hair-splitting between Islamism and Islam runs the risk of doing exactly what we must avoid doing: minimizing the challenge confronting us." It is amazing to see that McCarthy, who is not favorable to Islam at all, approvingly quotes the founder of Islamism, Hasan al-Banna, who believes his Islamist ideology to be true Islam. McCarthy comments, "Banna was right," and supports this allegation with the argument that if all Muslims and Islamists share the belief that "shari'a is obligatory," then there exists no distinction between Islam and Islamism. Yet in chapter 6 of this book I elaborate on the Islamist invention of shari'a tradition, acknowledging that the Islamist shari'a al-Banna advocates is not classical shari'a. Furthermore, McCarthy quotes the Turkish prime minister Recep T. Erdoğan's comment that the distinction between Islam and Islamism is "offensive and an insult to our religion." "Is it wrong, then," McCarthy asks, "to shrink from the conclusion that the real problem is

Islam?" He answers this question by quoting Andrew Bostom, who contends that "Islam and Islamism were synonymous."[1] My answer to McCarthy's question is that he and Bostom are wrong: Islamism is not Islam.

Three Basic Distinctions

I have in this book argued that for a proper understanding of Islamism, one needs to look at three basic distinctions:

1. *Political religion and the problematic of political order.* Islamism emanates from a politicization of religion. If this politicized religion were simply an indication of cultural differences, we could make room for it in the name of diversity. But Islamism, as an Islamic variety of the global phenomenon of religious fundamentalism, is uniquely focused on the international order. Islamists mobilize on religious grounds in the pursuit of not only an Islamic state but a remaking of the world. The jihadists among them engage in irregular war as a means of establishing a totalitarian order. The shari'a state is not an Islamic variety of constitutionalism but the nucleus of an order embedded in the Islamist quest for a global *pax Islamica.* This goal is shared by nonviolent as well as jihadist Islamists.

2. *The practice of violence as a holy terror and irregular war of nonstate actors.* Not all Islamists are jihadists, but all jihadists are Islamists, who fight for their goals not by political means but on a battlefield whose definition—abhorrently to non-Islamists—has been expanded to include office buildings, subways, and urban sidewalks. While institutional Islamists forgo violence and publicly distance themselves from this jihadism, they have not abandoned their ambitions for Islamic governance and the Islamist order. On the other hand, jihadist Islamists practice violence as "holy terror" within a war of incompatible value systems. To be sure, all Islamists are Muslims, as they stand within Islam. To criticize them is not an offense, since non-Islamist Muslims are the majority of the "Islamic umma" of 1.7 billion people living across the globe.

3. *Islamism and the conceptual framework of religious fundamentalism.* Political Islam or Islamism (the terms are interchangeable) is conceptualized as a religious fundamentalism. Some scholars dispute the application of the term "fundamentalism" to Islam. For instance, Robert Lee confesses:

"I side with those who do not find this term helpful."[2] Unfortunately, he does not support this objection with any substantive arguments. It is true that the term has become a cliché, but beyond its considerable life as a sound bite it remains a useful concept for studying the politicization of religion. The Fundamentalism Project of the American Academy of Arts and Sciences establishes the concept's scholarly authority. The politicization of religion is a global phenomenon of which Islamism is an important instance.

In short, Islamism is a vision of a world order based on politicized religion, a movement that contains a branch committed to sacral violence, and an expression of the worldwide phenomenon of religious fundamentalism. These three aspects define Islamism as religionized politics. The nonstate actors of the jihadist branch of Islamism can never be countered by state armies, as the United States is still attempting to do in Iraq and Afghanistan with no success in sight. There is a need for more complex strategies—true also for dealings with Iran—where Islamism is in power. The West also needs a strategy for dealing with institutional nonviolent Islamism, which presents the most powerful opposition to several existing governments—and may have taken power in one or more nations by the time this book is published. Nonetheless, the West lacks such strategies.

Islamism, Europe, and the World at Large

Over the past few decades, Islamism has gone global; it exists both in the world of Islam and in its diaspora in the West. For a number of reasons, Europeans are more directly confronted by Islamism than the United States is. Among these reasons are the geopolitical neighborhood—the world of Islam is at Europe's borders—and the rapidly increasing size of the Islamic segment of Europe's population (23 million in 2010). Europe needs to learn how to live with Islam and truly engage its Muslim immigrants by granting them a citizenship of substance, beyond merely giving them passports. In Europe there is a process of ethnicization of Islam, from which Islamism not only benefits but actively takes advantage.[3] This can be averted only by integrating Muslim immigrants into full citizenship, by making them "citizens of the heart." Just as democracy is hollow if it exists only at the ballot box and is not a part of people's everyday values and expectations, citizenship is hollow if it exists only on paper. By the same token, Muslim passport Europeans are not real Europeans if they reject Western values and prefer to live in enclaves legitimated as communitarian parallel societies.

The totalitarian movement of Islamism acts within a geopolitical triangle consisting of the Islamic states, Europe, and the Muslim diasporic culture in the West. There is a need for policy—not for policing, and certainly not a "war on terror"—to better integrate relations among these three sides. Of course one has to counter jihadist terrorism, but the rhetoric of crusade only defeats that purpose. To deal effectively with Islamism and Islam, the United States and Europe—despite being allies—need different strategies because they are in utterly different situations and do not share entirely the same interests.

There is, of course, a Muslim community in the Unites States, and while part of it is sympathetic to Islamism,[4] that group is a small fraction of the Muslim population, and it presents less difficult problems than does European Islamism. Muslims have certainly faced discrimination in the United States, but because they are among many immigrant populations in a country with a long tradition of (eventually) accepting newcomers, they are not as ghettoized as they are in Europe. The U.S. approach to Islamism is more focused on foreign policy. President Obama's first two visits to Islamic countries, in April and June 2009, promised a wind of change, and the mere fact of such visits and significant speeches so early in his presidency testified to his (and the United States') sense of the region's importance. I repeat the combination of applause and criticism: the Obama administration aims to bridge the divide, but it fails to account for the distinction between Islam and Islamism and does not deliver what it promises.

The challenge of Islamism for Europe is tougher than for the United States,[5] and there is no wind of change. Europe is host to a tremendously growing yet barely integrated Islamic diaspora, and Europe is next door to the Islamic world. As a longtime resident of Germany, I can testify to the Europeans' failure to win the hearts and souls of Muslim immigrants, to integrate them as true Europeans, or even to see that this is something at which they should make an effort.[6] The contradictory extremes of policing and facile goodwill pronouncements aside, Europe is doing little to avert the hijacking of the diaspora, especially its youth, by Islamism.

Some authors view Europe today as the battlefield of Islamism, while others see it as the place where Islam can be reformed and made compatible with the principles of civil society. Islamists have been successful in abusing their religious rights in European civil society to establish Islamic enclaves where fundamentalists can gain influence. This European connection is pertinent, but it should not conceal the fact that the threat of Islamism is not restricted to Europe but is general and even global.[7] To fight radical ideologies of all sorts, including political Islam, one needs a strategy that avoids entrenchments. In Europe I have put forward the concept of Euro-Islam[8] as a bridge between civil Islam and enlightened inclusionary Europe. The values of the open society[9] are to be unambiguously stated and protected. For the world at large one needs a cross-cultural morality to prevent "the clash of civilizations."

Is Islamism Anti-Islamic?

Given that Muslims constitute more than one quarter of humanity, the competition between civil Islam and Islamist totalitarianism matters to everyone. It certainly matters to those who live with Islam, whether within their own borders or in their geopolitical neighborhood. The bottom line for living together in peace is to solve Islam's predicament with modernity.[10] This requires that the Islamic world not only free itself from the misery of authoritarian regimes and embrace secular democracy but also resist Islamism's presentation of itself as "the alternative," or al-hall al-Islami, the Islamic solution.

Islamism is not an alternative for a civil society because it does not accept the core values that, in a civil society, must be shared by all. Islamists refuse to share power, and therefore the pluralism of civil Islam is alien to them. Islamist ideology rejects modernity, democracy, and civic culture.[11] Nonviolent Islamists pay lip service to a democracy that is reduced to a procedure of a ballot box, but vehemently dismiss its values. They do not abandon the hopeless goal of Islamization. Only non-Islamist Muslims can solve the crisis Islamic civilization is undergoing, but they must avoid solutions that only deepen the crisis.

Given that Islamism is the new totalitarianism, Muslims cannot afford to let Islamists speak for their civilization. Above all, they cannot put their future in the hands of a movement that leads them nowhere. The message to the West is that it must forgo the luxury of cultural blind spots it can no longer afford. The Enlightenment produced countless benefits, but it also led Westerners to adopt a particular view of the proper relation between the secular and the sacred—and then to absorb this view so thoroughly that they seem to forget that it is not universally shared. While in London in January 2008 for the opening of the University of London's new Center for the Study of Radicalization, I heard an address given by Jacqui Smith, then the Labour British secretary of the Home Office. The next day, the *Daily Mail* gave this account of her speech: "Ministers have adopted a new language for declarations on Islamic terrorism. In future fanatics will be referred to as pursuing 'anti-Islamic activity.' Home Secretary Jacqui Smith said that extremists were behaving contrary to their faith. . . . Miss Smith repeatedly used the phrase *anti-Islamic*. . . . Her words were chosen to reflect a new government strategy on labeling terrorists and their recruiting agents."

This prompted an editorial comment in the same issue: "If al-Qaeda attacks tomorrow, the bombers should, according to Miss Smith, not be described as Islamic terrorists, but as engaging in anti-Islamic activity. It is like describing the Nazis as being engaged in anti-German activity. Goebbels would have been proud of such doublespeak."[12]

To give the home secretary credit for honesty, her concern should be cited: "Linking terrorism to Islam is inflammatory and risks alienating mainstream Muslim opinion." But this is precisely why we need to grasp the distinction between Islamism and Islam. One must be able to condemn Islamist terror while respecting the religion of Islam. Otherwise we are simply buying into the jihadists' self-definition as representing all of Islam. Smith, like most other Western politicians—including President Obama's counterterrorism adviser, John Brennan—misses this point. If scholars were to follow her absurd characterization, then Islamists could continue to defame any criticism as Islamophobia and make a false parallel between antisemitism and anti-Islamism to camouflage their quest for an Islamic world order.[13]

Among the great disadvantages of secularization is that it results in profanation. This is what makes so many people blind to the distinction between Islam as a religion and Islamism as religionized politics. The British government, which could not separate the jihadists from Islam except by resorting to the unbelievable assertion that the former are "anti-Islamic," exemplifies the larger problem. Europeans (and some American scholars) no longer understand the meaning of religion and its use in politics. As the Dutch scholar Johannes Jansen argues, these people think the combination of religion and politics "should simply not exist. If it is political, it can be fought. If it is religious, constitution or conscience dictates that it should be tolerated. By being both, Islamic fundamentalism forcefully demonstrates the weakness . . . of the modern world itself."[14]

This is exactly what many people in the West fail to understand. Islamism is not only a quest for a political order, it is also a "messianic religious dream." Though Islamist leaders themselves fervently believe in this dream, they also know how to employ doublespeak; they present their political agenda as a legitimate religion to which they are entitled as a right by Western constitutional standards. They rebuff Western constitutionalism but take advantage of its privileges to further a war of ideas against it. Lenin remarked that "the capitalists will sell us the rope with which we hang them"; his successors in totalitarianism similarly hope to use the West against itself.[15]

Understanding how Islamism is related to Islam may help us change the balance in favor of open civil society, an effort in which civil Islam is an ally. Ultimately the Islamists must have their day. Political and cultural pluralism is a universal good,[16] but one of the prices we pay for it is susceptibility to short-term manipulation. A liberal democracy cannot censor or exclude institutional Islamists. They must be given the chance to embrace in deeds the democratic political culture to which they have paid so much lip service (for example, the AKP in Turkey). At that point they will be revealed for what they truly are. As Karl Popper has argued, open society must then have the right to defend itself through democratic responses, because intolerance cannot be admitted in the name of tolerance.[17] Totalitarian movements do not last forever: they fade on a scale of decades rather than centuries. We may hope that the present phase of the crisis of Islamic civilization[18] will give way to religious reforms and cultural changes that will lead to true democracy. I have suggested that Islamism is a response to a civilizational crisis, but it is not the movement that will resolve this crisis. In defending the universal values of cultural enlightenment against the counterenlightenment of Islamism, we must look to the humanism that has always been a part of the heritage of Islam.[19]

Who Are the Moderate Islamists?

The mainstream of Islamism consists of nonviolent institutional Islamists, who present themselves in the garb of "moderate Islam." One finds this institutional Islamism in Egypt and Turkey, among other countries. In Egypt the Muslim Brothers have abandoned the radical language that once gave the government a pretext for persecuting them. They have not changed their mindset. Despite continuing electoral fraud by the Mubarak government, the Islamists have managed to put several of their leaders into the Egyptian parliament. It is not only President Obama and some Washington policymakers who see the Muslim Brothers as partners in promoting Egyptian democracy. Reliable sources tell me that the EU leadership in Brussels has been seeking contact with the Muslim Brothers through back channels in a questionable effort at cultural diplomacy. European think tanks feed the illusion that "Europe's engagement with moderate Islamists" could help curtail "Islamist radicalization."[20] This is disturbingly myopic, but this myopia is becoming the rule since the Arab Spring of 2011.

In Turkey three Islamist parties existed from the early 1970s until the late 1990s: Selamet, Refah, and Fazilet. Each in turn was banned by the supreme courts as unconstitutional. Turkish Islamists learned from this history. Their new party, the AKP, abandoned all Islamist rhetoric and since 2002 has ruled the country almost as a one-party state. The AKP uses the discourse of democracy to camouflage its politics of creeping Islamization.[21] It employs no Islamist jargon but instead presents itself as an "Islamic conservative" party comparable to Germany's Christian-Democratic Union. But despite the AKP politicians' claim that they are no longer Islamists, the support they receive from American and European leaders alienates the West from liberal Muslims and secularists. As I showed in Chapters 1 and 4, the AKP has been successful in moving Turkey in an Islamist direction. In 2010 some Western politicians started to reconsider their positive views about the AKP and its leader, Recep Tayyip Erdoğan, following Turkey's rapprochement toward Iran, Hamas, and Hezbollah, and its suppression of press freedoms[22] and interference with the judicial system.

Before their apparent conversion from religious fundamentalism to moderate Islamic conservatism, Turkish Islamists were less inclined to hide what was on their minds. At a rally in December 1997 in the city of Siirt, Erdoğan, then the mayor of Istanbul, quoted an Islamist poem approvingly: "The mosques are our barracks; the minarets are our bayonets. The domes are our helms. The believers are our soldiers." After a formal indictment by the state prosecutor on grounds of inflammatory speech, the Ankara High Court forced Erdoğan to step down as mayor and sentenced him to jail. Upon his release, he declared his intent to "continue the struggle to return to the political scene even more powerful than before."[23] The Turkish Supreme Court then issued a ban on Erdoğan's party, Fazilet Partisi. This is the experience that underlay the founding of the AKP in 2002. From then on Erdoğan styled himself a "Muslim-conservative European" rather than a "neo-Ottoman pan-Turkish Islamist." But it is not clear that the leopard actually changed his spots. Zeyno Baran convincingly shows that the substance of AKP politics since 2002 consists of lip service to Kemalist secularism alongside the intent to "reshape the republic, chiefly along Islamist lines" as pursued in a politics of a "creeping . . . top-down Islamization."[24]

The AKP cannot yet publicly state its Islamist commitments. Any such declaration would prompt its legal banning. Turkey is not yet completely in Islamist hands: it still has a secular constitution and a constitutional court. Yet the recent constitutional referendum suggests that the tension between the AKP's clear Islamist tendencies and the secular elements of Turkish society is bound to increase. The WikiLeaks disclosures cited in Chapter 4 show that U.S. diplomats in Ankara are aware of the true leanings of the AKP's leaders. It is possible that once the new constitution is in effect, with a weakened judiciary and reconfigured Supreme Court, these leaders will be more outspoken about their mindset and more aggressive in pursuing Islamist policies. In fact, developments in the spring and summer of 2011 have tended in that direction. There has been a shake-up in the Turkish court system, with some judges forced to accept early pensions and others exiled to rural areas, and the constitutional court stripped of its independence from the government, all as part of an AKP effort to weaken the judiciary. Meanwhile, in the other pillar of the secular republic, the entire officer command of all branches of the armed forces of Turkey resigned in July 2011 to protest AKP prosecution of the bogus "Ergenekon" conspiracy, a pretext to arrest and hold without trial opposition judges, officers, and journalists.[25]

Modernity, Islam, and Enlightenment

Modernity must be understood in the terms of the European Enlightenment set out by Immanuel Kant. As Jürgen Habermas phrased it, "Kant . . . installed reason in the supreme seat of judgment before which anything that made a claim to validity has to be justified."[26] Lest this be seen as Eurocentric, I would note that this recognition of the primacy of reason also existed in medieval Islamic rationalism.[27] Thus the rationalist view of the world can be shared cross-culturally by people of different civilizations. As the late Moroccan philosopher Mohammed al-Jabri argued, Islamic rationalism is in line with modernity. Clearly, Islamism is not "the other modernity," because it is totalitarian.[28]

The Islamist worldview is not in line with the tradition of Islamic rationalism founded on the work of Avicenna and Averroës. This tradition should be considered a genuine enlightenment[29] even if it did not ultimately move the Islamic world into modernity. I refer again to the great Islamic rational philosopher Mohammed al-Jabri of the University of Rabat, Morocco, to argue with him that the rationalist spirit of Averroism "is adaptable to our era because it agrees with it on more than one point: rationalism, realism, axiomatic method, and critical approach." Jabri writes of "the universality and historicity of knowledge" approved by Averroës and contends that the Islamic revival must be specific to "the survival of our philosophical tradition, i.e., what is likely to contribute to our time, [which] can only be Averroist."[30] The existence of this variety of Islamic philosophy supports the contention that there can be only one, cross-cultural modernity, based on a shared recognition of the primacy of reason.

The humanist scholar Zeev Sternhell, in *The Anti-Enlightenment Tradition*,[31] mounts a strong defense of this rationalist modernity. Sternhell extensively discusses Hannah Arendt and defends her work against critiques, in particular Isaiah Berlin's objection that an analysis originally developed around fascism could not then be applied to Soviet communism. Sternhell sees Arendt's theory, which I have extended further, as fully generalizable. In Sternhell's view, the totalitarian impulse Arendt identified, whose purest expression was in the concentration camps and Gulags, emerges from a long history of cultural counterenlightenment that has developed alongside the rationalist tradition. He confines the debate to the intellectual history of Europe, but I want to extend his approach to view Islamism not as an "other modernity" but rather as an antimodernity, a counterenlightenment. I have largely confined my application of Arendt's approach to the two levels of ideology and movement—theory and practice, if you will—but Sternhell's analysis adds a third layer: totalitarianism as part of the antienlightenment tradition. As the new totalitarianism, Islamism would return the individual to the straitjacket of an allegedly divine collectivity. Islamism contradicts not only European Enlightenment but also the rationalist tradition of Islamic humanism.

The political order of hakimiyyat Allah, God's rule, by demanding that its followers dismiss popular sovereignty in the name of Islam, in effect contests the rule of humans over themselves as free individuals. Following an invented tradition of Islamic law, Islamists subject humanity to a constructed and essentialized supranatural will of God. The *aql* (reason) and its authority are replaced by the authority of *wahi* (revelation) fixed in scripture. The revelation is, of course, a strictly Islamist interpretation, arbitrary and highly selective, of the text.

For many decades to come, the West will be challenged by the problems of the world of Islam, including Islamism. This world is characterized by the diversity of local cultures. The political theorist John Brenkman sees "an uncomfortable truth . . . to be faced: most of the dangers are coming from the Muslim world. . . . Europe must learn how to deal with . . . conflicts generated within and between Muslim countries, and between radical Muslims and the West. . . . The crisis of Muslims' relations to the West is condensed."[32]

Some may dismiss this assessment as Islamophobic, but it is only a strategic overview of the present state of the world. What to do? One has to talk to Muslims, and President Obama did the right thing in his speech of June 4 when he invited Muslims in Cairo to join in a dialogue. Still, no proper politics can be pursued without considering the distinction between Islamism and Islam; one has to ensure that one has one's dialogue with the right party. There is a need for bridging, but how and on what foundations, and above all, with whom? At this juncture, we may note that the West cannot afford to overlook the distinction between Islam and Islamism, as well as the tensions between civil liberal Islam and Islamism. Whatever garb Islamists may appear in, they are not a pro-democracy movement.

Politics and the Ambivalence of the Sacred

The task is to acknowledge the place of Islam and Islamism in the present global conflict without overlooking the need for secular solutions. Others have different solutions; they upgrade the sacral in politics. For instance, Scott Appleby, formerly the cochairman of the Fundamentalism Project of the American Academy of Arts and Sciences, seems to have forgotten the pitfalls of politicized religion. In *The Ambivalence of the Sacred,* Appleby argues that if the sacral is the problem, it has to be included in the solution. "Religion . . . inspired, legitimated, and exacerbated deadly conflicts," he writes, but it "contributes consistently to their peaceful resolution." Appleby believes that men and women of political religion "without sacrificing their unique identity . . . as religious actors, . . . must become central players."[33] Is this an approval of religionized politics and an abandonment of the need to separate religion from politics? I doubt that any solution along these lines is feasible. Take the case of Malaysia, an ethnically and religiously diverse nation where Muslims make up a little more than 50 percent of the population but nearly monopolize political power. Exclusively Muslim solutions to religious conflict will surely not be acceptable to the country's Hindus, Buddhists, and Christians, yet fundamentalism admits no compromise. The Middle East is another case: the solutions proposed by Hamas and Hezbollah are not acceptable to Jews or to liberal secular Muslims. Religionized politics not only creates an impasse but entrenches it. Again, solutions to conflict have to be secular if they are to be accepted by all players.

This is not an ideology of secularism, but rather recognition that secular solutions can be shared by people of different faiths. This prospect seems to be more promising than the religionized politics that Islamism tries to impose. Sternhell concludes his book this way: "To prevent people of the twenty-first century from sinking into a new ice age of resignation, the enlightenment vision of the individual as creative of his or her present and hence of his or her future is irreplaceable."[34]

A liberal civil Islam supports this secular option. Enlightened Islam has a tradition of Islamic humanism. Islamism, by contrast, insists on religionized politics and dismisses enlightenment as an "imported solution." In the past four decades, having traveled throughout the world of Islam, I know of many Muslims who prefer rationalism to religionized politics. While writing an early draft of this chapter I went to two cities to discuss the future of Islam. In Fez, Morocco, prominent Arab-Muslim thinkers and opinion leaders gathered at the invitation of a Berber-Muslim professor, Moha Ennaji, under the patronage of the liberal Muslim king of Morocco, Mohammed VI, to discuss diversity and pluralism in the world of Islam. For the first time in my life I heard educated Arabs publicly acknowledging not only European and other non-Muslim sources of Arab culture but also Jewish sources.

The second event took place in Jakarta, Indonesia, under the patronage of the Indonesian Ministry of Religious Affairs and the graduate school (UIN) of the Hidayatullah Islamic State University. This conference carried the challenging title Debating Progressive Islam. It was made clear that a progressive Islam—one that approves the separation of religion and politics, pluralism, individual human rights, and secular democracy—stands in clear opposition to Islamism. One of the mentors of civil Islam in Indonesia, Azyumardi Azra, a major opinion leader and the former president of Hidayatullah University, was among the speakers. He clearly rejected political Islam and its ideology of an "Islamic shari'a state" in favor of a civil Islam "compatible with democracy."[35] Similarly, M. Syafi'i Anwar, who runs the Center for the Promotion of Pluralism, argued for a progressive liberal democratic Islam that approves secular pluralism. These are highly promising statements. It is sad to see that many Western academics view these exemplary liberal Muslims as a "small slice," to be written off.[36]

If the West were to construe Islamism as somehow representative of all of Islam, it would be a tragedy on multiple levels. First would be the failure to recognize the liberal Muslims who should be the secular rationalists' natural allies.[37] Second would be the success of the war of ideas Islamism has waged for so many decades. Finally, and by far the most important, would be the tragedy of the people forced to live under a system that perverts their faith into a form of totalitarian rule. I have written this book to enlighten readers about the danger of this multiple tragedy. This message is meant not only for Western readers, but also for the "other Muslims"[38] who are the true revivalists of the classical heritage of Islam[39] that underpinned one of the most developed civilizations of the world.[40] We must understand the call for an Islamic revival as breathing life into the buried tradition of Islamic civilization. Our goal must not be a restoration of the supremacist glory of medieval times, when it was—as the late scholar of Islam Marshall G. S. Hodgson stated—"supposed that the human world was on the verge of becoming Muslim . . . based . . . on the strategic and political advantages of Muslims . . . [and] also on the vitality of their general culture."[41]

In their nostalgia for the past greatness of Islamic civilization, combined with their resistance to cultural change,[42] Muslims today suffer what Daryush Shayegan, an Iranian Muslim scholar who has taught in Teheran and Paris, diagnoses as "cultural schizophrenia." This syndrome results from being torn "between ideas based on nostalgia for a golden age and psychological behavior patterns rooted in centuries of laicism and secularization."[43]

The invented tradition of Islamism is an expression of this cultural schizophrenia. It is not a solution to the predicament. There exist genuine Islamic alternatives.[44]

In place of Islamism's unresolvable tensions between an invented tradition and modern reality, I argue for cultural change in the Islamic civilization toward a mindset of pluralism,[45] in a world where all civilizations interact and respect one another on an equal footing. We liberal Muslims do not seek to replace the hegemony of the West with the hegemony of a united Islamicate. The Kantian idea of democratic peace is nobler than the agenda of global jihad.[46]

Coda

My editor at Yale University Press keeps reminding me that a book cannot stop history: even if it is completely up to the minute when the proofs are finished and sent to the printer, something will happen the next day and the day after that. The world overtakes it even before the ink is dry on the paper. I have therefore tried not to give the most recent events too much weight.

Yet the Arab Spring of 2011 and the Islamist movements' successful efforts to use it to climb the ladder of power are not ordinary events but a development of world-historical significance. Therefore, it is fitting that I close this book, the last one of my forty-year academic career, with some final thoughts about the challenge the Islamist rise to power poses to the findings presented here. The competition between civil Islam and Islamism will determine the future of democracy in the Middle East in the shadow of the Arab Spring. What will follow in the wake of the toppled authoritarian regimes in the Arab core of Islamic civilization? Will there be a truly democratic order committed to pluralism?

In his book *Fi shar'iyat al-Ikhtilaf* (On the legitimacy of discord and dissent), the Moroccan Muslim philosopher Ali Oumlil offered what I believe is the most persuasive criterion for assessing what happens in the years to come. Oumlil wrote the book in 1991, when the priority among Arab Muslims in postcolonial development was "national unity." The

Islamists translated this dictum into "Unity of the Umma" and used the idea to suppress dissent based on disagreement (*al-Ikhtilaf*). In response, Oumlil wrote that "today we need to turn to recognizing diversity instead of unity" because the right to *ikhtilaf* is the substance of democracy. He added: "Every democratic system not only admits diversity, but also rests on its legitimacy as a system based on pluralism. . . . Arab Muslims do not need unity, but rather three basics: democracy, pluralism and individual human rights."[47]

The *Nizam al-Islami* of the shari'a state does not support any of these three values. Will the shari'a state be the outcome of the Arab Spring? In Tunisia, the Islamist al-Nahda (Ennahda) Party has been voted into power. In Libya the Islamists, with Western military support, toppled Qadhafi and executed him. In Egypt, the Muslim Brothers appear poised to take control of the government. In all three cases, the commitment to the shari'a state has been made unambiguously clear. Will these Islamists, once they are in power, honor Oumlil's three basic values of democracy, pluralism, and individual human rights?

The Arab Spring was initiated not by Islamists but by ordinary Arab Muslims who finally became fed up with authoritarian rule. But Islamists, who are better organized than any other political groups, have so far been the revolts' chief beneficiaries. Will they allow space in their shari'a state for the democratic idealists who launched the Arab Spring? Or will the moderate face Islamism shows the West turn ugly? Most of us can only wait and see.

Notes

In order to reduce the number of notes, multiple citations from one source in a single paragraph have usually been consolidated into a single note. For full publication information see the Bibliography.

1. Why Islamism Is Not Islam

1. This aspect of Islamism (political Islam) is not well understood in most contributions of Western scholarship to this theme. The mainstream U.S. literature on political Islam is not only controversial and flawed but also at times charged with misleading assessments. The same applies even to a higher degree to the state of the art in Europe, in particular to the French contributions by two authors who dominate the field also in the United States through the citation of their books in English translations: Olivier Roy, *The Failure of Political Islam,* and even to a greater extent Gilles Kepel, *Jihad.* Both pundits seem to fail to understand properly the dual nature of Islamism as religionized politics in pursuit of a divine order, the shari'a state. This duality is better understood by the Dutch scholar Johannes Jansen, *The Dual Nature of Islamic Fundamentalism.* The most influential and at the same time most flawed contributions in the United States are the numerous books published one after the other mostly in a short time span by John Esposito. In contrast to this kind of work, the older monograph by the late Muslim scholar Nazih Ayubi, *Political Islam,* continues to be more useful as an introduction. In Germany there are almost no basic scholarly books on this subject worth mentioning. In Arabic the central critical book on Islamism is by the former state court judge Said M. al-Ashmawi, *al-Islam al-Siyasi.*

2. I acknowledge the impact of the Fundamentalism Project of the American Academy of Arts and Sciences (1989–95) on my work. See B. Tibi, *The Challenge of Fundamentalism* and the fives volumes of the project referenced in Chapter 2.

3. The primary source of this debate is the lecture by Daniel Bell, "The Return of the Sacred," presented in 1977 at the London School of Economics and published in his book *The Winding Passage,* 324–54. This debate has been resumed in the 2005 edition of my book *Islam between Culture and Politics,* chapter 11, written in the aftermath

of the attacks of September 11, 2011. This book has been published in association with Harvard University's Weatherhead Center for International Affairs. One aspect of "The Return of the Sacred" is the revival of particular calendars based on religion and thus the contestation of what has earlier been considered as "world time"; each civilization refers to its own time context. For instance there exist Jewish, Muslim, and other creed-based calendars. The term "world time" refers to the European expansion and to the globalization it generated. Under the impact of these processes the understanding of time changed in that Europeanization has created along the new global structures a "world time." This expansion "promoted the spread of European civilization across the entire globe" to the extent of establishing "the dimension of 'world time,'" as Theda Skocpol writes in *States and Social Revolution,* 21–23. The revival of "Islamic time" (the *hijra* year, 622 c.e., is the first year of the Islamic calendar) by the Islamists happens under the adverse conditions of world time.

4. In his authoritative multi-volume history of early Islam, van Ess writes that "umma" in early Islam did not have the meaning attributed to it in current times. This is an important and authoritative statement: van Ess is the most distinguished German professor of Islamic studies in thetwentieth century. Josef van Ess, *Theologie und Gesellschaft im 2. und 3. Jahrhundert Hidschra.*

5. The classic book that the Holocaust survivors Max Horkheimer and Theodor W. Adorno wrote in U.S. exile, *Dialektik der Aufklärung* (Dialectics of Enlightenment), presents a much misunderstood view of the Enlightenment. Many scholars—failing to read the work carefully—incorrectly impute to Adorno and Horkheimer the thesis that fascism grew from the Enlightenment.

6. Eric Hobsbawm and Terence Ranger, *The Invention of Tradition,* introduction.

7. Josef van Ess, *Theologie und Gesellschaft im 2. und 3. Jahrhundert Hidschra.*

8. Benedict Anderson, *Imagined Communities.*

9. The volume edited by Eric Patterson and John Gallagher, *Debating the War of Ideas,* includes my chapter on an Islamic humanism–based "peace of ideas" viewed as the alternative to the Islamist war of anti-Western propaganda. See also Walid Phares, *The War of Ideas.* Some discard this thinking as an expression of Said's Orientalism (*al-istishraq*); Edward Said, *Orientalism.* The truth is that the use of the notion predates the work of Said; the former Sheykh of al-Azhar, Mohammed al Bahi, coined the term in *al-fikr al-Islami al hadith wa silatuhu bi al-isti'mar al-gharbi*; he connected "Orientalism" with clearly antisemitic sentiments toward world Jewry. Al-Bahi earned his Ph.D. in Hamburg in 1936, when Germany was under Nazi rule. The contemporary use of "Orientalism" is related to Said's impact dubbed as Saidism. Said's book was timely when it was first published, as it challenged the dreadful Eurocentrism then in vogue. However, it was grossly distorted by the U.S. Middle East studies community. As the U.S.-educated Arab-Muslim scholar Sadik J. al-Azm suggests, Said's thinking has been subverted to justify an

"Orientalism in reverse." See Sadiq Jalal al-Azm, *Dhihniyyat al-tahrim*, 17–86. Unfortunately, the powerful criticism by al-Azm did not resonate in Western scholarship and was simply ignored. For a comprehensive survey on this issue, see also chapter 4 on the Orientalism debate in my *Einladung in die islamische Geschichte*, 136–90.

10. Sayyid Qutb, *Ma'alim fi al-tariq*, 201; translations are my own unless otherwise specified. Most of the writings of Qutb circulate in millions of copies of illegal printings distributed in the underground, or in informal translations in the diaspora and at home. The Western reader has access to Qutb's texts through this anthology: Albert Bergesen, ed., *The Qutb Reader*.

11. Sayyid Qutb, *al-Salam al-'alami wa al-Islam*, 172–73. In this pivotal Islamic source Qutb views global jihad as a civilizational project for a remaking of the world. This Islamism is not simple terrorism but rather a public choice committed to changing world order. Without a reference to Qutb the contemporary moderate Islamist Hasan al-Hanafi has put forward a claim for an Islamic lead articulated in this phrasing: "In the past, Islam found its way between two falling empires, the Persian and the Roman. Both were exhausted by wars. Both suffered moral and spiritual crises. Islam, as a new world order, was able to expand as a substitute to the old regime. Nowadays, Islam finds itself again a new power, making its way between the two superpowers in crises. Islam is regenerating, the two superpowers are degenerating. Islam is the power of the future, inheriting the two superpowers in the present." Quoted by Martin Kramer, *Arab Awakening and Muslim Revival*, 155–56. The quoted statement predates the decline and fall of the Soviet Union. Islamists claim to have brought down the Soviet superpower in the first Afghanistan war. Today, al-Qaeda wants to continue this mission in the envisioned toppling of the only remaining superpower, the United States, as a step toward a "return of history."

12. Robert Leiken and Steven Brooke, "The Moderate Muslim Brotherhood," 107–22, is a poorly informed article that runs against all facts and is highly ignorant about the Movement of the Muslim Brothers. The significance of the article is not its quality but the fact that it upgrades the Islamist Muslim Brothers to pure "moderate Muslims." The same wrong assessment is continued in another article published later in the powerful journal *Foreign Affairs*, which is also read by U.S. policymakers, in the article "Veiled Truth," by Marc Lynch (2010). For solid information see the classic on this subject by Richard Mitchell, *The Society of the Muslim Brothers*, which continues to be the authoritative source on the Muslim Brotherhood. A useful recent book on this movement is by Lorenzo Vidino, *The New Muslim Brotherhood in the West*. See the section on the Muslim Brotherhood in Chapter 4 of this book.

13. For a clarification and some corrections see B. Tibi, "Religious Extremism or Religionization of Politics?" in Hillel Frisch and Efraim Inbar, *Radical Islam and International Security*, 11–37.

14. This classification is baseless, but it is done in the poor contributions included in Barry Rubin, *Revolutionaries and Reformers;* much more informative is the book on this subject by the Egyptian historian Abdulazim Ramadan, *Jama'at al-Takfir fi misr. Al-Usul.* Some U.S. Middle East pundits do not read these original sources and are obsessed with their own projections.

15. On the Shi'ite doctrine of taqiyya see Moojan Momen, *An Introduction into Shi'a Islam,* 183. Momen states this deception is "lawful in Shi'ism." Sunni Islamists adopt today this sentiment but give it another name: iham, or deception of the infidels.

16. See the book by the Islamist Mohammed Imara, *al-Sahwa al-Islamiyya.* Among those who confuse revivalism and Islamism one finds Tariq Ramadan, *Aux Sources du Renouveau Musulman,* who views his grandfather Hasan al-Banna as a "revivalist"; in fact, al-Banna invents tradition and clearly revives nothing.

17. Raymond Baker, *Islam without Fear.*

18. See, for instance, John Esposito and John Voll, *Islam and Democracy.* In my book review in the *Journal of Religion,* 667–69, I demonstrate that Esposito and Voll deal in fact with Islamism, but they always speak of Islam in general. This flaw also exists in John Esposito, *The Islamic Threat.*

19. See William McNeill, *The Rise of the West.*

20. Eric Wolf, *Europe and the People without History.*

21. On this medieval tradition of a reason-based Islamic enlightenment see B. Tibi, *Der wahre Imam,* part II; for more information and sources see also Chapter 7 in this book. On the Islamic history of ideas see Peter Adamson and Richard Taylor, *The Cambridge Companion to Arab Philosophy,* and also my comprehensive monograph *Der wahre Imam.*

22. See the definition of Enlightenment by Jürgen Habermas, *The Philosophical Discourse of Modernity,* 18.

23. Jakob Burckhardt, *Die Kultur der Renaissance in Italien.* On the Renaissance placed in an Islamic context see B. Tibi, *Kreuzzug und Djihad,* chapter 5.

24. Lee Harris, *The Suicide,* 205.

25. Ibid., 206.

26. Bruce Bawer, *Surrender: Appeasing Islam, Sacrificing Freedom.*

27. This writing-off of a "liberal Islam" is amazingly shared between someone like Bruce Bawer, who fears Islamism, and Marc Lynch, who in "Veiled Truth" romanticizes it. Even worse is the upgrading of some Islamists to "liberals" in the questionable reader: *Liberal Islam: A Sourcebook,* ed. Charles Kurzman.

28. See the knowledgeable but unfortunately flawed and biased anthologies edited by Andrew Bostom, *The Legacy of Jihad* and *The Legacy of Islamic Antisemi-*

tism. One source of the flaws is the confusion first between Islam and Islamism, and second between jihad and jihadism. Bostom's work is cited by Andrew C. McCarthy, *The Grand Jihad,* as an authoritative source for the view that Islam and Islamism are the same. For a criticism see Chapter 9 of this book.

29. Hasan al-Banna, "Risalat al-Jihad," in *Majmu'at Rasa'il al-Imam al-Shahid Hasan al-Banna* [Collected essays of the Martyr Imam al-Banna], 271–92; the quotation is compiled from 289–91.

30. See note 12.

31. B. Tibi, "Turkey's Islamist Danger," 47–54; Zeyno Baran, *Torn Country: Turkey between Secularism and Islamism.*

32. Matthew Levitt, *Hamas,* is highly recommended. Among the few useful books on jihad and jihadism are David Cook, *Understanding Jihad,* and Laurent Murawiec, *The Mind of Jihad,* but the best is John Kelsay, *Arguing the Just War in Islam.*

33. See August R. Norton, *Hezbollah.* Norton is unfortunately among these Western apologetics who promote favorable views about Islamism, including Hezbollah. For a contrast see the chapter on Hezbollah by Eithan Azani in Katherina von Knop and Martin van Creveld, eds., *Countering Modern Terrorism,* 71–86.

34. On Islamist Shi'a parties in Iraq see Faleh A. Jabar, *The Islamist Shi'ite Movement in Iraq.*

35. Klaus-Michael Mallmann and Martin Cüppers, *Nazi Palestine.* For more on the findings included in this book see Chapter 3.

36. Richard Schultz and Andreas Dew, *Insurgents, Terrorists, and Militias,* chapter 7 on post-Saddam Iraq.

37. See the following reports: "Turkish Parliament Approves Bill to Overhaul Judiciary and Role of Military," *New York Times,* May 7, 2010, A12; Sebnem Arsu, "Turkey Sets Its Sights on a Whole New Constitution," *International Herald Tribune* (global ed. of *New York Times*), September 14, 2010.

38. In addition to the new book by Zeyno Baran, *Torn Country,* see the following new books: Ali Carkoglu and Ersin Kalaycioglu, *The Rising Tide of Conservatism in Turkey,* in particular the section "Consequences for the Relations with the EU," 121–40; William Hale and Ergun Özbudun, *Islamism, Democracy, and Liberalism in Turkey;* and Arda Can Kumbaracibasi, *Turkish Politics and the Rise of the AKP.*

39. See "Turkey's Radical Drift," *Wall Street Journal,* June 4, 2010.

40. Marshall G. S. Hodgson, *The Venture of Islam,* 2: 12–61.

41. The seminal work on this subject is Charles Tilly, *The Formation of National States in Western Europe.*

42. See the historical overview by Adam Watson, *The Evolution of International Society,* chapter 11 on the Islamic system and chapter 17 on Westphalia; see also the valuable contributions in Hedley Bull and Adam Watson, *The Expansion of International Society,* in particular the chapter by Hedley Bull, "The Revolt against the West."

43. See John Kelsay, *Arguing the Just War in Islam.*

44. Jürgen Habermas, *The Philosophical Discourse of Modernity.* On the Frankfurt School from which Habermas emanates see Martin Jay, *The Dialectical Imagination.* The recent book by Zeev Sternhell, *The Anti-Enlightenment Tradition,* revives rationalist modernity as an enlightenment against antienlightenment, of which Islamism is a powerful variety.

45. B. Tibi, *Islam's Predicament with Modernity.*

46. Turan Kayaoglu, "Westphalian Eurocentrism in International Relations Theory." This interpretation is defensive-cultural. On the notion of defensive culture in the context of crisis see B. Tibi, *The Crisis of Modern Islam,* 1–8.

47. Jadul-Haq Ali Jadul-Haq, *Bayan li al-nas,* 1: 273–91.

48. Joseph Schacht, *An Introduction to Islamic Law,* 54–55.

49. The late Naser Hamed Abu Zaid, in *al-Tafkir fi asr al-Takfir* [Thinking in the age of the accusation of heresy], was among liberal Muslims who were harassed by Islamists; takfir is the accusation of heresy; Abu Zaid died in July 2010. Among other critics of Islamism is Abdulazim Ramadan, *Jama'at al-Takfir fi misr,* not to be confused with Tariq Ramadan. Unlike some Western pundits who positively classify Islamists in categories such as "revolutionaries and reformers," Abdulazim Ramadan views Islamists as takfiris. See also Dharif, *al-Islam al-Siyasi fi al-Watan al-Arabi.* These Muslim scholars are more informative about Islamism than are some Western. The notorious lack of knowledge of sources in Arabic often damages Western books. For a contrast see the excellent introduction into Islamism in Arabic by Halah Mustafa, *al-Islam al-Siyasi fi Misr.* American pundits also confuse politics in Islam with Islamism. For an insightful study of Islam and politics that is not Islamism see Husain F. al-Najjar, *al-Islam wa al-Siyasa.* See also B. Tibi, "Between Islam and Islamism."

50. Thomas Farr, "How Obama Is Sidelining Religious Freedom," *Washington Post,* June 25, 2010, A17.

51. Patrick French, "Touting Religion, Grabbing Land," *New York Times,* March 16, 2009, A27.

52. Donald Emmerson, "Inclusive Islamism: The Utility of Diversity," 22; Daniel Varisco, "Inventing Islamism: The Violence of Rhetoric," 45, both in Martin in association with Barzegar, *Islamism;* Paul Berman, *The Flight of the Intellectuals,* 285.

2. Islamism and the Political Order

1. The principle of din wa dawla was conceived by the founder of the Muslim Brotherhood, Hasan al-Banna. His major writings are collected in one volume: *Majmu'at Rasa'il al-Imam al-Shahid.* Today this tradition is continued by the Egyptian Islamist Mohammed Imara, *author of Ma'rakat al-Islam wa Usul al-Hikm.* The best survey of this Islamist ideology was completed by the Moroccan Muslim scholar Mohammed Dharif, *al-Islam al-Siyasi fi al-Watan al-Arabi;* see in particular 253–62.

2. On the ambition of all religious fundamentalisms for a remaking of the order of the state in a unity of religion and politics see Martin Marty and Scott Appleby, *The Fundamentalism Project,* vol. 3. The project conducted at the American Academy of Arts and Sciences and led by Marty and Appleby has had a great impact on this chapter, but the underlying knowledge was obtained in the world of Islam itself. I am a contributor to volume 2 of the five volumes of this project. It is most deplorable to state that in most writings on political Islam as a movement, as well as on the ideology of Islamism, Western authors flatly ignore the findings of this research project.

3. The shari'a state that Islamism proposes to establish is an order placed on top of the agenda of Islamist movements. This fact is authoritatively reflected in the Islamist contributions published in Arabic by Mustafa A. Fahmi, *Fan al-hukm fi al-Islam,* and the more influential book by Mohammed Salim al-Awwa, *Fi al-Nizam al-Siyasi lil dawla al-Islamiyya.*

4. Maajid Nawaz, "Dangerous Concepts and the Struggle Within," 49.

5. On shari'a and on the invention of its tradition in the Islamist shari'atization agenda, see Chapter 6 and the references cited there.

6. On this notion see the preceding chapter and Eric Hobsbawm and Terence Ranger, *The Invention of Tradition,* 1–14. See also the authoritative introduction to Islam by Mahmoud Zakzouk, the German-educated former dean of the Shari'a faculty of the stage-setting al-Azhar University in Cairo, *Einführung in den Islam.* There is no mention of an Islamic state or government in this introduction.

7. I elaborate upon the notion of "world disorder" in *The Challenge of Fundamentalism.*

8. Charles Tilly, *The Formation of the National States,* 45.

9. See Milton-Edwards, *Islam and Politics in the Contemporary World.*

10. John Brenkman, *The Cultural Contradictions of Democracy,* 165–70.

11. The premature prediction of Francis Fukuyama's *The End of History* has been repudiated by the claims of Islamism in its call for a "return of history"; for more details see B. Tibi, *Political Islam,* introduction and chapter 5. Already in 1995,

in *Der Krieg der Zivilisationen,* 28–29, I contested Fukuyama's view of an End of History and argued instead that the Islamist claim for a return of history is a serious challenge. This combination of a contestation and a claim occurs in the shape of constructing collective memories about the historical competition between rival civilizational models. The conflict that results from these tensions is a civilizational value-based conflict that should not be confused with Huntington's "clash." On this issue see B. Tibi, "Islam between Religious-Cultural Practice and Identity Politics."

12. Hedley Bull, "The Revolt against the West," 223.

13. Daniel Philpott, "The Challenge of September 11."

14. As I have mentioned, the research on this chapter rests on my participation in the Fundamentalism Project. The work done in that project was carried out in the years 1989–93, and the findings were published in five volumes by the chairpersons, Martin Marty and Scott Appleby, acting as editors. My essay "The Worldview of Sunni-Arab Fundamentalists" was published as chapter 4 of vol. 2, *Fundamentalisms and Society.* The other volumes are *Fundamentalisms Observed, Fundamentalisms and the State, Accounting for Fundamentalisms,* and *Comprehending Fundamentalisms.* My book *The Challenge of Fundamentalism* relates also to this project.

15. The work of this Culture Matters Research Project was published in two volumes: Lawrence Harrison and Jerome Kagan, *Developing Cultures: Essays on Cultural Change,* and Lawrence Harrison and Peter Berger, *Developing Cultures: Case Studies.* I am a contributor to both volumes.

16. Hasan Hanafi, in contrast to his Arabic book *a-Usuliyya al-Islamiyya,* states in his chapter in the U.S. book *Islamism,* edited by Richard C. Martin in association with Abbas Barzegar, that the notion of usuliyaa (fundamentalism) reflects "a Western invention" (64).

17. See B. Tibi, "Worldview of Sunni-Arab Fundamentalists."

18. See B. Tibi, "Islam between Religious-Cultural Practice and Identity Politics," and the introduction to my *Islam's Predicament.*

19. The challenge addressed by the Islamist Mohammed Imara, *al-Sahwa al-Islamiyya wa al-Tahddi al-Hadari,* creates a predicament and a related crisis. This issue has been a research focus in my work in the course of the past four decades. See my *Islam's Predicament with Modernity* and, earlier, by the same *The Crisis of Modern Islam.* This kind of reasoning is also continued by Hichem Djaït, *Islamic Culture in Crisis.*

20. The publication by each of three authoritative encyclopedias of an entry the length of a journal article on fundamentalism based on the finding of the Fundamentalism Project of the American Academy of Art and Sciences is a sign of grow-

ing recognition of the phenomenon. See my entries in Seymour Martin Lipset, *The Encyclopedia of Democracy;* Mary Hawkesworth and Maurice Kogan, *Routledge Encyclopedia of Government and Politics;* and Marc Bevier, *The Encyclopedia of Political Theory.* In these entries it is argued that Islamism is not the other modernity, but rather the Islamic variety of religious fundamentalism viewed as antienlightenment in its nature as a totalitarian ideology.

21. See chapter 7 on pluralism in B. Tibi, *Islam's Predicament with Modernity.*

22. See Nikkie Keddie's edited writings of al-Afghani published under the title *An Islamic Response to Imperialism.* Tariq Ramadan, *Aux sources du renouveau musulman: D'al Afghani à Hasan al-Banna. Un siècle de réformisme islamique,* establishes a wrong continuity between the revivalist al-Afghani and the Islamist al-Banna. For a criticism see Paul Berman, *The Flight of the Intellectuals.* The Berlin-based liberal Muslim immigrant Ralph Ghadban, *Tariq Ramadan und die Islamisierung Europas,* accuses Ramadan of engaging in an "Islamization of Europe." Ramadan denies this, but the French feminist writer Caroline Fourest, *Brother Tariq: The Doublespeak of Tariq Ramadan,* contends that Ramadan's statements depend on the audience he addresses. In my view it seems to be a fallacy when this Islamist thinking is presented as a reform. See Tariq Ramadan, *Radical Reform.*

23. Traditional, pre-Islamist, classical shari'a is characterized by diversity. It differs in many ways from the reinvented shari'a as represented by political Islam. On this debate see Chapter 6 and B. Tibi, *Islam between Culture and Politics.*

24. For more details see B. Tibi, "The Return of the Sacred to Politics as Constitutional Law."

25. John Kelsay, *Arguing the Just War in Islam,* 165–66. On this subject see also my most recent article, "John Kelsay and Shari'a Reasoning in Just War in Islam."

26. See Albert Bergesen, *The Qutb Reader.* In terms of influence and lasting impact, the major work of Sayyid Qutb in Arabic is *Ma'alim fi al-tariq,* especially 5–10 and 201–2. On Qutb see also Roxanne Euben, *Enemy in the Mirror,* 54–55. On Hasan al-Banna see Chapter 5 and his collected essays in one volume, *Majmu'at Rasa'il al-Imam al-Shahid Hasan al-Banna.* Unlike Qutb, who was a thinker and acted in his numerous writings as the intellectual authority in the philosophical foundation of Islamism, al-Banna was a simpleminded practitioner of jihadism, not a pillar of a *Renouveau Musulman* as his grandson Tariq Ramadan contends. Basically, al-Banna was a propagandist of the first Islamist movement. Among his writings is the most influential text on jihad; ibid., 271–92. This text is the cornerstone of the ideology of jihadism as a new interpretation of jihad. New, archivally based disclosures by the historian Jeffrey Herf reveal a connection between al-Banna and the antisemitic Mufti of Jerusalem Amin al-Husseini, who met and closely worked with Hitler. See Herf, *Nazi Propaganda for the Arab World.*

27. Paul Cliteur, *The Secular Outlook.*

28. In traditional Islamic shari'a non-Muslim territoriality—such as Europe—is classified as *dar al-harb,* abode of war. Tariq Ramadan, viewed by some as "moderate Islamist," but accused by others of "double-speak," no longer views Europe as "Dar al-harb" but defines it as dar al-shahadah; the shift is considered a liberalization by ill-informed Europeans, who seem not to understand the implication of Ramadan's formula. Ramadan's new label for Europe is another term for "house of Islam." Thus the presence of Muslims in Europe makes Europe an Islamic territoriality. On this issue see B. Tibi, "Ethnicity of Fear?"

29. This application has been criticized in the debate published in English by the European online magazine Signandsight.com. Euro-Islam understood as Europeanized Islam is the alternative to the approach of Ramadan. Some of the basic contributions of the cited debate—including mine—were published in German in a book edited by Thierry Chervel, *Islam in Europa.*

30. On this decisive epoch see B. Tibi, *Conflict and War in the Middle East,* chapters 3 and 4, as well as the new chapter 12 added to the second edition. The seminal book on the ensuing legitimacy crisis is by Fouad Ajami, *The Arab Predicament,* 50–75 (on fundamentalism), reprinted a dozen of times. The classical book by Hudson, *Arab Politics,* in particular the introduction, 1–30, continues to be worth reading.

31. For more details see Carry Rosefsky Wickham, *Mobilizing Islam.* For an overview on Egypt as a model: Tibi, "Egypt as a Model of Development."

32. See B. Tibi, "Secularization and De-Secularization in Islam," chapter 6, on secularization, in *Islam's Predicament with Modernity.*

33. Hedley Bull, "Revolt against the West," 222.

34. See Zeyno Baran, "Fighting the War of Ideas"; and Walid Phares, *The War of Ideas;* and more recently the contributions in Eric Patterson and John Gallagher, *Debating the War of Ideas.*

35. On Islamism and political order see the books by the influential "moderate" Egyptian Islamists: Mustafa A. Fahmi *Fan al-hukm fi al-Islam,* and Mohammed Salim al-Awwa, *Fi al-Nizam al-Siyasi lil dawla al-Islamiyya.*

36. Roxanne Euben, *Enemy in the Mirror,* 55, and for similar evidence on Qutb's impact see also David Cook, *Understanding Jihad,* 102–6.

37. On the AKP see Zeyno Baran, *Torn Country,* chapters 2, 3, and 5. During my tenure as a visiting professor at Bilkent University in Ankara, 1995, one of my able Turkish students, Ayşegül Keçeçiler, completed a fully referenced thesis, "Qutb and His Influence on Turkish-Islamic Intellectuals" (unpublished). On Turkish Islamism see B. Tibi: "Turkey's Islamist Danger."

38. See Daniel Philpott, "Challenge of September 11," and my contribution to Efraim Inbar and Hillel Frisch, *Radical Islam and International Security,* "Religious Extremism or Religionization of Politics?"

39. In this venture I wrote a chapter, "International Morality and Cross-Cultural Bridging," for the response by Roman Herzog and others to Samuel Huntington, *Preventing the Clash of Civilizations.* By the time of the publication, Herzog was the president of the Federal Republic of Germany. See also my contribution, "Euro-Islam," to Zeyno Baran's *The Other Muslims.*

40. See Chapter 4 and for a survey on this history see my comprehensive monograph *Kreuzzug und Djihad,* in which this history is subdivided—in terms of historical sociology—into eight great epochs. A biased but well-informed study is the book by Efraim Karsh, *Islamic Imperialism.*

41. Geoffrey Parker, *The Military Revolution and the Rise of the West;* Philip Curtin, *The World and the West.*

42. The earlier book by my academic teacher Jürgen Habermas, *The Philosophical Discourse of Modernity,* continues to be a major source of inspiration for my work. Modernity matters in understanding Islamism as it does with regard to any other religious fundamentalism. The exposure to modernity is the overall context of the phenomenon. The feature of Islamist nostalgia reflects a modern invention of tradition undertaken under conditions of this exposure. On this Islamic nostalgia see John Kelsay, *Islam and War,* 114–18.

43. On Islam and cultural pluralism see Anthony Reid and Michael Gilsenan, *Islamic Legitimacy in Plural Asia,* including my chapter, "Islam and Cultural Modernity," and chapter 7 in B. Tibi, *Islam's Predicament with Modernity.*

44. See Bat Ye'or, *Islam and Dhimmitude.*

45. Samuel P. Huntington, *The Third Wave,* 13.

46. Charles Tilly, *Coercion, Capital, and European States,* 191.

47. The reader is reminded of the fact that nation-states emerged as new states in the non-Western world in the course of the process of decolonization, but without any parallel real nation-building underlying the process. Therefore, the new emerging states are weak states; for more details see Robert Jackson, *Quasi-States.* It is not an exaggeration to describe this process in the Arab world as an emergence of "nominal states" that are practically ruled by tribes with national flags. For an elaboration and more details see B. Tibi, "The Simultaneity of the Unsimultaneous."

48. For more details see Michael Barnett, *Dialogue in Arab Politics,* and Beverly Milton-Edwards, *Contemporary Politics in the Middle East.* See also my *Das arabische Staatensystem.*

49. See B. Tibi, *Arab Nationalism.*

50. The confusion of Islamist internationalism and pan-Islamism can even be found in the work of such established scholars as James Piscatori of Oxford. In his chapter in Shahram Akbarzadeh and Fethi Mansouri, *Islam and Political Violence,* he confuses these realities and the related notions, but he is contradicted in the same volume in by B. Tibi "Jihadism and Intercivilizational Conflict." See also Fernand Braudel, *A History of Civilizations,* 41–114, for a historical overview of the background from which the contemporary civilizational conflict emerges.

51. Today, Yusuf al-Qaradawi acts as the heir of Sayyid Qutb and his tradition. His three-volume work *al-hall al-Islami* has been reprinted in numerous editions. The first volume bears the title *al-Hulul al-Mustawrada* [The imported solutions].

52. Charles Kurzman, *Liberal Islam.*

53. See Frank J. Lechner and John Boli, *The Globalization Reader,* part VIII, in particular 358–63.

54. See B. Tibi, *Kreuzzug und Djihad,* chapters 1 and 4, and Fred Donner, *The Early Islamic Conquests.* This book published decades ago by Donner is more enlightening than his recent book adjusted to the new mindset of U.S.-Islamic studies: *Muhammad and the Believers.* Much better than both is the book by Yahya Blankinship, *The End of the Jihad State.* See also Ephraim Karsh, *Islamic Imperialism,* a most provocative book on this subject that could have been more valuable if it were more sound, but Karsh's book has a point and is closer to the historical truth than is the new book by Donner.

55. These terms, "Islamicate" (synonymous for Islamdom), "international civilization," and "international order," were coined by Marshall Hodgson in *The Venture of Islam,* vol. 2.

56. On the industrialization of warfare see the respective chapter in Anthony Giddens, *A Contemporary Critique of Historical Materialism,* vol. 2, *Nation-State and Violence.*

57. On the significance of Qutb's pamphlet "our struggle against the Jews" as the major source for Islamist antisemitism see Chapter 3 and the references cited there.

58. It follows that Islamism is about the order of the world, but in two rival visions. On Islamist internationalism and the Sunni-Shi'i competition, see B. Tibi, *Political Islam, World Politics, and Europe,* part II.

59. Eric R. Wolf, *Europe and the People without History.*

60. Francis Fukuyama, "Identity, Immigration, and Liberal Democracy." See also Fukuyama's earlier *End of History.*

61. Ernest Gellner, *Religion and Postmodernism,* 84.

62. See the proceedings of the Erasmus Foundation, *The Limits of Pluralism,* which includes this controversy between Ernest Gellner and Clifford Geertz next to contributions by Schlomo Avineri and this author, among others.

63. I was there in May 1994 and witnessed these tensions in the Gellner-Geertz controversy. The quotation is based on my notes during the conference.

64. Therefore Turan Kayaoglu, "Westphalian Eurocentrism in International Relations Theory," is wrong—see the debate in Chapters 1 and 4.

65. See Feldman, *Fall and Rise of the Islamic State.* For a different interpretation of the Islamist shari'a state, see chapters 6–8 in my *Challenge of Fundamentalism.*

3. Islamism and Antisemitism

1. See the recent most remarkable books on this issue, by Robert Wistrich, *Lethal Obsession,* and by Anthony Julius, *Trials of the Diaspora.* New books that relate these issues to the Holocaust are cited in subsequent notes to this chapter. This chapter is based on my evaluation of representative Arab-Islamist sources collected during several research trips to the Middle East. It was completed between 2008 and 2010 at the Center for Advanced Holocaust Studies of the U.S.-Holocaust Memorial Museum in Washington, D.C. In spring 2008 and again in summer 2010 I was designated as the Judith B. and Burton P. Resnick Scholar for the Study of Antisemitism in that institution.

2. Edward Rothstein, "A Hatred That Resists Exorcism." *New York Times,* July 5, 2010, C1, C5. Rothstein discusses the books cited in note 1. The present chapter continues my earlier research on this subject matter; see "Public Policy and the Combination of Anti-Americanism and Antisemitism in Contemporary Islamist Ideology" and *From Sayyid Qutb to Hamas.*

3. Edward Rothstein, "A Hatred That Resists Exorcism," C5.

4. Bernard Lewis, "The New Antisemitism." 25–26. Lewis's *The Jews of Islam* is the most authoritative and highly appreciated source for the study of this subject. See also Bernard Lewis, *Semites and Antisemites.*

5. The reader edited by Andrew Bostom, *The Legacy of Islamic Antisemitism,* is on the one hand highly knowledgeable, but on the other it is based on untenable generalizations that lack nuances and distinctions, then become wrong.

6. See the report in *Süddeutsche Zeitung,* August 20–21, 2005.

7. On secular Arab nationalism see B. Tibi, *Arab Nationalism.*

8. See Robert Wistrich, *Lethal Obsession;* Anthony Julius, *Trials of the Diaspora;* and Andrei Markovits, *Uncouth Nation.* One source of Islamist anti-Americanism is the prejudice that the Jewish lobby rules the United States. Unbelievably, at least two

prominent American professors unwittingly support this prejudice; see John Mearsheimer and Stephen Walt, *The Israel Lobby and U.S. Foreign Policy,* which Islamists quote to support their anti-Americanism.

9. In addition to the most important book on anti-Americanism, by Andrei Markovits, cited in the previous note, one needs to mention the book edited by Peter Katzenstein and Robert Keohane, *Anti-Americanism in World Politics,* though it includes an extremely weak chapter on Islam and the Middle East by Marc Lynch. This chapter does a disservice to an otherwise fine volume.

10. Maxime Rodinson, *Peuple juif ou problème juif?* 135–52.

11. B. Tibi, *Die Verschwörung,* introduction and chapter 1.

12. Bernard Lewis's *The Jews of Islam* is the best record for "The Judeo-Islamic Tradition" (chapter 2, 67–106) and its "End" (chapter 4, 154–92).

13. See Martin Kramer, *The Jewish Discovery of Islam.*

14. In May 2010 Insani Yardim Vakfi (IHH), an Islamist charity with close ties to the AKP, sent a flotilla of vessels carrying humanitarian aid to challenge the Israeli naval blockade of Gaza. After Israeli commandoes boarded one vessel, the *Mavi Marmara,* nine Turkish activists—one carrying a U.S. passport—were killed and several dozen injured, and seven Israeli soldiers were wounded. Israel claimed to have found no humanitarian supplies on board the ship and to have responded to an armed attack. The flotilla turned around; the incident sparked an international uproar and was generally viewed as a public relations disaster for Israel. See "Sponsor of Flotilla Tied to Elite of Turkey," *New York Times,* July 16, 2010, A4; "Islamic Charity," *Washington Post,* June 10, 2010, A8; Steven Rosen, "Erdogan and the Israel Card," *Wall Street Journal,* June 10, 2010, A21. Rosen's article cites "the 2009 PEW global attitudes survey" that found that "73% of Turks rated their opinions of Jews as negative." AKP Prime Minister T. Erdoğan plays this card in his election campaign; he made use of Israel's mistake and exploited the popularity of this issue to freeze all relations to the Jewish state and to upgrade Turkey's relationship to Hamas. The *Washington Post* of July 5, 2010, A7, reported, "the prime minister's autocratic tendencies . . . to arrest journalists and Erdogan's allegations that some Turkish columnists are agents of Israel"; as a result, "journalists are jailed," in most cases with no trial.

15. For more details on cultural Arab Germanophilia see the third edition of my *Arab Nationalism;* for details about the Nazi link to some Arab nationalists see Jeffrey Herf, *Nazi Propaganda for the Arab World.* The classic by Lukas Hirszowicz, *The Third Reich and the Arab East,* continues to be worth reading.

16. See Zvi Elpeleg, The *Grand Mufti al-Husaini,* and the published Ph.D. dissertation by Klaus Gensicke, *Der Mufti von Jerusalem und die Nationalsozialisten,* as well as Jeffrey Herf, *Nazi Propaganda for the Arab World.* Paul Berman, *The Flight of*

the Intellectuals, chapters 2–4, discusses at length Islamist antisemitism. Berman has been defamed by Marc Lynch, "Veiled Truth" for this "pathological obsession," but he was praised by Anthony Julius, "The Pretender," *New York Times,* May 14, 2010. This imported antisemitism explains the change Meir Litvak and Ester Webman deal with in *From Empathy to Denial.*

17. Bernard Lewis, "The New Anti-Semitism."

18. Muhammed Y. Muslih, *The Origins of Palestinian Nationalism,* and Zvi Elpeleg, *The Grand Mufti.*

19. See B. Tibi, *Arab Nationalism.*

20. For a powerful example see Faruq Abdul-Salam, *al-Ahzab al-Siyasiyya wa al-Fasl bayn al-din wa al-Dawla,* 23.

21. I discuss this Islamist argument in more detail in "Der djihadistische Islamismus."

22. See chapter 6 on secularization and desecularization in B. Tibi, *Islam's Predicament with Modernity,* 178–208.

23. For some examples see Walter Laqueur, *The Changing Face,* 125–50 and 191–206, as well as Bernard Harrison, *The Resurgence of Antisemitism,* 1–26. Phyllis Chesler, *The New Antisemitism,* is also worth reading, though it is also charged with this flaw.

24. Robert Wistrich, *Muslim Antisemitism,* 44; similar mistakes are made by Walter Laqueur, *The Changing Face,* 141 and 197, and Mattias Küntzel, *Jihad and Jew-Hatred.* Despite this minor criticism, I acknowledge the great significance of Wistrich's contribution to the future study of antisemitism in his new magisterial book *A Lethal Obsession.* The spelling "antisemitism," with no hyphen or capitalization, which also has been adopted by the Center for Advanced Holocaust Studies in Washington, D.C., is derived from Laqueur. I refer to Hannah Arendt's views in refuting Andrew Bostom, *The Legacy of Islamic Antisemitism,* and in rejecting his equation of antisemitism with Judeophobia. In contrast, Arendt argues in the preface to *The Origins of Totalitarianism* that "antisemitism is not simply Jew-hatred." Bostom's anthology includes a disturbingly Islamophobic chapter by the German right-wing author Hans Peter Raddatz, "Antisemitism in Islam," 643–49.

25. Sayyid Qutb, *Ma'rakatuna ma'a al-Yahud,* 15 ("not for the sake of any material benefits"), 36 ("this is an enduring war").

26. Ibid., 21.

27. Walid Phares, *War of Ideas,* and the alternative to this war: Tibi, "Inter-Civilizational Conflict between Value Systems and Concepts of Order."

28. Sayyid Qutb, *Ma'rakatuna ma'a al-Yahud,* 31.

29. Ibid., 33.

30. Ibid., 32.

31. Ibid., 27.

32. Ibid., 33 ("there is a crusader-Zionist war"), 23 ("The Jews were the instigator").

33. Salah A. al-Khalidi, *Amerika min al-dakhil bi minzar Sayyid Qutb.* See also my "Public Policy and the Combination of Anti-Americanism and Antisemitism in Islamist Ideology."

34. Quoted in "House-Negro Job Is Just Another of al-Qaeda Lies," *USA Today,* November 25, 2008.

35. "America Seeks Bonds to Islam, Obama Insists," *New York Times,* April 7, 2009, A1. This message was repeated by Obama with more substance and vigor as well in his historical address to the people of Islamic civilization delivered in Cairo on June 4 of the same year. See the coverage of *International Herald Tribune,* June 5, 2009, A1, A4.

36. Walter Laqueur, *The Changing Face,* 10. The phenomenon Laqueur addresses is one feature of the ethnicization of the Islamic diaspora in Europe. For more details see my chapter, on the Islamic diaspora in Europe and also the chapters on Jewish communities in Europe in Roland Hsu, *Ethnic Europe.*

37. Walter Laqueur, *The Changing Face,* 200. See also B. Tibi, *Die Verschwörung,* about the origin of this Arab *"Verschwörung*/conspiracy"-driven mindset.

38. See the contributions in Patterson and Gallagher, *Debating the War of Ideas.*

39. On this most consequential perception see Graham Fuller, *A Sense of Siege.*

40. Ali M. Jarisha and Mohammed Sh. Zaibaq, *Asalib al-Ghazu al-Fikri lil alam al-Islami,* 3–4.

41. Sayyid Qutb, *Ma'arakatuna ma'a al-Yahud,* 21.

42. Ali M. Jarisha and Mohammed Sh. Zaibaq, *Asalib al-ghazu al-fikri lil alam al-Islami,* 150.

43. On this distinction see Leslie Lipson, *The Ethical Crisis of Civilizations,* 62–66, and B. Tibi, *Kreuzzug und Djihad,* chapter 5.

44. Ali M. Jarisha and Mohammed Sh. Zaibaq, *Asalib al-Ghazu al-Fikri lil alam al-Islami,* 9.

45. For evidence of the Jewish-Islamic alliance, see Steven Runciman, *History of the Crusades.*

46. Ali M. Jarisha and Mohammed Sh. Zaibaq, *Asalib al-Ghazu al-Fikri lil alam al-Islami,* 20.

47. See the festschrift for Bernard Lewis edited by Martin Kramer, *The Jewish Discovery of Islam.*

48. Mohammed al-Bahi, *al-Fikr al-Islami al-Hadith wa silatuhu bi al-ist'mar al-Gharbi.* The book includes an appendix on Orientalism, 528–53, that lists the names of European Orientalists, some of them resentfully identified and profiled as "Jews." The late Azhar-Sheykh al-Bahi completed his Ph.D. in Germany at the University of Hamburg in the year 1936 under Nazi rule. In that dissertation his name is transliterated as al-Bahy.

49. Ali M. Jarisha and Mohammed Sh. Zaibaq, *Asalib al-ghazu al-fikri lil alam al-Islami,* 37–39.

50. Ibid., 110–11, 150.

51. Ibid., 202. This is evidence for the predicament of Islam with pluralism. On this issue see B. Tibi, *Islam's Predicament with Modernity,* chapter 7.

52. Ali M. Jarisha and Mohammed Sh. Zaibaq, *Asalib al-ghazu al-fikri lil alam al-Islami,* 179.

53. Ibid., 203; see also Daniel Pipes, *The Hidden Hand,* and B. Tibi, *Die Verschwörung,* introduction and chapter 1.

54. On this religionization see B. Tibi: "Islam between Religious-Cultural Practice and Identity Politics."

55. On Islam's place in the Middle East conflict see Rifaat S. Ahmed, *al-Islam wa qadaya al-Sira' al-Arabi al-Israeli.* On this issue see also Milton-Edwards, *Islamic Politics in Palestine,* and Jacob Lassner and Ilan Troen, *Jews and Muslims in the Arab World.*

56. Muhsin al-Antawabi, *Limatha narfud al-Salam ma'a al-Yahud.*

57. Matthias Küntzel, *Jihad and Jew-Hatred,* 109. For more details on Hamas as a terrorist movement see Matthew Levitt, *Hamas,* as well as Richard Cohen, "Hamas, a Threat to Its Own People," *Washington Post,* June 29, 2010, A19. The Palestinian Khalid Hurub, based in Cambridge, defamed and distorted Levitt's book in his review "Hamas Viewed in American Eyes." The review was published in the Arab-Saudi sponsored newspaper *al-Hayat.* The charter of Hamas is quoted from its original text in Arabic; the translation is my own. The full text of the charter in Arabic is included in Ahmed Izzuldin, *Harakat al-Muqawamha al-Islamiyya Hamas,* 43–82.

58. See Matthew Levitt, *Hamas,* 30.

59. Hamas Charter.

60. Ibid.

61. Paul McGough, "The Changing Face of Hamas," *International Herald Tribune,* April 13, 2009.

62. The three volumes of Yusuf al-Qaradawi, *Hatmiyyat al-hall al-Islami,* have been cited in the preceding chapters.

63. Quoted in Walter Laqueur, *The Changing Face,* 199.

64. On this third-worldism see B. Tibi, "The Legacy of Max Horkheimer and Islamist Totalitarianism." One also encounters an equation of Muslims in Europe with Jews; see B. Tibi, "Foreigners: Today's New Jews?"

65. See B. Tibi, "Public Policy and the Combination of Anti-Americanism and Antisemitism in Islamist Ideology" and the references in note 9 above.

66. Andrei Markovits, *Uncouth Nation,* 180.

67. See B. Tibi, "Ethnicity of Fear?" and Roland Hsu, *Ethnic Europe.*

68. See Andrei Markovits, *Uncouth Nation,* 195, and Tibi, "Foreigners: Today's New Jews?"

69. Andrei Markovits, *Uncouth Nation,* 180 ("While these immigrants awakened"), 194 ("raised their voices").

70. Jeffrey Herf, *Antisemitism and Anti-Zionism in Historical Perspective;* see in particular the introduction to the volume by Herf, x–xix, and the chapter by Markovits.

71. Hanif Kureishi, "Der Karneval der Kulturen. Ein Plädoyer gegen fundamentalistische Wahrheitsbegriffe," *Neue Zürcher Zeitung,* August 11, 2005.

72. On the British diaspora of Islam see Melanie Phillips, *Londonistan.*

73. This point is not well understood by Jonathan Lawrence and Justin Vaisse in their questionable book *Integrating Islam,* 233. For a contrast see B. Tibi, "A Migration Story." My article includes a section on Islamic diasporic antisemitism. The contention of "integrating Islam" is belied by the reality of the failed integration of Muslims in Europe. For evidence and on the related challenges see B. Tibi, *Political Islam,* chapters 5 and 6, and B. Tibi, "Ethnicity of Fear?"

74. This is the phrasing of Lawrence and Vaisse.

75. See Seyran Ateş, *Der Multikulti-Irrtum,* 253.

76. Jeffrey Herf, preface to Matthias Küntzel, *Jihad and Jew-Hatred,* vii–xvii.

77. B. Tibi, "Der Islamismus ist genauso gefährlich wie der Rechtsradikalismus," *Die Welt,* January 15, 2001, 2. On the Islamist radicalization in the Islam diaspora in Europe see Marc Sageman, *Leaderless Jihad,* 71–88. Sageman fails, however, to understand the ideology and the movement involved.

78. See B. Tibi, "Europeanizing Islam or the Islamization of Europe."

79. See Caroline Fourest, *Brother Tariq,* and Paul Berman, The *Flight of the Intellectuals.*

80. See, for instance, Marc Lynch, "Veiled Truth"; in contrast, Paul Berman, *The Flight of the Intellectuals,* provides a better understanding of Islamism. See also my critique of Ramadan in my chapter to Zeyno Baran, *The Other Muslims,* 157–74. Jeffrey Herf and Paul Berman published lengthy rejoinders in the subsequent issue (September 2010) of *Foreign Affairs,* in which Lynch's "Veiled Truth" appeared.

81. These voices are documented by liberal Muslims in Zeyno Baran, ed., *The Other Muslims.*

82. On Islamist networks in Europe see Lorenzo Vidino, *Al-Qaeda in Europe* and, more recently, *The New Muslim Brotherhood in the West.* To be sure, there is no Holocaust in contemporary Europe against Muslims. Ester Webman, the Israeli historian and author of the book *From Empathy to Denial,* coined the formula "Stealing the Holocaust from the Jews" as the title of her paper presented to the International Conference on Antisemitism and Holocaust Denial in Dublin, November 18–19, 2010, to characterize a variety of denial pursued by Islamists.

83. B. Tibi, "Bringing Back the Heterogeneity of Civilizations."

84. Klaus-Michael Mallmann and Martin Cüppers, *Nazi Palestine.* See also Zvi Elpeleg, *The Grand Mufti al-Husaini,* and Klaus Gensicke, *Der Mufti von Jerusalem und die Nationalsozialisten,* as well as Jeffrey Herf, *Nazi Propaganda for the Arab World.*

85. Jeffrey Herf, *Nazi Propaganda for the Arab World,* 225; see also 198–200.

86. Ibid., 243–44; see also 253.

87. Ibid., 265.

88. Quoted ibid., 244.

89. Ibid.

90. Klaus-Michael Mallmann and Martin Cüppers, *Nazi Palestine,* 124 ("The example of the Einsatzgruppen"), 125 ("A vast number of Arabs"), 124 ("friction"), 166 ("Hitler had planned in 1941").

91. Ibid. 111 ("that such a terrorist"), 15 ("the acceptance of the universal values"). The critical reference pertains to the work of Gudrun Krämer.

92. Ibid., 217–18.

93. See Bat Ye'or, *Islam and Dhimmitude,* and Andrew Bostom, *The Legacy of Islamic Antisemitism.*

94. On Islamic tolerence see Yohanan Friedman, *Tolerance and Coercion in Islam.*

95. On the classification of Jews as dhimmi, see Bat Ye'or, *Islam and Dhimmitude.*

96. See Ali Mohammed Jarisha and Mohammed Sharif Zaibaq, *Asalib al-ghazu al-fikri lil alam al-Islami,* and B. Tibi, *Islam's Predicament with Modernity.* To be sure, traditional Islamic tolerance does not solve this flaw.

97. A most deplorable example of this trend is the highly questionable book by Gilbert Achcar, *The Arabs and the Holocaust: The Arab-Israeli War of Narratives* (see also the critical review by the historian Jeffrey Herf in the *New Republic,* www.tnr .com). Achcar does not deny the existence of Arab antisemitism, but—in the name of fighting prejudice and Islamophobia—ends up belittling of this evil to the extent of defaming scholars who straightforwardly address the issue. These scholars, how-ever, provide a better analysis. I restrict this positive reference to Meir Litvak and Esther Webman, *From Empathy to Denial,* and Küntzel, *Jihad and Jew-Hatred.*

Achcar is among those who outlaw the dealing with Islamism as Islamophobia: "Islamophobia has found a means of large-scale sublimation to what has come to be called Islamism" (268). Based on this prejudice he writes further: "For a few years now Bassam Tibi has been one of the authors who serve certain writers as warrant for this Islamophobia" (296). As a devout Muslim who descends from the Islamic Kadi/Mufti aristocracy of Damascus, I prefer to refrain from commenting on this defamation, but quote it to demonstrate the mine field that the present book enters.

98. Michael Borgstede, "Angriff auf den Frieden," *Die Welt,* September 11, 2011, 8.

4. Islamism and Democracy

1. In its July 2008 issue the *Journal of Democracy* published a debate that re-volves around this question addressed in eight contributions.

2. On this issue see the debate covered in Chapter 3 and the related references there, as well as Hannah Arendt, *The Origins of Totalitarianism,* xi–xvi and–120. In Chapter 8, employing Arendt's approach, I conceptualize Islamism as the most re-cent variety of totalitarianism.

3. B. Tibi, "Islamist Parties"; see also the other seven contributions to the de-bate in the July 2008 issue of the *Journal of Democracy.*

4. Marc Lynch, "Veiled Truths." See also the debate on Islamism in the review article by Andrew F. March, "Arguments: *The Flight of the Intellectuals* and Tariq Ramadan" and the response to it by Paul Berman, "Arguments: The Response to Andrew F. March," both published in *Dissent* in 2010.

5. Ibid.

6. The Western scholarly debate on these issues in which I have participated re-lates basically to my contributions to three research projects to be acknowledged be-cause this chapter draws on them: (a) the project at Boston University chaired by Alan Olson, who edited the volume *Educating for Democracy;* (b) the Center for European

Policy Studies, an EU think tank for which Michael Emerson edited *Democratization in the Neighborhood;* and (c) the international congress organized by the Club of Madrid one year after the assaults in that city of March 11, 2004, from which a volume edited by Leonard Weinberg grew: *Democratic Responses to Terrorism.* A more general debate about Islam and democracy can be found in my "Democracy and Democratization in Islam."

7. Contrary to Marc Lynch's assertion, liberal Muslims are not an "insignificant slice." Their pivotal contribution to the debate on democracy is documented in the proceedings of the Arab Congress Azmat al-democratiyya fi al-watan al-Arabi, (Crisis of democracy in the Arab world), published and edited in Arabic by the Center of Arab Unity Studies. This chapter also reflects the Islamic reasoning on democracy earlier pursued in the volume that grew from the November 1982 meeting of seventy leading Arab thinkers and opinion leaders, myself among them, in Limassol, Cyprus, to discuss Azmat al-demoqratiyya fi al-Watan al-Arabi (Crisis of democracy in the Arab world). We were denied a venue at which to convene in any Arab country. No Islamists were invited. My chapter in Arabic is included in that volume, 73–87. Before that Limassol congress a smaller group of leading Arab democrats, to which I also belonged, met in Tunis in October 1980 to discuss the "Arab Future." The host institution, Centre d'Études et de Récherches Economiques et Sociales, acted as an editor to the volume *Les Arabes face à leur destin.*

8. Marc Lynch, "Veiled Truths."

9. Yusuf al-Qaradawi, *Hatmiyyat al-hall al-islami.* Qaradawi views democracy as an "import from the West" and dismisses it. See the important contribution by Ana B. Soage, "Yusuf al-Qaradawi."

10. Sayyid Qutb, *Ma'alim fi al-tariq,* 6–7, emphasis added.

11. Abu al-A'la al-Mawdudi, *al-Islam wa al-Madaniyya al-haditah,* as reprinted verbatim in Mohammed Dharif, *al-Islam al-siyasi fi a-Watan al-Arabi,* 98–99, emphasis added.

12. These quotations are from Yusuf al-Qaradawi, *Hatmiyyat al-Hall al-Islami,* 1: 53–56, 61–73, 111–24.

13. For instance, John Esposito and John Voll do this in *Islam and Democracy.* See my critical review in the *Journal of Religion.*

14. For more details see B. Tibi, *Islam's Predicament with Modernity,* and chapter 10, on "Shura," in B. Tibi, *Der wahre Imam.*

15. On this debate with more details see chapter 7, "Democracy and Democratization in Islamic Civilization," in B. Tibi, *Islam, World Politics, and Europe.*

16. On the first Afghanistan war of the 1980s see Barnett Rubin, *The Fragmentation of Afghanistan,* part III. See also Ahmed Rashid, *The Taliban.*

17. See Raymond Baker, *Islam without Fear,* on the Egyptian Islamists organized in the movement of the Muslim Brotherhood. For a contrast see Lorenzo Vidino, *New Muslim Brotherhood,* and Barry Rubin, *Muslim Brotherhood.*

18. Stephen Larrabee, "Turkey's Broading Crisis," *International Herald Tribune,* July 26–27, 4.

19. Zeyno Baran, *Torn Country,* 140–41. It is worth mentioning that in 2008 the then chief prosecutor of Turkey requested this ban in his 162-page indictment of the AKP as a suspected Islamist party. In that year this view was partly shared by the Constitutional Court, which admitted the indictment but stopped short a verdict of banning. See the report by Sebnem Arsu, "Against Ban on Turkey's Top Party: Judges Cut Financing with Strong Warning," *International Herald Tribune,* July 31, 2008. I argue that the AKP is an Islamist, not an Islamic-conservative party, as it successfully camouflages itself in the West. See also the earlier article by Zeyno Baran, "Turkey Divided," and B. Tibi, "Turkey's Islamist Danger." The AKP takes revenge against the secular judiciary and the supreme court in the new constitution. Turkish Islamists weaken the independent judiciary, and also target the supreme court.

20. Sebnem Arsu, "Turkey Sets Its Sights on a Whole New Constitution" *International Herald Tribune* (global ed. of *New York Times*), September 14, 2010.

21. "Turkish Parliament Approves Bill to Overhaul Judiciary," *New York Times,* May 7, 2010.

22. Marc Champion, "Turkey Faces Rap on Media Curbs," *Wall Street Journal,* November 8, 2010.

23. *Der Spiegel,* November 29, 2010, in particular the article "Volkstribun aus Anatolien: Der NATO-Partner Türkei," 116–17, the source of the following quotations.

24. Ibid.

25. Michael Martens, "Muslime an die Front," *Frankfurter Allgemeine Zeitung,* August 26, 2011.

26. For background on the Egyptian political situation before the uprising, see the chapter on Egypt in Lawrence Harrison, *Developing Cultures,* 2: 63–180, which stands in contrast to Raymond Baker's *Islam without Fear.* See also the classic by the late Richard P. Mitchell, *Society of the Muslim Brothers.*

27. The classic on this movement is by the late Richard P. Mitchell, *The Society of the Muslim Brothers.*

28. See Zeyno Baran, "The Brotherhood Network in the US."

29. On the Muslim Brotherhood in Europe see Lorenzo Vidino, *The New Muslim Brotherhood.*

30. Barry Rubin, *The Muslim Brotherhood.*

31. David Rich, "The Very Model of a British Muslim Brotherhood." On Tariq Ramadan see Caroline Fourest, *Brother Tariq: The Doublespeak of Tariq Ramadan.*

32. David Rich, "The Very Model of a British Muslim Brotherhood," 133.

33. Ana B. Soage, "Yusuf al-Qaradawi."

34. Paul Berman, *The Flight of the Intellectuals,* 92 ("Ramadan's admired hero"), 150 ("Muslim counterculture in the West"). This counterculture is an ethnicized Islam. See B. Tibi, "Ethnicity of Fear?"

35. B. Tibi, "Europeanizing Islam or the Islamization of Europe."

36. Lorenzo Vidino, *The New Muslim Brotherhood,* 222 ("deceitful actors"), 223 ("ample evidence" and "nonviolent Islamists"). On the theme of Islamist doublespeak, see Caroline Fourest, *Brother Tariq: The Doublespeak of Tariq Ramadan.*

37. Robert Hefner, *Civil Islam.*

38. On political ethics in Islam see the contributions included in Sohail Hashmi, *Islamic Political Ethics,* including my chapter 9.

39. This statement was made by Professor Ibrahim in public in Madrid in 2005, during the commemoration of the victims of the terrorist attack of March 11, 2004, the European equivalent to 9/11 in the United States. There, the Club of Madrid organized a huge congress (see note 6). Among the organizers was Professor Peter Neumann of London, who is also the editor of the three volumes that emerged from this venture. I was among the speakers at this Madrid meeting and contributed to the second volume of the papers, edited by Leonard Weinberg, *Democratic Reponses to Terrorism.*

40. See B. Tibi, "Religious Extremism, or Religionization of Politics?"

41. See B. Tibi, *Political Islam, World Politics, and Europe,* as well as the contributions in Zeyno Baran, *The Other Muslims.*

42. Editorial, *Financial Times,* December 28, 2005.

43. Fouad Ajami, *The Foreigner's Gift;* on Iraq's Shi'a see the authoritative study by Yitzhak Nakash, *The Shi'is of Iraq;* more recent, but more biased, is Faleh A. Jabar, *The Shi'ite Movements in Iraq.*

44. On Hamas see also the most informed and enlightening monograph by Matthew Levitt, *Hamas,* and earlier, Shaul Mishal and Avraham Sela, *The Palestinian Hamas.* The overall context is addressed by Beverly Milton-Edwards, *Islamic Politics in Palestine.*

45. See Loren D. Lybarger, *Identity and Religion,* and Amal Jamal, *The Palestinian National Movement.*

46. On Hezbollah see the questionable study by Augustus R. Norton, *Hezbollah.*

47. On this unlucky war see Amos Harel and Avi Issacharoff, *34 Days.*

48. On democracy in the Middle East see the references in note 7 above. More promising on democracy in Indonesia is Robert Hefner, *Civil Islam;* on the one-dimensional interaction between Southeast Asia and the Arab Middle East for the favor of the Middle East see Fred R. von der Mehden, *Two Worlds of Islam,* 97.

49. The book by Jocelyne Cesari, *When Islam and Democracy Meet,* ignores all facts on the ground (Islamist networks placed in Europe) and baselessly claims to see "in the West a reformist trend . . . in Islamic thought," 159. One finds this kind of wishful thinking also in a book by Jytte Klausen, *The Islamic Challenge.*

50. For an example of enlightened Arab-Muslim thought, see Saad Eddin Ibrahim, *Egypt, Islam, and Democracy,* in particular chapter 12, on civil society and the prospects of democratization in the Arab world. See also Beverly Milton-Edwards, *Contemporary Politics in the Middle East,* 145–72, and on the way pre-Islamist modern Muslims made efforts to accommodate democracy, see Hamid Enayat, *Modern Islamic Political Thought,* 125 ff.

51. Leslie Lipson, *The Ethical Crises of Civilization,* 62. On the two waves of the Hellenization of Islam see Watt, *Islamic Philosophy and Theology,* parts II and III. On the Islamic heritage see the classic by Franz Rosenthal, *The Classical Heritage of Islam.*

52. Albert Hourani, *Arabic Thought in the Liberal Age.*

53. Rifa'a Rafi' al-Tahtawi, *Takhlis al-ibriz fi talkhis Paris;* see also B. Tibi, *Der wahre Imam,* 221–51.

54. See the contributions in Philipp Khoury and Joseph Kostiner, *Tribes and State-Formation in the Middle-East.*

55. On military regimes in the Arab world see Eliezer Be'eri, *Army Officers in Arab Politics and Society,* part VI, and B. Tibi, *Militär und Sozialismus in der Dritten Welt.*

56. On "cultural development" see Lawrence Harrison, *Developing Cultures.* I am a contributor to both volumes. On institution building as "political development" see the classic by Samuel P. Huntington, *Political Order in Changing Societies.*

57. For more details see Fouad Ajami, *The Arab Predicament*—reprinted more than a dozen times—herein in particular the chapter on political Islam, 50–75. Sadik J. al-Azm, *Al-naqd al-dhati ba'd al-hazima,* is among the works by critical Arab thinkers appreciated by Fouad Ajami (*The Arab Predicament,* 30–37).

58. The core idea of Islamism is that Islam prescribes a state order; for more details see B. Tibi, *The Challenge of Fundamentalism,* in particular chapters 7 and 8.

See also my "Islamic Law, Shari'a, and Human Rights," and "Return of the Sacred to Politics."

59. Yechi Dreazen, "Iraqi Charter Causes Alarm: Bush Allies Raise Concern over the Role of Islam," *Wall Street Journal,* September 19, 2005, A15.

60. Zeyno Baran, "Turkey Divided," 57.

61. See Matthew Levitt, *Hamas,* and, on the roots of Palestinian Hamas in Muslim Brotherhood, Ziad Abu-Amr, *Islamic Fundamentalism in the West Bank and Gaza.*

62. See the references in note 7.

63. United Nations Development Program, *Arab Human Development Report.*

64. See Hisham Sharabi, *Arab Neo-Patriarchy,* and Hudson, *Arab Politics,* in particular 1–30.

65. The Arab-Muslim Yale-educated Enlightenment philosopher al-Azm writes in *Dhihniyyat al-tahrim,* 17–128, of "*al-Istishraq Ma'kusan*"—Orientalism in reverse— and unravels this as a conspiracy-driven thinking.

66. On conspiracy-driven Arab political thought see B. Tibi, *Die Verschwörung,* and the Spanish edition, *La conspiración.* Later Daniel Pipes published *The Hidden Hand,* not only without acknowledging this previously published work, but also with a different mindset.

67. This question is the point of departure for traditional Muslims and it determines the intellectual history of Islam. See B. Tibi, *Der wahre Imam,* and Fuad Khuri, *Imams and Emirs,* on the role of the imams in creating sectarian divisions within the umma.

68. Al-Farabi, *al-Madina al-Fadila* [On the Perfect State], trans. and ed. Richard Walzer.

69. Barrington Moore, *The Social Origins of Dictatorship and Democracy.*

70. Hasan Sa'b, *al-Islam tijah tahidiyat al-hayat al-'asriyya,* 123.

71. This is an argument against and a criticism of the "postsecular society" of Jürgen Habermas, who fails to understand the reality of religionized politics, as shown in B. Tibi, "Habermas and the Return of the Sacred."

72. Zeyno Baran, "Turkey Divided" and *Torn Country.*

73. John Kelsay, *Arguing the Just War in Islam,* chapter 2. See also B. Tibi, "John Kelsay and Shari'a Reasoning."

74. John Kelsay, *Arguing the Just War in Islam,* 72.

75. Ibid., 165.

76. Zeyno Baran, "Turkey Divided."

77. For an example of these shifts see the autobiographical book by Ed Hussain, *The Islamist.*

78. This was also the view of Abdullahi An-Nai'im, expressed in his first book. Like some other Muslims, An-Na'im swings in a pendulum on this hot-bottom issue: his two books contradict each other. In his 1990 book he adopts a critical view of shari'a, while his 2008 book is an apologetics of it. This puzzling U-turn makes one wonder how the same person could have written so inconsistently. See *Towards an Islamic Reformation* and *Islam and the Secular State.* For a criticism of An-Nai'im see B. Tibi, *Islam's Predicament with Modernity,* 95–129 and 178–208.

79. See B. Tibi, "Turkey's Islamist Danger," 47–54.

80. Zeyno Baran, "Turkey Divided."

81. Larry Diamond, *The Spirit of Democracy.* The late Samuel P. Huntington coined the term "third wave of democratization" in *The Third Wave.*

82. On the view that the order of a shari'a state contradicts individual human rights see B. Tibi: "Islamic Law, Shari'a, and Human Rights," and "The Return of the Sacred to Politics as Constitutional Law." This interpretation rebukes the views of Noah Feldman, *Fall and Rise of the Islamic State.*

83. See the contributions in Eric Patterson and John Gallagher, *Debating the War of Ideas.*

84. Thomas Friedman, "Pay Attention," *International Herald Tribune* (global ed. of *New York Times*), May 30, 2011, 9.

85. Anthony Shadad, "Arab Spring Turns to Blazing Summer," *International Herald Tribune* (global ed. of *New York Times*), August 26, 2011, 5.

86. *International Herald Tribune,* February 5–6, 2011, 3.

87. *International Herald Tribune,* February 4, 2011, 3.

88. *Financial Times,* January 31, 2011, 9.

89. Ibid.

90. Thomas Friedman, "Pay Attention."

91. See my essay "Islamism in the Arab Spring" on the Telos Press blog, http://www.telospress.com/main/index.php?main_page=news_article&article_id=445.

92. *Wall Street Journal,* February 2, 2011, 15. A more accurate transcription of the Arabic is al-Barad'i.

93. *International Herald Tribune,* February 4, 2011, 6.

94. *Frankfurter Allgemeine Zeitung,* February 13, 2011, 2.

95. *International Herald Tribune,* February 3, 2011, 6.

96. Ibid.

97. "Islamists' Role Fuels a Debate," global edition of *New York Times* (*International Herald Tribune*), September 15, 2011 (front page, continued p. 4).

98. Associated Press, "Erdogan in Cairo Touts Turkey as Model for All Arab Nations," *Haaretz* (supplement to *International Herald Tribune,* September 15, 2011), 2.

99. Nabil Abdel Fattah, quoted in "Erdogan in Cairo," *Jerusalem Post,* September 14, 2011.

100. Quoted in Anthony Shadid, "Arab World Turns to Defining Islam after Revolt," global edition of *New York Times* (*International Herald Tribune*), September 30, 2011 (front page, continued p. 7).

101. John Stuart Mill, "On Liberty" (1859), in *On Liberty and Other Essays,* ed. John Gray (Oxford: Oxford University Press, 1998), 9. On "Political Islam and Democracy's Decline to a Voting Procedure," see chapter 7 of my *Political Islam, World Politics, and Europe* (New York: Routledge, 2008), 216–34.

5. Islamism and Violence

1. B. Tibi, *Violence and Religious Fundamentalism in Political Islam.*

2. As is true of any part of Muslim belief, knowledge about the religious obligation to jihad is incorporated in Islamic patterns of socialization equally in family, school, and society. This principle can also be applied to my own upbringing in Damascus. I was first inspired to research jihad and jihadism, however, as part of a project conducted in Jerusalem by the American Ethicon Institute. The findings were published by Terry Nardin as *The Ethics of War and Peace.* The present chapter continues the research for my contribution to that volume.

3. On the reinvention see Hasan al-Banna, "Risalat al-jihad."

4. See volume 1, *Politics and War,* in Bernard Lewis, *Islam.* See also B. Tibi, *Kreuzzug und Djihad,* and my chapter "War and Peace in Islam" in Terry Nardin, *Ethics of War and Peace.*

5. It is pertinent here to remember the work of Max Weber, *Politik als Beruf,* in which he argues that responsibility ethics combined with professional knowledge is part of the profession of policymakers. John Brenkman, *The Cultural Contradictions of Democracy,* outlines a new context most pertinent to Western policy, but most policymakers seem to ignore this. See Henry Kissinger, "How to Repair Our Afghan Strategy," *Washington Post,* June 24, 2010, A21.

6. See Barak Mendelsohn, *Combating Jihadism.* On the recognition that Islamism and security are interrelated, see the contributions in Hillel Frisch and Efraim Inbar, *Radical Islam and International Security.*

7. John Brennan, "A New Approval to Safeguarding Americans," lecture at CSIS, Washington, D.C., August 6, 2009, and repeated elsewhere, http://www.white house.gov/the-press-office/remarks-assistant-president-homeland-security-and -counterterrorism-john-brennan-csi.

8. John Kelsay, *Arguing the Just War in Islam.*

9. David Cook, *Understanding Jihad;* Laurent Murawiec, *The Mind of Jihad.*

10. For historical overviews see Alan Jamieson, *Faith and Sword,* and B. Tibi, *Kreuzzug und Djihad.*

11. On this lecture by the pope and the related story see Knut Wenzel, *Die Religionen und die Vernunft.* The prose of the Regensburg lecture by Pope Benedict in its original German text is known only in sound bites to most protesting Muslims. So it is safe to state that only a few Muslims read it. The text was published under the title "Vernunft baut auf Glauben" in the Christian weekly *Rheinischer Merkur,* issue 37, 2006, 25. This issue was taken up again in a project at the University of Zurich on religion and violence, where I addressed the pope's lecture in more detail. The findings were published by Christiane Abbt and Donata Schoeller, *Im Zeichen der Religion,* including my "Gewalt, Krieg und die Verbreitung der Religion des Islam," specifically 215–21.

12. See note 11.

13. Yahya Blankinship, *The End of the Jihad State.*

14. See Bernard Lewis, *Islam,* vol. 1, *Politics and War;* B. Tibi, *Kreuzzug und Djihad;* Tibi, "War and Peace in Islam"; David Cook, *Understanding Jihad;* Alan Jamieson, *Faith and Sword;* and Efraim Karsh, *Islamic Imperialism.*

15. Bat Ye'or, *Islam and Dhimmitude.*

16. On rules and permitted targets of classical jihad as tenets basic to the distinction between jihad and jihadism see B. Tibi, "War and Peace in Islam." It is unfortunate that Fawaz A. Gerges, the author of *The Far Enemy,* fails to understand this distinction between jihad and jihadism. The distinction in point is not about "going global" (jihad and jihadism are both global). It is about the honoring of rules and complying with limiting targets (irregular war in contrast to regular war).

17. The term "irregular war" that I coined in my first book on Islamism, *The Challenge of Fundamentalism,* 86–88, is a notion that clarifies jihadism and intercivilizational conflict in an understanding of post-Clausewitzian war. See B. Tibi, *Violence and Religious Fundamentalism in Political Islam.*

18. Along the sectarian divides in Islam there exist two varieties of jihadism, one Shi'ite and state-sponsored (Iran), the other Sunni and represented by nonstate actors. For more details on both see B. Tibi, *Political Islam,* chapters 3 and 4.

19. Hedley Bull, "The Revolt Against the West," in particular, 223.

20. See the most interesting article by Daniel Philpott, "The Challenge of September 11."

21. See Mark Juergensmeyer, *Terror in the Mind of God,* and his earlier *The New Cold War.*

22. See "Nasrallah Wins the War," cover story of the *Economist,* August 19, 2006.

23. The change of the nature of war from an interstate conflict to a new post-Clausewitzian warfare waged by nonstate actors is also addressed, however, in different terms by Martin van Creveld, *The Transformation of War,* Kalevi J. Holsti, *The State, War, and the State of War,* and B. Tibi, *Conflict and War in the Middle East,* in particular chapter 12. Some scholars boast of their discovery of "the new wars" (see, e.g. the German professor Herfried Münkler) after 9/11, though without acknowledging the origin of the debate in the cited works.

24. The basic differences between Islam and Islamism explained in Chapters 1 and 2 are also pertinent to a perspective of security; on this see B. Tibi, "Islam and Islamism."

25. See Hasan al-Banna, "Risalat al-jihad," in particular the quotation on 289–91, which I have included in Chapter 1.

26. On the related real history see Bernard Lewis, *Islam,* vol. 1, *Politics and War;* B. Tibi, "War and Peace in Islam"; David Cook, *Understanding Jihad;* Alan Jamieson, *Faith and Sword;* Efraim Karsh, *Islamic Imperialism;* and Walter Kaegi, *Byzantium and the Early Islamic Conquests.* In his Regensburg lecture Pope Benedict did refer to this imperial expansion, unspecifically, quoting Manuel II. In real history the Muslims' violent conquest of Constantinople in 1453 is most essential. This jihad war ended the history of Byzantium. For more details see Steven Runciman, *The Fall of Constantinople.* See also B. Tibi, *Kreuzzug und Djihad,* especially chapter 1 on the early Arab-Muslim jihad conquests and chapter 4 on their continuation by Ottoman Turks. These futuhat were wars of Islamization; in short, the da'wa was not pursued peacefully.

27. See the pertinent chapters in Martin Marty and Scott Appleby, *Fundamentalism and the State.*

28. Peter Neumann, "Europe's Jihadist Dilemma." On jihadist Islamism as a transnational religion that matters to European politics see my *Political Islam, World Politics, and Europe.*

29. Sayyid Qutb, *al-Salam al-Alami wa al-Islam,* 171–73, and Qutb, *al-Jihad for Sabil Allah.* The "war of ideas" is a central part of the issue. See B. Tibi, "Countering Terrorism als Krieg der Weltanschauungen."

30. Eric Hoffer, *The True Believer.*

31. See for instance the flawed survey by Michael Banner, *Jihad in Islamic History.* The reference to al-Banna, 161, is, for instance, fairly meaningless. There are

general contributions like Bruce Lincoln, *Holy Terrors,* with poor knowledge about Islam. More helpful and more comparative are Juergensmeyer, *Terror in the Mind of God,* Cook, *Understanding Jihad,* and Murawiec, *Mind of Jihad.*

32. Books like Dale Eickelmann and James Piscatori, *Muslim Politics,* ignore all basic issues. Political science is not to be confused with anthropology, as Eickelmann does. Piscatori, a political scientist, confuses pan-ideologies (e.g., nationalism) with internationalism, and thus fails to draw a line between what is pan-Islamic and the Islamist internationalism. This confusion gives reasons to mistrust the understanding that underlies what "Islamic Politics" is all about.

33. B. Tibi, *Violence and Religious Fundamentalism in Political Islam.*

34. Marc Sageman, *Understanding Terror Networks* and *Leaderless Jihad.* Unlike Sageman, there are experts who look at jihadism in terms of ideology and movement, not simply technically as "terror networks."

35. In earlier contributions to this theme, such as in Grant Wordlaw, *Political Terrorism,* one finds no reference to Islam or to jihad at all. In contrast, recent books like Bruce Hoffman, *Inside Terrorism,* deal with this issue. Among the more topical contributions are: David J. Whittacker, *The Terrorism Reader,* and Paul R. Pillar, *Terrorism and U.S. Foreign Policy.* In the United States jihadist terror is bizarrely treated by some as a taboo in established Islamic studies. At the same time in popular publications terrorism is identified indiscriminately with Islam, with no distinction between jihad and jihadism. Most professional scholars in the field either remain silent and fail to enlighten, or deny.

36. On Islamic nostalgia see John Kelsay, *Islam and War,* 25–26. This Islamist nostalgia is not a mere romanticism but is associated with a claim for a return of Islamic glory in the new shape of the envisioned Islamist world order.

37. See my entry on jihad in Roger S. Powers and William Vogele, *Protest, Power, and Change.*

38. The seminal work on world order continues to be Hedley Bull's classic, *The Anarchical Society.*

39. See B. Tibi, *From Islamist Jihadism to Democratic Peace?* and on democratic peace, Bruce Russet, *Grasping Democratic Peace.* The origin of the concept is Immanuel Kant, "Zum ewigen Frieden."

40. This notion of disorder is used in the subtitle of my *Challenge of Fundamentalism,* published in 1998 and updated 2002. Stanley Hoffmann, *World Disorders,* also employs the term, but without any reference to religion and fundamentalism, or to earlier research, thus overlooking the basic issue pertinent to this topic. Politicized religion is one of the major sources of disorder and is a threat to security, as I argue throughout the present book.

41. For more details see Rohan Gunaratna, *Inside al-Qaeda,* and his recent book written with Michael Chandler, *Countering Terrorism.* On the Taliban as a case of jihadism see Rashid, *The Taliban.*

42. This allegation of "une vaste conspiration juif-chrétienne" is made by the Algerian Islamist Mohammed Y. Kassab, *L'Islam face au nouvel ordre mondial.* Not only Islamists but also some Germans, left and right, have claimed in best-selling books that September 11 was a homemade U.S. conspiracy. The German news magazine *Der Spiegel,* in its special issue *Verschwörung* (Conspiracy), no. 37, 2003, criticized these best-sellers, some of which were not only anti-American but also antisemitic.

43. Hedley Bull, "The Revolt against the West," 223.

44. See Mohammed Salim al-Awwa, *fi al-Nizam al-Siyasi li al-dawla al-Islamiyya.*

45. Johannes J. G. Jansen, *The Dual Nature of Islamic Fundamentalism,* 1–25.

46. See Barry Buzan, *People, States, and Fear.*

47. Robert Pape, *Dying to Win.*

48. On the traditional origins of this concept and its current relevance see John Kelsay, *Islam and War,* chapter 5, and James T. Johanson, *The Holy War Idea in Western and Islamic Tradition.* The issue has to be placed in the study of civilizations in the tradition of Sir Hamilton Gibb, *Studies on the Civilization of Islam,* who established Islamic Studies at Harvard.

49. On this Sunni-Shi'i conflict carried out, e.g., by shi'ite movements in Iraq after Saddam's fall, see Faleh A. Jabar, *The Shi'ite Movements in Iraq.* In an earlier contribution, Andrew Cockburn and Patrick Cockburn, *Out of the Ashes,* analyzed this issue under Saddam's rule.

50. See B. Tibi, *Political Islam, World Politics, and Europe,* chapter 4.

51. On the rise of Iran to a regional superpower and on the empowering of shi'a pursuant to the Iraq war of 2003 see Alireza Jafarzadeh, *The Iran Threat,* and on the related rise of shi'a, Yitzhak Nakash, *Reaching for Power.*

52. B. Tibi, "Jihadism and Inter-Civilizational Conflict."

53. John Kelsay, *Islam and War,* 117.

54. Leonore Martin, *New Frontiers in Middle Eastern Security,* introduction.

55. See B. Tibi, "Europeanizing Islam or the Islamization of Europe" and "Islamization of Europe." J. Millard Burr and Robert O. Collins, *Alms for Jihad,* in which the latter chapter appears, discloses terror financing and—in contestation of the disclosure—was withdrawn from the market after a successful Saudi lawsuit.

56. See the contributions in Roland Hsu, *Ethnic Europe,* including my "The Return of Ethnicity to Europe via Islamic Migration?"

57. B. Tibi, "Ethnicity of Fear?"

58. Souat Mekhennet, "Young Muslims Travel Route from Germany to Radicalism," *New York Times,* July 31, 2010. These "young Muslims" do not resort to jihadism only because of "grievances" but also as a result of Islamist indoctrination. On Jihadist Islam in Europe see also Russel Berman, *Freedom or Terror,* and also B. Tibi, *Die islamische Herausforderung,* as well as the two books by Lorenzo Vidino cited in the following note.

59. See Lorenzo Vidino, *Al-Qaeda in Europe* and *The New Muslim Brotherhood in the West.*

60. See the paper by B. Tibi, "The Mosques in Germany between Freedom of Faith and Parallel Societies," presented to the conference Secularism in the Muslim Diaspora at the Wilson Center in Washington, D.C., and published in the Occasional Paper Series (Summer 2009) of the Center, 4–10.

6. Islamism and Law

1. Joseph Schacht, *An Introduction to Islamic Law,* 1. The research for this chapter goes back to my Harvard University affiliation in several appointments and continued at the Asia Research Institute, National University of Singapore. My findings have been presented in lectures delivered at Cornell University Law School, and at Carthago University, Tunis, during the International Humanities Convention in July 2006, as well as the Japanese Association for Comparative Constitutional Law in Tokyo. See also my "Return of the Sacred to Politics." I acknowledge that my understanding of Islamic shari'a law is based on borrowings from the work of Schacht. Though I share the spirit (but not the outcome) of the critique of Orientalism, I strongly dismiss turning the table to an Orientalism in reverse. Therefore I deplore the intrusion of Islamic identity politics into the field that disqualifies what non-Muslims write about Islam. As a Muslim, I defend Schacht against the work of Wael Hallaq. Among the questionable books of Hallaq are *The Origins and Evolution of Islamic Law* and *History of Islamic Legal Theories.*

2. See the chapter by John Kelsay on shari'a reasoning in *Arguing the Just War in Islam.* Islamist shari'a reasoning happens in an invention of tradition; see Terence Ranger and Eric Hobsbawm, *The Invention of Tradition,* 1–14.

3. Mahmoud Zaqzuq has a German Ph.D. and therefore he wrote his introduction in German but published it in Cairo; see *Einführung in den Islam,* chapter 3 on diversity and chapter 4 on spirituality.

4. Personal communication in Cairo. On the tatbiq al-shari'a debate see Salah al-Sawi, *al-Muhawara.*

5. On this issue see Mohammed Said al-Ashmawi, *al-Shari'a al-Islamiyya wa al-qanun al-misri.* For more details see the chapter on Egypt in Tibi, *Islam and the*

Cultural Accommodation of Social Change, and chapter 9 in Lawrence Harrison and Peter L. Berger, *Developing Cultures* 163–80.

6. Yusuf al-Qaradawi, *al-Hall al-Islami,* vol. 2 of the three-volume *Hatmiyyat al-Hall al-Islami,* 82–83.

7. See the book by the Sheykh al-Azhar, Mahmud Schaltut, *al-Islam, Aqida wa Shari'a,* 9–13. Another Sheykh of al-Azhar, Jadul-Haq Ali Jadul-Haq, edited the authoritative al-Azhar textbook *Bayan li al-nas,* in which *taschr'i* (legislation) is equated with *wahi* (revelation).

8. Bell's *Introduction to the Qur'an,* completely revised and enlarged by William M. Watt, 162. The numbering of the Qur'anic verses in the present book follows the authoritative German edition by Rudi Paret, *Der Koran.*

9. On the madhahib shari'a schools see Joseph Schacht, *An Introduction to Islamic Law,* chapters 6 and 9, and Joseph Schacht and Clifford Bosworth, *The Legacy of Islam,* chapter 9.

10. On hudud law see Ahmad Fathi Bohnasi, *al-Jara'im fi al-fiqh al-Islami.*

11. According to the founder of Islamic studies at Harvard (before that at Oxford), Sir Hamilton Gibb, the religious foundations of the Islamic caliphate were always based on a post eventum legitimation. See Hamilton A. R. Gibb, *Studies on the Civilization of Islam,* in particular part II.

12. Joseph Schacht, *An Introduction to Islamic Law,* 54 ("to apply and to complete the sacred law"), 54–55 ("a double administration"). Another authoritative source is N. J. Coulson, *A History of Islamic Law.*

13. Hamid Enayat, *Modern Islamic Political Thought,* 67 ("there is no such thing"), 99 ("not . . . any rigid code of laws"), 131 ("was never implemented").

14. Mohammed Said al-Ashmawi, *Usul al-shari'a.*

15. See ibid. and Mohammed Said al-Ashmawi, *al-Islam al-Siyasi,* 177–92.

16. See my paper presented in Tokyo at the International Conference on Comparative Constitutional Law, jointly organized by the Japanese Association for Comparative Constitutional Law in 2005, "Islamic Shari'a as Constitutional Law?" Based on my research for this essay I argue that Noah Feldman is wrong when he takes Islamist shari'a reasoning at face value. See his *The Fall and Rise of the Islamic State,* chapter 3.

17. In his challenge to Max Weber the Harvard sociologist Daniel Bell puts forward the notion of "the return of the sacred." This is a lecture given in 1977 at the London School of Economics and published in his *The Winding Passage.* Weber's notion of "disenchantment of the world" appears in *Soziologie—Weltgeschichtliche Analysen—Politik,* 317. See Bryan S. Turner, *Weber and Islam,* and Wolfgang Schluchter, *Max Webers Sicht des Islam.*

18. See my 1980 contribution "Islam and Secularization" and twenty years later "Secularization and De-Secularization in Modern Islam." The final outcome of this reasoning appears in chapter 6 of my *Islam's Predicament with Modernity*.

19. On the call for tatbiq al-shari'a, the implementation of shari'a, see Salah al-Sawi, *al-Muhawara*, and B. Tibi, *The Challenge of Fundamentalism*, 158–78.

20. Abdullahi an-Na'im, *Towards an Islamic Reformation*, 100 ("the Qur'an does not mention"), 99 ("unattainable under shari'a").

21. See Tibi, *Islam between Culture and Politics*, chapters 7 and 11.

22. Ali Abdelraziq, *al-Islam wa usul al-hukm*. For a French translation see *Revue des Études Islamiques* 7 (1933) and 8 (1934). On Abdelraziq, see B. Tibi, *Arab Nationalism*, 170–77. See also Mohammed Said al-Ashmawi, *al-Khilafah al-Islamiyya*.

23. Mark Juergensmeyer, *The New Cold War?*

24. See Daniel Bell, "Return of the Sacred"; Max Weber, *Soziologie—Weltgeschichtliche Analysen—Politik*, 317; Bryan S. Turner, *Weber and Islam;* and Wolfgang Schluchter, *Max Webers Sicht des Islam*.

25. Nekki Keddie, *An Islamic Response to Imperialism*.

26. Sayyid Qutb, *Ma'alim fi al-tariq*, 5–7.

27. Sayyid Qutb, *al-Salam al-Alami wa al-Islam*, 171–73.

28. See chapters 2 on knowledge and chapter 6 on secularization in B. Tibi, *Islam's Predicament with Modernity*.

29. John Kelsay, *Islam and War*, 117; see also John Kelsay, *Arguing the Just War in Islam*.

30. Ibn Taymiyyah, *al-Siyasa al-Shari'yya*, reprinted in many editions and published by many presses. On Ibn Taymiyyah see B. Tibi, *Der wahre Imam*, chapter 5. The early Abdullahi an-Na'im in *Towards an Islamic Reformation* once offered an alternative to Ibn Taymiyyah and his contemporary followers, but An-Na'im later changed his mindset. Emmanuel Sivan, *Radical Islam*, points at the impact of medieval Ibn Taymiyyah on modern Islamism.

31. This coinage leans on the famous formula of Eric Hobsbawm, "invention of tradition."

32. On this rationalism in Islam see B. Tibi, *Der wahre Imam*.

33. In contrast, Westernization was viewed positively earlier, for instance by Theodore von Laue, *The World Revolution of Westernization*. Today, no scholar could write such a book, have it published by a university press, and go unscathed. On the de-Westernization of law see my paper published by the law school of the University of Frankfurt, "Die Entwestlichung des Rechts."

34. This is an argument put forward by the Iranian born scholar Mehrzad Boroujerdi in *Iranian Intellectuals and the West.*

35. This notion was coined by Jürgen Habermas *in Glauben und Wissen;* for a critique see Tibi, "Habermas and the Return of the Sacred." Habermas has never responded to this criticism.

36. See the contributions included in Y. Raj Isar and Helmut Anheier, *Conflicts and Tensions,* in particular my chapter, "Islam between Religious-Cultural Practice and Identity Politics."

37. *Al-Hayat,* May 7, 2005. See the commentary by B. Tibi, "The Clash of Sharia and Democracy," *International Herald Tribune,* September 17–18, 2005.

38. B. Tibi, "Islamic Law, Shari'a, and Human Rights" and "European Tradition of Human Rights and the Culture of Islam."

39. Dale Eickelmann and James Piscatori, in chapter 2 of *Muslim Politics,* acknowledge "the invention of tradition in Muslim politics" but utterly fail to grasp the shari'atization of politics, nor do they distinguish between Islam and Islamism, or classical shari'a and the invention of its tradition.

40. Mohammed al-Ghazali, *Huquq al-insan bain al-Islam wa I'lan al-umam al-mutahhidah;* Mohammed Imara, *al-Islam wa huquq al-insan.*

41. See Abdullahi An-Na'im, *Towards an Islamic Reformation,* and in contrast Abdullahi An-Na'im, *Islam and the Secular State.*

42. See Bat Ye'or, *Islam and Dhimmitude,* and B. Tibi, "The Pertinence of Islam's Predicament with Democratic Pluralism."

43. See Abdulazim Ramadan, *Jama'at al-Takfir.*

44. This is acknowledged by Sami Zubaida, *Law and Power in the Islamic World,* chapter 3, who nonetheless as a Marxist has great problems with understanding the meaning of religion beyond power and economics.

45. See, e.g., Najib al-Armanazi, *al-Shar' al-duwali fi al-Islam.*

46. See ibid., Mohammed Said al-Ashmawi, *Usul al-shari'a,* Abdullahi A. An-Na'im, *Towards an Islamic Reformation,* and Subhi al-Salih, *Ma'alim al-shari'a al-Islamiyya.* Al-Salih was the vice mufti of Lebanon, killed by Shi'ite gunmen in Beirut.

47. My understanding of international society in world politics has been shaped by Hedley Bull, *The Anarchical Society,* 13. Bull argues that international society exists "when a group of states conscious of certain common interests and common values form a society." The values of shari'a do not fulfill this requirement.

48. On this notion see my chapter in Robert Fortner and Mark Fackler, *Handbook of Global Communication.*

49. On the Saudi-sponsored shari'a universalism see Stephen Schwartz, *The Two Faces of Islam*. For a contrast see Paul Cliteur, *The Secular Outlook*.

50. H. L. A. Hart, *The Concept of Law*, 221. See also Michael Akehurst, *A Modern Introduction to International Law*, 21 ff.; F. S. C. Northrop, *The Taming of the Nations*; and Terry Nardin, *Law, Morality, and the Relations of States*.

51. For more details on the Sunni and Shi'ite varieties of this Islamist internationalism see B. Tibi, *Islam, World Politics, and Europe*, part II.

52. See the contributions to Tore Lindholm and Kari Vogt, *Islamic Law Reform and Human Rights*.

53. See chapter 3 on law in B. Tibi, *Islam's Predicament with Modernity*.

54. Abdullahi An-Na'im, *Islam and the Secular State*, 290–91.

55. Theodor Viehweg, *Topik und Jurisprudenz*, 118. This is allowed by Salih, *Ma'alim al-shari'a*, 122 ff., but not by Yusuf al-Qaradawi, *al-Halal wa al-haram fi al-Islam*.

56. On the notion of cross-cultural morality and its meaning for bridging see my chapter in Roman Herzog et al., *Preventing the Clash of Civilizations*.

57. On this classical binary see Najib al-Armanazi, *al-Shar' al-duwali fi al-Islam*; W. M. Watt, *Islamic Political Thought*, 91; and Tibi, "War and Peace in Islam."

58. See B. Tibi, "Bridging the Heterogeneity of Civilizations."

59. See the articles by Ann E. Mayer, Abdulaziz Sachedina, and Norman Caldor on "Islamic Law" in John Esposito, *Oxford Encyclopedia of the Middle Eastern World*, 2: 450–72.

60. See B. Tibi, *Islam and the Cultural Accommodation of Social Change*, 76–101, and Ann E. Mayer, "Law and Religion in the Muslim Middle East."

61. See Donald E. Smith, *Politics and Social Change in the Third World*.

62. Rudi Paret, *Mohammed und der Koran*; Bell and Watt, *Introduction to the Qur'an*; N. J. Dawood, *The Koran*, 320 ff.; and Johan Bouman, *Gott und Mensch im Qur'an*.

63. See W. M. Watt, *Islamic Revelation in the Modern World*.

64. N. J. Coulson, *A History of Islamic Law*, 5–7. See also part III, "Islamic Law in Modern Times."

65. For an example see Sabir Tu'aima, *al-Shari'a al-Islamiyya fi asr al-ilm*, 208 ff.

66. Malcolm Kerr, *Islamic Reform*. Kerr was murdered by Islamist Shi'ite fanatics in Beirut in January 1984, while president of the American University of Beirut. Kerr is defamed by Muslehuddin, *Philosophy in Islamic Law and the Orientalists*, 242, 247.

67. See B. Tibi, *Islam's Predicament with Modernity,* 95–129, and my chapters in Lawrence Harrison, *Developing Cultures,* 1: 245–60, and 2: 163–80.

68. More on this in B. Tibi, *Islam between Culture and Politics,* 159–66.

7. Islamism, Purity, and Authenticity

1. The fashionable notion of authenticity on which the claim to identity politics rests is a contemporary drive that is central to Islamism. My work on this subject has been associated with an effort to introduce the social-scientific study of religion and culture in international relations. As I have pointed out, interest in the new discipline of Islamology grew rapidly only after 9/11. The pilot projects on this issue area that have been pertinent for the completion of this chapter are the Culture and Globalization Research Project, chaired by Y. Raj Isar and Helmut Anheier, and the Culture Matters Research Project, chaired by Lawrence Harrison. I am a coauthor of the volumes in which the research findings of both projects are published: Y. Raj Isar and Helmut Anheier, *Conflicts and Tensions,* and Lawrence Harrison, *Developing Cultures.* Those projects provided the research background for this chapter, as well as to chapter 8 on authenticity in my *Islam's Predicament with Modernity.* Here I develop the arguments included there, but with a further focus on Islamism and purity.

2. The classic on this subject is the book by David Apter, *The Politics of Modernization.* On Westernization see Theodore von Laue, *The World Revolution of Westernization.*

3. Yusuf al-Qaradawi, *Bayinat al-hall al-Islami wa shabahat al-ilmaniyyin wa al-Mustaghribin.*

4. Faruq Abdul-Salam, *al-Ahzab al-siyasiyya wa al-fasl bain al-din wa al-siyasa,* 4.

5. Ibid., 137. For more details on this issue see B. Tibi, "Secularization and De-Secularization in Islam," and chapter 6 in B. Tibi, *Islam's Predicament with Modernity.*

6. See the interesting but not so critical book by Robert Lee, *Overcoming Tradition and Modernity: The Search for Islamic Authenticity.* The authoritative—but also uncritical—work on this subject is Charles Taylor, *The Ethics of Authenticity.*

7. Anwar al-Jundi, *Min al-tabai'iyya ila al-asalah,* 184.

8. Anwar al-Jundi, *Ahdaf al-taghrib;* on the conspiracy 11–29.

9. Mohammed Sharif Zaibaq and Ali Mohammed Jarisha, *al-Ghazu al-fikri lil alam al-Islami.*

10. Anwar al-Jundi, *al-Mu'asarah fi itar al-asalah,* 35. All of the following quotations, if not otherwise referenced, originate from that book and are translated from Arabic by the author.

11. Albert Hourani, *Arabic Thought in the Liberal Age.*

12. For the research on this inner-Islamic conflict in the history of ideas, see B. Tibi, "Politisches Denken im mittelalterlichen Islam zwischen Philosophie (Falsafa) und Religio-Jurisprudenz (Fiqh)."

13. On these questions see the bright answers given by Mohammed al-Jabri, *Arab-Islamic Philosophy*.

14. See John Kenny, *The Politics of Identity*. See also my chapter on Islamic identity politics in H. Anheier and Y. Raj Isar, *Conflicts and Tensions*.

15. This view is shared with the late Mohammed Abed al-Jabri, *Arab-Islamic Philosophy:* The best elaboration of the notion of cultural modernity is Jürgen Habermas, *The Philosophical Discourse of Modernity*. In the aftermath of 9/11 Habermas retreated and proclaimed a "postsecular society." This deplorable retreat amounts to a setback, as I have argued in "Habermas and the Return of the Sacred."

16. See B. Tibi, "Politisches Denken im mittelalterlichen Islam zwischen Philosophie (Falsafa) und Religio-Jurisprudenz (Fiqh)." In my comprehensive intellectual history of Islam, *Der wahre Imam,* I contrast the fiqh and falsafa traditions to demonstrate two rival discourses throughout Islamic history.

17. See Franz Rosenthal, *The Classical Heritage of Islam*. This heritage is based on Hellenization with seeds of enlightenment. Contemporary Islamism claims to be an Islamic revival, but it is not based on this heritage.

18. Jürgen Habermas, *The Philosophical Discourse of Modernity,* 18.

19. Robert Lee, *Overcoming Tradition and Modernity,* 191.

20. George Makdisi, *The Rise of the Colleges*.

21. For a survey on these efforts see the most valuable work of Anke von Kugelgen, *Averroës und die arabische Moderne*.

22. Mohammed al-Jabri, *Arab-Islamic Philosophy,* 124.

23. Herbert A. Davidson, *Averroes, al-Farabi, and Avicenna on Intellect*. On Hellenization of Islam see W. M. Watt, *Islamic Philosophy and Theology,* parts II and III.

24. For more details B. Tibi, "The Worldview of Sunni Arab Fundamentalists."

25. Emmanuel Sivan, *Militant Islam*. To be sure, in Islam fiqh is not kalam (theology) and therefore Sivan is wrong!

26. Robert Lee, *Overcoming Tradition and Modernity,* 191, 193.

27. Ibid., 177.

28. Rifa'a R. al-Tahtawi, *Takhlis al-ibriz fi talkhis Paris*. There is an excellent German translation by Karl Stowasser, *al-Tahtawi*.

29. B. Tibi, *Islam's Predicament with Modernity,* chapter 2.

30. On this accusations of Muslims of *jahl,* ignorance, by al-Afghani see the edition by Mohammed Imara, *al-A'mal al-Kamila li al-Afghani,* 448; see also 327–28.

31. See Hasan al-Banna's collected writings in one volume, *Majmu'at Rasa'il al-Imam al-Shahid.*

32. Science was highly developed in classical Islam. For more details see Edward Grant, *The Foundations of Modern Science in the Middle Ages,* 29 ff., 176 ff.; and Toby E. Huff, *The Rise of Early Modern Science,* 47 ff. On the Islamic tradition of science see also Howard Turner, *Science in Medieval Islam.*

33. Gerald Holton, *Science and Anti-Science.*

34. See Max Weber, *Soziologie, weltgeschichtliche Analysen, Politik,* 317.

35. See David Lindberg, *The Beginnings of Western Science,* in particular chapters 8–10; quotation is from 168.

36. See chapter 2, "Knowledge" in: B. Tibi, *Islam's Predicament with Modernity;* and Yusuf al-Qaradawi, *Bayinat al-hall al-Islami wa shabahat al-ilmaniyyin wa al-Mustaghribin.* For a contrast see Yusuf al-Qaradawi, *Bayinat al-hall al-Islami wa shabahat al-ilmaniyyin wa al-Mustaghribin.*

37. See Ziauddin Sardar, *Islamic Futures,* 85–86; see also Ziauddin Sardar, *Exploration in Islamic Science.*

38. David Lindberg, *The Beginnings of Western Science,* 170–71.

39. See Richard Martin, Mark R. Woodward, and Dwi S. Atmaja, *Defenders of Reason in Islam.*

40. The formula *"bi al-wahi aw bi al-aql"*—Either by revelation or by reason—was coined and given authenticity by Abu al-Hassan al-Marwadi, *Kitab al-ahkam al-sultaniyya* [Book of rules on the Sultanic government].

41. David Lindberg, *The Beginnings of Western Science,* 174. See also 180.

42. See ibid., as well as Edward Grant, *Foundations of Modern Science in the Middle Ages;* Toby E. Huff, *Rise of Early Modern Science;* and Howard Turner, *Science in Medieval Islam.*

43. Robert Wuthnow, *Meaning and Moral Order,* 265–98.

44. International Institute of Islamic Thought, *Islamiyyat al-ma'rifah.*

45. See the second report of the United Nations Development Program on Arab Human Development 2003, *Building a Knowledge Society* (New York: United Nations, 2003). Instead of a search for knowledge, apologetic authors like C. A. Qadir, *Philosophy and Science in the Islamic World,* and Abdulrawiq Nawfal, *al-Muslimun wa al-ilm,* prefer to praise the Islamic collective self.

46. Among these accomplishments is the masterpiece of the medieval-Islamic philosopher al-Farabi, translated by Richard Walzer as *Al-Farabi on the Perfect State.*

Basic texts by al-Farabi are included in the most valuable reader edited by Ralph Lerner and Muhsin Mahdi, *Medieval Political Philosophy*. See also David Reisman, "al-Farabi and the Philosophical Curriculum," and the Farabi chapter in Tibi, *Der wahre Imam,* 133–50, as well as Ian Richard Netton, *al-Farabi and His School.*

47. Jamal al-Afghani, *al-A'mal al-kamila,* 448.

48. Niklas Luhmann, *Funktion der Religion,* 87.

49. On the Islamic dream, or illusion, of semimodernity see chapter 11 in B. Tibi, *Islam's Predicament with Modernity.*

50. For example the major Islamic reformer Mohammed Abduh, *al-Islam wa al-Nasraniyya bain al-Ilm wa al-Madaniyya.*

51. Sadik J. al-Azm, *Naqd al-fikr al-dini.*

52. Mohammed al-Jabri, *Arab-Islamic Philosophy,* 128.

53. International Institute of Islamic Thought, *Islamiyyat al-ma'rifah.*

54. David C. Lindberg, *The Beginnings of Western Science,* 180.

55. Robert R. Reilly, *The Closing of the Muslim Mind.* Reilly, who has a point and rightly draws a line between the Islamic past and present, overstretches, however, Asha'rism (Islamic orthodoxy) and fails to draw a line between Islam and Islamism.

56. John Waterbury, "Social Science Research and Arab Studies in the Coming Decade."

57. John Waterbury and Alan Richards, *A Political Economy of the Middle East,* chapter 14, "Is Islam the Solution?" 346–65.

8. Islamism and Totalitarianism

1. The interpretation in this book of political religions as totalitarian ideologies has been inspired by the participation in a research project on this issue conducted at the Hannah Arendt Center for the Study of Totalitarianism at the University of Dresden. In addition, my activity since 2007 as a consulting editor of the journal *Totalitarian Movements and Political Religions* had an impact on my thinking. This journal focuses on related research and also publishes my work. Other editors of *TMPR,* in particular Jeff Bale and Roger Griffin, have been inspiring. The journal published in its issue no. 1 of 2007 my study on Islamist totalitarianism "The Totalitarianism of Jihadist Islamism." Jeffrey Bale and I were in charge for the *TMPR* special issue on Islamism (vol. 10, 2009). At the Hannah Arendt Institute for Research on Totalitarianism, I contributed to the volume on political religion edited by Gerhard Besier and Hermann Lübbe, *Politische Religion und Religionspolitik.* The bilingual journal of the Center, *Religion-Staat-Gesellschaft,* has published since its establishment in 2000 several of my articles on Islamism interpreted as a political religion both in English and in German.

2. Raymond Aron, *Paix et guerre entre les nations*. Chapter 8 includes this prediction made at the height of bipolarity and its binary of the East-West blocs.

3. Francis Fukuyama, *The End of History and the Last Man*. This assumption reflected a premature forecast. At the time of its publication, shortly after the end of the East-West conflict, most Western international relations scholars overlooked the challenge by Islamism in its claim for the restoration of Islamic supremacy as a return of history; for more details see my *Political Islam, World Politics, and Europe,* the introduction and chapter 5. Larry Diamond, *The Spirit of Democracy,* continues to assume a global democratization.

4. In all respect due to the late Samuel Huntington and in an unforgettable gratitude for his invitation to join Harvard in 1982, I deplore his deliberate negligence of my work in which I express disagreement with his "clash of civilizations." Huntington knew of my book *Krieg der Zivilisationen* and wrote me a friendly letter on March 30, 1995, with this positive feedback: "In skimming through the book, I could see that you have developed powerful arguments on the roles of civilizations, religion and of the West and Islam in the contemporary world. I trust the book will get a favorable reception." Nevertheless, the late Huntington chose to ignore my book, which predates his, as well as the expression of disagreement, which is a violation of scholarly standards. I elaborated on our differences in the new edition of that book republished in 1998 (Munich: Heyne Verlag, expanded 1998), which includes a new chapter (305–33) in which I dissociate my thinking about civilizations from any Huntingtonization of the civilizational conflict, though without engaging in the ritual of a demonization of Huntington, which I reject. This mindset is reflected in "International Morality and Cross-Cultural Bridging," my contribution to the volume of Roman Herzog, by then the president of Germany, *Preventing the Clash of Civilizations,* 107–26.

5. In this regard the most authoritative and highly competent case study on Egypt—which is also the most important country in the Middle East for the study of Islamism—is the impressive book by John Waterbury, *Egypt under Nasser and Sadat*. Also see chapter 14 on political Islam, both acting in opposition and when in power, in Alan Richards and John Waterbury, *A Political Economy of the Middle East*.

6. In *The Cultural Contradictions of Democracy,* 165–70, John Brenkman coins in a short section the term "Islam's civil war," which turns into a "geo-civil war," though he fails to provide any further elaboration of the notion. In *Islam's Predicament with Modernity* I address the same issue, but argue that there are intra-Islamic tensions related to the predicament indicated in the title of the book; when these tensions become politicized then they develop into sources of conflict (see chapter 5). This process happens not only locally and regionally, but also on a global level. This is the substance of what could be termed Islam's "geo-civil war."

7. Lawrence Harrison and Jerome Kagan, *Developing Cultures: Essays on Cultural Change*. This is vol. 1 of the publication of the Culture Matters Research

Program at the Fletcher School, Tufts University; vol. 2 is Lawrence Harrison and Peter L. Berger, *Developing Cultures: Case Studies.*

8. This crisis is addressed in four books, three of them by Muslim scholars. These are, chronologically, B. Tibi, *The Crisis of Modern Islam;* Bernard Lewis, *The Crisis of Islam;* Ali A. Allawi, *The Crisis of Islamic Civilization;* and Hichem Djaït, *Islamic Culture in Crisis.*

9. B. Tibi, "Islam: Between Religious-Cultural Practice and Identity Politics."

10. See Wilfried C. Smith, The *Meaning and the End of Religion.*

11. The coinage "al-hall al-Islami" originates in the trilogy bearing that title by Yusuf al-Qaradawi.

12. This argumentation appears in the repeatedly quoted, highly influential Yusuf al-Qaradawi, *al-Hall al-Islami.*

13. For references on Iran see Alireza Jafarzadeh, *The Iran Threat,* on Afghanistan, Ahmed Rashid, *The Taliban,* and on Sudan, Dan Petterson, *Inside Sudan.*

14. For more details see B. Tibi, *Political Islam, World Politics, and Europe,* chapters 5 and 6, and my chapter on Islam in Roland Hsu, *Ethnic Europe,* 127–56.

15. See, for instance, the flawed studies by Jonathan Lawrence and Justine Vaisse, *Integrating Islam;* Jytte Klausen, *The Islamic Challenge;* and Jocelyne Cesari, *Where Islam and Democracy Meet.*

16. See B. Tibi, "Ethnicity of Fear?"; B. Tibi, *Political Islam, World Politics, and Europe;* B. Tibi, "The Return of Ethnicity to Europe via Islamic Migration?"; and Lorenzo Vidino, *al-Qaeda in Europe.*

17. Noah Feldman, *The Fall and Rise of the Islamic State,* 124 ("disaster waiting to happen"), 119 ("compatibility of shari'a and democracy"). For a competing view on the notion of the "Islamic state" and for a different understanding of politicized shari'a see my *The Challenge of Fundamentalism,* chapters 7 and 8. In Chapter 6 of this book on the shari'atization in Islamist politics I also discuss the "shari'a state." For a critical assessment of politicized shari'a see my contribution to the following legal authoritative publications: Mashood A. Baderin, *International Law and Islamic Law,* chapter 16, and Japanese Association of Comparative Constitutional Law, *Church and State: Towards Protection for Freedom of Religion,* 126–70.

18. On Islamism and democracy see Chapter 4 and also my *Political Islam, World Politics, and Europe,* chapter 7.

19. This assessment does not discount crisis and dissent in that country; see John Bradley, *Saudi Arabia Exposed,* and earlier Mamoun Fandy, *Saudi Arabia and the Politics of Dissent.*

20. John Waterbury, *Egypt under Nasser and Sadat.*

21. See the report "Turkey Sets Its Sights on a Whole New Constitution," *International Herald Tribune* (global ed. of *New York Times*), September 14, 2010, 3. See also the report "Turkey Faces Rap (by EU) on Media Curbs," *Wall Street Journal,* November 8, 2010, and the commentary "Turkey's Radical Drift," *Wall Street Journal,* June 4–6, 2010, 2. On early AKP influence see Zeyno Baran, "Turkey Divided," and B. Tibi, "Turkey's Islamist Danger"; see also Zeyno Baran, *Torn Country.*

22. Carrie Rosefsky Wickham, *Mobilizing Islam.*

23. See John Cooley, *Unholy Wars.* This book, published in 1999, includes on its cover a picture of Osama bin Laden, who was not yet well known in the United States. See also the earlier disclosure in Kurt Lehbeck, *Holy War, Unholy Victory.*

24. See the documentation of the European-German-Afghan connection that led to the 9/11 assaults that was filed by the editors of the German magazine *Der Spiegel:* Stefan Aust and Cordt Schnibben, *11. September.* See also on the Hamburg cell of al-Qaeda Rohan Gunarattna, *Inside al-Qaeda,* 129–31.

25. Emad El Din Shahin, "Egypt's Moment of Reform," in *Democratization in the European Neighborhood,* 123. The same volume, edited by Michael Emerson, includes B. Tibi, "Islam, Freedom, and Democracy in the Arab World," with a different assessment of Islamism.

26. Emad El Din Shahin "Egypt's Moment of Reform," 128, 129 ("institutional guarantees"); see also Shahin, *Political Ascent.*

27. Robert Leiken and Steven Brooke, "The Moderate Muslim Brotherhood."

28. Raymond Baker, *Islam without Fear,* and Bruce Rutherford, *Egypt after Mubarak,* as well as Marc Lynch, "Veiled Truth."

29. See the historical survey on the Weimar Republic by Hagen Schulze, *Weimar Deutschland.*

30. See the editorial "People Ignore Predictions They Dislike," *Financial Times,* December 30, 2008, 7, whose author posits that the financial crisis of 2009 was predicted, but that the prediction was disliked and therefore ignored. This theory sheds light on the stance of opinion leaders in the West toward Islamism: they ignore predictions about Islamists in power (e.g., Hamas in Gaza) because they dislike these alerts.

31. Karl Wittfogel, *Oriental Despotism.*

32. Paul Berman, The *Flight of the Intellectuals*, and Jeffrey Herf, *Nazi Propaganda for the Arab World.*

33. Hannah Arendt, The *Origins of Totalitarianism,* ix.

34. Max Horkheimer, a Holocaust survivor and the founder of the Frankfurt School of Critical Theory, who was my academic teacher, argued that supporters of his critical theory must pledge to combat any totalitarianism. See B. Tibi, "The Political

Legacy of Max Horkheimer and Islamist Totalitarianism." In this tradition and following both Arendt and Horkheimer, I published 2004 in German my book on Islamism
bearing the title *Der neue Totalitarismus.*

35. Elisabeth Young-Bruehl, *Why Arendt Matters,* is a superb study that upholds
the continued topicality of Arendt's theorizing about totalitarianism.

36. See note 1 above on totalitarian ideologies based on political religion and the
reference to the Hannah Arendt Institute for the Study of Totalitarianism–based
study edited by Gerhard Besier, who was then HAIT director. The major theorist on
political religions is Emilio Gentile, *Politics as Religion.*

37. Elisabeth Young-Bruehl, *Why Arendt Matters,* 266, 281.

38. Ibid., 35–36 ("a kind of imperialism"), 56 ("the Muslim Brotherhood led by
the Egyptian Hasan al-Banna" and "one of the most threatening ways").

39. See Jean Charles Brisard, *Zarqawi.*

40. Daniel Benjamin and Steven Simon, "Zarqawi's Life after Death," *International Herald Tribune,* June 10–11, 2006, 4; see also the special issues on this subject
"After Zarqawi," *Newsweek,* June 19, 2006, and *Time,* the same date.

41. B. Tibi, "The Totalitarianism of Jihadist Islamism"; see also B. Tibi, "Political Legacy of Max Horkheimer and Islamist Totalitarianism," and *Der neue Totalitarismus.*

42. Hannah Arendt, *The Origins of Totalitarianism,* ix ("totalitarianism is not
merely dictatorship"), 281 ("the permanent domination"), 326 ("totalitarian movements").

43. Ibid., 308 ("aim at and succeed"), 359 ("The motive of a global conspiracy").

44. On the terror of Hamas see the excellent study by Matthew Levitt, *Hamas,*
chapters 2 and 5.

45. Hannah Arendt, *The Origins of Totalitarianism,* 312.

46. Zeyno Baran, *Torn Country.*

47. Hannah Arendt, *The Origins of Totalitarianism,* 391–92.

48. Ibid., 331; see also chapter 13, "Ideology and Terror."

49. Ibid., 465.

50. Eric Hoffer, *The True Believer.*

51. See Eric Patterson and John Gallagher, *Debating the War of Ideas.* See also
B. Tibi, "Countering Terrorism als Krieg der Weltanschauungen."

52. For a prominent example of this flaw see Robert Pape, *Dying to Win.*

53. B. Tibi, "Islamism and Democracy."

54. Lorenzo Vidino, *The New Muslim Brotherhood in the West.*

55. See the deceptive and misleading selection of text in the reader of Charles Kurzman, *Liberal Islam,* in which the heir of Sayyid Qutb, namely Yusuf al-Qaradawi, becomes a representative of "liberal Islam."

56. Francis Fukuyama, "Identity, Immigration, and Liberal Democracy." See also B. Tibi; "Ethnicity of Fear?"; B. Tibi, *Political Islam, World Politics, and Europe;* B. Tibi, "The Return of Ethnicity to Europe via Islamic Migration?"; and Lorenzo Vidino, *The New Muslim Brotherhood in the West.*

57. Jürgen Habermas, *Glauben und Wissen;* see B. Tibi, "Habermas and the Return of the Sacred."

58. In Hedley Bull's seminal work *The Anarchical Society,* the study of order is placed at the center of international relations; see in particular part I. For an appreciation of Bull, see the essay "Bull and the Contribution to International Relations" in Stanley Hoffmann, *World Disorders,* 13–34.

59. Sayyid Qutb, *al-Islam wa Mushkilat al-Hadarah,* 191; the reference to the enemies is on 186. Qutb combines theology with politics, leading to the religionized politics that underpin Islamism as a political religion.

60. Without a reference to Hannah Arendt, Emanuel Sivan, *Radical Islam: Medieval Theology and Modern Politics,* uses the term as a subtitle for his book. The related worldview is analyzed by B. Tibi, *Islam between Culture and Politics,* 53–68.

61. See B. Tibi; "Ethnicity of Fear?"; B. Tibi, *Political Islam, World Politics, and Europe;* B. Tibi, "The Return of Ethnicity to Europe via Islamic Migration?"; Lorenzo Vidino, *New Muslim Brotherhood in the West;* and Peter Katzenstein and Timothy Byrnes, *Religion in an Expanding Europe,* which introduced the concept of "transnational religion" into the discipline of international relations in a project conducted at Cornell University 2003–6 in which I participated, contributing the chapter "The Europeanization of Islam or the Islamization of Europe."

62. The origin of this concept is included in Sayyid Qutb, *Ma'alim fi al-Tariq,* published in millions of copies in Arabic as well as in diverse translations to other Islamic languages. I use the 13th legal edition.

63. Sayyid Qutb, *al-Salam al-'alami wa al-Islam,* 171–73. See Chapter 5 and my "Jihad."

64. Jean Bethke Elshtain, *Just War against Terror.*

65. Hedley Bull, "The Revolt against the West"; Bull's interpretation is supported by the Muslim Brother Muhhamed Imarah in *al-Sahwa al-Islamiyya wa al-Tahaddi al-Hadari* (The Islamic awakening and the civilization challenge) (Cairo: Dar al-Shuruq, 1991), in which he argues for a "revolt against the West" in this

sense: the revolt is not only against the hegemony of the West, it is against its civilization as such and its values; see 30–40 and, on the Muslim Brothers, 41–83.

66. See the remarkable article by Daniel Philpott, "The Challenge of September 11 to Secularism in International Relations."

67. This idea was put forward at first in a project of the German Council for Foreign Affairs on postbipolar German policy; see the resulting three-volume publication edited by Karl Kaiser and colleagues, *Deutschlands neue Außenpolitik*, including my contribution "Die Revolte gegen den Westen in der neuen internationalen Umwelt."

68. Benedict Anderson, *Imagined Communities*, provides the best framework for conceptualizing this drive.

69. See the contributions in Adeed Dawisha, *Islam in Foreign Policy*, and more recently Graham Fuller and Ian Lesser, *A Sense of Siege*, and B. Tibi, *Political Islam, World Politics, and Europe*, 130–52.

70. John Kelsay, *Islam and War*, 117.

71. Stanley Hoffmann, *World Disorders*; on the term "disorder," with reference to religion and fundamentalism, and on "disorder" as a threat to security, see B. Tibi, *The Challenge of Fundamentalism*.

72. Paul Berman, The *Flight of the Intellectuals*, 285.

73. See Salim al-Awwa, *fi al-Nizam al-Siyasi li al-dawla al-Islamiyya*.

74. B. Tibi, "Bridging the Heterogeneity of Civilizations." On the roots of Islamic humanism see Joel Kraemer, *Humanism in the Renaissance of Islam*.

75. See Eric Patterson and John Gallagher, *Debating the War of Ideas*, which includes my chapter "Intercivilizational Conflict between Value Systems and Concepts of Order."

76. John Kelsay, *Islam and War*, 117.

77. Naika Foroutan, *Kulturdialoge zwischen dem Westen und der islamischen Welt*; John Brenkman, *The Cultural Contradictions of Democracy*.

78. Zeyno Baran, *The Other Muslims*.

79. The forthcoming collection of my revised research papers to which I refer at the beginning of the acknowledgments revolves around these issues: *Islam in Global Politics: Conflict and Cross-Civilizational Bridging* (New York: Routledge, 2012).

9. Civil Islam as an Alternative to Islamism

1. Andrew McCarthy, *The Great Jihad*, 40 ("I'm not a Muslim"), 39 ("Is it wrong"). See also Andrew Bostom, "Islamism or Islam," *The American Thinker*, November 14, 2009.

2. Robert Lee, *Overcoming Tradition and Modernity,* 21.

3. See B. Tibi, "The Return of Ethnicity to Europe via Islamic Migration?" and "Ethnicity of Fear?" On Islam in Europe see also chapters 5 and 6 in my *Political Islam, World Politics, and Europe,* and two books by Lorenzo Vidino, *Al-Qaeda in Europe* and more recently *The New Muslim Brotherhood in the West.* On Islam in the United States see Zuhdi Jasser, "Americanism vs. Islamism."

4. The Palestinian Hamas-variety of political Islam also receives support in the Islamic diaspora of the United States; for more details see Matthew Levitt, *Hamas,* 145–55, and for a more general overview see Jane Smith, *Islam in America.* For an alternative see the liberal U.S. Muslim M. Zudhi Jasser, "Americanism vs. Islamism."

5. The title and subtitle of the book by the former federal prosecutor Andrew McCarthy are hyperbolic: *The Grand Jihad: How Islam and the Left Sabotage America.* McCarthy's misconception results from his missing the distinction between Islam and Islamism.

6. The result of this missed effort is described in the *New York Times* report on German-Muslim jihadists who fight in Afghanistan and Pakistan: Souad Mekhennet, "Young Muslims Travel Route from Germany to Radicalism," July 31, 2010, A4, A6.

7. Daniel Philpott, "The Challenge of September 11 to Secularism in International Relations."

8. The source of this concept is my paper presented in Paris 1992, "Les Conditions d'Euro-Islam." See also the report on Dalil Boubakir, the imam of the Paris grand mosque, who supports Euro-Islam: Katrin Bennhold, "Muslim and French and Proud to Be Both," *International Herald Tribune,* March 16, 2006, 2. On this issue one reads in *Time,* December 24, 2001, 49: "Bassam Tibi . . . who coined the term Euro-Islam, insists on the integration of Europe's Muslims," 49. On the debate on Islam in Europe see B. Tibi, "Between Communitarism and Euro-Islam," and "Euro-Islam."

9. The classic by Karl Popper, *The Open Society and Its Enemies,* is highly pertinent for a liberal response against totalitarian Islamism. This is the intellectual underpinning for my plea for an "open Islam" reflected in my concept of Euro-Islam.

10. B. Tibi, *Islam's Predicament with Modernity.*

11. On democracy, Islamism, and Islam see chapter 7 of my *Political Islam, World Politics, and Europe;* on the overall context that has shaped my life's work, see my *Islam's Predicament with Modernity,* in particular the section "Between Four Worlds" in the introduction.

12. See the report by James Slack, "Terrorism? We'll Call It Anti-Islamic Activity," *Daily Mail,* January 18, 2008, ridiculing the "new language" of Jacqui Smith, who by then was secretary of the British home security department. One can safely compare this British politician with Obama's counterterrorism adviser John Brennan, with whom I took issue in Chapter 5.

13. This Islamist propaganda effort is employed in a war of ideas. See my chapter in Eric Patterson and John Gallagher, *Debating the War of Ideas.*

14. Johannes J. G. Jansen, *The Dual Nature of Islamic Fundamentalism,* 2.

15. François Revel, *Democracy against Itself,* chapter 12 on Islamism.

16. This "universal good" is best established in Indonesia as civil Islam. The global success of Islamism also occurs in Southeast Asia, but Indonesia seems to be an exception; see Robert Hefner, *Civil Islam.* Indonesia is the Islamic country with the largest Muslim population in the world (235 million). There it was possible for me, in teaching, lecturing, and writing in the media, to discuss pending issues with my coreligionists in Jakarta on several occasions. One of these occasions was the international conference on Debating Progressive Islam: A Global Perspective at Universitas Islam Negeri (UIN) in Jakarta, July 2009. It was a forum for liberal Muslims to express the need for pluralism in Islamic civilization. UIN is the graduate school of Hidayatullah Islamic State University, which allowed me during my tenure there in 2003 to teach a course on my concept of a reform Islam. I also published several books in Bahasa, Indonesia, the language of the country. On pluralism and dialogue see the UIN volume edited by Karlina Helmanita et al., *Dialogue in the World of Disorder,* which includes my chapter "Islamic Civilization and the Quest for Democratic Pluralism." Indonesia is also the country where U.S. president Barack Obama spent a part of his childhood. It is noteworthy to quote the report of The *International Herald Tribune* of April 25–26, 2009, from Jakarta about the April 2009 election in Indonesia: "From Pakistan to Gaza and Lebanon, militant Islamist movements have gained ground rapidly in recent years, fanning Western fears of a consolidation of radical Muslim governments. But here in the world's most populous Muslim-majority nation, just the opposite is happening. . . . In parliamentary elections . . . voters punished Islamic parties. . . . The largest Islamic party, the Prosperous Justice Party . . . squeezed out a gain of less than 1 percent over its showing in 2004. . . . Indonesians overwhelmingly backed the country's major secular parties even though more of them are continuing to turn to Islam in their private lives." This is a hopeful coverage about a civil Islam against Islamism. In 2005 I continued my work in Southeast Asia in a project at the National University of Singapore. This research was published in the related volume edited by Anthony Reid and Michael Gilsenan, *Islamic Legitimacy in Plural Asia,* which includes my chapter "Islam and Cultural Modernity." Earlier in Jakarta I contradicted the ambassador of Iran to Indonesia Shaban S. Moaddab, who presented there his country as a model that Indonesia might emulate. His speech was included for politeness in the UIN volume *Dialogue in the World of Disorder,* 149–58, followed by mine (159–201) as a rejoinder not only at more length but also with arguments and evidence instead of Iranian state propaganda, which dominated the ambassador's contribution.

17. Karl Popper, *Open Society and Its Enemies;* see also the contributions in Leonard Weinberg, *Democratic Responses to Terrorism,* including my chapter, "Islam, Islamism, and Democracy."

18. See Ali Allawi, *The Crisis of Islamic Civilization.* I have addressed this crisis in *Crisis of Modern Islam.* See also the Muslim voice of Hichem Djaït, *Islamic Culture in Crisis.*

19. B. Tibi, "Bridging the Heterogeneity of Civilizations."

20. The EU-sponsored volume on Islamist radicalization edited by Michael Emerson and Kristina Kausch, *The Challenge for Euro-Mediterranean Relations,* includes this misguided view.

21. Zeyno Baran, *Torn Country.*

22. See the report from Istanbul by Janine Zacharia, "Press Freedom," *Washington Post,* July 5, 2010, A7, and on the response of the EU to curbing the freedom of the press by the AKP see Marc Champion: "Turkey Faces Rap on Media Curbs," *Wall Street Journal,* November 8, 2010, A10. Steven Rosen, "Erdogan and the Israel Cord," *Wall Street Journal,* June 10, 2010, A21, also touches on this issue; see also Don Bilefsky and Sebnem Arsu, "Sponsor of Flotilla Tied to the Elite of Turkey," *New York Times,* July 16, 2010, A4. It has been proven that IHH (Humanitarian Relief Foundation), which led the flotilla of May 2010 to Gaza in support of Hamas, is an Islamist charity and that this action was supported by the AKP government.

23. Marvine Howe, *Turkey Today,* 191.

24. Zeyno Baran, "Turkey Divided," 55, 57, 69.

25. *International Herald Tribune* (global ed. of *New York Times*), September 14, 2010. See also Ali Carkoglu and Ersim Kalaycioglu, *The Rising Tide of Conservatism in Turkey;* William Hale and Ergun Özbudun, *Islamism, Democracy, and Liberalism in Turkey;* and Arda Can Kumbaracibasi, *Turkish Politics and the Rise of the AKP.*

26. Jürgen Habermas, *The Philosophical Discourse of Modernity,* 18.

27. Herbert Davidson, *Averroës, Al-Farabi, and Avicenna on Intellect.*

28. On Islamic humanist rationalism see Mohammed Abed al-Jabri, *Arab-Islamic Philosophy,* and in contrast on totalitarian Islamism see B. Tibi, *Der neue Totalitarismus. "Heiliger Krieg" und westliche Sicherheit.* This interpretation is also shared with the Muslim scholar Mehdi Mozaffari, "The Rise of Islamism in the Light of European Totalitarianism" and *Globalization and Civilizations,* as well as with Jeffrey Bale, "Islamism and Totalitarianism."

29. On this Islamic enlightenment see B. Tibi, *Der wahre Imam,* part II.

30. Mohammed al-Jabri, *Arab-Islamic Philosophy,* 124.

31. Zeev Sternhell, *The Anti-Enlightenment Tradition.*

32. John Brenkman, *The Cultural Contradictions of Democracy,* 165.

33. Appleby, *The Ambivalence of the Sacred,* 7 ("Religion . . ."), 305–6 ("without sacrificing").

34. Zeev Sternhell, *The Anti-Enlightenment Tradition.*

35. Azyumardi Azra, *Indonesia, Islam, and Democracy,* 213–15.

36. This is the view of Marc Lynch, "Veiled Truths." In this review of Paul Berman, *Flight of the Intellectuals,* Lynch writes (on his first page) of Berman's "obsession . . . [that] approaches the pathological."

37. See the contributions in Zeyno Baran, *The Other Muslims.*

38. Ibid.

39. Franz Rosenthal, *The Classical Heritage of Islam.*

40. Marshall G. S. Hodgson, *Rethinking World History:* "Until the Seventeenth Century of our era, the Islamicate society . . . was the most expansive society in the Afro-Asian hemisphere and had the most influence on other societies" (97). See also Zeyno Baran, ed., *The Other Muslims;* Franz Rosenthal, *The Classical Heritage of Islam.*

41. Marshall G. S. Hodgson, *Rethinking World History,* 97. Hodgson is the author of the—in my view—best history of Islamic civilization published in three volumes under the title *The Venture of Islam.*

42. My thinking on cultural change in Islamic civilization can be found in chapter 14 of Lawrence Harrison and Jerome Kagan, *Developing Cultures.* The most complete expression of my understanding of diversity attached to pluralism of religions is *Islam's Predicament with Modernity,* 209–36; see also the references in the long note 16 above. To be sure, my critique of Islam and Islamism dismisses the rhetoric of a "clash of civilizations"; in my plea for "International Morality and Cross-Cultural Bridging," I suggest a thinking different from that of Huntington.

43. Daryush Shayegan, *Cultural Schizophrenia,* 75.

44. See the Tunisian-French Muslim writer Abdelwahab Meddeb, *Sortir de la Malédiction,* who employs this term. Meddeb's ideas are discussed at length in Paul Berman, *The Flight of the Intellectuals,* 45–50.

45. See especially B. Tibi, *Islam's Predicament with Modernity,* 209–36.

46. Therefore, I chose for *Political Islam, World Politics, and Europe* the subtitle *Democratic Peace and Euro Islam versus Global Jihad* to express my commitment to Immanuel Kant's "Zum ewigen Frieden."

47. Ali Oumlil, *Fi shar'iyat al-Ikhtilaf,* 12, 89.

Glossary of Arabic Terms

ahl-al-kitab	people of the book: Jews and Christians
al-arkan al-khamsah	five pillars of Islam
al-asalah	authenticity
al-hall al-Islami	Islamic solution
al-hall huwa al-Islam	Islam is the solution
al-hulul al-mustawradah	imports from the West
al-Islamiyya	Islamism
al-istishraq	Orientalism
al-kuffar al-yahud	Jewish unbeliever
al-nusus al-qat'iyya	absolute divine texts
al-sahwa al-Islamiyya	Islamic awakening
al-sahyuniyya al-alamiyya	world Zionism
al-yahudiyya al-'alamiyya	world Jewry
al-yahud wa al-salibiyun	Jews and crusaders
anzimat al-hazima	regimes of defeat
aql	reason
ashraf	Muslim nobility
awqaf	religious affairs
azmat al-democratiyya	crisis of democracy
bid'a	destructive innovation
butlan	invalidity
dar al-harb	abode of war
dar al-Islam	abode of peace
dar al-shahadah	Islamic territoriality
da'wa	proselytization
dawla	state

dawla Islamiyya	Islamic shari'a-based state
dhimmi	protected monotheist minorities
din	religion
din-wa-dawla	unity of state and religion
dönme	hidden Jews
dustur	constitution
falsafa	rationalism
faqihs, fuqaha'	jurists
farida	obligation
farida ghaibah	neglected duty
fatwa	legal judgment
fiqh	orthodoxy
fitna	sexual danger, violence among Muslims
futuhat	opening
gharb salibi	crusader West
ghazu fikri	intellectual invasion of the world of Islam
hadith	canonical accounts of what the Prophet said and did
hadj	pilgrimage
hafat al-hawiya	brink
hajji (m), hajja (f)	pilgrim
hakimiyyat Allah	God's rule
halal	permitted
haram	forbidden
harb, hurub (pl)	war
harb al-afkar	war of ideas
hijra	migration of the Prophet to Mecca
hisab	agenda
hudna	temporary peace
hudud	penal code
hukuma Islamiyya	Islamic government
hulul mustawrada	imported solutions
ibadat	cult rules
'idwan	aggression of unbelievers
iham	deception

ijma'	consensus doctorum
ijtihad	free reasoning
iman	belief
Islamiyyat	Islamicity
jahiliyya	pre-Islamic ignorance
jahl	ignorance
jihad al-nafs	self-exertion
jizya	tax on Christians and Jews
kalam	theology
khair umma	chosen people
khiyana uzma	great treason
kuffar	infidels
kufr	unbelief
la'ama	wickedness
madhahib	Sunni shari'a schools
ma'rakatuna ma'a al-yahud	our fight against the Jews
mu'amalat	civil law
mu'amarah	conspiracy
mu'amarat al-istishraq	conspiracy of Orientalism
mukhabarat	secret police
mukhtat yahudi	Jewish master plan
mustaghribun	Westernizers
mutakalimun	theologian
nizam Islami	new Islamic order, state order
nizam salih	just system
qital	physical fighting against the kuffar for the spread of Islam
qiyama	resurrection
qiyas	conclusion by analogy
rabbaniyya	theocentrism
ra's hurbah	spearhead
riddah	apostasy
sahwa Islamiyya	Islamic revival
sahyuniyyun	Zionists
salat	daily prayers
salibiyyun	crusaders

shahadah	unity of God and the acknowledgment of Mohammed as His messenger; allegiance to Islam
shahdid	martyrs
sheykh	religious or tribal leader
shura	consultation
shurk	heresy
simat al-yahud	basic traits of the Jews
siyadat al-Islam	dominance of Islam
siyasa	politics
tadhiya	sacrifice
taghrib	agenda of Westernization
takfir	excommunication from the umma
takfiri	person or group that accuses Muslims of kufr (unbelief) in pursuit of excommunication from the umma, often followed by execution
takhtit al-yahudi al-alami	Jewish world master plan
taqiyya	dissimulation
taschr'I	legislation
tatbiq al-shari'a	implementation of shari'a
thawrah	revolution
thawrah alamiyyah	world revolution
ulema	men of knowledge, informal clergy
umma	worldwide Muslim community
wahi	revelation
waqf Islami	nonnegotiable divinity
yahud	Jews
zakat	alms

Bibliography

Abbt, Christiane, and Donata Schoeller, eds. *Im Zeichen der Religion: Gewalt und Friedfertigkeit in Christentum und Islam*. New York: Campus, 2008.

Abdelraziq, Ali. *al-Islam wa usul al-hukm* [Islam and patterns of government]. 1925; rpt. Beirut: Maktabat al-Hayat, 1966.

Abdelwahab, Meddeb. *Sortir de la malédiction: L'Islam entre civilization et barbarie*. Paris: Seuil, 2008.

Abduh, Mohammed. *al-Islam wa al-Nasraniyya bain al-Ilm wa al-Madaniyya* [Islam and Christianity between science and civilization]. Beirut: Dar al-Hadatha, rpt. 1983.

Abdul-Salam, Faruq. *al-Ahzab al-Siyasiyya wa al-Fasl bayn al-din wa al-dawla* [Political parties and the separation between religion and politics]. Cairo: Qalyub, 1979.

Abu-Amr, Ziad. *Islamic Fundamentalism in the West Bank and Gaza: Muslim Brotherhood and Islamic Jihad*. Bloomington: Indiana University Press, 1994.

Abu Zaid, Naser Hamed. *al-Tafkir fi asr al-takfir* [Thinking in the age of the accusation of heresy]. Cairo: Madbuli, 1995.

Achcar, Gilbert. *The Arabs and the Holocaust: The Arab-Israeli War of Narratives*. London: Saqi, 2010.

Adams, Charles. *Islam and Modernism in Egypt: A Study of the Modern Reform Movement*. 1933; rpt. London, 1968.

Adamson, Peter, and Richard Taylor, eds. *The Cambridge Companion to Arab Philosophy*. Cambridge: Cambridge University Press, 2006.

Afghani, Jamal al-. *al-A'mal al-kamila*. Cairo: al-Mu'assasa al-Misriyya, 1968.

Ahmed, Rifaat S. *al-Islam wa qadaya al-sira' al-Arabi al-Israeli* [Islam and conflict: Studies on Islam and the Arab-Israel conflict]. Cairo: Dar al-Sharqiyya, 1989.

Ajami, Fouad. *The Arab Predicament: Arab Political Thought and Practice since 1967*. Cambridge: Cambridge University Press, 1981.

———. *The Foreigner's Gift: The Americans, the Arabs, and the Iraqis in Iraq*. New York: Free Press, 2006.

Akbarzadeh, Shahram, and Fethi Mansouri, eds. *Islam and Political Violence: Muslim Diaspora and the Radicalization in the West.* London: Tauris, 2007.

Akehurst, Michael. *A Modern Introduction to International Law.* 6th ed. London: Unwin Hyman, 1987.

Allawi, Ali. *The Crisis of Islamic Civilization.* New Haven: Yale University Press, 2009.

AlSayyad, Nezar, and Manuel Castells, eds. *Muslim Europe or Euro-Islam.* New York: Lexington, 2002.

Anderson, Benedict. *Imagined Communities.* New ed. London: Verso, 1991.

Anderson, Norman. *Law Reform in the Muslim World.* London, 1976.

An-Na'im, Abdullahi A. *Towards an Islamic Reformation.* Syracuse, N.Y.: Syracuse University Press, 1990.

———. *Islam and the Secular State: Negotiating the Future of Shari'a.* Cambridge: Harvard University Press, 2008.

Antawabi, Mushin al-. *Limatha narfud al-Salam ma'a al-Yahud* [Why we reject peace with Jews]. Cairo: Kitab al-Mukhtar, n.d.

Appleby, Scott. *The Ambivalence of the Sacred: Religion, Violence, and Reconciliation.* Lanham, Md.: Rowman and Littlefield, 2000.

Apter, David. *The Politics of Modernization.* Chicago: University of Chicago Press, 1965.

Arendt, Hannah. *Vita Activa.* Stuttgart: Piper, 1960.

———. *The Origins of Totalitarianism.* New York: Harcourt, rpt., 1979.

Arkoun, Mohammed. *Rethinking Islam.* Boulder, Colo.: Westview, 1994.

Armanazi, Najib al-. *al-Shar' al-duwali fi al-Islam* [International law in Islam]. London: Riad El-Rayyes, 1990.

Aron, Raymond. *Paix et guerre entre les nations.* Paris: Calmann-Lévy, 1962.

Ashmawi, Mohammed Said al-. *Usul al-shari'a* [The origins of shari'a]. Cairo: Madbuli, 1983.

———. *al-Shari'a al-Islamiyya wa al-qanun al-misri* [Islamic shari'a and Egyptian law]. Cairo: Sina, 1988.

———. *al-Islam al-Siyasi* [Political Islam]. Cairo: Sina, 1989.

———. *al-Khilafah al-Islamiyya* [Islamic Caliphate]. Cairo: Sina, 1990.

Ateş, Seyran. *Der Multkulti-Irrtum.* Berlin: Ullstein, 2007.

Aust, Stefan, and Cordt Schnibben, eds. *11. September: Geschichte eines Terrorangriffs.* Stuttgart: DVA, 2002.

Awwa, Mohammed S. al-. *Fi al-Nizam al-Siyasi lil dawla al-Islamiyya* [On the political system of the Islamic state]. 6th ed. Cairo: al-Maktab al-Masri, 1983.

Ayubi, Nazih. *Political Islam.* London: Routledge, 1991.

Azm, Sadiq Jalal al-. *al-naqd al-dhati ba'd al-hazima* [Self-critique after the defeat]. Beirut: al-Tali'a, 1968.

———. *Naqd al-fikr al-dini* [Critique of religious thought]. Beirut: Dar al-Talia, 1969.

———. *Dhihniyyat al-tahrim* [The mentality of taboos]. London: El Rayyes, 1992.

Azra, Azymardi. *Indonesia, Islam, and Democracy.* Jakarta: Solstice / Asia Foundation, 2006.

Bahi, Mohammed al-. *al-Fikr al-Islami al hadith wa silatuhu bi al-isti'mar al-gharbi* [Modern Islamic thought and its relationship to Western colonialism]. 4th ed. Cairo: Maktabat Wahba, n.d.

Baker, Raymond. *Islam without Fear: Egypt and the New Islamists.* Cambridge: Harvard University Press, 2003.

Bale, Jeffrey. "Islamism and Totalitarianism." *Totalitarian Movements and Political Religions* 10, no. 2 (2009): 73–96.

Banna, Hasan al-. *Majmu'at Rasa'il al-Imam al-Shahid Hasan al-Banna* [Collected essays of the Martyr Imam al-Banna]. New legal ed. Cairo: Dar al-Da'wa, 1990.

Banner, Michael. *Jihad in Islamic History.* Princeton: Princeton University Press, 2006.

Baran, Zeyno. "Fighting the War of Ideas." *Foreign Affairs* 84, no. 6 (2005): 68–79.

———. "The Brotherhood Network in the US." *Current Trends in Islamist Ideology* 6 (2008): 95–122.

———. "Turkey Divided." *Journal of Democracy* 19, no. 1 (2008): 55–69.

———. *Torn Country: Turkey between Secularism and Islamism.* Stanford: Hoover Institution Press, 2010.

———, ed. *The Other Muslims: Moderate and Secular.* New York: Palgrave Macmillan, 2010.

Barnett, Michael. *Dialogue in Arab Politics.* New York: Columbia University Press, 1998.

Bawer, Bruce. *Surrender: Appeasing Islamism, Sacrificing Freedom.* New York: Doubleday, 2009.

Be'eri, Eliezer. *Army Officers in Arab Politics and Society.* New York: Praeger, 1969.

Bell, Daniel. "The Return of the Sacred." In *The Winding Passage: Sociological Essays and Journeys,* 324–54. New York: Basic, 1980.

Bell, R., and W. M. Watt. *Introduction to the Qur'an.* Edinburgh: Edinburgh University Press, 1977.

Bellah, Robert, ed. *Religion and Progress in Modern Asia.* New York: New York University Press, 1965.

Benz, Wolfgang, and Juliane Wetzel, eds. *Antisemitismus und radikaler Islamismus.* Essen: Klartext Verlag, 2007.

Bergesen, Albert, ed. *The Qutb Reader: Selected Writings on Politics, Religion, and Society.* New York: Routledge, 2008.

Berman, Paul. *The Flight of the Intellectuals.* Brooklyn: Melvillehouse, 2010.

Berman, Russell A. *Freedom or Terror: Europe Faces Jihad.* Stanford: Hoover Institution Press, 2010.

Bernard, Cheryl, and Zalmay Khalilzad. *The Government of God: Iran's Islamic Republic.* New York: Columbia University Press, 1984.

Besier, Gerhard, and Hermann Lübbe, eds. *Politische Religion und Religionspolitik: Zwischen Totalitarismus und Bürgerfreiheit.* Göttingen: Vandenhoek and Ruprecht, 2005.

Bevir, Marc, ed. *Encyclopedia of Political Theory.* 3 vols. Thousand Oaks, Calif.: Sage, 2010.

Bistolfi, Robert, and François Zabbal, eds. *Islams d'Europe: Intégration ou insertion communitaire.* Paris: Editions de l'Aube, 1995.

Blankinship, Yahya. *The End of the Jihad State.* Albany: SUNY Press, 1994.

Bohnasi, Ahmad Fathi. *al-Jara'im fi al-fiqh al-Islami* [Criminal law in Islamic fiqh]. 6th ed. Cairo: Dar al-Shuhruq, 1988.

Boroujerdi, Mehrzad. *Iranian Intellectuals and the West: The Tormented Triumph of Nativism.* Syracuse, N.Y.: Syracuse University Press, 1996.

Bostom, Andrew, ed. *The Legacy of Jihad.* Amherst, N.Y.: Prometheus, 2005.

———, ed. *The Legacy of Islamic Antisemitism.* Amherst, N.Y.: Prometheus, 2008.

Bouman, Johan. *Gott und Mensch im Qur'an: Eine Strukturform religiöser Anthropologie anhand des Beispiels Allah und Muhammad.* Darmstadt: Wissenschaftliche Buchgesellschaft, 1977.

Bradley, John. *Saudi Arabia Exposed.* New York: Palgrave, 2005.

Braudel, Fernand. *A History of Civilizations.* New York: Allen Lane, 1994.

Brenkman, John. *The Cultural Contradictions of Democracy: Political Thought since September 11.* Princeton: Princeton University Press, 2007.

Brisard, Jean-Charles. *Zarqawi: The New Face of al-Qaeda.* New York: Other, 2005.

Bull, Hedley. *The Anarchical Society: A Study of Order in World Politics.* New York: Columbia University Press, 1977.

———. "The Revolt against the West." In Bull and Watson, *Expansion of International Society,* 217–28.

Burckhardt, Jakob. *Die Kultur der Renaissance in Italien.* 11th ed. Stuttgart: Kröner, 1988.

Burgat, François, and William Dowell. *The Islamic Movement in North Africa.* Austin: University of Texas Press, 1993.

Burr, J. Millard, and Robert O. Collins, eds. *Alms for Jihad.* Cambridge: Cambridge University Press, 2006.

Buzan, Barry. *People, States, and Fear: An Agenda for International Security Studies in the Post–Cold War Era.* Boulder, Colo.: Lynne Rienner, 1991.

Carkoglu, Ali, and Ersin Kalaycioglu. *The Rising Tide of Conservatism in Turkey.* New York: Palgrave Macmillan 2009.

Center for Arab Unity Studies, ed. *Azmat al-democratiyya fi al-Watan al-Arabi* [Crisis of democracy in the Arab world]. Beirut: Markaz Dirasat al-Wihda al-Arabiyya, 1983.

Centre d'Études et de Récherches Economiques et Sociales, ed. *Les Arabes face à leur destin.* Série Études Sociologiques no. 6. Tunis: CERES, 1980.

Cesari, Jocelyne. *When Islam and Democracy Meet: Muslims in Europe and the United States.* New York: Palgrave, 2004.

Chervel, Thierry, ed. *Islam in Europa.* Frankfurt am Main: Suhrkamp, 2007.

Chesler, Phyllis. *The New Antisemitism.* San Francisco: Jossey-Bass, 2003.

Chubin, Shahram. *Iran's Nuclear Ambitions.* Washington, D.C.: Carnegie Endowment for International Peace, 2006.

Cliteur, Paul. *The Secular Outlook: In Defense of Moral and Political Secularism.* Oxford: Wiley-Blackwell, 2010.

Cockburn, Andrew, and Patrick Cockburn. *Out of the Ashes: The Resurgence of Saddam Hussein.* New York: HarperCollins, 1999.

Cook, David. *Understanding Jihad.* Berkeley: University of California Press, 2005.

Coulson, N. J. "The Concept of Progress and Islamic Law." In Bellah, *Religion and Progress in Modern Asia,* 74–92.

———. *Conflicts and Tensions in Islamic Jurisprudence.* Chicago: University of Chicago Press, 1969.

———. *A History of Islamic Law.* 3rd ed. Edinburgh: Edinburgh University Press, 1978.

Coulson, N. J., and Norman Anderson. "Modernization: Islamic Law." In *Northern Africa: Islam and Modernization,* ed. Michael Brett, 73–83. London: Cass, 1973.

Creveld, Martin van. *The Transformation of War.* New York: Free Press, 1991.

Creveld, Martin van, and Katharina von Knop, eds. *Countering Modern Terrorism: History, Current Issues, and Future Threats.* Bielefeld: Bertelsmann, 2005.

Curtin, Philip. *The World and the West: The European Challenge.* Cambridge: Cambridge University Press, 2000.

Davidson, Herbert. *Averroës, al-Farabi, and Avicenna on Intellect.* New York: Oxford University Press, 1992.

Dawisha, Adeed, ed. *Islam in Foreign Policy.* Cambridge: Cambridge University Press, 1983.

Dawood, N. J. *The Koran.* Harmondsworth: Penguin, 1974.

Deng, Francis, and Abdullahi An-Na'im. eds. *Human Rights: Cross-Cultural Perspectives.* Washington, D.C.: Brookings Institution, 1990.

Dharif, Mohammed, ed. *al-Islam al-Siyasi fi al-Watan al-Arabi* [Political Islam in the Arab world]. Casablanca: Maktabat al-Umma, 1992.

Diamond, Larry. *The Spirit of Democracy: The Struggle to Build Free Societies throughout the World.* New York: Times Books, 2008.

Djaït, Hichem. *Islamic Culture in Crisis: A Reflection on Civilizations in History.* Trans. Janet Fouli. New Brunswick, N.J.: Transaction, 2010.

Docker, John, and Gerhard Fischer, ed. *Adventures of Identity: European Multicultural Experiences and Perspectives.* Tübingen: Stauffenberg, 2001.

Donner, Fred M. *The Early Islamic Conquests.* Princeton: Princeton University Press, 1981.

———. *Muhammad and the Believers: The Origins of Islam.* Cambridge: Harvard University Press, 2010.

Eickelmann, Dale, and James Piscatori. *Muslim Politics.* Princeton: Princeton University Press, 1996.

Elpeleg, Zvi. *The Grand Mufti al-Husaini: Founder of the Palestinian National Movement.* London: Cass, 1993.

Elshtain, Jean Bethke. *Just War against Terror.* New York: Basic, 2003.

Emerson, Michael, ed. *Democratization in the Neighborhood.* Brussels: CEPS, 2005.

Emerson, Michael, and Kristina Kausch, eds. *The Challenge for Euro-Mediterranean Relations.* Brussels: CEPS, 2009.

Emmerson, Donald. "Inclusive Islamism: The Utility of Diversity." In Martin in association with Barzegar, *Islamism,* 17–32.

Enayat, Hamid. *Modern Islamic Political Thought.* Austin: University of Texas Press, 1982.

Erasmus Foundation, ed. *The Limits of Pluralism: Relativism and Neoabsolutism.* Amsterdam: Praemium Erasmianum Foundation, 1994.

Esposito, John. *The Islamic Threat: Myth or Reality?* New York: Oxford University Press, 1992.

———, ed. *The Oxford Encyclopedia of the Middle Eastern World.* 4 vols. New York: Oxford University Press, 1995.

Esposito, John, and John Voll. *Islam and Democracy*. New York: Oxford University Press, 1996.

Ess, Josef van. *Theologie und Gesellschaft im 2. und 3. Jahrhundert Hidschra: Eine Geschichte des religiösen Denkens im frühen Islam*. Vol. 1. Berlin: De Gruyter, 1991.

Esser, Josef. *Vorverständnis und Methodenwahl in der Rechtsfindung*. Frankfurt: Athenäum Verlag, 1970.

Euben, Roxanne. *Enemy in the Mirror: Islamic Fundamentalism and the Limits of Modern Rationalism*. Princeton: Princeton University Press, 1999.

Faber, Klaus, Julius Schoeps, and Sacha Stawski, eds. *Neu-alter Judenhass: Antisemitismus*. 2nd ed. Berlin: Verlag Brandenburg, 2007.

Fahmi, Mustafa, ed. *Fan al-hukm fi al-Islam* [The art to govern in Islam]. Cairo: al-Maktab al-Masri, [c. 1981].

Fandy, Mamoun. *Saudi Arabia and the Politics of Dissent*. New York: Palgrave, 1999.

Feldman, Noah. *The Fall and Rise of the Islamic State*. Princeton: Princeton University Press, 2008.

Foroutan, Naika. *Kulturdialoge zwischen dem Westen und der islamischen Welt: Eine Strategie zur Regulierung von Zivilisationskonflikten*. Wiesbaden: Deutscher Universitäts-Verlag, 2004.

Fortner, Robert, and Mark Fackler, eds. *Handbook of Global Communication*. 2 vols. Oxford: Blackwell, 2011.

Fourest, Caroline. *Frère Tariq: Discours, stratégie, et méthode de Tariq Ramadan*. Paris: Grasset, 2004.

———. *Brother Tariq: The Doublespeak of Tariq Ramadan*. Trans. Ioana Wieder and John Atherton. London: Encounter, 2008.

Fradkin, Hillel. "Academic Word Games." In Martin in association with Barzegar, *Islamism,* 74–80.

Friedman, Yohanan. *Tolerance and Coercion in Islam: Interfaith Relations in the Muslim Tradition*. New York: Cambridge University Press, 2003.

Frisch, Hillel, and Efraim Inbar, eds. *Radical Islam and International Security*. New York: Routledge, 2008.

Fukuyama, Francis. *The End of History and the Last Man*. New York: Avon, 1992.

———. "Identity, Immigration, and Liberal Demcracy." *Journal of Democracy* 17, no. 2 (2006): 5–20.

Fuller, Graham. *The Center of the Universe Iran: The Geopolitics of Iran*. Boulder, Colo.: Westview, 1991.

———. *A Sense of Siege: The Geopolitics of Islam and the West*. Boulder, Colo.: Westview, 1995.

————. *The Future of Political Islam.* Boulder, Colo.: Westview, 2003.

Gellner, Ernest. *Religion and Postmodernism.* London: Routledge, 1992.

Gensicke, Klaus. *Der Mufti von Jerusalem und die Nationalsozialisten.* Darmstadt: WBG, 2007.

Gentile, Emilio. *Politics as Religion.* Trans. George Staunton. Princeton: Princeton University Press, 2006.

Gerges, Fawaz A. *The Far Enemy: Why Jihad Went Global.* New York: Cambridge University Press, 2005.

Ghadban, Ralph. *Tariq Ramadan und die Islamisierung Europas.* Berlin: Schiler, 2006.

Ghazali, Mohammed al-. *Huquq al-insan bain al-Islam wa I'lan al-umam al-mutahhidah.* [Human rights between Islam and the universal declaration of human rights]. Cairo: Dar al-Kutub al-Islamiyya, 1984.

Gibb, Hamilton A. R. *Studies on the Civilization of Islam.* 1962; rpt. Princeton: Princeton University Press, 1982.

Giddens, Anthony. *A Contemporary Critique of Historical Materialism.* Vol. 2, *The Nation-State and Violence.* London: Macmillan, 1985.

Grant, Edward. *The Foundations of Modern Science in the Middle Ages: Their Religious, Institutional, and Intellectual Contexts.* Cambridge: Cambridge University Press, 1996.

Gress, David. *From Plato to NATO: The Idea of the West and Its Opponents.* New York: Free Press, 1998.

Gunaratna, Rohan. *Inside al-Qaeda: Global Network of Terror.* New York: Columbia University Press, 2002

Gunaratna, Rohan, and Michael Chandler. *Countering Terrorism.* London: Reaction, 2007.

Habermas, Jürgen. *The Philosophical Discourse of Modernity: Twelve Lectures.* Trans. Frederick G. Lawrence. Cambridge: MIT Press, 1986.

————. *Glauben und Wissen.* Frankfurt: Suhrkamp, 2001.

Hale, William, and Ergun Özbudun. *Islamism, Democracy, and Liberalism in Turkey.* London: Routledge, 2010.

Hallaq, Wael. *History of Islamic Legal Theories.* New York: Cambridge University Press, 1997.

————. *The Origins and Evolution of Islamic Law.* New York: Cambridge University Press, 2005.

Hanafi, Hasan al-. *al-Usuliyya al-islamiyya* [Islamic fundamentalism]. Cairo: Madbuli, 1989.

————. "Islamism. Whose Debate Is It?" In Martin in association with Barzegar, *Islamism,* 63–66.

Harel, Amos, and Avi Issacharoff. *34 Days: Israel, Hezbollah, and the War in Lebanon.* New York: Palgrave, 2008.

Harris, Lee. *The Suicide of Reason: Radical Islam's Threat to the Enlightenment.* New York: Basic, 2007.

Harrison, Bernard. *The Resurgence of Antisemitism.* New York: Rowman and Littlefield, 2006.

Harrison, Lawrence, and Peter L. Berger, eds. *Developing Cultures: Case Studies.* New York: Routledge, 2006.

Harrison, Lawrence, and Jerome Kagan, eds. *Developing Cultures: Essays on Cultural Change.* New York: Routledge, 2006.

Hart, H. L. A. *The Concept of Law.* Oxford: Clarendon, 1970.

Hashmi, Sohail. *Islamic Political Ethics: Civil Society, Pluralism, and Conflict.* Princeton: Princeton University Press, 2002.

Hasseini, Ziba Mir, and Richard Tapper. "Islamism—Ism or Wasm?" In Martin in association with Barzegar, *Islamism,* 81–92.

Hawkesworth, Mary, and Maurice Kogan, eds. *Routledge Encyclopedia of Government and Politics.* 2 vols. 2nd ed. London: Routledge, 2004.

Hefner, Robert. *Civil Islam: Muslims and Democratization in Indonesia.* Princeton: Princeton University Press, 2000.

Helmanita, Karlina, ed. *Dialogue in the World Disorder.* Jakarta: Hidayatullah Islamic State University, 2004.

Herf, Jeffrey, ed. *Antisemitism and Anti-Zionism in Historical Perspective.* New York: Routledge, 2007.

———. *Nazi Propaganda for the Arab World.* New Haven: Yale University Press, 2009.

Herzog, Roman. *Preventing the Clash of Civilizations: A Peace Strategy for the Twenty-First Century.* Ed. Henrik Schmiegelow. New York: St. Martin's, 1999.

Hirszowicz, Lukas. *The Third Reich and the Arab East.* London: Routledge, 1966.

Hobsbawm, Eric, and Terence Ranger, eds. *The Invention of Tradition.* New York: Cambridge University Press, rpt. 1983.

Hodgson, Marshall G. S. *The Venture of Islam: Conscience and History in a World Civilization.* 3 vols. Chicago: University of Chicago Press, 1974.

———. *Rethinking World History: Essays on Europe, Islam, and World History.* Cambridge: Cambridge University Press, 1995.

Hoffer, Eric. *The True Believer: Thoughts on the Nature of Mass Movements.* 1951; rpt. New York: Perennial, 2002.

Hoffman, Bruce. *Inside Terrorism.* New York: Columbia University Press, 1998.

Hoffmann, Stanley. *World Disorders: Troubled Peace in the Post–Cold War Era.* New York: Rowman and Littlefield, 1998.

Holsti, Kalevi J. *The State, War, and the State of War.* Cambridge: Cambridge University Press, 1996.

Holton, Gerald J. *Science and Anti-Science.* Cambridge: Harvard University Press, 1993.

Horkheimer, Max, and Theodor W. Adorno. *Dialektik der Aufklärung.* (Amsterdam: Querido, 1947).

———. *Dialectic of Enlightenment.* Trans. Edmund Jephcott. Stanford: Stanford University Press, 2002.

Hourani, Albert. *Arabic Thought in the Liberal Age.* London: Oxford University Press, 1962.

Howe, Marvine. *Turkey Today: A Nation Divided over Islam's Revival.* Boulder, Colo.: Westview, 2000.

Hsu, Roland, ed. *Ethnic Europe: Mobility, Identity, and Conflict in a Globalized World.* Stanford: Stanford University Press, 2010.

Hudson, Michael. *Arab Politics: The Search for Legitimacy.* New Haven: Yale University Press, 1977.

Huff, Toby E. *The Rise of Early Modern Science: Islam, China, and the West.* Cambridge: Cambridge University Press, 1993.

Huntington, Samuel P. *Political Order in Changing Societies.* New Haven: Yale University Press, 1968.

———. *The Third Wave: Democratization in the Twentieth Century.* Norman: University of Oklahoma Press, 1991.

———. *The Clash of Civilizations and the Remaking of the World Order.* New York: Simon and Schuster, 1996.

Hussain, Ed. *The Islamist: Why I Joined Radical Islam.* London: Penguin, 2007.

Ibrahim, Saad Eddin. *Egypt, Islam and Democracy.* Cairo: AUC Press, 1996.

Imara, Mohammed. *al-A'mal al-Kamila li al-Afghani* [Collected writings]. Cairo: Dar al-Katib al-Arabi, 1968.

———. *al-Islam wa huquq al-insan* [Islam and human rights]. Cairo: Dar al-Shuruq, 1989.

———. *Ma'rakat al-Islam wa Usul al-Hikm* [The battle of Islam on governance]. Cairo: Dar al-Shuruq, 1989.

———. *al-Sahwa al-Islamiyya al-tahddi al-hadari* [The Islamic awakening and the civilizational challenge]. Cairo: Dar al-Shuruq, 1991.

International Institute of Islamic Thought, ed. *Islamiyyat al-ma'rifah* [Islamization of knowledge]. Cairo: al-Ahram lil Tawzi', 1986.

Isar, Y. Raj, and Helmut Anheier, eds. *Conflicts and Tensions.* Los Angeles: Sage, 2007.

Izzuldin, Ahmed. *Harakat al-Muqawamha al-Islamiyya Hamas* [The Islamic resistance movement Hamas]. Cairo: Dar al-Tawzi' al-Islamiyya, 1998.

Jabar, Faleh A. *The Shi'ite Movement in Iraq.* London: Saqi, 2003.

Jabri, Mohammed A. al-. *al-Turath wa al-hadatha* (Heritage and modernity). Beirut: al-Markaz al- Thaqaf, 1991.

———. *Arab-Islamic Philosophy.* Trans. Aziz Abbassi. Austin: CMES, 1999.

Jabri, Mohammed A. al-, and Hasan Hanafi. *Hiwar al-Mashriq al-Maghrib* (Dialogue between the Arab East and the Arab West). Casablanca, Tobical 1990.

Jackson, Robert. *Quasi-States: Sovereignty, International Relations, and the Third World.* Cambridge: Cambridge University Press, 1990.

Jacoby, Tami A., and Brent Sasley, eds. *Redefining Security in the Middle East.* New York: Palgrave, 2002.

Jadul-Haq, Jadul-Haq Ali, ed. *Bayan li al-nas* [Declaration to humanity]. 2 vols. Cairo: al-Azhar, 1984, 1988.

Jafarzadeh, Alireza. *The Iran Threat: President Ahmadinejad and the Coming Nuclear Crisis.* New York: Palgrave, 2007.

Jamal, Amal. *The Palestinian National Movement.* Bloomington: Indiana University Press, 2005.

Jamieson, Alan. *Faith and Sword: A Short History of Christian-Muslim Conflict.* London: Reaktion, 2006.

Jansen, Johannes J. G. *The Dual Nature of Islamic Fundamentalism.* Ithaca, N.Y.: Cornell University Press, 1997.

Japanese Association of Comparative Constitutional Law, ed. *Church and State: Towards Protection for Freedom of Religion.* Tokyo: Nihon University Press, 2006.

Jarisha, Ali Mohammed, and Mohammed Sharif Zaibaq. *Asalib al-ghazu al-fikri lil alam al-Islami* [The methods of intellectual invasion of the world of Islam]. Cairo: Dar al-I'tisam, 1978.

Jasser, M. Zuhdi. "Americanism vs. Islamism." In Baran, *The Other Muslims,* 175–91.

———. "Political Islam, Liberalism, and the Diagnosis of a Problem." In Martin in association with Barzegar, *Islamism,* 104–9.

Jay, Martin. *The Dialectical Imagination: A History of the Frankfurt School and the Institute of Social Research.* Berkeley: University of California Press, 1996.

Johanson, James T. *The Holy War Idea in Western and Islamic Tradition.* University Park: Pennsylvania State University Press, 1997.

Juergensmeyer, Mark. *The New Cold War? Religious Nationalism Confronts the Secular State.* Berkeley: University of California Press, 1993.

———. *Terror in the Mind of God: The Global Rise of Religious Violence.* Berkeley: University of California Press, 2000.

Julius, Anthony. *Trials of the Diaspora: A History of Antisemitism in England.* New York: Oxford University Press, 2010.

Jundi, Anwar al-. *Ahdaf al-taghrib* [The goal of Westernization]. Cairo: al-Azhar Press, 1987.

———. *al-Mu'asarah fi itar al-asalah* [Modernity in the framework of authenticity]. Cairo: Dar al-Sahwa, 1987.

———. *Min al-tabai'iyya ila al-asalah* [From dependency to authenticity]. Cairo: Dar al-I'tisam, n.d.

Kaegi, Walter. *Byzantium and the Early Islamic Conquests.* Cambridge: Cambridge University Press, 1992.

Kagan, Robert. *The Return of History and the Ends of Dreams.* New York: Knopf, 2008.

Kaiser, Karl, Steffen Angenendt, Hanns W. Maull, and Gabriele Brenke, eds. *Deutschlands neue Außenpolitik: Herausforderungen.* 3 vols. Munich: Oldenburg Verlag, 1995.

Kant, Immanuel. "Zum ewigen Frieden." In *Friedensutopien,* ed. Zwi Batscha and Richard Saage, 37–82. Frankfurt: Suhrkamp, 1979.

Karsh, Efraim. *Islamic Imperialism.* New Haven: Yale University Press, 2006.

Kassab, Mohammed Y. *L' Islam face au nouvel ordre mondial.* Algiers: Editions Salama, 1991.

Katzenstein, Peter, and Timothy Byrnes, eds. *Religion in an Expanding Europe.* Cambridge: Cambridge University Press, 2006.

Katzenstein, Peter, and Robert Keohane. *Anti-Americanism in World Politics.* Ithaca, N.Y.: Cornell University Press, 2006.

Kayaoglu, Turan. "Westphalian Eurocentrism in International Relations Theory." *International Studies Review* 12, no. 2 (2010): 193–217.

Keddie, Nikkie, ed. *An Islamic Response to Imperialism.* Berkeley: University of California Press, 1983.

Kelsay, John. *Islam and War.* Louisville, Ky.: John Knox, 1993.

———. *Arguing the Just War in Islam.* Cambridge: Harvard University Press, 2007.

Kenny, John. *The Politics of Identity.* Cambridge: Polity, 2004.

Kepel, Gilles. *Jihad: Expansion et déclin de l'islamisme.* Paris: Gallimard, 2000.

———. *Jihad: The Trail of Political Islam.* Trans. Anthony F. Roberts. Cambridge: Harvard University Press, 2002.

Kerr, Malcolm. *Islamic Reform: The Political and Legal Theories of Muhammad Abduh and Rashid Rida.* Berkeley: University of California Press, 1966.

Khalid, Osama. *al-Mustaqbal al-Arabi fi al-asr al-Ameriki* [The future of Arabs in the age of American dominance]. Cairo: Markaz al-Qada, 1992.

Khalidi, Salah A. al-. *Amerika min al-dakhil bi minzar Sayyid Qutb* [America viewed from inside through the lenses of Sayyid Qutb]. al-Mansura, Egypt: Dar al-Manara, 1987.

Khalil, Samir al-. *Republic of Fear: The Politics of Iraq*. Berkeley: University of California Press, 1989.

Khoury, Philip, and Joseph Kostiner, eds. *Tribes and State-Formation in the Middle-East*. Berkeley: University of California Press, 1990.

Khuri, Fuad. *Imams and Emirs: State, Religion and Sects in Islam*. London: Saqi, 1990.

Klausen, Jytte. *The Islamic Challenge: Politics and Religion in Western Europe*. New York: Oxford University Press, 2005.

Kraemer, Joel. *Humanism in the Renaissance of Islam*. Leiden: Brill, 1986.

Kramer, Martin. *Arab Awakening and Muslim Revival*. New Brunswick, N.J.: Transaction, 1996.

———, ed. *The Jewish Discovery of Islam: Studies in Honor of Bernard Lewis*. Tel Aviv: Tel Aviv University Press, 1999.

Kugelgen, Anke von. *Averroës und die arabische Moderne: Ansätze zu einer Neubegründung des Rationalismus im Islam*. Leiden: Brill, 1994.

Kumbaracibasi, Arda Can. *Turkish Politics and the Rise of the AKP*. London: Routledge, 2009.

Küntzel, Matthias. *Jihad and Jew-Hatred: Nazism and the Roots of 9/11*. New York: Telos, 2007.

Kurzman, Charles. ed. *Liberal Islam: A Sourcebook*. New York: Oxford University Press, 1998.

Laqueur, Walter. *The Changing Face of Antisemitism*. New York: Oxford University Press, 2006.

Laskier, Michael. "Islamic Radicalism and Terrorism in the European Union: The Maghrabi Factor." In Frisch and Inbar, *Radical Islam and International Security*, 93–120.

Lassner, Jacob, and Ilan Troen. *Jews and Muslims in the Arab World: Haunted by Pasts Real and Imagined*. Lanham, Md.: Rowman and Littlefield, 2007.

Laue, Theodore von. *The World Revolution of Westernization*. New York: Oxford University Press, 1988.

Lawrence, Jonathan, and Justin Vaisse. *Integrating Islam*. Washington, D.C.: Brookings Institution, 2006.

Lechner, Frank J., and John Boli. *The Globalization Reader*. Malden, Mass.: Blackwell, 2008.

Lee, Robert. *Overcoming Tradition and Modernity: The Search for Islamic Authenticity*. Boulder, Colo.: Westview, 1997.

Lehbeck, Kurt. *Holy War, Unholy Victory: The CIA's Secret War in Afghanistan.* Washington, D.C.: Regenery Gateway, 1993.

Leiken, Robert, and Steven Brooke. "The Moderate Muslim Brotherhood." *Foreign Affairs* 86, no. 2 (2007): 107–22.

Lerner, Ralph, and Muhsin Madi. *Medieval Political Philosophy.* Ithaca, N.Y.: Cornell University Press, 1972.

Levitt, Matthew. *Hamas: Politics, Charity, and Terrorism in the Service of Jihad.* New Haven: Yale University Press, 2006.

Lewis, Bernard. *The Jews of Islam.* Princeton: Princeton University Press, 1984.

———. *Semites and Antisemites.* 1986; rpt. New York: Norton, 1999.

———. *The Crisis of Islam: Holy War and Unholy Terror.* London: Weidenfeld and Nicholson, 2003.

———. "The New Anti-Semitism: First Religion, Then Race, Then What?" *American Scholar* 75, no. 1 (2006): 25–26.

———, ed. *Islam: From the Prophet Muhammad to the Capture of Constantinople.* New York: Harper and Row, 1974.

Lincoln, Bruce. *Holy Terrors: Thinking about Religion after September 11.* Chicago: University of Chicago Press, 2003.

Lindberg, David C. *The Beginnings of Western Science.* Chicago: University of Chicago Press, 1992.

Lindholm, Tore, and Kari Vogt. eds. *Islamic Law Reform and Human Rights: Challengers and Rejoinders.* Copenhagen: Nordic Human Rights, 1993.

Lipset, Seymour Martin, ed. *The Encyclopedia of Democracy.* 4 vols. London: Routledge, 1995.

Lipson, Leslie. *The Ethical Crisis of Civilizations.* London: Sage, 1993.

Litvak, Meir, and Ester Webman. *From Empathy to Denial: Arab Responses to the Holocaust.* New York: Columbia University Press, 2009.

Lüderssen, Klaus, ed. *Aufgeklärte Kriminalpolitik oder Kampf gegen das Böse.* Baden-Baden: Nomos, 1998.

Luhmann, Niklas. *Funktion der Religion.* Frankfurt am Main: Suhrkamp, 1977.

Lybarger, Loren D. *Identity and Religion: The Struggle between Islamism and Secularism in the Occupied Territories.* Princeton: Princeton University Press, 2007.

Lynch, Marc. "Veiled Truths." *Foreign Affairs* 89, no. 4 (2010).

Mahdi, Muhsin. *Al-Farabi and the Foundation of Islamic Political Philosophy.* Chicago: University of Chicago Press, 2001.

Makdisi, George. *The Rise of the Colleges: Institutions of Learning in Islam and the West.* Edinburgh: Edinburgh University Press, 1981.

Mallmann, Klaus-Michael, and Martin Cüppers. *Nazi-Palestine: The Plans for the Extermination of the Jews in Palestine*. New York: Enigma in association with U.S. Holocaust Memorial Museum, 2010.

Mandaville, Peter. *Transnational Muslim Politics: Reimagining the Umma*. New York: Routledge, 2004.

Markovits, Andrei. "An Inseparable Tandem of European Identity? Anti-Americanism and Anti-Semitism in the Short and Long Run." In Herf, *Antisemitism and Anti-Zionism in Historical Perspective*, 71–91.

———. *Uncouth Nation: Why Europe Dislikes America*. Princeton: Princeton University Press, 2007.

Martin, Leonore, ed. *New Frontiers in Middle Eastern Security*. New York: St. Martin's, 1999.

Martin, Richard C., in association with Abbas Barzegar, eds. *Islamism: Contested Perspectives on Political Islam*. Stanford: Stanford University Press, 2010.

Martin, Richard C., and Mark R. Woodward, with Dwi S. Atmaja. *Defenders of Reason in Islam: Mu'tazilism from Medieval School to Modern Symbol*. Oxford: Oneworld, 1997.

Marty, Martin, and Scott Appleby, eds. *The Fundamentalism Project*. Vol. 1, *Fundamentalisms Observed*. Chicago: University of Chicago Press, 1991.

———. *The Fundamentalism Project*. Vol. 2, *Fundamentalisms and Society*. Chicago: University of Chicago Press, 1993.

———. *The Fundamentalism Project*. Vol. 3, *Fundamentalisms and the State*. Chicago: University of Chicago Press, 1993.

———. *The Fundamentalism Project*. Vol. 4, *Accounting for Fundamentalisms*. Chicago: University of Chicago Press, 1994.

———. *The Fundamentalism Project*. Vol. 5, *Comprehending Fundamentalisms*. Chicago: University of Chicago Press, 1995.

Marwadi, Abu al-Hassan al-. *Kitab al-ahkam al-sultaniyya* [Book of rules on the sultanic government]. Cairo: several editions, n.d.

Mawdudi, Abu al-A'la al-. *al-Islam wa al-Madaniyya al-haditah* [Islam and modern civilization]. Rpt., Cairo.

Mayer, Ann. "Law and Religion in the Muslim Middle East," *American Journal of Comparative Law* 35, no. 1 (1987): 127–84.

McCarthy, Andrew C. *The Grand Jihad: How Islam and the Left Sabotage America*. New York: Encounter, 2010.

McNeill, William. *The Rise of the West: A History of Human Community*. Chicago: University of Chicago Press, 1965.

Mearshheimer, John, and Stephen Walt. *The Israel Lobby and U.S. Foreign Policy*. New York: Farrar, Straus and Giroux, 2008.

Mehden, Fred von der. *Two Worlds of Islam: Interaction between Southeast Asia and the Middle East.* Tampa: University of Florida Press, 1993.

Mendelsohn, Barak. *Combating Jihadism: American Hegemony and Interstate Cooperation in the War on Terrorism.* Chicago: University of Chicago Press, 2009.

Milton-Edwards, Beverley. *Islamic Politics in Palestine.* London: Tauris, 1999.

———. *Contemporary Politics in the Middle East.* Cambridge: Polity, 2000.

———. *Islam and Politics in the Contemporary World.* Cambridge: Polity, 2004.

Mishal, Shaul, and Avraham Sela. *The Palestinian Hamas.* New York: Columbia University Press, 2000.

Mitchell, Richard P. *The Society of the Muslim Brothers.* London: Oxford University Press, 1969.

Momen, Moojan. *An Introduction into Shi'a Islam.* New Haven: Yale University Press, 1985.

Moore, Barrington. *Social Origins of Dictatorship and Democracy.* Boston: Beacon, 1966.

Mozaffari, Medhi, ed. *Globalization and Civilizations.* Routledge, 2002.

———. "The Rise of Islamism in the Light of European Totalitarianism." *Totalitarian Movements and Political Religions* 10, no. 1 (2009): 1–13.

Murawiec, Laurent. *The Mind of Jihad.* New York: Cambridge University Press, 2008.

Muslehuddin, Muhammad. *Philosophy in Islamic Law and the Orientalists: A Comparative Study of Islamic Legal Systems.* Lahore, n.d.

Muslih, Mohammed Y. *The Origins of Palestinian Nationalism.* New York: Columbia University Press, 1988.

Mustafa, Halah. *al-Islam al Siyasa fi Misr* [Political Islam in Egypt]. Cairo: al-Ahram, 1992.

Najjar, Husain F. al-. *al-Islam wa al-Syasa* [Islam and politics]. Cairo: Dar al-Sha'b, 1977.

Nakash, Yitzhak. *The Shi'is of Iraq.* Princeton: Princeton University Press, 1994.

———. *Reaching for Power: The Shi'a in the Modern Arab World.* Princeton: Princeton University Press, 2006.

Nardin, Terry. *Law, Morality, and the Relations of States.* Princeton: Princeton University Press, 1983.

———, ed. *The Ethics of War and Peace: Religious and Secular Perspectives.* Princeton: Princeton University Press, 1993.

Nawaz, Maajid. "Dangerous Concepts and the Struggle Within: Reclaiming State and Politics from Islamists." In Patterson and Gallager, *Debating the War of Ideas,* 35–53.

Nawfal, Abdulraziq. *al-Muslimun wa al-ilm al-hadith* [Muslims and modern science]. Cairo: Dar al-shuruq, 1988.

Netton, Ian Richard. *al-Farabi and His School*. London: Routledge, 1992.

Neumann, Peter. "Europe's Jihadist Dilemma." *Survival* 48, no. 2 (2006): 71–84.

Northrop, F. S. C. *The Taming of the Nations: A Study of the Cultural Basis of International Policy*. Woodbridge, Conn.: Ox Bow, 1987.

Norton, Augustus R. *Hezbollah: A Short Story*. Princeton: Princeton University Press, 2007.

Olson, Alan, ed. *Educating for Democracy*. Lanham, Md.: Rowman and Littlefield, 2005.

Oumlil, Ali. *Fi shar'iyat al-Ikhtilaf*. Rabat: Majlis al-Qaumi, 1991.

Pape, Robert. *Dying to Win: The Strategic Logic of Suicide Terrorism*. New York: Random House, 2005.

Paret, Rudi. *Mohammed und der Koran*. Stuttgart: Kohlhammer, 1976.

———. *Der Koran*. Stuttgart: Kohlhammer, 1979.

Paris, Jonathan. "Explaining the Causes of Radical Islam in Europe." In Frisch and Inbar, *Radical Islam and International Security,* 121–33.

Parker, Geoffrey. *The Military Revolution and the Rise of the West, 1500–1800*. Cambridge: Cambridge University Press, 1988.

Patterson, Eric, and John Gallager, eds. *Debating the War of Ideas*. New York: Palgrave, 2010.

Petterson, Dan. *Inside Sudan: Political Islam, Conflict, and Catastrophe*. Boulder, Colo.: Westview, 2003.

Phares, Walid. *The War of Ideas: Jihadism against Democracy*. New York: Palgrave, 2007.

Phillips, Melanie. *Londonistan*. New York: Encounter, 2006.

Philpott, Daniel. "The Challenge of September 11 to Secularism in International Relations." *World Politics* 55, no. 1 (2002): 66–95.

Pillar, Paul R. *Terrorism and U.S. Foreign Policy*. Washington, D.C.: Brookings Institute, 2001.

Pipes, Daniel. *The Hidden Hand: Middle East Fears of Conspiracy*. Basingstoke: Macmillan, 1996.

Piscatori, James. "Imaging Pan-Islamism." In Akbarzadeh and Mansouri, *Islam and Political Violence,* 27–38.

Popper, Karl. *The Open Society and Its Enemies*. 2 vols. London: Routledge, 1945.

Powers, Roger, and William B. Vogele, eds. *Protest, Power, and Change: An Encyclopedia of Nonviolent Action*. New York: Garland, 1997.

Qadir, C. A. *Philosophy and Science in the Islamic World*. London: Routledge, 1988.

Qaradawi, Yusuf al-. *Hatmiyyat al-hall al-islami* [The Islamic solution]. Vol. 1, *al-Hall al-Islami wa al-Hulul al-mustawradah* [The imported solutions]. Beirut: al-Risala, rpt. 1980.

———. *Hatmiyyat al-hall al-islami.* Vol. 2, *al-hall al-Islami: Farida wa darura* [The Islamic solution: A religious duty and necessity]. Cairo: Matba'at Wahba, 1987.

———. *Hatmiyyat al-hall al-islami.* Vol. 3, *Bayinat al-hall al-Islami wa shabahat al-ilmaniyyin wa al-Mustaghribin* [The characteristics of the Islamic solution and the suspicions of the Westernized elites]. Cairo: Matba'at Wahba, 1988.

———. *al-Halal wa al-haram fi al-Islam* [The permitted and the forbidden in Islam]. Cairo: Wahba, 1991.

Qutb, Sayyid. *al-Islam wa Mushkilat al-Hadarah* [Islam and the problems of civilization]. 9th legal ed. Cairo: Dar al-Shuruq, 1988.

———. *Ma'alim fi al-tariq* [Signposts along the road]. 13th legal ed. Cairo: Dar al-Shuruq, 1989.

———. *Ma'rakatuna ma'a al-Yahud* [Our struggle against the Jews]. 10th legal ed. Cairo: Dar al-Shuruq, 1989.

———. *al-Jihad for Sabil Allah* [Jihad on the path of Allah]. Cairo: Dar al-Asma', rpt. 1992.

———. *al-Salam al-'alami wa al-Islam* [World peace and Islam]. Cairo: Dar al-Shuruq, rpt. 1992.

Raddatz, Hans Peter. "Antisemitism in Islam: Europe in the Conflict between Tolerance and Ideology." In Bostom, *Legacy of Islamic Antisemitism,* 643–49.

Ramadan, Abdulazim. *Jama'at al-Takfir fi misr: al-Usul al-Tarikhiyya* [The Islamist groups and their origin in Egypt: The historical origins]. Cairo: al-Hay'a al-Misriyya, 1995.

Ramadan, Tariq. *Aux sources du renouveau musulman: D'al Afghani à Hasan al-Banna; Un siècle de réformisme islamique.* Paris: Bayard, 1998.

———. *Radical Reform: Islamic Ethics and Liberation.* Oxford: Oxford University Press, 2009.

Rashid, Ahmed. *Taliban: Militant Islam, Oil, and Fundamentalism in Central Asia.* New Haven: Yale University Press, 2000.

Rayyes, Mohammed D. al-. *al-Nazariyyat al-siyasiyya al-Islamiyya* [Islamic political theories]. Cairo, 1953.

Reid, Anthony, and Michael Gilsenan, eds. *Islamic Legitimacy in Plural Asia.* New York: Routledge, 2007.

Reilly, Robert R. *The Closing of the Muslim Mind: How Intellectual Suicide Created the Modern Islamist Crisis.* Wilmington, Del.: Intercollegiate Studies Institute, 2010.

Reisman, David. "al-Farabi and the Philosophical Curriculum." In Adamson and Taylor, *Cambridge Companion to Arab Philosophy,* 52–71.

Revel, François. *Democracy against Itself: The Future of the Democratic Impulse.* New York: Free Press, 1993.

Rich, David. "The Very Model of a British Muslim Brotherhood." In Rubin, *Muslim Brotherhood,* 117–36.

Richards, Alan, and John Waterbury. *A Political Economy of the Middle East.* 2nd ed. Boulder, Colo.: Westview, 1996.

Rodinson, Maxime. *Mohammed.* Frankfurt: Bucher, 1975.

———. *Peuple juif ou problème juif?* Paris: Maspero, 1981.

Rosenthal, Franz. *The Classical Heritage of Islam.* London: Routledge, 1992.

Roy, Olivier. *The Failure of Political Islam.* Cambridge: Harvard University Press, 1994.

Rubin, Barnett. *The Fragmentation of Afghanistan.* New Haven: Yale University Press, 1995.

Rubin, Barry, ed. *Revolutionaries and Reforms: Contemporary Islamist Movements in the Middle East.* Albany: SUNY Press, 2003.

———, ed. *The Muslim Brotherhood: The Organization and Policies of a Global Islamist Movement.* New York: Palgrave, 2010.

Runciman, Steven. *History of the Crusades.* Cambridge: Cambridge University Press, 1954.

———. *The Fall of Constantinople.* New York: Cambridge University Press, 1990.

Russet, Bruce. *Grasping Democratic Peace.* Princeton: Princeton University Press, 1993.

Rutherford, Bruce. *Egypt after Mubarak.* Princeton: Princeton University Press, 2008.

Sageman, Marc. *Understanding Terror Networks.* Philadelphia: University of Pennsylvania Press, 2004.

———. *Leaderless Jihad: Terror Networks in the Twenty-First Century.* Philadelphia: University of Pennsylvania Press, 2008.

Said, Edward. *Orientalism.* New York: Vintage, 1979.

Salih, Subhi al-. *Ma'alim al-shari'a al-Islamiyya* [Essential characteristics of Islamic law]. Beirut: Dar al-Ilm Lilmalayin, 1975.

Sardar, Ziauddin. *Islamic Futures: The Shape of Ideas to Come.* London: Mensell, 1985.

———. *Exploration in Islamic Science.* London: Mensell, 1989.

Sawi, Salah al-. *al-Muhawara: Musajalah fikriyya haul qadiyyat tatbiq al-shari'a al-Islamiyya [Dialogue: A conversation about the problematic of the implementation of the Shari'a].* Cairo: Dar al-A'lam, 1992.

Schacht, Joseph. *An Introduction to Islamic Law.* Oxford: Clarendon, rpt. 1979.

Schacht, Joseph, and Clifford Bosworth, eds. *The Legacy of Islam.* Oxford: Clarendon, 1974.

Schaltut, Mahmud. *al-Islam, Aqida wa Shari'a* [Islam is a religious doctrine and law]. 10th ed. Cairo: al-Shuruq, 1980.

Schluchter, Wolfgang, ed. *Max Webers Sicht des Islam.* Frankfurt am Main: Suhrkamp, 1987.

Schmiegelow, Michèle, ed. *Democracy in Asia.* New York: Campus, 1997.

Schultz, Richard, and Andreas Dew. *Insurgents, Terrorists, and Militias.* New York: Columbia University Press, 2006.

Schulze, Hagen. *Weimar Deutschland, 1917–1933.* Berlin: Siedler, 1982.

Schwartz, Stephen. *The Two Faces of Islam: The House of Sa'ud from Tradition to Terror.* New York: Palgrave, 2002.

Scruton, Roger. *The West and the Rest: Globalization and the Terrorist Threat.* Wilmington, Del.: ISI, 2002.

Shadhli, Saad Eddin al-. *al-Harb al-Salibiyya al-Thamina* [The eighth crusade]. Casablanca: al-Jadida, 1991.

Shahin, Emad E. *Political Ascent: Contemporary Islamic Movements in North* Africa. Boulder, Colo.: Westview, 1997.

———. "Egypt's Moment of Reform." In Emerson, *Democratization in the European Neighborhood,* 117–30.

Sharabi, Hisham, ed. *The Next Arab Decade.* Boulder, Colo.: Westview, 1988.

———. *Arab Neo-Patriarchy: A Theory of Distorted Change in Arab Society.* New York: Oxford University Press, 1992.

Shayegan, Daryush. *Cultural Schizophrenia: Islamic Societies Confronting the West.* London: Saqi, 1992.

Silverstein, Paul A. *Algeria in France.* Bloomington: Indiana University Press, 2004.

Sivan, Emmanuel. *Radical Islam: Modern Politics and Medieval Theology.* New Haven: Yale University Press, 1985.

Skocpol, Theda. *States and Social Revolution.* New York: Cambridge University Press, rpt. 1979.

Smith, Donald E. *Religion, Politics, and Social Change in the Third World.* New York: Free Press, 1971.

Smith, Jane. *Islam in America.* New York: Columbia University Press, 1999.

Smith, Wilfred C. *The Meaning and End of Religion.* New York: Harper and Row, 1963.

Soage, Ana B. "Yusuf al-Qaradawi: The Muslim Brothers' Favorite Ideological Guide." In Rubin, *Muslim Brotherhood,* 19–38.

Spencer, Robert. *Onward Muslim Soldiers: How Jihad Still Threatens America and the West.* New York: Regnery, 2003.

Sternhell, Zeev. *The Anti-Enlightenment Tradition.* New Haven: Yale University Press, 2009.

Stowasser, Karl, ed. *al-Tahtawi. Ein Muslim entdeckt Europa.* Munich: C. H. Beck, 1989.

Tahtawi, Rifa'a Rafi' al-. *Takhlis al-ibriz fi talkhis Paris* [Tahtawi's Paris diary]. Beirut: Dar Ibn Zaidun, rpt., n.d.

Taylor, Charles. *The Ethics of Authenticity.* Cambridge: Harvard University Press, 1991.

Tibi, Bassam. *Militär und Sozialismus in der Dritten Welt.* Frankfurt am Main: Suhrkamp, 1973.

———. "al-kuttab al-arab wa azmat al-mujtam'at al Arabiyya" [Arab writers and the crisis of Arab societies]. In Centre d'Études et de Récherches Economiques et Sociales, *Les Arabes face à leur destin,* 177–215.

———. "Islam and Secularization: Religion and the Functional Differentiation of the Social System." *Archives for Philosophy of Law and Social Philosophy* 66 (1980): 207–22.

———. "Islam and Social Change in the Modern Middle East." *Law and State* 22 (1980): 91–106.

———. "al-bina' al-iqtisadi al-ijtima'i lil democratiyya [The socioeconomic underpinning of democracy]. In Center for Arab Unity Studies, *Azmat al-democratiyya fi al-Watan al-Arabi,* 73–87.

———. "Politisches Denken im mittelalterlichen Islam zwischen Philosophie (Falsafa) und Religio-Jurisprudenz (Fiqh)." In *Pipers Handbuch der politischen Ideen,* ed. I. Fetscher, 2: 87–140. Munich: Piper Verlag, 1987.

———. *The Crisis of Modern Islam.* Salt Lake City: University of Utah Press, 1988.

———. *Arab Nationalism: Between Islam and the Nation State.* 3rd ed. 1990; New York: St. Martin's, 1997.

———. "The European Tradition of Human Rights and the Culture of Islam." In Deng and An-Na'im, *Human Rights,* 104–32.

———. "The Simultaneity of the Unsimultaneous: Old Tribes and Imposed Nation-States in the Modern Middle East." In Khoury and Kostiner, *Tribes and State Formation in the Middle East,* 127–52.

———. *Islam and the Cultural Accommodation of Social Change.* Boulder, Colo.: Westview, 1990.

———. *Conflict and War in the Middle East: From Interstate War to New Security.* 2nd ed. 1993; New York: St. Martin's, 1998.

———. "The Worldview of Sunni-Arab Fundamentalists: Attitudes toward Modern Science and Technology." In Marty and Appleby, *Fundamentalism Project,* 2: 73–102.

————. *Die Verschwörung. Das Trauma arabischer Politik.* 2nd ed. 1993; Hamburg: Hoffmann and Campe, 1994.

————. "Islamic Law, Shari'a, and Human Rights: Universal Morality and International Relations." *Human Rights Quarterly* 16, no. 2 (1994): 277–99.

————. "Les conditions d'Euro-Islam." In Bistolfi and Zabbal, *Islams d'Europe,* 230–34.

————. "Culture and Knowledge: The Politics of Islamization of Knowledge as a Claim to De-Westernization," *Theory, Culture, and Society* 12, no. 1 (1995): 1–24.

————. "Fundamentalism." In *The Encyclopedia of Democracy,* ed. Seymour Martin Lipset, 2: 507–10. London: Routledge, 1995.

————. *Der Krieg der Zivilisationen: Politik und Religion zwischen Vernunft und Fundamentalismus.* Hamburg: Hoffmann and Campe, 1995.

————. "Die Revolte gegen den Westen in der neuen internationalen Umwelt." In Kaiser, Angenendt, Maull, and Brenke, *Deutschlands neue Außenpolitik,* 2:61–80.

————. *Das arabische Staatensystem.* Mannheim: Bibliographisches Institut, 1996.

————. *La Conspiratión: El Trauma de la Politica Arabe.* Barcelona: Herder, 1996.

————. "Foreigners, Today's New Jews?" In Wank, *Resurgence of Right-Wing Radicalism,* 85–102.

————. *Der wahre Imam.* Munich: Piper, 1996.

————. "War and Peace in Islam." In Nardin, *Ethics of War and Peace,* 128–45.

————. "Democracy and Democratization in Islam." In Schmiegelow, *Democracy in Asia,* 127–46.

————. "Jihad." In Powers and Vogele, *Protest, Power, and Change,* 277–81.

————. *The Challenge of Fundamentalism: Political Islam and the New World Disorder.* Updated ed. 1998; Berkeley: University of California Press, 2002.

————. "Die Entwestlichung des Rechts: Das Hudud-Strafrecht der islamischen Schari'a." In Lüderssen, *Aufgeklärte Kriminalpolitik oder Kampf gegen das Böse,* 21–30.

————. Review of *Islam and Democracy,* by John Esposito and John Voll. *Journal of Religion* 78, no. 4 (1998): 667–69.

————. "International Morality and Cross-Cultural Bridging." In Herzog, *Preventing the Clash of Civilizations,* 107–26.

————. *Kreuzzug und Djihad: Der Islam und die christliche Welt.* Munich: Bertelsmann, 1999.

————. *Fundamentalismus im Islam: Eine Gefahr für den Weltfrieden?* 3rd ed. 2000; Darmstadt: Primus Verlag, 2002.

————. "Secularization and De-Secularization in Modern Islam." *Religion-Staat-Gesellschaft: Journal for the Study of Beliefs and Worldviews* 1, no. 1 (2000): 95–117.

————. "Between Communitarism and Euro-Islam: Europe, Multicultural Identities, and the Challenge of Migration." In Docker and Fischer, *Adventures of Identity,* 45–60.

————. *Einladung in die islamische Geschichte.* Darmstadt: Primus, 2001.

————. *Islam between Culture and Politics.* 2nd enlarged ed. 2001; New York: Palgrave, 2005.

————. "Between Islam and Islamism: A Dialogue with Islam and a Security Approach vis-à-vis Islamism." In Jacoby and Sasley, *Redefining Security in the Middle East,* 62–82.

————. "Habermas and the Return of the Sacred: Is It a Religious Renaissance or the Emergence of Political Religion as a New Totalitarianism?" *Religion-Staat-Gesellschaft: Journal for the Study of Beliefs and Worldviews* 3, no. 2 (2002): 205–96.

————. "War and Peace in Islam." In Hashmi, *Islamic Political Ethics,* 175–93.

————. "Fundamentalism." In Hawkesworth and Kogan, *Routledge Encyclopedia of Government and Politics,* 1: 184–204.

————. "Islamic Civilization and the Quest for Democratic Pluralism." In Helmanita, *Dialogue in the World Disorder,* 159–201.

————. *Der neue Totalitarismus: "Heiliger Krieg" und westliche Sicherheit.* Darmstadt: Primus, 2004.

————. "Countering Terrorism als Krieg der Weltanschauungen." In Creveld and Knop, *Countering Modern Terrorism,* 131–72.

————. "Education and Democratization in an Age of Islamism." In Olson, *Educating for Democracy,* 203–19.

————. *From Islamist Jihadism to Democratic Peace? Islam at the Crossroads in Post-Bipolar International Politics.* Ankara paper 16. London: Taylor and Francis, 2005.

————. "Islam, Freedom, and Democracy." In Emerson, *Democratization in the Neighborhood,* 93–116.

————. "Politischer Konservatismus der AKP als Tarnung für den politischen Islam? Die Türkei zwischen Europa und dem Islamismus." In Besier and Lübbe, *Politische Religion und Religionspolitik,* 229–60.

————. "Egypt as a Model of Development for the World of Islam." In Harrison and Berger, *Developing Cultures,* 163–80.

————. "Europeanizing Islam or the Islamization of Europe: Political Democracy versus Cultural Difference." In Katzenstein and Byrnes, *Religion in an Expanding Europe,* 204–24.

———. "Islamic Shari'a as Constitutional Law? The Reinvention of the Shari'a and the Need for Islamic Law Reform." In Japanese Association of Comparative Constitutional Law, *Church and State,* 126–70.

———. "Die Mär des Islamismus von der jüdischen und kreuzzüglerischen Weltverschwörung gegen den Islam." In Faber, Schoeps, and Stawski, *Neualter Judenhass,* 179–202.

———. "The Pertinence of Islam's Predicament with Democratic Pluralism," *Religion-Staat-Gesellschaft: Journal for the Study of Beliefs and Worldviews* 7, no. 1 (2006): 83–117.

———. "Der djihadistische Islamismus, nicht der Islam ist die Quelle des neuen Antisemitismus." In Benz and Wetzel, *Antisemitismus und radikaler Islamismus,* 43–69.

———. *Die islamische Herausforderung: Religion und Politik im Europa des 21. Jahrhunderts.* Darmstadt: Primus, 2007.

———. "Islam and Cultural Modernity: In Pursuit of Democratic Pluralism." In Reid and Gilsenan, *Islamic Legitimacy in Plural Asia,* 28–52.

———. "Islam between Religious-Cultural Practice and Identity Politics." In Isar and Anheier, *Conflicts and Tensions,* 221–31.

———. "Jihadism and Intercivilizational Conflict: Conflicting Images of the Self and the Other." In Akbarzadeh and Mansouri, *Islam and Political Violence,* 39–64.

———. "A Migration Story: From Immigrants to Citizens of the Heart." *Fletcher Forum of World Affairs* 31, no. 1 (2007): 147–68.

———. "Gewalt, Krieg und die Verbreitung der Religion des Islam." In Abbt and Schoeller, *Im Zeichen der Religion,* 206–23.

———. "Islam, Islamism, and Democracy: The Case of the Arab World." In Weinberg, *Democratic Responses to Terrorism,* 41–62.

———. "Islamist Parties: Why They Can't Be Democratic." *Journal of Democracy* 19, no. 3 (2008): 43–48.

———. *Political Islam, World Politics, and Europe: Democratic Peace and Euro-Islam vs. Global Jihad.* New York: Routledge, 2008.

———. "Public Policy and the Combination of Anti-Americanism and Antisemitism in Islamist Ideology." *Current* 12 (2008): 123–46.

———. "Religious Extremism or Religionization of Politics?" In Frisch and Inbar, *Radical Islam and International Security,* 11–37.

———. "The Return of the Sacred to Politics as Constitutional Law: The Case of Shari'atization of Politics in Islamic Civilization." *Theoria: A Journal of Social and Political Theory* 55, no. 115 (2008): 91–119.

———. *Violence and Religious Fundamentalism in Political Islam: The New Irregular War.* EKEM paper 11. Athens: Hellenic Center for European Studies, 2008.

———. "Bridging the Heterogeneity of Civilizations: Reviving the Grammar of Islamic Humanism." *Theoria: A Journal of Social and Political Theory* 56, no. 120 (2009): 65–80.

———. "Euro-Islam." In Baran, *Other Muslims,* 157–74.

———. "Islamism and Democracy: On the Compatibility of Institutional Islamism and the Political Culture of Democracy." *Totalitarian Movements and Political Religions* 10, no. 2 (2009): 135–64.

———. *Islam's Predicament with Modernity: Cultural Change and Religious Reform.* New York: Routledge, 2009.

———. "Political Islam as a Forum of Religious Fundamentalism and the Religionization of Politics: Islamism and the Quest for a Remaking of the World." *Totalitarian Movements and Political Religions* 10, no. 2 (2009): 97–120.

———. "The Political Legacy of Max Horkheimer and Islamist Totalitarianism." *Telos* 148 (2009): 7–15.

———. "Turkey's Islamist Danger: Islamists Approach Europe." *Middle East Quarterly* 16, no. 1 (2009): 47–54.

———. "Ethnicity of Fear? Islamic Migration and the Ethnicization of Islam in Europe." *Studies in Ethnicity and Nationalism* 10, no. 1 (2010): 126–57.

———. *From Sayyid Qutb to Hamas: The Middle East Conflict and the Islamization of Antisemitism.* YIISA working paper. New Haven: Yale University Press, 2010.

———. "Fundamentalism." In Bevir, *Encyclopedia of Political Theory,* 2: 536–40.

———. "Global Communication and Cultural Particularisms: The Place of Values in the Simultaneity of Structural Globalization and Cultural Fragmentation." In Fortner and Fackler, *Handbook of Global Communication.*

———. "Inter-Civilizational Conflict between Value Systems and Concepts of Order: Explaining the Islamic Humanist Potential for a Peace of Ideas." In Patterson and Gallager, *Debating the War of Ideas,* 157–74.

———. "The Politicization of Islam into Islamism in the Context of Global Religious Fundamentalism." *Journal of the Middle East and Africa* 1, no. 2 (2010): 153–70.

———. "The Return of Ethnicity to Europe via Islamic Migration? The Ethnicization of the Islamic Diaspora." In Hsu, *Ethnic Europe,* 127–56.

———. "John Kelsay and Shari'a Reasoning in Just War in Islam: An Appreciation and a Few Propositions." *Journal of State and Church* 53, no. 1 (2011): 4–26.

Tilly, Charles, ed. *The Formation of National States in Western Europe.* Princeton: Princeton University Press, 1975.

———, ed. *Coercion, Capital, and European States.* Cambridge, Mass.: Blackwell, 1990.

Tu'aima, Sabir. *al-Shari'a al-Islamiyya fi asr al-ilm* [Islamic law in the age of science]. Beirut: Dar al-jil, 1979.

Turner, Bryan. *Weber and Islam*. London: Routledge, 1974.

Turner, Howard R. *Science in Medieval Islam*. Austin: University of Texas Press, 1995.

United Nations Development Program. *Arab Human Development Report: Creating Opportunities for Future Generations*. New York: United Nations, 2002.

———. *Arab Human Development Report: Building a Knowledge Society*. New York: United Nations, 2003.

Varisco, Daniel. "Inventing Islamism: The Violence of Rhetoric." In Martin in association with Barzegar, *Islamism,* 33–50.

Vidino, Lorenzo. *Al-Qaeda in Europe: The New Battleground of International Jihad*. Amherst, N.Y.: Prometheus, 2006.

———. *The New Muslim Brotherhood in the West*. New York: Columbia University Press, 2010.

Viehweg, Theodor. *Topik und Jurisprudenz: Ein Beitrag zur rechtswissenschaftlichen Grundlagenforschung*. Munich: C. H. Beck, 1974.

Walzer, Richard, trans. *Al-Farabi on the Perfect State*. Oxford: Oxford University Press, 1985.

Wank, Ulrich, ed. *The Resurgence of Right-Wing Radicalism in Germany*. New Jersey: Humanities, 1996.

Waterbury, John. *Egypt under Nasser and Sadat: The Political Economy of Two Regimes*. Princeton: Princeton University Press, 1983.

———. "Social Science Research and Arab Studies in the Coming Decade." In Sharabi, *The Next Arab Decade,* 293–302.

Waterbury, John, and Alan Richards. *A Political Economy of the Middle East*. Boulder, Colo.: Westview, 1990, rpt. 1996.

Watson, Adam, *The Evolution of International Society: A Comparative Historical Analysis*. London: Routledge 1992.

Watt, W. M. *Islamic Philosophy and Theology*. 1962; rpt. Edinburgh: Edinburgh University Press, 1979.

———. *Islamic Political Thought: The Basic Concepts*. Edinburgh: Edinburgh University Press, 1969.

———. *Islamic Revelation in the Modern World*. Edinburgh: Edinburgh University Press, 1969.

———. *Muhammad at Medina*. Oxford: Oxford University Press, 1977.

Watt, W. M., and R. Bell. *Introduction to the Qur'an*. Edinburgh: Edinburgh University Press, 1970.

Weber, Max. *Soziologie, weltgeschichtliche Analysen, Politik.* Stuttgart: Kröner, 1964.

——. *Politik als Beruf.* 9th ed. Berlin: Dunker und Humblot, 1991.

Weinberg, Leonard, ed. *Democratic Reponses to Terrorism.* New York: Routledge, 2008.

Wenzel, Knut, ed. *Die Religionen und die Vernunft: Die Debatte um die Regensburger Vorlesung des Papstes.* Freiburg: Herder, 2007.

Whittacker, David J., ed. *The Terrorism Reader.* London: Routledge, 2001.

Wickham, Carrie Rosefsky. *Mobilizing Islam: Religion, Activism, and Political Change in Egypt.* New York: Columbia University Press, 2002.

Wistrich, Robert. *Muslim Antisemitism.* New York: American Jewish Committee, 2002.

——. *A Lethal Obsession: Antisemitism from Antiquity to Global Jihad.* New York: Random House, 2010.

Wittfogel, Karl. *Oriental Despotism: A Comparative Study of Total Power.* New Haven: Yale University Press, 1957.

Wolf, Eric R. *Europe and the People without History.* New ed. Berkeley: University of California Press, 1997.

Wordlaw, Grant. *Political Terrorism.* 2nd ed. 1982; Cambridge: Cambridge University Press, 1989.

Wuthnow, Robert. *Meaning and Moral Order.* Berkeley: University of California Press, 1987.

Ye'or, Bat. *Islam and Dhimmitude: When Civilizations Collide.* Cranbury, N.J.: Associated Universities Press, 2002.

Young-Bruehl, Elisabeth. *Why Arendt Matters.* New Haven: Yale University Press, 2006.

Zakzouk, Mahmoud. *Einführung in den Islam.* Cairo: Public Ministry of Awqaf/ Religious Affairs (Egypt), 2000.

Zubaida, Sami. *Law and Power in the Islamic World.* London: Tauris, 2003.

Index

JUN   2012